Anne Gregg's love affair with France began as a teenager when she first took the train to Marseille and woke up to the garlic-and-Gauloises smells of the seductive south. Since then, she has visited almost every corner of the country, written numerous travel articles about it and been editor of *The Traveller in France* magazine for the French Tourist Office for the past 25 years. Between times, her stint as presenter of the BBC *Holiday* programme as well as other television and radio work also often took her to France.

TARRAGON & TRUFFLES

A Guide to the Best French Markets

Anne Gregg

Photographs by Ken Wright

BANTAM BOOKS

LONDON • TORONTO • SYDNEY • AUCKLAND • JOHANNESBURG

TARRAGON & TRUFFLES
A BANTAM BOOK: 0553816233
9780553816235

First publication in Great Britain

PRINTING HISTORY
Bantam edition published 2006

3 5 7 9 10 8 6 4 2

Copyright © Anne Gregg 2006
Photographs by Ken Wright

The right of Anne Gregg to be identified as the author of
this work has been asserted in accordance with sections 77
and 78 of the Copyright Designs and Patents Act 1988.

Bantam Books are published by Transworld Publishers,
61–63 Uxbridge Road, London W5 5SA,
a division of The Random House Group Ltd,
in Australia by Random House Australia (Pty) Ltd,
20 Alfred Street, Milsons Point, Sydney, NSW 2061, Australia,
in New Zealand by Random House New Zealand Ltd,
18 Poland Road, Glenfield, Auckland 10, New Zealand
and in South Africa by Random House (Pty) Ltd,
Isle of Houghton, Corner of Boundary Road & Carse O'Gowrie,
Houghton 2198, South Africa.

Design by Fiona Andreanelli.

Printed in Scotland by Scotprint.

Papers used by Transworld Publishers are natural, recyclable products made from wood grown in sustainable forests. The
manufacturing processes conform to the environmental regulations of the country of origin.

For my Mum

Some Useful Contacts

Brittany Ferries Tel 08705 360 360 www.brittanyferries.com
Eurostar Tel 08705 186 186 www.eurostar.com
Eurotunnel Tel 08705 35 35 35 www.eurotunnel.com
P&O Ferries Tel 08705 202 020 www.POferries.com
Rail Europe Tel 08705 848 848 www.raileurope.co.uk
SeaFrance Tel 08704 431 685 www.seafrance.com
Maison de la France, 178 Piccadilly, London W1J 9AL. France Information
Line: Tel 09068 244123 (9am–5pm, Monday to Friday; calls charged at 60p per
minute). E-mail info.uk@franceguide.com Web site: www.franceguide.com

Note: The market lists were supplied by the region's *départements* and
were correct at the time of going to press. However, while some markets
have existed for hundreds of years, others may suddenly stop through lack
of custom or be moved for a revamp of urban design. If you happen to find
any incorrectly listed, the author would be pleased to know.

Key

✪   To do/see

ⓘ   Tourist information

↘   Place to stay

🖰   Website

☎   Telephone number

◎   Market

ACKNOWLEDGEMENTS

My biggest thank you goes to Christine Fenley who, when at the French Tourist Office in London, read and checked every chapter, pouncing on blips in my French, calling up *départements* to unravel obscure facts and adding extra nuggets of information – especially about the markets in her native Auvergne. Christine has now moved to Brussels and I miss her hugely. Thank you also to Annie Jenkins who first prompted me to write the book (as we sat wasting time at a beachside café in Normandy) and to my editor Francesca Liversidge at Transworld Publishers who took up the idea and ran with it, then supported me so good-naturedly when the writing became somewhat sporadic due to a protracted illness. Also to Mari Roberts for her sensitive and restrained line-editing and to Fiona Andreanelli who made such a splendid job of the design.

I am grateful to everyone connected with the regional tourist offices of France who took the trouble to collate the market lists for me, particularly to those who hosted me on research trips and went the extra kilometre in guiding me to the gems: Stéphanie Chénet-Tissier and Chantal Guibert in Champagne-Ardenne; Christine Rigolot in Lorraine; Barbara Gris-Pichot in Franche-Comté; Isabelle Faure in Rhône-Alpes; Isabelle Stierlin in Limousin; Annie Dumoulin in Alsace; Solenne Odon in Mid-Pyrénées; Perrine Armandary in Aquitaine; Régine Turgis in Normandy and Marie-Stella Ray, who at the time represented Picardy. Staff in Nord-Pas de Calais and Languedoc-Roussillon I must also single out for special thanks.

Many friends living in France have been kind enough to make recommendations, gather maps and brochures or accompany me round their local favourites – so thank you to Monique Prunet, Peter and Dominique Glynn-Smith, Anne and Jeremy Towler, George and Stella Metaxas, Peter Danton de Rouffignac, Juliana Uhart and Maurice Blackbourne. Gleanings from fellow writers such as Robin Dewhurst, Audrey Stevenson and Perrott Phillipps were also much appreciated, as were those from Claudia Corallo, Roger Day, John Miller and Susi Golding. Sincere thanks are also due to my girlfriends (known as 'the sorority'): Jenny Paton, who came to the rescue when the endless and sometimes hard-to-decipher market lists had to be word-processed and I was running out of steam; Prue Gearey, who on occasion became an enthusiastic accompanying 'market researcher'; and Pat Houlihan, who could always be relied upon to take one's mind off the task when it weighed too heavily.

Finally, I am deeply indebted to P&O Ferries, SeaFrance, Brittany Ferries, Eurostar, Rail Europe and Eurotunnel for generously providing tickets for both me and my colleague Ken Wright, who is responsible for all the wonderful photographs in the book and who also helped with the research in ways too numerous to mention.

CONTENTS

INTRODUCTION

To market, to market . . .

I can't remember which came first. My love of France or my passion for markets. I do know that I became a francophile long before going there – breathing its air, touching and tasting it through the books of Elizabeth David, that doyenne of cookery writers. When I eventually made it across the Channel, the markets seemed to embody so much of what the country was about. Keeping faith with tradition. Savouring rural pleasures. Maintaining a quality of life. Making the simple look special. And, of course, wonderful food. I could never resist dawdling if I caught a glimpse of scalloped awnings and little white vans. Even now, after I've been steeped in the subject, a market can still make my pulse beat faster. Indeed, I'm quite put out if I arrive somewhere as one is packing up. Whether or not I want to buy anything is immaterial. I'm miffed at having missed the show.

Markets are theatre: each a performance whose cast of traders moves in like travelling players to unload props and dress the set. Bright sprigged cottons spread on makeshift trestle tables, wooden bowls for the olives, seaweed and lemons for the fish . . . Then, cue the practised sales patter to attract the audience. No applause, but they win smiles, gain approval, get paid, and are only as good as their last gig. At the finale, the church bell chimes and it's all got to be stowed away before the troupe hits the road again – until next time. Pick a town – any town – and however delightful or dreary it might be, a market will boost its appeal 200 per cent. Over the coffee and croissants one morning at a bed-and-breakfast near Auch, I sat next to a sparky little woman who said, 'Le jour du marché, la ville est toute animée' – on market day, a town is completely alive.

Exactly. Perhaps as alive as it was even a thousand years ago. Many French markets have been held in the same place for centuries and there's a wonderful sense of continuity as history creeps into the foreground, peopling the streets of some arcaded town square with characters who, if you peel away their 21st-century trappings, are fundamentally the same as they've always been – out and about in search of a bargain, a baguette, a new knife, an old lamp or just company. In country areas, the market is often the social event of the week. Watch from the sidelines and you'll see the little knots of gossipers; children gallivanting among the forest of legs; young girls flirting with the hunky jeans vendor; a frail old man spinning out the conversation over some minor purchase; the buxom *femme d'un certain âge* chatting up a lugubrious farmer and getting the best eggs from the back of his van. If you're a visitor, it's a chance to plug in to the local scene, try out your French – actually connect with people.

The gastronomic treasures of France are never more apparent than at markets of high-quality fresh local produce, and these attract discerning shoppers from all walks of life – top chefs and shop assistants, counts and happy campers. The appeal to the senses is intense. You admire, you touch and you sniff but most importantly you listen – to the *fromager* eloquently describing how he matures his cheeses, to the honey lady explaining the need to move her beehives from one season to the next, to the mushroom seller's recipe suggestions flung in for good measure as he weighs his *morilles* or *girolles*. Even if you don't understand every word, their gestures alone convey the passion these country people have for what they produce.

Of course, you don't just learn about food. At a big general market, everything from old farm tools among the bric-a-brac to the kind of hand-woven baskets that are on offer will drop hints about the local climate, crops, traditions, preoccupations and prosperity.

'Aren't all French markets much the same – seen one, seen 'em all?' is a question I've parried more than once in the throes of writing this guide. Absolutely not! Each corner of France has its own specialities and character, influenced as much as anything else by its close neighbours. That's why you get espadrilles and paella in the south west, *choucroute* (sauerkraut) in Alsace and cuckoo clocks in Savoy. There are flea markets and oyster markets, fish markets and truffle markets, massive everything-including-the-kitchen-sink markets and magical Christmas markets. What's more, the settings are so different, and this book is as much about places as it is about markets – places I've discovered and delighted in over time.

I've been a bit of a pedant about sticking to the proper geographical/political regions of France – the equivalent of counties in England or states in the US – giving each a chapter to itself (except for Côte d'Azur which, because it is so tiny, I added to Provence). Many guidebooks tend to bend and blur the boundaries, referring vaguely to 'the Loire' or 'the Dordogne'. I just felt it would be more helpful to give the right regional names so that everyone can easily source follow-up information. I've also assumed a certain degree of knowledge of France on the part of the reader, using abbreviations such as AOC for Appellation d'Origine Contrôlée, the accolade for state-of-the-art produce.

Having long had professional links with France, I didn't have to start from scratch with my research. Even so, I can't claim to have been to every market in the land, so my selection is far from definitive. It's haphazard and highly personal, made up of markets I've fallen upon by accident, sought out because of their reputation or included as a result of a tip-off. If there are a few I haven't checked out in person, be assured I know a man or woman who has.

My yardstick was to choose either brilliant markets worth a detour or exceptional locations with good markets. In most instances, you get both. This doesn't guarantee, I'm afraid, that every market recommended will be precisely the same on the day you go there. Markets are organic. They move locations if the town hall is being renovated or the road is up. Merchandise changes with the seasons. If it rains, maybe only two-thirds the usual quota of stallholders will claim their pitches. Sometimes a merchant or grower will decide not to make an encore. I've seen the same olives man consistently in several markets around the Luberon, but the seller who brought Agen prunes to Forcalquier only came once.

There are bound to be scores of terrific markets I haven't singled out – France, twice the size of Britain, has literally thousands. If you're a francophile too, you'll have your own favourites. But with this book as a prompt, I hope you'll discover lots more, as well as many new-to-you special places to see and to stay.

*Outsize bargains, mushrooms with blue feet and
scents you've never heard of*

She must have been well into her eighties. From her weather-buffed complexion, hands roughened by hard work and bosom encased in one of those all-enveloping pinnies, I guessed she was – or had been – a farmer. As I paused by her little stall, a shy '*Bonjour*' was uttered and her eyes crinkled hopefully. Laid out for sale on a yellow cloth were a straw basket containing about fifteen eggs, two smaller ones each with a different kind of dried bean in it, a single slab of butter and four pots of red jelly – '*C'est groseille, m'dame*'. That was the sum total of her stock at the onset of Etaples's Tuesday market. She had made the redcurrant jelly herself? '*Oui, fait maison.*'

How could I not? My purchase was wrapped slowly in a brown paper bag, and we exchanged a few comments about the likelihood of rain. Moving away, I wondered if the profit she would make in a morning would really be worth the effort? Was it perhaps more just for the sake of coming – to keep her hand in, augment her pension, enjoy the buzz of activity around her? All I can tell you is her redcurrant jelly was the best I've ever tasted.

You don't collect moments like this off a shelf in the hangars of Intermarché, Carrefour or Auchan. I'm not knocking the supermarkets – like anyone else who frequently slips across to Nord-Pas de Calais, I dive into them with gusto to collect bargain dollops of Dijon mustard in recyclable glass jars or the latest chic in picnic plates – but somehow when you get a little earth clinging to vegetables just pulled out of the ground that morning, or an extra macaroon flung into the bag after it's been weighed, or a few *bon mots* from an old countrywoman selling her home-made preserves, it gives you a better sense of *la différence*.

I often think how remarkable it is that despite this most northern bit of France poking its nose, so to speak, across the neck of the English Channel, it remains so quintessentially unlike southern Britain. Leaving aside the commonalities of hypermarkets and spaghetti junctions, you only have to shift down a gear and peel off into the countryside to feel well and truly *en France*. Cohorts of poplars march single-file along the brow of hills. Eurostar shoots like an arrow past dawdling cars. Shops signs make plain what it is they sell – *Boucherie, Boulangerie, Epicerie, Fleurs* – instead of merely flagging up the name of the owner. And there's that special spidery writing reserved for *plat du jour* menus chalked on blackboards outside restaurants and cafés, where in most weathers parasols stay optimistically in place over pavement tables.

Markets here are as authentic as anywhere further on in. Even familiar fishy Boulogne has a Gallic swagger about it that instantly draws you in, to touch, sniff and taste, or at the very least admire all those wonderful still-lifes – the little oyster cart, the rough-hewn boulders of rustic bread, the Van Dyck perfection of Philippe Olivier's cheese displays outside his shop in Rue Thiers.

It may be a small region with only two *départements*, but Nord-Pas de Calais is not short on variety. Pockets of it would surprise you if you've previously registered only the melancholy flats of old Flanders and those long straight shuttered villages that punctuate long straight stretches of *routes nationales*. Yes, some of it *is* dull, but there are also dense forests, glimmering marshlands and secretive rivers burbling between the soft agricultural hills of the Sept Vallées. My friends Anne and Jeremy Towler live in the valley of the Canche, in a charming hamlet which shall be nameless to protect their privacy. It has a church on the slope, a rambling garden-cum-nursery by the river and rose-covered cottages, two of which are shops in disguise, crammed full of treasures for house and garden. Oh, all right then, it's Boubers-sur-Canche! There isn't a market there, but it was through Anne and Jeremy that I discovered the gem of nearby Hesdin's.

Specialities

Nord-Pas de Calais is inclined to hide away its treasures, but they're not hard to find if you know where to look, and some of them are markets. With the country's premier fishing port (Boulogne) dominating the coast, **seafood** here is hardly a speciality – it's a staple. And what they do with it is endlessly inventive. Among my 'bring backs' is often one of the ready-made dishes that fishmongers make plenty of on market days – scallops already *gratiné*-ed, stuffed crab or lobster terrine. I wish they'd also do that splendid Flemish fish stew *waterzoï au poisson,* but I've only ever had it in a restaurant.

The **Flemish influence** is strongest the closer you get to Belgium. Try getting your tongue round words like *potje vleesch* – it's a terrine of veal, ham and rabbit – before you order some to taste. Beer rather than wine goes into casseroles of *carbonade flamande* (beef) and *coq à la bière* (chicken) – and the beer is locally brewed. Names to look for are La Choulette, Abbatiale de St-Armand, Goudale, and the latest, Saint-Landelin, which claims to be the only abbey-brewed ale in France. Houlle distils the best-known Flanders *genièvre* – gin, basically – made with juniper berries and a mix of rye, oats and barley. The towns of Loos and Wambrechies have their own versions.

Nord-Pas de Calais boasts another prime number – it supplies the world with chicory, or *endive*. Ideal conditions exist in the **marshland market gardens**, especially around Orchies, south of Lille, where the crisp, bitter salad leaves are cultivated by the *brouckaillers* (marsh dwellers) who still go to work by boat along the water channels. The markets are full of them.

The marshland also provides peat for the **smokehouses**. If you see plaits of sulphury-tinged garlic, it is not past its sell-by date but smoked. In the town of Arleux, it was discovered that smoking garlic would make it keep longer. Peat was the chosen fuel, first dried out under straw. They say smoking gives bulbs the shelf life of a year. This I would dispute – mine lasted longer than fresh garlic but, in the atmosphere of a normal kitchen, I think a year is a little optimistic. Smoking also imparts a mellower flavour. Every year 3000 tons of garlic are smoked in Arleux, and celebrated at an annual fair in September, during which they appoint a Miss Garlic – a title which must be something of a cross to bear!

Of the many excellent farmhouse **cheeses** made here, few are well known outside the region. The exception is Maroilles, one of my all-time favourites. Produced since the 10th century, it comes in chalky ridged squares like thick ceramic tiles and gets its slight dusting of 'terracotta' from being soaked in beer. The inside is creamy and pungent. If you see *tarte au Maroilles* for sale, pounce on it; made with equal quantities of Maroilles and *fromage blanc*, this can be demolished hot or cold, but warmed through it positively melts in the mouth. Other good local cheeses to sniff out are Bergues (very low fat as it's repeatedly washed in beer); mild *rollot* from Créquy; orange-crusted *forme d'Antoine*; and soft-textured Vieux Lille, which is pretty whiffy, but nothing to compare with *boulette d'Avesnes*, which they say makes strong men weep.

Ever since they made tapestries in Arras, the north has been known for its **textiles**. The manufacture of fabrics and ready-to-wear fashion really took off when the mining industry played itself out, and few general street markets are without whole sections, not just one or two stalls, of dress and furnishing fabrics – often in extra-wide measure so you can make large curtains without seams. There's plenty of extra-wide fashion too – Nord-Pas de Calais seems to appreciate that not everyone is size 10 and tube-shaped. Where the clientele is chicer, expect to see top label off-the-peg stuff at knock-down prices. Leather goods too are a bargain, well made and stylish. Some of my smartest, sturdiest and cheapest handbags have been bought in markets here.

A possible explanation for the glut of voluminous fashions is the temptations on offer for the **sweet-toothed**. Coconut macaroons are shovelled from mountainous heaps. *Tarte au sucre* (sugar tart), *tarte à la Cassonade* (brown sugar tart), *gaufres* (waffles) and chocolate-covered pastries called *Ryssels* are all too visible. To say nothing of huge baskets of garishly wrapped bonbons – chewy Sottises from Valenciennes and Bêtises (striped humbugs) from Cambrai. Chocolate seduction lurks in the *halles* or *pâtisseries* rather than in outdoor markets: give in to Coeur de Miss violet-flavoured chocs, and Germinal's flavoured with chicory.

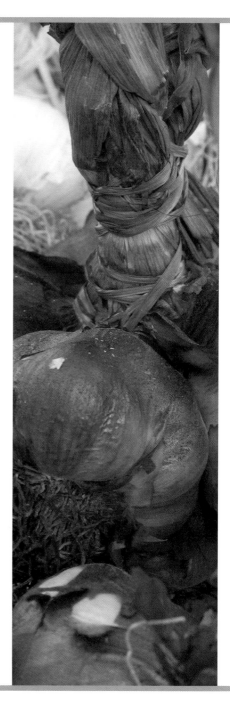

Etaples (Pas de Calais)

Tuesday and Friday, fish market almost every day

A bridge across the River Canche separates the fishing port of Etaples from smart Le Touquet. On Tuesday and Friday mornings its pavements are as crowded as Oxford Street. Those heading for Etaples have empty baskets. Those on the return have several bags full. Although Le Touquet itself has a superb market, there are, I suspect, more bargains in Etaples.

The town is bright and businesslike. Trawlers in for careening rest up on 'the hard' and almost every morning, depending on the catch, the fish cabins along the estuary are open. Each belongs to a local boat-owner whose name appears on creamy tiles – Pater Noster, Galaxie, Marie-Lise – and as you queue to buy you can marvel at the experts' skill in skinning and gutting a spotted sole in three swift moves and as many seconds.

This daily fish market is reason enough to visit Etaples. The attractions of its twice-weekly general market are a further bonus. Waft through a street lined with striped tops and sundresses (or sweaters in winter) to the packed, wedge-shaped main square where, under the gaze of the mauve-shuttered *mairie*, you have a huge selection of food, fashion and flowers. As *beignets de crevettes* – prawn fritters – are plunged into a cauldron of smoking oil, their aroma gives way to the fainter odour of a stall of smoked garlic,

hung aloft and heaped in boxes. Besides toys, tablecloths and barbecue sets, there are hills of french beans in green, pale-green and yellow, and waxy *ratte du Touquet* potatoes. A big cheese van, then a small cheese table – an artisan farmer's offerings. Fake orchids and fresh tarragon. Fancy underwear and industrial-strength corsets. Truly something for everyone.

Don't miss

✪ The big *poissonnerie* of Aux Pêcheurs d'Etaples, which sells the A to Z of fresh seafood among a glistening garnish of crushed ice and lemons. From the *traiteur* section, take home prepared fish pâtés and oysters by the dozen packed in wooden crates. Upstairs, the restaurant will serve you a meal fit for Neptune at a very reasonable price. The whole outfit is supplied and run by the Etaples Shipping Co-operative (☎ 03 21 94 06 90).

✪ Maréis, which engages children's interest in the life of fishermen with hands-on exhibits and audio-visuals.

✪ Maison de la Miniature's model of the port.

✪ The Etaples Military Cemetery, where almost 10,774 white crosses mark the graves of First World War Commonwealth casualties.

✪ Le Touquet (*see* Best of the Rest).

ⓘ Boulevard Bigot Descelers.

Somewhere to stay

↘ Charles VIII, modest two-chimney Logis de France in town, near the bridge. ☎ 03 21 09 00 44.

↘ Westminster, the absolute tops in Le Touquet, palatial 1930s red brick with Art Deco salon and rooms. Expensive, but worth it. ☎ 03 21 05 48 48.

Lille (Nord)
Daily except Monday, but Sunday morning the best

For antique-hunters, the corker to visit in Nord-Pas de Calais is Lille's annual Braderie, which fills the centre of the old town over the first weekend in September, but the next best thing is Wazemmes. There are plenty of bygones to browse among every Sunday morning in this ethnically diverse quarter just 15–20 minutes' walk from Vieux Lille (or Métro it to Gambetta). Wazemmes not only offers the whole span from second-hand junk to bric-a-brac to quite large collectables, it has bargain new clothes, novelties, fabrics, furniture and food as well. This is an outdoor supermarket with entertainment thrown in – robotic clowns, accordion players, North African drummers and demos of gadgets that may never work at home. You can eat your way around it, snacking on fabulous chips, Chinese spring rolls, waffles and Tunisian pastries. There'll be a paella steaming away, spit-roasted chicken, couscous and *tartiflette*, that wicked mix of potatoes, cream and bacon. By lunchtime, all you'll want is a chilled Leffe beer from Lille's own brewery. Find a table at the Café Nouvelle Aventure and watch the market skilfully pack up and melt away. By 2 o'clock it's as if it had never been.

Doing Wazemmes is the perfect way to round off a weekend in the Nord's lively capital (a breeze to get to by Eurostar), for on Sunday other shops are shut – even the big Euralille mall. There are markets in the Wazemmes district every day except Monday, but only Sunday's has the flea market.

If you're in Lille on the first Saturday of the month there's a small flea-market in Place Léon-Trulin. And Lille's Christmas market runs through all of December – chalets crowd Place Rihour, a big wheel turns in the Grand' Place, lights festoon the trees and outline the medieval stock exchange.

Don't miss

✪ French and Flemish masterpieces as well as cutting-edge contemporary work at the Palais des Beaux Arts (a collection second only to the Louvre's).

✪ Watteau paintings and Flemish interiors in the 17th-century Hospice Comtesse.

✪ A lusty *carbonnade flamande* at Alcide (on the Grand' Place), or posh fish at l'Huitrière, an Art Deco gem in the tiny Rue des Chats-Bossus (humpbacked cats).

✪ Café Méert (27 Rue Esquermoise) – somewhere to collapse when all passion and money are spent. It's a *chocolaterie/pâtisserie/salon de thé* where the waffles with hot chocolate are worth sinning for (but closed on Sunday).

ⓘ Place Rihour.

Somewhere to stay

❯ **Alliance**. A clever conversion of a 17th-century convent by the canal. Very contemporary and smart with a huge atrium garden and chic restaurant. ☎ 03 20 30 62 62.

❯ **Paix**. Comfy 18th-century townhouse hotel with a nice friendly feel. The patron is an art lover, hence the plethora of reproductions on the walls. He did the breakfast room mural himself. ☎ 03 20 54 63 93.

St-Omer (Pas de Calais)
Saturday

Rising above the Clairmarais marshlands, with some of its Vauban battlements still in place, St-Omer is a likeable and approachable town. It preserves an air of calm, both along the canalized river Aa, where low workers' cottages watch barges idle by, and in its historic centre. Even on Saturday when the market fills the cobbled Place Foch, people sprawl contentedly in the cafés and just-married brides and grooms pose for photographs on the steps of the 19th-century town hall (locally known as the 'coffee mill') before making an unromantic exit past the cut-price DVDs.

Rue Louis Martel's *marché du terroir* (farmers' market) is the place to trawl for the freshest local vegetables and fruit (once floated in by water). In this street too, farmers' wives at small trestle tables proffer their own home-baked sugar tarts and jars of *potje vleesch*, the three-meats terrine.

In the main square, in June, I found pots of pure white honey, the first of the season (such a light, scented sweetness), and wild mushrooms – crinkly morels, *pieds bleus* with lavender stalks and fragile *pleurottes*. The *pleurottes* were also made up into a quiche, cut in bite-size pieces. *'Vous voulez essayer?'* I tried, and it was good.

St-Omer seems to be big on outsize fashion. Among the usual eclectic selection of mattresses, nightdresses, mobile phone covers and sewing machines, racks of voluminous numbers are labelled *'spécial grande taille'*. I've also noticed it goes in for bumper bottles of obscure scents such as Wagner's Attitude and Lannis's Aujourd'hui. Chanel it ain't, but look and sniff anyway.

At just under an hour from Calais, St-Omer is well worth aiming for on a day trip across the Channel.

Don't miss

✪ The massive basilica of Notre Dame, which shelters Saint Omer's tomb. The nave is 13th century, the enormous tower 15th.

✪ Musée Henri Dupuis, an 18th-century mansion with an ornately tiled Flemish kitchen and fascinating natural history collection of beetles, shells, etc.

✪ Flemish and Dutch paintings, ceramics and tapestries in the Sandelin Museum.

✪ Good antique shops in Rue de Calais – Au Vieux Soldat, for military stuff, and Au Petit Camelot.

✪ The lovely public gardens which have a heated swimming pool open from early June to late September.

✪ At a distance of 8 km, the Cristallerie d'Arques factory shop which sells seconds in Luminarc and Cristal d'Arques glassware.

ⓘ by the cinema in Rue du Lion d'Or.

Somewhere to stay

↘ Ibis. An unusual member of the modestly priced chain, this one is tucked inside an ancient building near the cathedral. Unpretentious restaurant. ☎ 03 21 93 11 11.

↘ Hostellerie St-Hubert at Hallines, around 7km away. Beautiful old manor with delicious cuisine.
☎ 03 21 39 77 77.

Montreuil (Pas de Calais)
Saturday

On my first and most recent visits to this engaging medieval walled town on a hill, the Château de Montreuil hotel was pivotal. Twenty-five years ago, Roux-brothers-trained Christian Germain and his delightful English wife Lindsay had just taken it over and were running winter cookery classes to keep going. When I went back to celebrate a big-number birthday, they had become a Relais & Châteaux and the restaurant was Michelin-starred. Today, year round, they have to turn people away. I can't imagine going to Montreuil without at least dining if not staying there.

The market on Saturday is, however, not incidental to the pleasure of Montreuil. It draws people from miles around because the setting is so picturesque, the town's own specialist food shops are so classy, and there are plenty of atmospheric cafés and restaurants to congregate in before or after filling their baskets. And there's easy car-parking. A gem of a place to shop in an unfussed way. Merchandise ranges from cutlery to well-cut toddlers' jeans, rush-seated chairs to live chickens, and there's lots of farm produce and home-made treats. Particular local goodies to look out for include *saucisses* and terrines flavoured with chicory, a sparkling redcurrant wine called Perlé de Groseille, and a beer named after Jean Valjean, who really existed. The character around whom Victor Hugo worked his tale of *Les Misérables* was once Mayor of Montreuil.

Don't miss

✪ A walk round the fortress ruins (signs say 'La Citadelle') and the 3km of grass-topped ramparts. The views are lovely. Once Montreuil was 'sur-Mer', but like its rival Rye on the English coast, it is now about 15km inland.

✪ The abbey church of St Saulve and the Hôtel Dieu, all filigree stonework.

✪ Earl Douglas Haig's statue in front of the theatre – the British General's HQ were nearby during the First World War and 5000 British troops occupied Montreuil.

✪ *Gâteau battu* from L'Atelier du Goût pâtisserie/chocolatier, Rue Pierre Ledent.

✪ Great wine store, La Cave, in Place Général de Gaulle.

✪ Nice locally-woven baskets from Deroussent in the lower town.

ⓘ 21 Rue Carnot.

Somewhere to stay

↘ Château de Montreuil, not a castle but a country house built by an Englishman at the turn of the 19th century. In lovely grounds with heated swimming pool. Posh and pricy but welcoming.
☎ 03 21 81 53 04.

↘ Auberge de la Grenouillère, an old riverside inn oozing character in La Madelaine-sous-Montreuil, a mile or so out of town. The 'froggery' has excellent food and four rooms.
☎ 03 21 06 07 22.

Arras (Pas de Calais)
Wednesday and Saturday

As befits the capital of Pas-de-Calais, Arras holds the biggest Saturday market in the region (Wednesday's is half the size). For centuries its location has been in the heart of the city, the part bombed to pieces in 1916 but now beautifully restored. Tall stone and brick Flemish-style buildings rise above the arcades that surround all three of the market squares – Place des Héros, where the town hall is, the Grand' Place and the smaller Place de la Vaquerie. The architectural detailing is very pleasing – stepped gables, coats of arms and guild signs. In all but the coldest weather, the brasseries and cafés install their tables under the arcades, so you can take time to gaze upwards and admire. In any case, you need somewhere to recover after negotiating the traffic to get into the centre of town (plenty of space in underground car parks).

Arras has a bit of everything – from knife-sharpeners to shoes, waffles to scooters, live rabbits and cheeping chicks to the long-dead voices of Edith Piaf and Jacques Brel in sun-dried cassette boxes. Canopied fruit and vegetable sections are enormous and charcuterie and cheeses hail from all over France (for those who like milder cheeses, *coeur d'Arras* is one to try). Amateur decorators home in on the mammoth selection of furnishing fabrics and the haberdashery, while bag ladies pounce on the quality leather goods. There's a huge choice of both. A piece of Arras blue china might make a nice souvenir, though possibly it won't be found on a market stall. But there are more than 730 shops within walking distance, including branches of the big department stores. Shopaholics love Arras – especially in December when the Grand' Place hosts a Christmas market for the two weeks up to Christmas Eve.

Don't miss

○ Les Boves, an extraordinary undergound warren of chalk passages which you can explore on a guided tour starting from the town hall cellars. Parts of this subterranean layer date back to the 10th century. The British Army ran a clearing hospital in it during World War One. And there are shops, restaurants and even a night club down there.

○ If you have the puff, a trip up the town hall belfry.

○ St-Vaast's vast abbey which also

houses the fine arts museum and a library.

○ A horse-drawn carriage ride (June, July, August).

ⓘ the town hall.

Somewhere to stay

↘ Univers, elegant ex-monastery, ex-hospital. An 18th-century shell with pretty rooms treated as individuals. Classic cooking. ☎ 03 21 71 34 01.

↘ Trois Luppars, in the oldest house on the Grand' Place, is right in the swirl of things. Quieter rooms at the back. ☎ 03 21 71 34 01.

Hesdin (Pas de Calais)
Thursday

The final frontier of Hapsburg rule in Flanders, Hesdin is a complete one-off: a delightful little town of neat, steep-roofed brick and stone houses, through which the River Canche meanders. So does the

Thursday market, as it has done for more than a century. Behind the church, under the lime strees, are big stone slabs which used to serve as fish counters. Now the fish is sold from a pristine *poissonnerie* van as EU rules dictate, but still in the same picturesque corner where three streets meet over the river.

Start in the main square, Place d'Armes, with its wonderfully ornate Hôtel de Ville – a palace built by Charles V for Marie of Hungary. Here group the canopied stalls of the mixed market – the usual novelties, from shoelaces to watch straps, plants to knitting wools, and a particularly good selection of fabrics (bolts of Liberty and Dormeuil at well-docked prices). Turn down Rue de la Paroisse for hardware. Then the food runs along the side of the church. For an edible souvenir look for Hesdin cheese, or Belval, a tasty cow's milk cheese named after the monastery that makes it. Four rôtisseries are kept busy with delicious pork ribs as well as chicken, and there are *chichis* (a kind of long doughnut like Spanish *churros*) in addition to waffles.

Hesdin has starred on the small screen. The TV drama series *Monsieur Renard*, in which the much-loved late John Thaw played a local priest quietly aiding the Resistance, was shot here, and the town was once used in a Maigret series too.

Don't miss

✪ The Spanish royal coat of arms flanked by the shields of Hesdin and Artois on the town hall balcony – you can visit the interior (the ballroom is now a theatre) and climb the belfry.

✪ The fabulous Renaissance-style stone portal of Notre Dame church.

✪ A wander through the web of little side streets, full of historical oddities.

✪ Azincourt, about 10km away, where the Battle of Agincourt was fought.

✪ Pépinières Jean-Pierre Hennebelle in Boubers-sur-Canche, 16km away, a magical nursery-garden of grasses, flowers and perfumed shrubs that's full of inspiration.

ⓘ Place d'Armes.

Somewhere to stay

↘ Flandres, right in the centre, small and spotless. Good grills and fresh fish. ☎ 03 21 86 80 21.

↘ Trois Fontaines, just out of town, rather bland and modern but comfortable and good value in peaceful garden setting. ☎ 03 21 86 81 65.

Best of the Rest

★ **Ambleteuse** Nice small resort on a hill between Boulogne and Calais. Market on Wednesday.

★ **Ardres** Just inland from Calais, the essence of France – a pretty, peaceful little town that time seems to have passed by. Market on Thursday in triangular cobbled square.

★ **Avèsnes-sur-Helpe** Elegant riverside town with Vauban fortifications a few miles from Belgium at the very eastern tip of the Nord *département*. Good market on Friday.

★ **Berck-sur-Mer** Busy French family favourite with a great beach and pedestrian shopping areas full of cafés and restaurants. Markets most mornings – not Thursday or Monday.

★ **Béthune** Baroque, Alsatian and Art Deco buildings jostle each other in the well-restored Grand' Place of this industrious town where mining once mixed with its (still-thriving) market gardening. Useful to know that it has a market on Monday (as well as Friday) mornings – when shops are usually closed in France. Béthune's shops also stay open during the market.

★ **Boulogne** Fish straight off the boats are sold on quayside stalls daily (except Sunday). Wednesday and Saturday mornings, the traditional market takes over Place Dalton, lower town. Mainly fresh regional produce. Don't miss the historic old town and the battlements. There's a smaller Sunday market in Place Vignon.

★ **Calais** Its traditional markets are as big a draw as the outlying hypermarkets. Wednesday and Saturday near Place d'Armes; Thursday and Saturday, Place Crêvecoeur. Last weekend in May there's a huge flea market, Les Puces Calaisiennes.

★ **Cambrai** Much repaired after war damage, the centre is beautiful, with old Spanish and Flemish-style houses cheek by jowl. Fine cotton was – and still is – its thing (cambric). Wednesday and Saturday markets in the main square.

★ **Cassel** Perched on a hill above the Flanders plain, this *ville fleurie* of much charm has a castle, a windmill, an old brick church and a small Thursday market. Stop at one of its *estaminets* (bar with food) for typical Flemish beer and cheer.

★ **Le Cateau-Cambrésis** Odd but likeable small town that was Wellington's HQ for the Battle of Waterloo. The main street dips towards the river Selle then climbs steeply upwards. There are nice old cobbled bits and a museum devoted to Matisse who was born here. Small fruit and vegetable markets Tuesday and Friday mornings and a huge market on 22 of each month.

★ **Douai** Its surroundings may be dreary but if you're heading this way, the centre of this ex-mining town is worth seeing. There are lovely old Flemish buildings, canal-side walks and an exuberant town hall belfry that tolls on the quarters. Markets on Wednesday, Friday and Saturday (best) mornings.

★ **Gravelines** Vauban's walls have been carefully rebuilt around this neat small port/resort that welcomes cruisers into the river Aa. Arrivals on Friday or Sunday can top up their galley supplies at morning markets.

★ **Le Touquet-Paris-Plage** A fabulous market on Thursday and Saturday morning, plus Monday from Whitsun to mid-September, centres on the wonderful 1920s purpose-built arcaded hall in Rue de Metz and in the car parks front and back of it. Everything is top quality: food – especially fish from nearby Etaples and Boulogne – kitchenware, dress jewellery. Stalls outside sell bargains in well-known makes of high-street fashion.

★ **Valenciennes** A lively cultural mecca, birthplace of the painter Watteau. Markets are in the splendid central square on Wednesday morning and Place Taffin on Thursday afternoon. Local luxury: *langue Lucullus*, a striped pâté composed of *foie gras* and duck filet.

★ **Wimereux** Bright, whistle-clean resort typical of the Côte d'Opale with a great beach, a boardwalk and good restaurants; also a good market on Tuesday and Friday mornings.

🖱 www.northernfrance-tourism.com

Markets at a glance: Nord-Pas de Calais

A
Abscon, *Tue*
Aire-sur-la-Lys, *Fri*
Ambleteuse, *Wed*
Anconnes-lez-Aubert, *Thu*
Aniche, *Fri*
Annay-sous-Lens, *Wed*
Annouellin, *Tue*
Anor, *Wed*
Anzin, *Tue*, *Fri*
Ardres, *Thu*
Arleux, *Tue*
Armentières, *Fri*
Arques, *Tue*
Arras, see Six of the Best
Auby, *Wed*
Auchel, *Tue*
Audruicq, *Wed*
Aulnoye-Aimeries, *Tue*
Auxi-le-Château, *Sat*
Avèsnes-lez-Aubert, *Sun*
Avèsnes-sur-Helpe, *Fri*
Avion, *Thu*
B
Bailleul, *Tue*
Bapaume, *Fri*
Barlin, *Wed*
La Bassée, *Thu*
Bauvin, *Fri*
Bavay, *Fri*
Berck-sur-Mer, *Tue*, *Wed*,
 Fri, *Sat*, *Sun*
Bergues, *Mon*
Berlaimont, *Thu*
Béthune, *Mon*, *Fri*
Beuvrages, *Sun*
Beuvry, *Fri*
Biache-Saint-Vaast, *Thu*
Billy-Montigny, *Sun*
Bollezéele, *Wed*
Bondues, *Thu*, *Sun*
Bouchain, *Thu*
Boulogne-sur-Mer, *Wed*, *Sat*,
 Sun
Bourbourg, *Tue*
Boussois, *Fri*
Bray-Dunes, *Thu*
Brébières, *Thu*
Bruay, *Fri*
Bruay-la-Buissière, *Sun*
Bruay-sur-l'Escaut, *Thu*, *Sun*

Bully-les-Mines, *Thu*, *Sat*
C
Calais, *Wed*, *Thu*, *Sat*
Calonne-Ricouart, *Thu*
Cambrai, *Wed*, *Sat*
Camiers, *Mon*, *Thu*
Carvin, *Sat*
Cassel, *Thu*
Le Cateau, *Tue*, *Fri*
Catillon-sur-Sambre, *Mon*
Cauchy, *Fri*
Caudry, *Tue*
Chocques, *Thu*
Comines, *Mon*
Conde-sur-Escaut, *Sat*
Condette, *Sun*
Coudekerque-Branche, *Tue*,
 Thu, *Fri*
Coulogne, *Mon*
Courcelles-les-Lens, *Sun*
Courrères, *Wed*
Cousolre, *Wed*
Croix, *Tue*, *Wed*, *Fri*, *Sat*, *Sun*
Cucq, *Wed* and *Sun*
 (Jun–Sep)
Cysoing, *Tue*
D
Dechy, *Tue*
Denain, *Thu*
Dèsvres, *Tue*
Deulemont, *Fri*
Divion, *Wed*
Douai, *Wed*, *Fri*, *Sat*
Douchy-les-Mines, *Sat*
Douvrin, *Mon*
Dunkerque, *Tue*, *Wed*, *Thu*,
 Sat, *Sun*
E
Ecourt-Saint-Quentin, *Wed*
Escaudin, *Mon*
Escautpont, *Fri*
Estaires, *Thu*
**Etaples-sur-Mer, see Six of
 the Best**
F
Faches-Thumésnil, *Thu*
Fauquembergues, *Thu*
Feignies, *Thu*
Fenain, *Sat*
Ferrière-la-Grande, *Sat*
Flers-en-Escrebieux, *Mon*, *Fri*

Fouquieres-lez-Lens, *Fri*
Fourmies, *Sat*
Frèsnes-sur-Escaut, *Tue*
Frétin, *Wed*
Frévent, *Tue*
Fruges, *Sat*
G
Gognies-Chaussée, *Tue*
Gommegnies, *Sun*
Grande-Synthe, *Tue*, *Thu*
Grand-Fort-Philippe, *Mon*
Gravelines, *Fri*, *Sun*
Grenay, *Tue*
Guines, *Fri*
H
Halluin, *Sat*
Harnes, *Thu*
Hasnon, *Thu*
Haspres, *Mon*
Haubourdin, *Fri*
Hautmont, *Tue*, *Fri*
Hazebrouck, *Mon*
Hellèmes, *Wed*, *Sat*
Hem, *Sat*
Hénin-Beaumont, *Tue*, *Fri*
Hesdin, see Six of the Best
Hondschoote, *Fri*
Houdain, *Thu*, *Sat*
I
Isbergues, *Thu*
Iwuy, *Tue*
J
Jeumont, *Thu*
L
Lallaing, *Mon*
Lambérsart, *Tue*, *Wed*, *Fri*
Landrecies, *Sat*
Lannoy, *Fri*
Lécluse, *Wed*
Leers, *Sat*
Leforest, *Wed*
Lens, *Tue*, *Fri*, *Sat*
Lésquin, *Thu*
Libercourt, *Thu*
Lievin, *Wed*, *Sun*
Ligny-en-Cambresis, *Wed*
Lille, see Six of the Best
Lillers, *Sat*
Linselles, *Fri*
Loison-sur-Lens, *Sat*
Lomme, *Wed*, *Sat*

Loon-Plage, *Sun*
Loos-en-Gohelle, *Thu*
Lourches, *Wed*
Louvroil, *Thu*
Lumbres, *Fri*
M
La Madeleine, *Mon*, *Wed*, *Fri*
Marchiennes, *Sat*
Marcq-en-Baroeul, *Tue*, *Sat*
Mariolles, *Tue*
Marles-les-Mines, *Sat*
Marq-en-Baroeul, *Tue*, *Fri*,
    Sat
Marquette-lez-Lille, *Wed*
Marquise, *Thu*
Maubeuge, *Mon*, *Wed*, *Sat*
Mazingarbe, *Wed*, *Fri*, *Sat*
Méricourt, *Sat*
Merlimont, *Mon*, *Fri*
Merville, *Wed*
Mons, *Thu*
Mons-en-Baroeul, *Sun*
**Montreuil, see Six of the
    Best**
Mortagne-du-Nord, *Wed*
Mouvaux, *Thu*
N
Neuville-en-Ferrain, *Wed*
Neuville-sur-Escaut, *Sat*
Noeux-les-Mines, *Tue*, *Fri*
Noyelles-Godault, *Thu*
O
Oignies, *Tue*
Onnaing, *Mon*
Orchies, *Fri*, *Sun*
Ostricourt, *Thu*
Outreau, *Mon*, *Thu*
Oye-Plage, *Wed* (+ *Sat*
    Apr–Oct)
P
Perenchies, *Sat*
Pernus-en-Artois, *Thu*
Petite-Synthe, *Thu*
Pont-à-Vendin, *Thu*
Le Portel, *Tue*, *Fri*
Q
Le Quesnoy, *Fri*
Quesnoy-sur-Deule, *Sun*
Quivrechain, *Thu*
R
Raches, *Thu*

Raismes, *Thu*
Recquencourt, *Tue*
Roeulx, *Fri*
Ronchin, *Thu*, *Sun*
Roncq, *Wed*, *Thu*
Roubaix, daily (not *Tue*)
Rouvroy, *Mon*
S
Saighin-en-Weppes, *Fri*
Sains-du-Nord, *Wed*
Sains-en-Gohelle, *Wed*
Saint-Amand-les-Eaux, *Fri*
Saint-André-lez-Lille, *Tue*
**Saint-Omer, see Six of the
    Best**
Saint-Pol-sur-Mer, *Sun*
Saint-Pol-sur-Ternoise, *Mon*
Sallaumines, *Mon*, *Sat*
Samer, *Mon*
Sars-Poteries, *Thu*
Séclin, *Mon*
La Sentinelle, *Wed*
Sin-le-Noble, *Fri*
Solèsmes, *Thu*
Solre-le-Château, *Tue*
Somain, *Thu*
Steenvoorde, *Sat*
T
Templeuve, *Mon*
Therouanne, *Tue*
Thiant, *Fri*
Thumeries, *Mon*
Toufflers, *Wed*
Le Touquet-Paris-Plage, *Thu*,
    Sat (+ *Mon* Jun–Sep)

Tourcoing, daily (not *Sun*)
Trelon, *Mon*
Trith-Saint-Lèger, *Fri*
V
Valen, *Sat*
Valenciennes, *Wed*, *Thu*
Vendin-le-Vieil, *Mon*, *Fri*
Vermelles, *Mon*
Viesly, *Sun*
Vieux-Condé, *Mon*
Villeneuve-d'Ascq, *Fri*, *Sat*
Villers-Outreaux, *Tue*
Vimy, *Sat*
Vitry-en-Artois, *Tue*
W
Walincourt-Selvigny, *Mon*
Wambrechies, *Sun*
Wasquehal, *Wed*, *Sat*
Watten, *Fri*
Wattignies, *Wed*
Wattrelos, *Thu*, *Fri*, *Sat*, *Sun*
Wavrin, *Sat*
Waziers, *Tue*
Wimereux, *Tue*, *Fri*
Wingles, *Wed*
Wissant, *Wed*

PICARDY

Beans and bygones, Chantilly porcelain and the beginning of bubbly land

The best motorway in France is the A16. Sweeping southwards from Calais just inland from the coast, it's not only quieter than the A26 but more scenic. In less than an hour, the vast green duvet of Picardy billows around you, villages with pen-nib church spires settled in the folds, hedges and dense copses on the rises. But slow down a minute. This is not just somewhere to pass through on the way to somewhere else. Picardy is beautiful. It has six of the country's most awesome Gothic cathedrals, riveting World War One reminders, the great châteaux of Chantilly, Compiègne and Pierrefonds, and pretty rural backwaters.

Until recently I was as guilty as anyone of bypassing its glories. Now I'm in danger of becoming a Picardy bore, not least because I found some great markets here. The landscape is well watered from above as well as by its rivers and marshland, so the quality of farm produce is without peer. The coast may be the shortest on the Channel, the mouth of the Somme taking a good bite out of it, but its fishermen net a rich haul. What's more, the region's proximity to Paris means a heightened demand for antiques. The twice-yearly Rederies of Amiens are among the oldest bygones fairs in northern France, and throughout the year there are umpteen *brocantes* and *vide-greniers* (literally 'empty attics', the equivalent of car boot sales) in the market towns and country villages of Picardy's three *départements*: Oise, Aisne and Somme.

My re-education started with an early summer trip by Eurotunnel on a stormy, rain-lashed day – the kind of weather in which a ferry crossing might have left me in no mood for lunch. As it was, 70 minutes after emerging smoothly from beneath the sea, I was in delightful Saint-Valery-sur-Somme contemplating a plate of oysters in the Relais Guillaume de Normandy. This hotel's name underlines the port's great historical moment when William of Normandy's ships finally departed from Saint-Valery en route for Hastings in 1066. Its fanciful style, topped by a curious tower, at first reminded me of another Norman – *Psycho*'s Norman Bates – but once inside the cheerful dining room with its misty views of herons doing a fly-past over the Bay of the Somme I decided this was the perfect pitch to await Saint-Valery's Sunday market (see Six of the Best).

Amiens and its canal-veined old centre were another pleasant surprise. Revisiting Senlis confirmed it as the town I'd most want to settle in in northern France. And a whole string of gems such as Longpont, La Ferté-Milon, the perched medieval city of Laon and the strange fortified churches of the Thiérache have whetted my appetite for seeing more of Picardy and the Picards.

Specialities

Antoine Auguste Parmentier did for France what Sir Walter Raleigh did for Britain – he played a pivotal role in the cultivation of **potatoes**. A statue of him stands in the market place of Montdidier, his home town, but his best memorial is *hachis parmentier*, the French refinement of cottage pie. My, spuds are good here – especially the ones that soak up chicken *jus* in those glass-fronted market *rôtisseries*. Indeed, such a cornucopia of vegetables thrives in Picardy's market gardens – leeks, carrots, cress, chicory, green beans, peas – that it is no surprise to discover the excellent Bonduelle label's canning factories are based at Saint-Quentin.

For some reason, Soissons is renowned for a variety of large **white bean**. No one can say why, except that it does rather well in the soil around this cathedral city. Soissons beans are sold dried, canned, bottled and even replicated in sugar-coated chocolate form. I half expected to hear, as you do in France, that their *raison d'être* sprouted from some medieval miracle. You know the kind of story – the citizens of a beseiged Soissons are saved from starvation when some saintly fellow sows a row of beans that shoot up into a forest of beanstalks overnight. Why else would I have found, close by the cathedral's west door, a small plot staked with bamboo and the sign, 'Jardin des Haricots'?

Picardy also grows bumper crops of red **berries** which make the first Sunday in July a red letter day in Noyon for the annual Marché aux Fruits Rouges. But the season for strawberries, raspberries and cherries is a long one, with plenty of spin-off tarts, jams, sorbets, apéritifs and refreshing fruit drinks sold at *marchés paysans*. These farmers' markets are also great sources of *foie gras*, *saucissons*, and terrines made from wild boar or locally

smoked eel or duck with honey. Look, too, for freshly made *chèvre* as well as three other cheeses: orange-skinned Maroilles (made here as well as in Nord-Pas de Calais), creamy *dauphin* (young Maroilles mixed with tarragon, chives and pepper) and heart-shaped *rollot*.

The **apple orchards** of the Thiérache produce a light, flat cider, but topping the drinks list is Picardy's **champagne**. A few parcels of vines cluster on the banks of the river Marne where the champagne vineyards begin in earnest (Reims and Epernay are no distance away in neighbouring Champagne-Ardenne). From here, you can follow part of the marked Route du Champagne, stopping to taste and buy. At Picardy's Château-Thierry, the *caves* where Champagne Pannier is stored are inside the rocky spur on which the castle is built. Curiously, you have to go up, not down, to access them as the reception area is at the bottom of the hill.

The best of Picardy 'buys' are either edible or have some connection with *l'art de la table*. There's delicate Chantilly porcelain to seek out in specialist shops if you go to Chantilly market. Sadly, the spidery black gossamer of Chantilly lace is no longer made, but with luck you might come across a vintage scrap at an antique fair. Early pieces of the distinctive blue-and white faïence de Sinceny are also much sought after by collectors. Crisp lace-trimmed linens, old and new, are good market buys, as are beautiful baskets and other artefacts woven from reeds that grow around the Bay of the Somme.

Six of the Best

Senlis

Tuesday and Friday mornings

If minded to choose 'six of the best' in the country as a whole, I would have to include Senlis. Surrounded by woods, only a few miles from Chantilly, this small medieval town of pale stone is utterly charming. It has little suburban sprawl and its centre is walkable from neat flower-trimmed car parks. A lot of very well-heeled shoppers flock to the high-quality twice-weekly market which practically fills the *vieille ville*, though it centres on the little Place de la Halle (no hall visible). Here, a fabulous fish stall takes pride of place outside the permanent *poissonnerie*. On a bright May morning, *bulots* from the north-east and *crevettes roses* from the south-west flanked glistening mackerel and spiky spider crabs, while a *terrine de saumon* layered with egg and spinach *en gelée* offered upmarket picnic potential.

Plenty of chic children's togs and toys and pretty embroidered tablecloths wafted in the sunshine, and there was a good selection of men's and women's casual clothes and accessories. But the food, as ever, took centre stage, the entire gastronomic gamut. Handmade pasta. A stall piled with pulses – chickpeas, Puy lentils, black-eye beans and speckled pink ones like small birds' eggs as well as the local Soissons beans. Quail, guinea fowl and corn-fed chickens all impeccably prepared for cooking . . . My eyes fell upon two microscopic dogs tied up outside the *épicerie*, their little bodies shivering nervously as if terrified of being snatched up and trussed for the oven too!

A collectables market is held every first Friday of the month in Espace Parinord.

Don't miss

✪ La Petite Cocotte, state-of-the-art kitchen shop.

✪ Notre-Dame, Place Parvis, begun in 1153 – before Notre-Dame in Paris.

✪ The Musée d'Art in the former bishop's palace (medieval sculptures; Corot and Boudin landscapes).

✪ Cobbled streets of fine old houses leading down to the river Nonette.

✪ Nearby, the Château de Chantilly.

ⓘ Place Parvis.

Somewhere to stay

⬏Hostellerie de la Porte Bellon, well-patronized Logis de France a minute's walk from the market (with parking space). ☎ 03 44 53 03 05.

⬏Auberge de Fontaine in the sleepy hamlet of Fontaine-Chaalis, 13km away. Run by charming young couple who serve unpretentious tasty food. Good wine list. The Mouton Rothschild which cost £45 when I was treated to it by a show-off photographer friend in the 1980s is now priced at over £200 – but there are more affordable labels. ☎ 03 44 54 20 22.

St-Valery-sur-Somme
Sunday morning

This extremely pleasant little port, which inspired painters Degas and Seurat and novelist Victor Hugo, stretches along the mouth of the river Somme opposite Le Crotoy. Steep streets lead to its fortified old town up on the hill. Shrimping is the main interest of its fishing community, who come in on the tide in boats called *sauterelliers*.

Naturally, the Sunday morning market in Place des Pilotes (normally a car park) offers up some just-caught shellfish as well as other quality local produce, confectionery, handicrafts, gadgets. A big event – even in winter there are some 50 vendors; this doubles in summer. There's also a Wednesday market in Place du Jeu de Battoir, but it is a shrimp by comparison. The place to collapse after shopping is Les Galettes de Tante Olympe, Rue de la Ferté, a *salon de thé* serving great sweet and savoury pancakes.

William the Conqueror's last port of call (to pick up troops) before the invasion of England, St-Valery is today invaded at weekends by Parisians (it's nearer than Le Touquet), so the standard of shops is high. An extensive prom along the quays, past jolly cafés, bars and ice-cream parlours, leads from the river to the Bay, then flanks a well-managed beach. Through an archway in the ancient walls you enter the medieval town. From the calvary at the top is a splendid view of the bay flecked with the sails of pleasure yachts – or sand-yachts when the tide is out – and you can see sheep seasoning themselves as they crop the grasses of the surrounding salt-soaked meadows.

Don't miss

✪ The picturesque ruins of the abbey – the 18th-century abbot's château still stands intact.

✪ The old Mariners' Chapel with its chequerboard stonework facade and the entombed leftovers of Saint Valery.

✪ The Courtgain district where bright fishermen's cottages huddle together.

✪ *Bonnes adresses* in Rue de la Ferté: Dame Tartine for fine foods, wine and cheese; Entre Ciel et Terre for better-class souvenirs.

✪ Au Samovar, Place des Pilotes, for teas and *tisanes*.

ⓘ Place Guillaume le Conquérant.

Somewhere to stay

↘ Relais Guillaume de Normandy, as mentioned. Welcoming 2-chimney Logis de France where early booking is advisable for weekends. Closed Tuesdays except from 15 July to 20 August. ☎ 03 22 60 82 36.

Amiens

Every day (Saturday and Sunday best)

Amiens boasts the largest Gothic cathedral in the land in a historic centre so well restored you would never know two-thirds of it was destroyed in World War Two. The *vieille ville* is now *so* attractive, with a lacework of little waterways and acres of water gardens called *les hortillonnages*, which harbour mallards, moorhens, musk rats and herons. Appealing quayside restaurants and trips in raised-bow boats (once used by the market gardeners to deliver their produce) give the city a permanent holiday air.

Saturday's market in Place du Beffroi (old belfry) takes some beating for ambiance as well as variety. Outside the permanent Les Halles, a cool modern building where fresh produce is sold daily, stalls crowd the square and offshoot streets. You can buy everything from Picarde specialities like leek tart and ready-to-heat *ficelle picarde* (a pancake filled with ham, mushrooms, cream and cheese) to leather goods, fabrics, clothes and novelties.

Also on Saturday, until noon, fruit and vegetables are sold by the waterside on Quai Parmentier. This is one of the most engaging corners of town, just a block from the cathedral, and it's fun to stroll along the river when the market gives it an edible herbaceous border. Once a year, usually on the third Sunday in June, the vendors don medieval dress and punt their produce alongside the embankment on traditional boats.

On the second Sunday of every month, Quai Parmentier hosts a flea market. Among the cornucopia of yesterday's knick-knacks, you'll often find World War One memorabilia. The Rederies, among the oldest bric-a-brac fairs in the country, take over the town centre twice a year, usually the first Sunday in October and last Sunday in April.

Don't miss

✪ The cathedral of Notre Dame, a World Heritage Site of mind-boggling statistics. Remarkable 16th-century carved reliefs. Nicolas Blasset's poignant sculpture of the Weeping Angel.

✪ The picturesque Saint-Leu district. This old artisans' quarter bisected by channels of the Somme is full of antiques shops (a glut in Passage Bleu), little restaurants and bars.

✪ *Les Hortillonnages* – 45-minute boat trips go from the Parc Saint-Pierre.

✪ Jules Verne's House, 2 Rue Charles Dubois.

ⓘ 6 bis, Rue Dusevel.

Somewhere to stay

↘ Hôtel-restaurant Le Prieuré, Rue Porion, a 'hôtel de charme' in a 17th-century house near the cathedral. ☎ 03 22 71 16 71.

↘ Relais Mercure Amiens Cathédrale, Place au Feurre, next to the police station. Very individual link in the Mercure chain. ☎ 03 22 22 00 20.

Fère-en-Tardenois
Wednesday morning

An unassuming country town on the river Ourcq, north-east of Château-Thierry's champagne territory, Fère is a place where not a lot happens – until market day. Then, it absolutely jumps. The main focus of activity is the 16th-century Halle aux Blés whose slate roof and venerable timbers are held in place by stone pillars. Originally, the upper half was a communal tithe barn. During World War One, it was badly dented. Now painstakingly restored, it leans nonchalantly in Place Aristide Briand, providing larder conditions for shade-loving produce.

The merchandise reflects the life of the surrounding countryside, where the preoccupations are farming, market gardening, river fishing and hunting. On an early summer morning, rows of chalky hand-made cheeses vied with trays of bedding plants. Bunches of baby lilac-tinged turnips and new carrots arrived with leaves still attached. While, down the Rue des Marchands, the fashion accessories ranged from waders, gumboots and serious-looking knives to purple sunglasses and 'granny' canvas shoes.

Like all country markets, Fère doubles as a social event with knots of farmers here and farmers' wives there, all chatting greedily. Stallholders too. The asparagus seller asked where I was staying, then whipped out a business card for her own *chambres d'hôtes*.

Don't miss

✪ 16th-century church with lovely carved wooden seating.

✪ The extraordinary ruin of the Château de Fère, just out of town. Once as grand as Chenonceaux, it fell into the hands of the *méchant* Duc d'Orléans on whom the finer points of its architecture were lost. A profligate and libertine who famously held court among the low life of Paris during the Revolution, he sold off his château bit by bit – furniture, roof tiles and stones from its galleried bridge – partly to show his egalitarian spirit but mainly to pay off his debts. The castle was soon dismantled, and the *duc* also – by Madame Guillotine. One wing was restored in the 19th century and is now a sybaritic hotel.

✪ A hearty meal in La Table Féroise, 67 Rue Carnot – the food is tastier than the decor.

ⓘ just off Place Aristide Briand.

Somewhere to stay

↘ The Château de Fère (see above) has a pool and a fine, if expensive, restaurant. ☎ 03 23 82 21 13.

↘ Résidence Clairbois *chambres d'hôtes* run by Mme Chauvin. Comfortable, spotless and good value if you don't mind curiosities. My facilities were truly en suite, with the toilet in part of the wardrobe. M. Chauvin is a mine of local lore. ☎ 03 23 82 21 72.

Compiègne
Wednesday and Saturday

Once, when cruising the river Oise, I arrived in Compiègne by boat, mooring – as you still can – just below the heart of town. I was impressed by it then and still am. With the oaks and beeches of the Compiègne Forest creeping up to its outskirts, a palace ranked third after Versailles and Fontainebleau, and streets of pale, elegant houses, it is a very likeable town.

The splendid late-Gothic Hôtel de Ville boasts a belfry from which three wooden clockwork figures, Les Picantins, emerge on the hours and quarters. Much of what stands between the Place de l'Hôtel de Ville and the river is relatively new and it's here that a spacious Place du Marché has been created in the centre of a pedestrian zone of shopping malls and cafés. This is the venue, all day Wednesdays and Saturdays, for a really buzzy market for clothes, accessories, gadgets and fripperies. With Compiègne being so close to Paris, there is little tat. Also on Wednesday and Saturday mornings are excellent food markets in Place du Change – a rectangular space in the lee of the library with ancient timbered buildings in one corner. This is foodie territory even on non-market days – several butchers and *charcutiers*, a big deli/greengrocer (Les Halles du Grenier de Sel), a chocolate shop called Aux Trois Ours and an irresistible cheese shop, La Boîte à Fromages. Before or after shopping you can be revived in the atmospheric Coq d'Or bar-brasserie or be coiffed in L'Hair du Temps.

Brocante in Place du Marché aux Herbes on the fourth Sunday in the month.

Don't miss

✪ The heroic statue of Joan of Arc in Place de l'Hôtel de Ville. Compiègne was her last stand before being captured by the Burgundians, sold to the English and burned at the stake in Rouen.

✪ The château, now the Galerie Nationale, with its sumptuous silk hangings, tapestries, porcelain, paintings and vintage car museum. Glorious grounds with rose garden and stone lions sporting Dolly Parton manes.

✪ The Clairière de l'Armistice, on the edge of the Compiègne Forest, where the Armistice of 1918 was signed in a railway carriage (the one you see is a sister of the original, which Hitler used as a humiliating venue for the French surrender in 1940 and later took to Berlin).

✪ Les Picantins *pâtissier-chocolatier* in Rue Jean Legendre. Speciality: chocolate-covered glazed nuts named after the figures on the belfry.

ⓘ Place de l'Hôtel de Ville.

Somewhere to stay

⬆ Hôtel le Harlay, on the river, 5 minutes from the Hôtel de Ville. Bland and modern but comfortable with the plus of a residents' car park. No restaurant. ☎ 03 44 23 01 50.

⬆ Hôtel de Flandres, other side of the Pont Solférino. ☎ 03 44 83 24 40. The Bistrot de Flandre (☎ 03 44 83 26 35) underneath is owned by different people but is superb.

Laon
Thursday

If everyone flashing past Laon on the A26 knew what a fascinating town it was, Laon would be overrun. As it is, the Ville Haute, elevated on a table-top spur overlooking the surrounding plain, is almost too busy for its own good. Discover it off-season. Capital of France when Paris was a mere village, it has a beautiful early-Gothic cathedral, one of the oldest in Europe. Seeing its intricate west facade for the first time against a cobalt sky one August evening, I was agog. Neck-cricked, I spotted what I supposed to be cows on its pinnacles. They apparently represent the muscular oxen which hauled the stones up the hill for the builders. With appealing cafés and restaurants, cobbled streets and sturdy ramparts, old Laon is a delight. Down the hill and beyond spreads the Ville Basse.

On Saturday morning, a tiny but picturesque market sells fruit, vegetables, fish and fowl in the Ville Haute's Place du Marché aux Herbes. A more extensive Saturday afternoon one is held in Place du 8 Mai 1945 (Ville Basse). But the biggie is on Thursday in the Ville Basse, when over 130 stalls take their stands in Place Victor Hugo in the Quartier des Vaux. A market that garners the best of Picardy – flowers and *produits du terroir*, chunky knits and unusual casuals, babies' wear and bovver boots, skeins of knitting wools and reams of bargain fabrics. Name it, it's here.

Over the fourth weekend in May, Laon holds Les Euromédiévales, a medieval market and fair.

Don't miss

✪ As well as the cathedral, the abbey church of St-Martin and the walk around the 16th-century *citadelle*.

✪ The pedestrianized Rue Châtelaine with great little shops like La Torréfaction (coffees, teas, jams, chocs and presents); also Rue du Bourg's Les Merlettes for fruit confits, preserved duck, rabbit and *foie gras*.

✪ A few miles south of town, the Chemin des Dames memorial museum on the ridge which saw one of the most drawn-out battles of World War One.

ⓘ Place du Parvis.

Somewhere to stay

⬆ La Bannière de France, popular charismatic old inn in the Ville Haute serving tasty traditional cooking. ☎ 03 23 23 21 44.

Best of the Rest

★ **Beauvais** Huge markets all day Wednesday and Saturday in the wide Place des Halles. Stunning unfinished early Gothic cathedral (a rib-vaulted nave that reaches for the heavens and an astrological clock). Ice cream to-die-for opposite.

★ **Chantilly** The horse-racing capital. Traditional markets on Wednesday and Saturday mornings in Place Omer Vallon. The fabulous château reflected in its lake is almost outdone by its stables, Les Grandes Ecuries. See the Museum of the Living Horse – different breeds on show, dressage displays.

★ **Le Crotoy** Friday morning; Tuesdays too from mid-June to mid-October. Good for fresh fish. Port almost as nice as St-Valery on the other side of the estuary.

★ **La Ferté-Milon** *Tiny* market Friday morning – just a couple of stalls (one fish) in Place du Mail – but go for the setting. An adorable little town on the river Ourcq with a bridge designed by Gustave Eiffel. Birthplace of Racine, haunt of artists and fishing enthusiasts.

★ **Montdidier** Parmentier's birthplace has a lively market on Thursday mornings gathered around the potato promoter's statue. Great crêpes and salads in Le Verger – fabric flowers and plastic mushroom decor notwithstanding.

★ **Le Nouvion-en-Thiérache** The Wednesday market here is the best in the Thiérache border country where fortified churches with witch's hat spires nestle among apple orchards – Picardy's 'little Normandy'. Le Nouvion is small, relaxed and offers lots of leisure options.

★ **Noyon** *Grands marchés* on Saturday mornings and on the first Tuesday of the month. The monthly one is the more special, with farmers bringing handmade cheeses and *charcuterie*, and live chickens and animals creating a stir. Tiny market on Wednesday.

★ **Pierrefonds** Beside the magnificent feudal château, reconstructed by Viollet-le-Duc for Napoleon III, is a pretty spa town where shopping in the Friday morning market is a particular pleasure.

★ **Rue** Saturday morning traditional market in Place de Verdun. Quiet town full of charm on the edge of the Marquenterre marshes (just off the D940). Nice food shops such as La Ferme St Christophe for locally raised meat and poultry, Guy Serquier for Picardy tarts and Jean-Bernard Miot for honey.

★ **St-Quentin** Good markets on Wednesday and Saturday mornings in the Place de l'Hôtel de Ville. Others on Friday in the Quartier de l'Europe and on Sunday in the Quartier Faubourg d'Isle. Big, busy town.

★ **Soissons** Wednesday and Saturday mornings (until noon), Les Halles and good general market by the cathedral Saint Pierre. The farm shop L'Angélus, in the square on the other side of the cathedral from the market, sells Soissons beans in big glass jars and ostrich products from the Thiérache.

★ **Vic-sur-Aisne** Nice little riverside town if you ignore the two disused grain silos. Market on Thursday mornings in Place Général de Gaulle overseen by a turreted donjon. Bar de l'Oeuf Dur *very* friendly.

www.picardy.org

Markets at a glance: Picardy

A
Abbeville, *Wed, Thu, Sat*
Ailly-sur-Noye, *Wed*
Airaines, *Fri* (+ alternate *Suns*)
Albert, *Sat* (+ 2nd *Wed*)
Amiens, see Six of the Best
Ault-Onival, *Sat* (+ *Wed* Jul/Aug)
B
Beaucamp-le-Vieux, *Wed*
Beauvais, *Wed, Sat*
Berneuil-en-Bray, 2nd *Sun*
Béthisy-Saint-Pierre, *Fri*
Blangy-sur-Bresle, *Sun*
Braine, *Fri*
Bray-sur-Somme, 1st *Wed*
Bresles, *Thu*
Breteuil, *Wed*
C
Camon, *Thu*
La Capelle, *Fri*
Cayeux-sur-Mer, *Tue, Fri, Sun*
Chambly, *Wed*
Chantilly, *Wed, Sat*
Charly-sur-Marne, *Thu*
Château-Thierry, *Tue, Fri*, 4th *Sat*
Chaulnes, *Thu*
Chauny, *Tue* (fruit & veg only), *Fri*
Chézy-sur-Marne, *Sat*
Clermont, *Sat*
Coincy-l'Abbaye, 2nd *Sun* (Apr–Oct)
Combles, 1st *Sun* (except Jan)
Compiègne, see Six of the Best
Condé-en-Brie, *1st Sun* (Apr–Oct)
Conty, *Fri*
Corbie, *Fri*
Coye-la-Forêt, *Sat*
Crècy-en-Ponthieu, *Mon*
Creil, *Wed, Thu, Sat*
Crépy-en-Valois, *Wed, Sat, Sun*
Crevecoeur-le-Grand, *Thu*
La-Croix-Saint-Ouen, *Sun*

Le Crotoy, *Fri* (+*Tue*, mid-Jun– mid-Oct)
Cuise-la-Motte, *Sun*
D
Doullens, *Thu*
E
Ermenonville, 2nd *Sun*
F
La Fère, *Sat*
Fère-en-Tardenois, see Six of the Best
La Ferté-Milon, *Fri*
Formerie, *Wed*
Fort-Mahon-Plage, *Tue* and *Fri* (Jul/Aug)
G
Gamaches, *Sat* (+ 1st *Wed*)
Gouvieux, *Thu, Sun*
Grandvilliers, *Mon*
Guignicourt, *Fri*
Guise, *Sat*
H
Ham, *Sat*
Hirson, *Mon, Thu*
L
Lamorlaye, *Tue, Sat*
Laon, see Six of the Best
Liancourt, *Wed*
Longueil-Annel, 1st *Sun*
M
Margny-lès-Compiègne, *Fri*
Marigny-en-Orxois, last *Sun* (Mar–Dec)
Marseille-de-Beauvaisis, *Fri*
Mers-les-Bains, *Mon, Thu*
Meru, *Fri, Sun*
Milly-sur-Therain, *Sun*
Montdidier, *Thu*
Montreuil-aux-Lions, 1st *Sun*
Moreuil, *Tue*
Mouy, *Sat*
N
Nesle, *Fri*
Neuilly-St-Front, *Sat*
Noailles, *Tue*
Nogent-l'Artaud, *Sun*
Nogent-sur-Oise, *Fri*
Le Nouvion-en-Thiérache, *Wed*
Noyon, *Sat* (+ 1st *Tue*)

O
Oisemont, *Sat*
P
Péronne, *Sat*
Picquigny, *Sun*
Pierrefonds, *Fri* (+ 1st *Sun*)
Plachy-Buyon, *Fri*
Plailly, *Thu*
Poix-de-Picardie, *Sun*
Pont-Sainte-Maxence, *Tue, Fri*
Q
Quend-Plage, *Mon* (+ *Thu* Jul–Sep)
R
Ressons-sur-Matz, *Wed*
Rivery, 1st *Sun*
Rocourt-Saint-Martin, 2nd *Sat*
Rosières-en-Santerre, *Tue*
Roye, *Fri* (+ 1st *Sun*)
Rue, *Sat*
S
Saint-Eugène, 2nd *Sun* (Apr–Oct)
Saint-Just-en-Chaussée, *Tue*
Saint-Leu-d'Esserent, *Wed*
Saint-Ouen, alternate *Suns*
Saint-Quentin, *Sun, Wed, Fri, Sat*
Saint-Valery-sur-Somme, see Six of the Best
Senlis, see Six of the Best
Soissons, *Wed, Sat*
T
Thourotte, *Thu*
V
Vailly-sur-Aisne, *Sun*
Val-de-l'Oise, 1st *Fri*
Vallée-de-l'Aisne, *Wed*
Verneuil-en-Halatte, *Fri*
Vic-sur-Aisne, *Wed*
Villers-Bretonneux, *Wed*
Villers-Cotterêts, *Thu*

Acres of fleas, the country come to town and knickers at a snip

The street markets of Paris are an integral ingredient in the capital's charismatic mix, as much part of the scene as the Eiffel Tower or the Tuileries. The famous Puces at Saint-Ouen. The Sunday twitter of the bird market on Ile-de-la-Cité. Avenue Matignon's stamp market – do you remember Cary Grant and Audrey Hepburn threading through it as they dodged the baddies in the original version of *Charade*? Even the food markets are a draw – not so much, in this instance, to strangers in town likely to carry off and cook things, but because each reflects the character of its *quartier*.

Long gone are the old Halles at Châtelet. Like many other city-centre covered market halls, they were scooped out and removed to a less appealing but more efficient site further out. A side effect of this bit of urban surgery was the loss of one of Paris's little rituals: that of repairing to a cosy Les Halles bistrot to sup onion soup in the small hours after a night on the town. I used to picture myself doing this with some lookalike Alain Delon, who would then wrap me inside his crumpled trenchcoat and steer me through a carpet of discarded cabbage leaves to a dawn of untold bliss. Alas, by the time I got to Paris, Les Halles was a building site, with the new Forum des Halles shopping mall beginning to burrow downwards. When this was eventually finished, I quite liked the way its glass caterpillar arcades echoed the flying buttresses of the lovely old church of St-Eustache on the skyline. But the onion soup dream drained away, totally disappearing down the spout when, *toute seule* one bitter October afternoon, I ordered some in a newish snack bar. A bowl of brownish liquid was set before me with what appeared to be a sodden scrap of old army blanket floating on top. The flavours of neither onions nor cheese adhered to it. Who says you can never get a bad meal in France?

Happily, the capital's other food markets have lost none of their quality or atmosphere. They are alive and thriving from Rue Lépic in Montmartre to Mouffetard in St Germain, Place d'Aligre in the Bastille area and the classy Rue Poncelet, a baguette's throw from the Champs Elysées. These markets are the country come to town – in fact, often the whole of the country come to town, for in them you can buy specialities from Lyon, the Landes or the Loire, as well as a bit of provincial peace when the buzz of the city begins to frazzle your nerve ends.

I love Paris to bits, but the last time I was there it was edgy, full of protest marches that were slowing the traffic and shortening tempers. I took the Métro

to Monge and walked up through the market in Rue Mouffetard on one of those still, bright spring mornings when the sky was swept clean, the bones of the buildings were veiled by a mesh of new green buds and lovers were already entwined on benches. Whatever mood the capital is in, a market like Mouffetard is guaranteed to give you a reassuring fix of core Paris. Shoppers come from the local *arrondissement* as well as from out of town. It's like a village – which of course it is: in the case of Mouffetard, the village of Saint Germain. And it's peaceful. With the distant traffic on Rue Monge a mere murmur, I could hear the scrape of a poodle's claws on the cobbles as it trotted past.

In Paris, as anywhere else, markets are brilliant for sourcing picnics. Over the years, they have provided some of my most memorable meals in the capital: simple picnics of pâté and crisp *ficelle* (thinner and lighter than a baguette), or a few baby quiches, some fruit and a bottle of wine (never travel without a corkscrew). These have been consumed variously on the *quais*, by the vineyard in Montmartre, in the Jardins du Palais Royal and, once, in a mossy corner of the Père Lachaise cemetery. We were a foursome aping Manet's painting 'Déjeuner sur l'herbe', complete with pristine tablecloth and large hats – except we all kept our clothes on.

The flea markets are, of course, very much tourist territory. St-Ouen's enormous expanses at Clignancourt are as full of browsers as buyers, spectators aiming cameras at the fascinating jumble –– which doesn't seem to bother the traders. But there are other markets in which to look for bygones and bargains – some out of town. The 'Petite Couronne', the ring of *départements* immediately surrounding Paris (i.e. the rest of Ile-de-France) are sadly neglected yet have so many engaging towns, like Versailles and Auvers-sur-Oise, as well as riverside pleasures and historical highlights.

For Paris, I have skipped the 'Don't miss' and 'Somewhere to stay' advice because there must be a Bibliothèque Nationale of guide books to the capital. And all the markets mentioned are accessible from wherever you're staying.

Six of the Best in Paris

Marché aux Puces de St-Ouen

Saturday, Sunday, Monday

The 'attic of the world', and Paris's best and oldest antique market, sprawls across some 15 sq km at the northern edge of the city: a priceless landfill of bygones.

If you get there via the Métro to Clignancourt it's a 10-minute hike running the gamut of a peripheral all-sorts market where combat jackets, African masks and endless novelties waylay you. This is not it. Persevere until you get to the overhang of the ring road. Here beginneth Les Puces: some fifteen different markets boasting over 2,000 traders. First, head for Rue des Rosiers and get a Plan-Guide from the paper seller at the entrance to the Marché Malassis. This also contains an index of stands by speciality.

Les Puces is a bit of a misnomer. With gilded Second Empire furniture, Meissen porcelain and rare Torah texts, very little at St-Ouen is 'cheap as chips'. The name 'fleas' derives from the rag-and-bone men who, regarded as unwanted parasites, were chased out of the city centre at the end of the 19th century. Ironically, when they began to gather at the Portes de Clignancourt, Montreuil and Vanves, the toffs soon twigged that the fleas' haul of cast-off merchandise might secrete a few treasures. Les Puces took off. On one of the St-Ouen stands, there's a motto: 'I buy junk but I sell antiques.' St-Ouen, however, is not that easily defined. You will find literally anything

here that is of value to someone, from old bayonets to fin-de-siècle bustiers, whole stone-carved auriole windows to Tiffany lamps, daggers to Dinky toys. Go to Marché Paul Bert for curly wrought-iron garden furniture, to Jules Vallès for posters, to Dauphine for ancient books, and to Biron for sheer opulence. The ritual of negotiating a deal is to be savoured, prolonged by a coffee, much chat – a 10 per cent reduction is the most you can hope for – and handshaking. Go with the flow and the resulting purchase will always bring back the moment, the mood and the surroundings.

If you aren't buying, just enjoy the show. There are dogs everywhere: not only inanimate Jack Russells forever glued to shell-shaped loudspeakers, but assorted pooches left to guard the premises while dealers nap in Louis XV armchairs or have gone to lunch. Each market is dotted with snack bars and cafés in which you too can get your second wind and watch the market's characters. I remember being riveted by a woman trader dressed in skimpy top, micro-shorts, turquoise tights and espadrilles, her pale hair piled high, Bardot-style. When she turned round, I guessed she must have been all of eighty. Open 7.00 to 19.30 Saturday, Sunday, Monday. Quiet in August.

La Mouff'
Every day

Guaranteed to make you feel you've just popped out for some pâté from your rooftop apartment, the market in Rue Mouffetard (affectionately known as La Mouff') is Saint-Germain's extended corner shop. Tidy men with hair as impeccably cut as their raincoats stroll through to buy a croissant at Steff's. Old ladies with baskets on wheels pore over dumps of cut-price fruit. Couples launch into intense discussions with the *poissonnier* about the size of sea bass they need for dinner.

Among a clutch of regional food specialists is Aux Produits d'Auvergne, where you can buy Le Puy green lentils, *morteau d'or* sausage and *aligot* cheese. Like the rest of the shops, it sets out its products on the narrow, sloping street which has a pavement barely wide enough to support a little brass-rimmed

table. But there are plenty of these.

My favourite café-bar is Le Mouffetard – for its version of *croque madame*. Here, this tartine of toasted cheese and ham plus egg is based on wholesome Poilâne bread. Le Verre à Pied, at 118, is another good stop – a wonderful old-fashioned wine bar where each table has a name.

In Rue Mouffetard, you can find 200 varieties of goat's cheese, live *petits gris* (small grey shrimps) from the coast, and fruit and vegetables as dewy fresh as in any *marché paysan* in Limousin. I can never stop myself buying something whether or not it's practical or I'm remotely peckish. Last time, it was a box of sweet little *fraises des bois* from Ardèche which lasted me all the way to the Boul' Mich'.

Open Tuesday to Saturday from 8.30 to 12.30 and 14.30 to 19.00, and on Sunday mornings.

Marché St-Pierre
Tuesday to Saturday

Located close to the bottom of Sacré Coeur steps, a group of cavernous department-style stores known as the Marché St-Pierre have been dedicated to the sale of cut-price fabrics and household linens since 1868. If you are handy with a sewing machine or just mad for a bargain, these are great places to rummage. There are bolts of novelty fabrics, big cat prints for chic cushion covers and mock gold and silver lamé in extra wide measure begging to be made up into school-play costumes – or brothel curtains? Fur fabric and sparkly

beloved, *à la* the iconic 1950s Robert Doisneau photograph of the couple kissing in a Paris street, then the most romantic place to buy one is the Marché aux Fleurs on Ile-de-la-Cité. Although this island in the Seine is almost submerged by the number of tourists who come to visit its key sights – Notre Dame, the Sainte-Chapelle, the Conciergerie, the Mémorial de la Déportation – leafy little Place Louis Lépine, which opens out where the Rue de la Cité meets the Quai de la Corse, is rarely overrun. Every day its stalls form herbaceous borders of the freshest – and priciest – bouquets in Paris.

On Sunday come the sound effects. The flower stalls are joined by the Marché aux Oiseaux, the bird market: a twittering, squawking aviary of wise grey parrots and vivid macaws, jittery canaries and suave cockatiels, black minahs and pastel budgerigars. These and even more exotic breeds can be seen pecking at the bars of their cages, fluffing up their wings and peering sideways at passers-by. Should you fancy taking home a little something for your own feathered friends, there are also bird accessories, seed and treats galore.

Flower market every day, birds on Sunday, 8.00 to 19.00.

brocades, duvet covers and lace curtains, take your pick – and all for a lot less than they would cost elsewhere.

You need to case each building before making a decision because the prices go from really dirt cheap to fairly reasonable, depending on quality. In one corner, there are cottons at a couple of euros a metre, while in another hand-embroidered damasks are marked at – and worth – considerably more, if still *bon marché*.

I'm told even big-name couturiers and interior designers seek inspiration at the Marché St-Pierre, as well as at the other specialist fabric, home accessory and dress shops close by in Rue Charles-Nodier and Rue d'Orsel.

Open shop hours, Tuesday to Saturday.

Flowers and birds, Ile-de-la-Cité
Flowers every day/birds Sunday

If you want to present a posy to your

Rue Lepic
Every day except Monday

There are faster ways to reach Sacré Coeur on the crest of Montmartre, but I can never resist getting out of the Métro – or a taxi – at Place Blanche and strolling

up through the food market on the lower section of Rue Lepic simply because it is so picturesque. I wander and I wonder if Van Gogh, who lived at 54 with his brother Theo when they first arrived from Holland, ever popped out to buy a cauliflower, or a bar of soap to clean his paint-stained fingers. And I stop for a coffee in the Brasserie des Deux Moulins, whose windmills are on the tiles behind its bar. It's not hard to imagine Audrey Tautou, star of the cult movie *Amélie*, perched on a stool next to me, for the interior was featured in the film.

The street is full of small restaurants which source their menus from the fresh goodies to hand, but I have a picnic site in mind. After the market, Rue Lepic dog-legs up the hill of La Butte, with Sacré Coeur playing now-you-see-me-now-you-don't between the roofs. Then comes Rue Norvins and Place du Tertre. A sharp turn to the left at La Bonne Franquette and down towards the Lapin Agile café-cabaret. Here is where I prepare to unwrap my cheese and pop my cork – appropriately, on a wall by the vineyard in the grounds of the Musée du Vieux Montmartre.

Village Saint-Paul

Anyone with neither the time nor the energy to trawl St-Ouen's acres can settle instead for a quiet wander round the antiques shops in this corner of the Marais near the church of Saint Paul. Over 25 dealers cluster together in a series of courtyards which you can enter off the Rue Saint Paul, Rue de l'Ave Maria, Rue des Jardins Saint-Paul or Rue Charlemagne. From time to time, wares are displayed outside as well as inside, and other collectables-sellers gather in the courtyard, which creates a market atmosphere. It is nevertheless very genteel.

Most shops specialize in just one commodity, such as art nouveau and deco, chandeliers, embroidered linen and lace, or garden furniture. I love Histoire de Tables (in the courtyard) with its exquisite historical pieces for table settings, and Au Petit Bonheur la Chance, 15 Rue Saint Paul, which has a compulsive clutter of kitchenalia both ancient and modern – enamel cafetières, pottery bowls, soup ladle stands etc.

Open 11.00 to 19.00, Thursday, Friday, Saturday, Sunday and Monday.

Best of the Rest in Paris

★ **Les Puces de Vanves** (Métro Porte de Vanves) Comes more into the bric-a-brac category, although it has furniture and paintings too. Open Saturday and Sunday, 7.00 to 19.00.

★ **Les Puces de Montreuil** (Métro Porte de Montreuil) Mainly second-hand clothes, domestic appliances, tools and crockery. Open Saturday, Sunday and Monday, 7.00 to 20.00.

★ **Marché aux Timbres** Just round the corner from the Rond Point on Avenue Matignon, philatelists can search for Mozambique purples and other rare stamps on Thursdays, Saturdays, Sundays and public holidays from 9.00 to 19.00. Even those uninterested in postage flock here to enjoy the ambiance and eat at Market, a wildly popular new-wave restaurant which fuses Asian and French cuisine.

★ **Marché de la Création** The capital's lively art and craft market in Boulevard Edgar-Quinet, at the foot of the Tour Montparnasse between Rues du Départ and de la Gaité. Sunday, 10.00 to 19.00.

★ **Marché d'Aligre** Near the Bastille. Bric-a-brac, second-hand clothes and exotic fruits and vegetables from North Africa occupy Place d'Aligre; the main produce market packs out Rue d'Aligre. Mornings except Monday.

★ **Rue Poncelet** A step from the Arc de Triomphe, the street market here augments some of the capital's choicest gourmet shops. People from all over Paris make pilgrimages to Alléosse for cheese, to Planète Fruits in Rue Bayen and to various other *pâtisseries* and *charcuteries*. Rue Poncelet is between Avenue des Ternes and Avenue de Wagram. Mornings except Monday.

★ **Marché Belleville** In the Boulevard de Belleville east of the Canal St-Martin. Mangoes and papayas, dates and kumquats, pulses from the Caribbean, spices from the orient – all at reasonable prices. One of the most exotic markets in Paris. Belleville is the colourful working-class neighbourhood east of the Canal St-Martin where Edith Piaf was born – legend has it – under a street lamp. Lots of artists' studios and galleries to case.

★ **Marché du Cuir et de l'Habillement** In the Carreau du Temple (Métro Temple or Arts et Métiers) even the chicest Parisians can be found pouncing on leather and second-hand clothes bargains. Tuesday to Friday, 9.00 to 13.30; Saturday 9.00 to 18.00 and Sunday 9.00 to 14.00.

Best of the Rest outside Paris

★ **Auvers-sur-Oise** Charming village where Van Gogh lies buried. The Auberge Ravoux, where he died, has now become a shrine, and the house of his friend and fellow-artist, Daubigny, which is covered from floor to ceiling with the most delicate murals, is sheer enchantment. Also a picture, the Saturday morning market in the *centre ville*.

★ **Bois-le-Roi** The Forêt de Fontainebleau may be sparser than it used to be, but the countryside in between is well sprinkled with beautifully kept villages like this one. Markets are on Thursday and Sunday mornings, Place de la Gare.

★ **Fontainebleau** The big draw in this pleasant town south of the capital is King François I's glorious hunting lodge (now the National Museum of the Renaissance) which houses treasures that represent 800 years of French history. One of the smaller draws is the creamy *fromage blanc* called Fontainebleau which comes in small pots lined with muslin and is yummy served with fresh summer berries. Look for it at the small local market on Tuesday, Friday or Sunday mornings.

★ **L'Isle-Adam** Classy town, close to Auvers, which makes the most of its position right on the Oise. With dripping willows and pleasure-boat trips, it is more like a resort. On a canal cruise, I once spent a Friday night moored by the pontoon and went shopping in the Saturday open-air market. I can still

taste the outsize pink prawns we carried back for lunch on board, complete with a carton of freshly made mayonnaise. L'Isle-Adam's covered market in Place Verdun opens on Tuesday, Friday and Sunday.

★ **Mantes-la-Jolie** On the Seine, a pretty town indeed, and proud of its onions – which are seriously fêted every first Wednesday of December. Plenty also make their way to the lively Wednesday and Saturday markets in the town centre, a big square flanked by lots of *jolie* – and jolly – restaurants, like Le Coq Hardi.

★ **Marly-le-Roi** They say the designer Nina Ricci makes the most beautiful lingerie in the world. You might just find one of her lacy bras or silk camisoles in Marly's Tuesday or Friday market (possibly not at the Sunday one). A really big stand selling classy underwear, Pringle cashmere and Liberty scarves at well-reduced prices joins the cohort of outdoor traders around the covered market behind the RER station. Marly, with a historic centre like a rural village, was Louis XIV's choice for summer living and the gardens of the château are delightful.

★ **Milly-la-Forêt** When Jean Cocteau lived here, he said, 'It was at Milly that I discovered the rarest thing in the whole world: a proper setting.' Known since the Middle Ages for the cultivation of medicinal herbs, this sweet village west of Fontainebleau is home to the National Conservatoire of Medicinal and Aromatic Plants (where you can also buy). A beautiful herb garden flourishes in the grounds of the Chapelle Sainte Blaise des Simples, and the regular produce market on Thursday mornings animates a 15th-century *halle* in Place du Marché. A shop not to miss is L'Herbier de Milly on the sidelines where everything is mint or mint-flavoured.

★ **Provins** With its stalwart ramparts and lofty Tour César, Provins's walled *haute ville* was once the capital of the Brie Plateau, home of the most ubiquitous French cheese in the world. As perfectly formed as that creamy cartwheel, the medieval town of Provins is the size of a mere village. Boutiques selling home accessories and *produits du terroir* huddle discreetly among quiet cobbled streets. The

Saturday market in Place Honoré-de-Balzac (lower town) will always have a stand selling the local rosehip jelly, grainy mustard from nearby Meaux and, of course, the best of Brie. A lovely Relais du Silence hotel, Aux Vieux Remparts, in the old town (☎ 01 64 08 94 00).

★ **St-Germain-en-Laye** Picturesque haunt of artists, with a fine château, the Débussy Museum and marvellous markets on Tuesday, Friday and Sunday mornings in Place du Marché. Treat yourself to lunch in the most seductive surroundings: the garden terrace of Cazaudehore (☎ 01 30 61 64 64) on the fringe of the Saint-Germain forest.

★ **La Varenne-St-Hilaire** This chic commuter village in a loop of the river Marne attracts serious bargain hunters to its Thursday and Sunday food/fashion markets in the square opposite the RER station (a half-hour from Paris). Mainly produce on Thursdays, mainly clothes on Sundays (cut-price designer labels like Cacharel). Le Petit Duc *pâtisserie* sells wonderful croissants and blueberry tarts, Ty-Breiz *crêperie* excellent pancakes and the Château des Isles hotel a good lunch in its riverside restaurant looking out on trailing willows.

★ **Versailles** There's much more to it than the Sun King's overwhelmingly vast and opulent palace and gardens. This airy town boasts rebuilt 19th-century *halles* all around the Place du

Marché Notre Dame. Some providers are open every day (very upmarket produce); an open-air food market fills the square on Tuesday, Friday and Sunday mornings, and clothes and household goods are sold on Wednesday and Friday mornings. In addition, there are flea markets on Saturday and Sunday in Passage de la Gréole, where antique shops cluster. In summer, keen gardeners might like to visit the Potager du Roi, the king's vegetable garden in Rue Hardy, which sells fruit and vegetables on Tuesday

and Friday mornings and plants and herbs Monday to Friday mornings. For a good booking try the Pavillon de la Maye, the most stylish of *chambres d'hôtes* in a 19th-century townhouse within walking distance of the palace. It is run by a retired manager of Maxim's, the celebrated Paris restaurant (☎ 01 39 23 21 00).

🖱 www.pidf.com

Markets at a glance: Paris & Ile-de-France

A

Achères, *Wed*, *Sat*
Angerville, *Tue*, *Sat*
Argenteuil, *Wed*, *Thu*, *Fri*, *Sat*, *Sun*
Arnouville-lès-Gonesse, *Thu*, *Fri*, *Sat*
Arpajon, *Fri*
Athis-Mons, *Thu*, *Sun*
Auvers-sur-Oise, *Sat*
Avernes, *Sat*
Avon, *Thu*

B

Ballancourt, *Thu*, *Sun*
Beauchamp, *Thu*, *Sun*
Beaumont-sur-Oise, *Tue*, *Thu*, *Sat*
Bessancourt, *Wed*, *Sat*
Beynes, *Thu*, *Sun*
Bezons, *Thu*, *Sun*
Bièvres, *Wed*, *Sat*
Bois-d'Arcy, *Wed*, *Sat*
Bois-le-Roi, *Thu*, *Sun*
Bondoufle, *Wed*, *Sat*
Bonnières-sur-Seine, *Sun*
Bouafle, *Fri*
Bouffémont, *Wed*, *Sat*
Bougival, *Wed*, *Sat*
Bourron-Marlotte, *Sat*
Boussy-St-Antoine, *Thu*, *Sun*
Boutigny-sur-Essonne, *Sat*
Bray-sur-Seine, *Fri*
Bretigny-sur-Orge, *Thu*, *Sun*
Breuillet, *Thu*, *Sun*
Bréval, *Fri*
Brie-Comte-Robert, *Tue*, *Fri*, *Sun*
Brunoy, *Thu*, *Sun*
Buc, *Sat*
Bûres-sur-Yvette, *Wed*, *Sat*
Butry-sur-Oise, *Tue*

C

Cannes-Ecluse, *Sun*
Cergy, *Wed*, *Sat*, *Sun*
Cerny, *Fri*
Carrières-sur-Seine, *Tue*, *Fri*
Celle-St-Cloud, daily (not *Mon*)
Chalo-Saint-Mars, *Fri*
Champagne-sur-Seine, *Thu*, *Sat*

La Chapelle-la-Reine, *Tue*
Chars, *Sat*
Château-Landon, *Thu*
Le Châtelet-en-Brie, *Tue*, *Sat*
Chatou, *Wed*, *Thu*, *Sat*, *Sun*
Le Chesnay, *Wed*, *Sat*
Chevry-Cossigny, *Wed*
Chilly-Mazarin, *Tue*, *Thu*, *Sun*
Les Clayes-sous-Bois, *Thu*, *Sun*
Combs-la-Ville, *Wed*, *Sat*
Conflans-Ste-Honorine, daily (not *Mon*)
Corbeil-Essones, daily (not *Mon*)
Cormeilles-en-Parisis, *Wed*, *Sat*
Courcouronnes, *Sun*
Croissy-sur-Seine, *Fri*, *Sun*
Crosne, *Fri*

D

Dammarie-les-Lys, *Thu*, *Sun*
Deuil-la-Barre, daily (not *Mon*)
Domont, *Thu*, *Sun*
Donnemarie-Dontilly, *Mon*
Dourdan, *Wed*, *Sat*
Draveil, *Tue*, *Thu*, *Fri*, *Sun*

E

Eaubonne, *Tue*, *Fri*, *Sun*
Ecquevilly, *Wed*, *Sat*
Elancourt, *Sun*
Enghien-les-Bains, *Tue*, *Thu*, *Sat*
Ennery, *Thu*
Epinay-sous-Sénart, *Wed*, *Thu*, *Sat*, *Sun*
Epinay-sur-Orge, *Tue*, *Fri*
Éragny-sur-Oise, *Thu*, *Sun*
Ermont, *Wed*, *Sat*
Les Essarts-le-Roi, *Tue*, *Fri*, *Sun*
Etampes, *Tue*, *Sat*
Etrechy, *Sun*
Evry, *Wed*, *Fri*, *Sat*, *Sun*
Ezanville, *Wed*, *Sat*

F

La Ferté-Alais, *Wed*, *Sat*
Fleury-Merogis, *Mon*
Fontainebleau, *Tue*, *Fri*, *Sun*
Fosses, *Tue*, *Thu*, *Sat*

Franconville, *Wed*, *Thu*, *Sat*
Frépillon, *Thu*
La Frette-sur-Seine, *Thu*, *Fri* eve, *Sun*

G

Galluis, *Fri*
Gargenville, *Fri*, *Sun*
Garges-lès-Gonesse, *Wed*, *Thu*, *Sat*, *Sun*
Gif-sur-Yvette, *Wed*, *Thu*, *Sat*, *Sun*
Gonesse, *Wed*, *Thu*, *Sat*, *Sun*
Goussainville, *Tue*, *Thu*, *Sat*, *Sun*
Les-Granges-le-Roi, *Sun*
Gretz-Armainvilliers, *Tue*, *Fri*
Grigny, *Thu*, *Sun*
Groslay, *Thu*, *Sun*
Guignes-Rabutin, *Fri*
Guyancourt, *Wed*, *Sat*

H

Herblay, *Tue*, *Fri*, *Sun*
Houdan, *Fri*

I

Igny, *Wed*, *Thu*, *Sat*, *Sun*
L'Isle-Adam, *Tue*, *Fri*, *Sat*, *Sun*
Itteville, *Fri*

J

Jouy-le-Moutier, *Wed*, *Sat*
Juvisy-sur-Orge, *Wed*, *Sat*

L

Lardy, *Fri*, *Sat*
Lésigny, *Wed*, *Sat*
Lieusaint, *Fri*
Limay, *Tue*, *Fri*
Limours, *Thu*, *Sun*
Lisses, *Tue*, *Thu*
Longjumeau, *Wed*, *Sat*
Longueville, *Thu*
Lorrez-le-Bocage-Preaux, *Wed*, *Sun*
Louvres, *Thu*, *Sun*

M

Magny-en-Vexin, *Sat*
Maisons-Laffitte, *Wed*, *Sat*
Maisse, *Wed*
Mantes-la-Jolie, *Wed*, *Sat*
Marcoussis, *Thu*, *Sun*
Marly-le-Roi, *Tue*, *Fri*, *Sun*
Marolles-en-Hurepoix, *Sat*
Massy, daily (not *Mon*)

Maule, *Sat*
Maurecourt, *Thu*
Maurepas, *Wed*, *Sat*
Melun, *Wed*, *Thu*, *Sat*, *Sun*
Mennecy, *Wed*, *Sat*
Menucourt, *Sat*
Mereville, *Fri*
Méry-sur-Oise, *Mon*
Le Mesnil-St-Denis, *Thu*, *Sun*
Meulan, *Mon*, *Fri*, *Sun*
Milly-la-Forêt, *Thu*
Moissy-Cramayel, *Wed*, *Sun*
Montereau-Fault-Yonne,
Wed, *Thu**, *Sat*, *Sun*
Montesson, *Thu*, *Sun*
Montfort-l'Amaury, *Thu*
Montgeron, *Wed*, *Sat*
Montigny-le-Bretonneux,
Tue, *Wed*, *Fri*, *Sat*, *Sun*
Montlhéry, *Mon*, *Thu*
Montmagny, *Sun*
Montmorency, *Mon*, *Wed*,
Thu, *Fri*, *Sun*
Montsoult, *Tue*, *Fri*
Moret-sur-Loing, *Tue*, *Fri*
Mormant, *Thu*
Morsang-sur-Orge, *Wed*, *Sat*
Les Mureaux, *Thu*, *Sat*, *Sun*
N
Nangis, *Wed*, *Sat*
Neauphle-le-Château, *Mon*,
Fri
Nemours, *Wed*, *Sat*
O
Orgerus, *Tue*
Orgeval, *Sat*
Orsay, *Tue*, *Fri*, *Sun*
Osny, *Sun*
Ozoir-la-Ferrière, *Wed*, *Sat*
P
Palaiseau, *Wed*, *Thu*, *Sat*, *Sun*
Paray-Vieille-Poste,*Wed*, *Sat*
Paris, detailed in text
Le Perray-en-Yvelines, *Fri*
Persan, *Wed*, *Sun*
Pierrelaye, *Thu*, *Sun*
Plaisir, *Tue*, *Fri*, *Sun*
Le Plessis-Bouchard, *Wed*,
Sat, *Sun*
Le Plessis-Pâté, *Mon*, *Wed*,
Thu, *Fri*, *Sat*

Poissy, *Tue*, *Thu*, *Fri*, *Sat*, *Sun*
Pontault-Combault, *Tue*, *Thu*,
Fri, *Sun*
Pontoise, *Tue*, *Wed*, *Thu*, *Fri*,
Sat
Provins, *Sat*
Puiseux-en-France, *Sun*
Q
Quincy-sous-Sénart, *Thu*,
Sun
R
Rambouillet, *Wed*, *Fri*, *Sat*,
Sun
Ris-Orangis, *Wed*, *Sat*
La Rochette, *Tue*, *Fri*
Roissy-en-France, *Sat*
Rosny-sur-Seine, *Thu*
S
Saint-Arnoult-en-Yvelines,
Sun
Saint-Brice-sous-Forêt, *Tue*,
Fri
Saint-Chéron, *Thu*
Saint-Cyr-l'Ecole, *Wed*, *Sat*
Saint-Fargeau-Ponthierry,
Thu, *Sun*
Sainte-Genevieve-des-Bois,
daily (not *Mon*)
Saint-Germain-en-Laye, *Tue*,
Wed, *Fri*, *Sat*, *Sun*
Saint-Germain-lès-Arpajon,
Wed
Saint-Gratien, *Wed*, *Sun*
Saint-Léger-en-Yvelines, *Sat*
Saint-Leu-la-Forêt, *Wed*, *Sat*
Saint-Mammes, *Sun*
Saint-Martin-du-Tertre, *Thu*,
Sun
Saint-Michel-sur-Orge, *Wed*,
Sat
Saint-Ouen-l'Aumône, *Wed*,
Sun
Sannois, *Tue*, *Thu*, *Sun*
Sarcelles, *Tue*, *Wed*, *Fri*, *Sat*,
Sun
Sartrouville, *Thu*, *Fri*, *Sat*, *Sun*
Savigny-le-Temple, *Wed*, *Sat*
Savigny-sur-Orge, *Tue*, *Thu*,
Fri, *Sat*, *Sun*
Soisy-sous-Montmorency,
Wed, *Fri*, *Sun*

Souppes-sur-Loing, *Sun*
T
Taverny, *Tue*, *Fri*
Le Thilay, *Fri*
Thomery, *Tue*
Tournan-en-Brie, *Wed*, *Sat*
Trappes, *Tue*, *Thu*, *Fri*, *Sat*,
Sun
Triel-sur-Seine, *Thu*, *Sat*
U
Les Ulis, *Tue*, *Fri*, *Sun*
V
La Varenne-Saint-Hilaire,
Thu, *Sun*
Varennes-sur-Seine, *Fri*
Vauréal, *Thu*, *Fri*
Vaux-sur-Seine, *Sat*
Verneuil-sur-Seine, *Wed*, *Sun*
Vernouillet, *Wed*, *Sat*
Verrières-le-Buisson, *Wed*,
Sat
Versailles, daily
Vert-Saint-Denis, *Tue*, *Fri*
Le Vesinet, daily (not *Mon*)
Vétheuil, *Thu*, *Fri*
Viarmes, *Wed*, *Sat*
Vigneux, *Wed*, *Fri*, *Sun*
Vigny, *Sat*
Villebon-sur-Yvette, *Thu*, *Sun*
Villennes-sur-Seine, *Thu*, *Sat*
Villepreux, *Wed*, *Sat*
Villiers-Saint-Georges, *Fri*,
Sun
Viroflay, daily (not *Mon*)
Viry-Châtillon, *Tue*, *Fri*, *Sat*,
Sun
Voisins-le-Bretonneux, *Sat*,
Sun
Vulaines-sur-Seine, *Sat*
W
Wissous, *Wed*, *Sat*
Y
Yerres, *Wed*, *Thu*, *Sat*, *Sun*

NORMANDY

Creamy cheeses, cider like champagne and the spirit that burns a hole in the stomach

On a sparkling morning of picture-postcard blue skies, the photographer and I head out to Falaise. Our mission: to get a stunning shot of William the Conqueror's birthplace. To save time, a picnic is hastily shopped for at a small roadside market we happen to pass en route. I buy a thick wodge of terrine marked *tête de veau* (calf's head), a few apples, some Camembert cheese, golden *pain de campagne* and a bottle of cider. When the time comes to open up our parcels and tuck in, we settle in the perfect spot: a bench by the river Ante which mirrors, on its spur above, walled Falaise and the forbidding square keep where France's and England's seminal monarch first saw daylight. An emotional moment follows – not because of the significance of the view but because I bite on something hard that shouldn't belong in a terrine. Removing it gingerly, I find myself staring at a tooth. Not my own, but a calf's. Well, it *is tête de veau*. Lest I should come across the odd eyelash or a splinter of embryo horn, I offer the rest to the birds.

Normandy is one of my favourite regions, and I find its food – usually – as moreish as the aromatic flavours of Provence. After all, it inspired that doyenne of cookery writers, Elizabeth David, to pen the first of her best-sellers. I also like immensely the Normans themselves who seem eternally enthusiastic in their welcome of British and American visitors – 1944 and all that, never mind 1066. Today, as you stroll along the miles of golden beaches, which during the D-Day Landings were blasted by artillery fire and pounded by tens of thousands of Allied boots, it seems as if that strategically brilliant, complex and costly assault never happened – until you come to an isolated gun emplacement or a small memorial. The coast is lovely, whether wild and white-cliffed, tamed as in Deauville or full of briny smells and character in fishing ports like Dieppe or St-Vaast-la-Hougue.

And I love the gardens – Giverny, of course, Monet's botanical masterpiece; also Gertrude Jekyll's Bois des Moutiers, the Château de Vendeuvre with its water tricks, and Christian Dior's terraces at Granville. Most of all I love the natural garden of the Pays d'Auge which swallows you up in its chocolate-box countryside. Here, roaming through tunnels of tousled hedges, past pink timbered manor houses and stud farms, you come upon the rustic vignette that says it all – well, almost all – about the kind of specialities you can expect to find in Normandy's markets. Fluffy brown and white cattle munching contentedly on juicy grass under apple trees . . .

Specialities

They're the *crème de la crème*, those Normandy cows (see the beauty parade at L'Aigle market in Six of the Best) and, my, do they give unstintingly of themselves in the cause of good eating. They are world-famous **cheeses** on the hoof – Camembert, light and soft with a delicate bloom; Livarot, creamy inside its orange crust; Pont l'Evêque, one of the oldest, and the not-so-well-known Pavé d'Auge, produced only around Lisieux. Fine **butter** is inevitably a by-product (Beurre d'Isigny the most highly thought-of), as is wonderful **cream**. Nowhere is cream used more in cooking. Here, you will find it rich, thick and fresh as well as slightly soured in crème fraîche. The same cows become excellent **beef** and awfully good **offal**. I'm not into tripe but since they prepare it rather appetizingly in Normandy you may feel like giving it a go. It is unbleached, and when flavoured with herbs, vegetables, cider and Calvados is rated one of the great regional dishes (*tripes à la mode de Caen*). A more likely purchase for visiting shoppers in the markets is the pork **charcuterie**, the *andouilles* from Vire – a kind of chitterling sausage that's been lightly smoked – and a succession of plump *terrines*, *galantines* and *ballotines*, not to mention *tête de veau*!

Aside from a froth of apple blossom in spring and the tantalising scent of ripening fruit in autumn, the gift of Normandy's orchards is **cider**. A much lighter cider than they distil in England's West Country, this is drier and has more the texture of champagne. Its corks are similarly wired to keep in the bubbles. Cider is the perfect drink for picnics, pork and pancakes, but it doesn't grace the tables of most restaurants. Normandy may not have vineyards, but with the Loire Valley on its doorstep, there are plenty of good labels both on wine lists and to buy.

Then there is **Calvados**, the fiery apple

brandy that takes its name from the Calvados *département*. This is what gives a kick to all those creamy sauces in dishes like *sole normande* and *poulet vallée d'Auge*, and without it, in neat form, no meal in Normandy can be brought to a respectable conclusion. Indeed, it can be called for halfway through to create *le trou normand*, that is, to burn a hole in the stomach to make room for more food. It's an incendiary spirit that deserves respect. I well remember the evening an over-generous *maître d'* at the Lion d'Or in Bayeux kept slipping extra measures of Vieux Calvados into my glass and afterwards I had to be helped into the car. Mercifully the passenger seat.

Pommeau is a more recent variant, an aperitif based on apple juice mixed with Calvados. Interesting as a foil to *foie gras*. **Apples** are, of course, everywhere: on sale all year round as well as in glistening *tarte aux pommes* with raisins or wrapped in pastry like English 'cobs'.

Blue-black mussels for *moules à la crème*, unruly crabs and tiny sweet scallops, pink langoustines and little grey shrimps – there on the canopied *poissonnerie* stalls is stacked the Channel's bounty. Sole, skate and mackerel too. **Seafood** could never be fresher, what with Dieppe being one of France's premier fishing ports and many smaller ones along the coast landing their catches daily. Trout from the rivers of Orne are in the swim too – to be poached, delectably, *au cidre* – as well as tanks of live oysters from Courseulles and Isigny.

No one would deny how delightful it is to indulge in a two-tiered *plateau de fruits de mer* at some quayside table, but if you don't want to fork out quite so many euros, just fish for your own in the markets. Buy the prawns, the lemon and the mayonnaise in a little tub and find somewhere to consume them where a salty breeze is wafting off the water.

This is a great area for **antiquing** – in the Calvados *département*, especially. Country *armoires* and refined *commodes* are better bargains here than they might be in Paris or the south, and there is a good quota of Sunday *brocantes*; in most cases on just one Sunday in the month, but it's a different Sunday in each case, so if you shift your ground you can find one every weekend (see end of chapter). Dealers, if asked nicely, can often produce a list of smaller collectables markets and *vide-greniers* in the vicinity. There are also regular flea markets in Rouen and Cherbourg.

Lace-making was once a going concern in the towns of Bayeux and Alençon, but sadly little is made now. Old pieces are worth foraging for in flea markets, though – edging square pillows or bolster covers or linen panels for windows. And there's a traditional blue-and-white porcelain, quite expensive in the shops, which again it's possible to find second-hand.

Finally, if you like to buy souvenirs for your garden, there is a wealth of lovely garden furniture and ornaments as well as seedlings and plants for sale in a region where gardening is as much of a passion as it is for the British. There are no restrictions on taking away rooted plants grown in any EU country.

Dieppe (Seine-Maritime)

Saturday

Dieppe is one of those places that never really loses its identity. The resiting of the ferry terminal a few years ago did a fine job of dissuading travellers arriving from Newhaven from accessing the heart of town. However, this atmospheric fishing port, which bubbles with life from morning to night, is worth the rambling detour to get back into the thick of things where the air smells of Gauloises and *sole dieppoise*. The *vieux port* is now a yachting marina, but the surrounding fish restaurants' platters are still as good value and the bustle of the market is guaranteed to give you that first- or last-minute fix of France.

There is a bumper one on Saturday morning spilling down Grande Rue and streets off it. The barrowfuls of fresh-caught fish and shellfish – especially scallops – are irresistible, though the creamy Normandy butter and cheeses from nearby farms may travel home more easily if you're on a day trip.

Among the clothes racks, the seafaring gear is almost as smart as it is in the surrounding boutiques – yellow waterproofs, sneakers, stripy sailor T-shirts and husky woollies. On the sidelines, the intoxicating drift of sweetness from the *chocolatiers* challenges the general fishyness. When your basket is full, the place to unwind is the Café des Tribunaux, as characterful as it was when artists such as Renoir, Monet and Pissarro sat here grasping their *ballons* of wine with oily fingers.

Don't miss

✪ The cache of artworks and collection of ivory in the castle up on the cliff – amazingly, this survived the World War Two bombs which rearranged other parts of town.

✪ A *marmite dieppoise*, the fish stew that is Normandy's answer to *bouillabaisse*, in the Marmite Dieppoise, best of the many fish restaurants.

✪ Out of town, the Benedictine Abbey at Fécamp where the monks still make Benedictine liqueur; and the Bois des Moutiers at Varengeville – Gertrude Jekyll designed the woodland garden and Edwin Lutyens the Arts & Crafts house.

ⓘ Pont Jehan Ango.

Somewhere to stay

↘ Les Hêtres, charming hotel-restaurant in the Pays de Caux just west of Dieppe. 17th-century Norman house in grounds dominated by beech trees.
☎ 02 35 57 09 30.

↘ Le Domaine Saint-Clair, a romantic clifftop villa and ivy-clad keep with artistic vibes (Proust, Monet, Flaubert and Offenbach once stayed), overlooking Etretat. Gorgeously turned out. ☎ 02 35 27 08 23.

St-Pierre-sur-Dives (Calvados)
Monday

This is a lovely old market town with a vast medieval covered hall, the oldest of its kind in Normandy. The first time I saw it, some years ago, a few of its stalwart rafters were rotting and the slate roof was in need of repair. On a recent visit, I found it had been wonderfully restored. When the Monday market traders gather here under the cool of its steeply pitched roof, as they have done for almost a thousand years, there is an intense feeling of continuity.

St-Pierre-sur-Dives is not very big, yet it has a beautiful abbey church which in its original state was founded by a great-aunt of William the Conqueror, and he himself attended its consecration in all his new glory as King of England. The church has, of course, been much rebuilt and what survives now is mostly 15th- and 16th-century.

On the fringe of the Pays d'Auge and within sniffing distance of places like Livarot and Camembert, not surprisingly apples and cheese feature prominently among market produce. So do apple juices, cider vinegar and jars of delicious apple jellies. It's a traditional market, however, so there's lots else to focus on

apart from food. Swags of fabric, casual shoes, babies' gear, baskets and bags. And masses of flowers and pot plants.

Every first Sunday in the month, the covered market hosts a flea market.

Don't miss

✪ The church – especially the carved choir stalls.

✪ Nearby, the Château de Vendeuvre with its collections of miniature furniture and antique dog/cat baskets. But most of all don't miss the watery surprises in the garden devised by the mischievous Comte.

✪ The Jardins du Pays d'Auge at Cambremer – a whole series of intimate herbaceous-bordered spaces connected by little thatched summer houses.

✪ The Cider Route – signs 'Cru de Cambremer' indicate the distilleries where you can stop and taste cider, Calvados and Pommeau.

ⓘ Rue St-Benoît.

Somewhere to stay

↘ Les Agriculteurs, very simple 1-chimney Logis de France offering simple cooking. ☎ 02 31 20 72 78.

↘ More of a treat, the 19th-century Château les Bruyères in Cambremer. Lovely period furniture and paintings. ☎ 02 31 32 22 45.

Rouen (Seine-Maritime)
Every morning except Monday

Like many major ports, Rouen has an unattractive industrial shell. But crack through it and you find the kernel of a medieval city, the magnificent twin-spired cathedral that Monet painted serially and the streets where Flaubert wandered as a boy. And what a concentration of half-timbered buildings. Troyes and Dijon are Rouen's only rivals in Middle-Aged spread. Restoring the old centre to its former glory has been a monumental but worthwhile task, many of the beams and gables repainted in historically accurate pastel shades.

The Place du Vieux-Marché, in the heart of the pedestrianized area, is enclosed by charming 16th- and 17th-century houses. In the middle, architectural exclamation marks recall the city's darkest moment: the burning of Joan of Arc in 1432. A 20-foot-high cross marks the spot and the starkly modern Eglise Ste-Jeanne-d'Arc was dedicated to her in 1979. Behind this stands a neo-medieval market hall, in and around which surge the daily morning markets (save Monday). It really is a splendid location.

Produce at a big city market like this comes not just from all over Normandy but all over France. Fish leads – we're 80 kilometres from the Channel. As well as the fresh stuff, look on the *traiteur* counters for delicious prepared fish dishes. At the *fromageries*, heart-shaped goat's cheese from Neufchatel-en-Bray is the local goody. A plentiful supply of ducklings is also guaranteed, some of whom will be destined for adjacent restaurants where *caneton rouennais* is both a speciality and a spectacle. The duckling, roasted rare, is brought to your table where a special device is clamped on to squeeze out the blood before your startled eyes. This, mixed with wine, serves as the sauce. I'd just rather they'd do it in the kitchen . . .

Rouen also provides rich pickings for antique-hunters: there is a big flea market every weekend (Friday, Saturday and Sunday morning) in Place St-Marc just east of St-Maclou.

Don't miss

✪ The Gros Horloge, straddling the street.

✪ The cathedral – every kind of Gothic from the 12th century.

✪ St Ouen Abbey.

✪ The Renaissance windows in the new church of Ste-Jeanne-d'Arc.

✪ A meal in Couronne, Place du Vieux Marché, which claims to be the oldest auberge in France.

✪ Fine Arts Museum.

✪ The Flaubert Museum in the author's birthplace.

✪ Within range: on the left bank of the Seine, the artists' haunt of La Bouille; on the right, at Villequier, the delightful Victor Hugo museum in Maison Vacquerie, former home of his daughter's in-laws.

✪ The haunting ruins of Jumièges Abbey.

ⓘ Place de la Cathédrale.

Somewhere to stay

↘ Hôtel Dandy, stylish and cosy, a 3-star in the centre not far from the Place du Vieux Marché. No restaurant.
☎ 02 35 07 32 00.

↘ Le Saint-Pierre in the village of La Bouille, just out of town, restaurant and some rooms looking out on the Seine.
☎ 02 35 18 01 01.

L'Aigle (Orne)

Tuesday

I found it hard to decide between L'Aigle and Verneuil-sur-Avre (see **Best of the Rest**) for my six best. L'Aigle won because . . . well, how can you ignore the 'third largest market in France'? One that includes a mammoth *marché aux bestiaux*, that is, livestock, mostly cattle but sheep too.

Down in the delightful Pays d'Ouche, the centre of L'Aigle is pleasant if unremarkable. On Tuesday mornings, it feels like the centre of the known universe. The excitement is palpable, the 'promo' prices jaw-dropping, the noises-off – and smells – farmyard. Before you hit the traditional sector, it's fun to wander round the pens (livestock market 7.30 to 9.30). Farmers with round stomachs and flat berets stand in little knots considering the finer points of Friesians, Charollais or the distinctive coffee-and-cream home breed. Others make decisions alone with a notebook. Fleece is prodded, flesh is pressed. A pet calf stands willingly to heel, held by his tail. Every picture tells a story.

The main market gets going at 9 as the cattle sales are winding down. There is a *place* for everything. Place St-Martin for butchers and *charcuteries*; Place Boislandry, fruit and veg; Place de Verdun, chickens; Rue de l'Abreuvoir St-Martin for fish and dairy stuff; Place de la Halle, flowers and pot plants; Place de l'Europe, Rue de Bec-Ham and Rue Gambetta for fabrics, clothes and the rest. Whether you're after cheap T-shirts, diaphanous curtains, sensible shoes or tarty hair ornaments, you'll find them here. For just a few hours, the whole town is taken over and transformed into a vast open-air hypermarket.

Grab something 'to go' as you may not easily find a restaurant table for lunch.

Don't miss

✪ The château, now the town hall, with its monumental staircase and museum of musical instruments.

✪ The church dating from the 12th century in Place St Martin.

✪ The eloquent little Museum of June 1944 (open Tuesday, Wednesday, Saturday and Sunday), Place Fulbert de Beina.

✪ Auberge St-Michel, a couple of miles away on the road to Dreux, for really good traditional food at reasonable prices.

ⓘ Place Fulbert-de-Beina.

Somewhere to stay

↘ Hôtel du Dauphin, charming old 3-star in the centre of L'Aigle with two fine restaurants which naturally make the most of fresh market produce.
☎ 02 33 84 18 00.

↘ Le Dauphin in nearby Sées, a pretty 2-star near its 13th-century cathedral.
☎ 02 33 27 80 07.

Honfleur (Calvados)

Saturday

I adore Honfleur. Of all small fishing ports in France this one at the mouth of the Seine is by far the most beguiling – and it remains unspoiled, however many visitors are there to soak up its charms. No wonder the painter Eugène Boudin was inspired by his home harbour and drew the likes of Monet to his side to fill canvases with bright blurry colours. Was it the wavering reflections of the fishing boats that gave him the idea for the Impressionist style? Who knows? Painters came here before them and painters are still eager to set up their easels on the quayside around the *vieux bassin*. Some look in the direction of the old salt depot and the restaurant tables teetering by the water. Others focus on the line of tall thin houses faced with slate or wood on the right.

It is entirely fitting that the market should be in a picturesque spot and it is: squeezed in around the unique oak stave church of Ste Catherine, just a step away from the harbour. Surrounded by antique and curiosity shops, little art galleries and souvenir shops, this is always a honeypot of interest. On Saturday mornings it's packed with the cream of fresh local produce (also on Thursday mornings when there's a *marché bio*), while clothes and other merchandise spill along the Cours des Fossés, Quai Saint Etienne and Rue de la Ville.

On the second Sunday in the month, Honfleur stages a marvellous *brocante* in the Parvis St Léonard, just behind the tourist office. It was from Honfleur that I once carried away a curvy rosewood bedside cupboard – far from Louis Quinze but very satisfyingly French.

Don't miss

✪ The Eugène Boudin Museum (collection donated by the artist includes works of his own as well as those of Monet, Dufy, Courbet and Jongkind).

✪ A good look at Ste Catherine's – built by shipwrights as a thanksgiving for the departure of the English after the Hundred Years' War.

✪ On the other side of the harbour, the Musée du Vieux Honfleur in St Etienne's church. It tells the story of the port's fishing prowess and its salt trade.

✪ Great little antiques and *produits du terroir* shops, some of the best tucked away in side streets.

✪ For a push-out-the-*bateau* meal, La Terrasse et l'Assiette (1 Michelin star).

ⓘ Quai Lepaulmier.

Somewhere to stay

➘ Hôtel les Loges, slate-fronted beauty in a quiet cobbled street with an interior that's swish and contemporary. Breakfast on fresh apple juice and local goat's cheese. ☎ 02 31 89 38 26.

➘ Ferme St-Siméon, overlooking the Seine estuary. A sign on the grass explains its previous life as the auberge of M. Toutin, where the Impressionists caroused as Mme Toutin '*versait généreusement le cidre sous les pommiers*'. Now it's a sybaritic Relais & Châteaux. ☎ 02 31 81 78 00.

Villedieu-les-Poêles (Manche)
Tuesday

Down the centuries, the hammering of metal has been the signature sound of this attractive town just east of Granville on the Cherbourg (or Cotentin) peninsula. Consider its curious name: 'God's town of the frying pan'. Long ago, Villedieu cornered the market in copper cookware – frying pans, saucepans, huge double-handled casseroles, fish kettles, you name it – and today world-famous restaurant kitchens in France and abroad are supplied by its craftspeople. The *ateliers de cuivre* (copper workshops) are an added incentive to shopping at Tuesday's morning market. You might see a promotion at the market (or not), but to make sure you get the stainless-steel lined, cast-iron-mounted quality product it's to the workshops you must go. I'm not marginalizing the market – it's a good one. Just a case of two birds with one stone. Stalls are loaded with prime seafood and produce from the peninsula: lush fruit and vegetables, oysters from St-Vaast-la-Hougue, scallops from Barfleur, lamb *pré-salé* from the flocks grazing on the salt marshes around Mont-St-Michel. Plus the usual excellent dairy produce (look for Coutances cheese, a Manche special).

Don't miss

✪ Atelier du Cuivre shop, 54 Rue du Général Huard, for the full range of hand-crafted copper ware.

○ The workshops, hiding away down cobbled lanes with intriguing names such as Court of Lilies and Court of Hell (from the days when the Knights of St John were working metal here).

○ The traditional bell foundry, also open to the public.

○ The special cleaner that makes light work of keeping your copper shining!

○ To the west, the engaging seaside town of Granville from where you can take boat trips to the fishermen's islands of Chausey.

ⓘ Place des Costis.

Somewhere to stay

↘ Le Fruitier, central, businesslike and friendy Logis with fruity murals in the dining room. ☎ 02 33 90 51 00.

↘ La Beaumonderie, just outside Granville at Breville-sur-Mer, elegant early-20th-century manoir which was General Eisenhower's HQ during D-Day operations. ☎ 02 33 50 36 36.

★ **Bayeux** Miraculously untouched by D-Day although less than 13km from the coast. As well as the tapestry, fabulous Gothic cathedral and pretty backwaters on the River Aure, it has two good markets, on Saturday in Place St-Patrice and Wednesday in Rue St-Jean.

★ **Beuvron-en-Auge** One of the most adorable – and visited – villages of the Pays d'Auge with a restored covered market in the centre and a market on Saturday afternoon.

★ **Caen** A city with sights worth seeing – two abbeys, a castle and the brilliant Museum of Peace – but easy to get lost in. Friday morning market in Place St-Sauveur and Sunday in Place St-Pierre.

★ **Cambremer** In the heart of cider country, with a 16th-century manor and church with outsize Romanesque tower, this is one of the villages that holds a *marché à l'ancienne* (crafts, local produce, collectables, music, sometimes a bit of dressing up in costume) on Sundays in July and August. **Pont-l'Evêque** and **Le Molay-Littry** indulge in similar Sunday events in summer, and **Lisieux** does it on Wednesdays.

★ **Courseulles** Much rebuilt after bearing the brunt of 1944 action, a resort of great fish restaurants. Daily fish market as the boats come in.

★ **Etretat** With its pebble beach dramatically flanked by the white cliffs and needles that were painted by Monet and other artists, this elegant resort is a great favourite for weekenders from Paris. Covered market on Thursday.

★ **Falaise** An approachable small market town, rebuilt with style: the historic part, stacked on a spur high above the River Ante, looks fantastic floodlit at night. William the Conqueror's birthplace, Falaise was the Germans' 'last stand' during the battle of Normandy. The Saturday market pulsates all day in Place Belle-Croix, but in the mornings only in the covered hall.

★ **Granville** The great couturier Christian Dior's choice for a *maison secondaire* by the sea. His former home is now a museum and he left his terraced cliff-top garden overlooking the coast to the town. Market on Saturday.

★ **Ouistreham** Covered fish market every day at the ferry port end. Flea market every second Sunday in the ancient Grange aux Dîmes in the old town centre a mile or two inland.

★ **Trouville-sur-Mer** Every day the fish market, La Poissonnerie de Trouville, does brisk business by the harbour in this relaxed family resort next to posh Deauville. General market days are Wednesday and Sunday.

★ **Verneuil-sur-Avre** On the way south, I once stayed in Verneuil's local Relais & Châteaux, a turreted mansion called the Hostellerie du Clos, and had to be forcibly dragged away next morning from the town's exuberant Saturday market. It burgeons in Place de la Madeleine, beneath a church like a cathedral with an elaborate 15th-century tower. Clothes, food and flowers are accompanied by music on the sidelines and, all around, slotted behind delightful medieval frontages, are super little shops. Don't miss the chequerboard brick library on Rue de la Madeleine and other beautiful historic buildings. The whole of the old part of town is surrounded by a moat.

★ **Vire** In the *bocage*, an untrammelled rural and wooded swathe of countryside, stands this once-ancient town on a hill. Pleasantly rebuilt (World War Two again), it preserves a wonderful 13th-century gateway with a musical clock. Vire is where they make *andouilles* and *andouillettes* sausages. Markets on Tuesday mornings in Place du Petit Marché, and on Friday mornings both here and in Place du Château.

Other significant flea markets

◉ **Bretteville-sur-Dives**, first Saturday and Sunday, town centre.

◉ **Cherbourg**, first Saturday, Place des Moulins.

◉ **Le Molay-Littry**, covered market third Sunday.

🖰 www.normandy-tourism.org

Markets at a glance: Normandy

A
Alençon, *Wed*, *Thu*, *Sat*, *Sun*
L'Aigle, see Six of the Best
Argentan, *Tue*, *Fri*
Auffay, *Fri*
Avranches, *Sat*
B
Bagnoles-de-l'Orne, *Tue*,
   Wed, *Fri*, *Sat*
Bayeux, *Wed*, *Sat*
Bellême, *Thu*
Bernay, *Sat*
Beuvron, *Sat*
Brionne, *Sun*
Briouze, *Mon*
Buchy, *Mon*
C
Cabourg, *Wed*, *Sun* (daily in
   summer)
Caen, *Fri*, *Sun*
Cambremer, *Sun* at Easter,
   Whit and in summer
Carentan, *Mon*
Carrouges, *Wed*
Caudebec-en-Caux, *Sat*
Cherbourg, *Tue*
Courseulles, daily (fish)

Coutances, *Thu*
D
Deauville, *Tue*, *Fri*, *Sat* (+
   daily in summer)
Dieppe, see Six of the Best
Dives-sur-Mer, *Tue*
   (summer)
Domfront, *Fri*
Ducey, *Tue*
E
Ecouche, *Fri*
Etretat, *Thu*
Eu, *Fri*
Evreux, *Wed*, *Sat*
F
Falaise, *Sat*
Fécamp, *Sat*
Ferrière-sut-Risle, *Sun*
La Ferté-Macé, *Thu*
Flers, *Wed*, *Sat*
Forges-les-Eaux, *Thu*
G
Gacé, *Sat*
Goderville, *Tue*
Granville, *Sat*
H
Harfleur, *Sun*

Honfleur, see Six of the Best
J
Jumièges, *Sun* in July
L
Lisieux, *Sat* (+ *Wed* in
   summer)
Louviers, *Sat*
Lyons-la-Forêt, *Sat*, *Sun*
M
Le Mêle-sur-Sarthe, *Wed*
Le Molay-Littry, *Sun*
   (Jul/Aug)
Mortagne-au-Perche, *Sat*
Mortain, *Sat*
N
Le Neubourg, *Wed*
O
Ouistreham, daily (fish)
P
Pont l'Évêque, *Sun* (Jul/Aug)
Putanges-Pont-Ecrepin, *Thu*
R
Rouen, see Six of the Best
Routot, *Wed*
S
Sainte-Mère-Eglise, *Thu*
Saint-Hilaire-du-Harcouet,
   Wed
Saint-James, *Mon*
Saint-Lô, *Sat*
**Saint-Pierre-sur-Dives, see
   Six of the Best**
Saint-Saëns, *Thu*
Le Sap, *Sat*
Sées, *Sat*
Soligny-la-Trappe, *Tue*
T
Tourouvre, *Fri*
Trouville-sur-Mer, *Wed*, *Sun*
   (+ fish daily)
V
Valognes, *Fri*
Verneuil-sur-Avre, *Sat*
Vernon, *Sat*
**Villedieu-les-Poêles, see
   Six of the Best**
Vimoutiers, *Mon*, *Fri*
Vire, *Tue*, *Fri*
Y
Yvetot, *Wed*

BRITTANY

A harvest from the sea, crêpes *for all seasons and the skirl of bagpipes*

I remember a gloriously hot summer when my brother, sister-in-law and I rented a gîte just inland from Brittany's Pink Granite Coast. We took our mother as well as the children, then just tiny tots. The gîte, a long, stone-built, typically Breton cottage, had been lovingly renovated by a local farmer for his own retirement, so it was perfect. With his grandchildren in mind, he had also created a beautiful rambling garden, a lake with a pedalo, wiggly paths and a trickling stream spanned by a little stone bridge – ideal for playing Pooh-sticks. So idyllic was the experience that my nephew, despite being only three at the time, has never forgotten 'Monsieur Gillou's house'. And I've never forgotten the picture of a very small boy tottering round Guingamp market carrying a baguette as long as he was tall.

Brittany is everyone's family favourite for its stunning beaches and coves ranged on three sides around the 'spout' of the 'teapot' shape of France. A wide peninsula poking out into the Atlantic, it is in many ways a land apart. Strange menhirs and dolmens, prehistoric standing stones, exude an enigmatic aura at Carnac and Lajatjar. Arthurian legends lend a magic that swirls around the inland swathe of forest, moorland and rivers known as the Argoat. Celtic roots have given the region a language, music and architecture of its own – extraordinary parish enclosures are peopled with Bible scenes in stonework. Food is distinctive too. Tourists battling with French are further foxed by something unpronounceably Breton on a restaurant menu or market stall. What is *kouign amann*, for goodness' sake? (Answer: a brioche-type of cake well worth trying.)

And the markets are different. With all that coastline and some of France's prime fishing fleets at work, some are devoted entirely to *fruits de mer* – such as Cancale's oyster market and Le Guilvinec's seafood mini-market where they offer you morsels of this and that to taste as experts show their skill in filleting fish and opening shells.

In village markets, it's not unusual to find live chickens running around or crates of cheeping yellow chicks. Farmers not only bring their produce to town (or village), they also hold their own *marchés à la ferme* – farm shops – once a week at the end of the day. It's a novel experience in this pre-packaged, standardized age to take along your own container to fill with still warm newly laid eggs, or buy flower-petal jam with a lacy 'cap' and hand-scribbled label. Buying direct from the producer is, of course, *bon marché* (good value) too, so look for the sign '*Bienvenue à la Ferme*', or ask local tourist offices for a list of participating farms. This is mostly a summer thing.

Then there are markets that are spectator sports as far as the general public is concerned. You have to pay a small entry fee to attend France's number one livestock market in fortified old Fougères (if you can get up early enough – it starts at 5am and finishes at nine!). Guided tours are offered to Paimpol's dial-system vegetable auction as well as to several major fish markets including Concarneau's.

Summer evening markets are something else – as much about entertainment as shopping. These are exuberant occasions often turning into a *fest noz* (night festival) complete with Breton music and revelry, eating and cider-swilling – marvellous events at which to get to know people, for when the light fades and the barbecues glow, don't think you'll escape being drawn into the dancing to bagpipes, bombarde and drums.

Specialities

It's impossible to think Brittany without thinking **fish**. Nowhere is more than 100km from the sea, so every market is guaranteed a catch of the day. Marvellous cod – they celebrate it with a festival at Binic – sublime sole and sea trout, skate, halibut, sea bass and bream, smoked sardines and haddock. And the shellfish is just knockout. All of the items that you see on those spectacular tiered *plateaux de fruits de mer* can be bought in the markets. Cooked *langoustines* (Brittany or Dublin Bay prawns), spider crabs (*tourteaux* or *dormeurs*) and small velvet crabs – fiddly to shell but so well-flavoured – as well as prawns (*crevettes grises* or *boucauds*), winkles, whelks and squat lobster (related to the *langoustine*). Then the species to be sold raw: oysters, Venus clams and carpet shells, clams, queen scallops and mussels. The only extra ingredients you need to make a meal of it are a few lemons, some fresh bread – white and rye – and loads of butter.

Breton **oysters** are, for many connoisseurs, without peer, traditionally eaten from September to April 'when there's an "r" in the month'. However, with today's state-of-the-art chilling techniques, oysters are available and good to eat year round. They are produced at Cancale, Paimpol, Tréguier, Morlaix, Nacre-des-Abers, Brest Bay, Aven-Belon, the Etel River, Gulf of Morbihan, Penerf and Le Croisic.

Pancakes are the Breton food 'to go'. They say the region has 4000 *crêperies* – I wonder if they counted the *crêpe* stands in the markets? You can always detect that delicious aroma as the butter sizzles

on the *pillig* – the circular iron griddle. The batter is poured and spread with a flick of the spatula. Steam rises, bubbles form and subside, and you wait, swallowing. Golden *crêpes de froment*, marbled with brown, are made with wheatflour and served as a sweet treat. The larger and greyer *galettes de sarrasin* (buckwheat pancakes) can be munched simply with *beurre salé*, locally churned butter with sea salt added, or filled with something savoury to make a more substantial snack – a *galette complète*. Quimper prides itself on its fine, lacy *crêpes*, while Gourin's are so especially delicate they are a *cause célèbre* for a festival each July.

Among other calorific goodies to sample is that *kouign amann* – 'butter cake' in Breton. Originally from Douarnenez, it is actually a yeast dough with lots of butter and sugar in it, folded like flaky pastry and cooked in the oven. Then there's the ubiquitous *far* or *farz forn*, a type of flan cooked in a glazed earthenware dish. More a pudding, *far* can be enriched with prunes, cinnamon, rum and vanilla. You can buy it ready-made.

Seaweed piled on fish stalls is not just

for decoration. Like the Welsh, Bretons regard it as a delicacy and use it in salads and terrines, on skewers with fish and even pickled.

From the land comes a cornucopia of **vegetables**. The mild climate and rich soil of the Côte d'Armor nurtures wonderful 'prince of Brittany' cauliflowers, artichokes – originally from Italy in the Middle Ages – and white haricot beans known as Paimpol 'cocos'. St-Malo boasts of its new potatoes, especially the nice knobbly waxy ones known as *rattes*. And, of course, in every market are stalls festooned with strings of white and purple garlic, and those juicy, tight-skinned onions in crimson and gold that the bicycling 'Onion Johnnies' used to hang on their handlebars and pedal from town to town – even across the Channel and around the south of England. Alas, rarely if ever these days.

Among the harvest of soft summer fruits, **strawberries** are supreme. Brittany, it's believed, is where they were first grown in Europe, when a Monsieur Frézier imported them from Chile in the 18th century. Did he also give his name to them? Since *fraisier* is French for strawberry plant, it seems more than likely. The best come from Plougastel, where local varieties have a distinctive flavour reminiscent of woodland strawberries. I like to eat them sun-warmed, straight from the punnet. Add rich cream or ice cream if you must, or indulge in one of those glazed strawberry tarts.

Apples come with strawberry pink cheeks. By the truckload, as in Normandy. From the apples comes Breton **cider**, very similar to Normandy cider – light, slightly fizzy (*bouché*) and refreshing – excellent with savoury pancakes. There are an infinite number of fruit juices and liqueurs, some very individual ones sold at farmers' markets, and a delicate honey wine which reminds me of the mead they make on Holy Island off Northumberland. The Breton version is less cloying: it's called *chouchen* or *hydromel*. Local beer – particularly barley beer – is good. But there is only one drink to accompany the seafood: a bottle of flinty dry **Muscadet** from the vineyards of neighbouring Western Loire.

The clarity of the light in Brittany, like that of Cornwall across the water, has drawn many **artists** to its most picturesque corners. Small-scale oils and watercolours are often on sale at markets, as well as ceramics and pots. Sculptors in granite display small pieces too, more often than not as an introduction to their larger works in studios and galleries. Worth knowing about is the annual Granite Festival in Louvigné-du-Désert which lasts the whole of August. Here, every day, you can watch local and international sculptors chipping away in the act of creation. Especially pleasing is Quimper faïence, hand-painted pottery with 17th-century patterns in soft primary colours; also glazed earthenware and carved wooden craftwork. Sometimes, at the edge of a market, country needlewomen sit stitching away at pieces of traditional embroidery and lace. A handkerchief or baby's bonnet makes an easy-to-pack as well as special souvenir.

Cancale (Ille-et-Vilaine)

Oysters every day, weekly market Sunday

At this charming little fishing port just east of St-Malo, oyster stalls with blue and white canvas awnings occupy a pitch by La Houle harbour every day of the year from 9 in the morning until 7 in the evening. Just below, on the foreshore, are the stone tanks in which the oysters clean themselves after being raised in the *parcs* further out. Many of the oysters you buy here are straight from the sea. Others may have come from Finistère out west or elsewhere, but they are always extra good. *'Venez comparer – qualité – prix'*, insist the words on the canopies as people queue for a dozen *pieds de cheval*, *plates* or *creuses* to take home, or a paper plate of six opened on the spot to scoff perched on the sea wall.

Believing in their aphrodisiac qualities, Louis XIV had them delivered from here by the cartload for midnight snacks at Versailles. Casanova is said to have guzzled fifty a day.

Cancale's traditional weekly market is on Sunday morning in the centre of town.

Don't miss

✪ A trip out to sea in a *bisquine*, a sturdy modern version of the old Breton fishing boat, or a stroll along the *sentier des douaniers* (coastguard's path) with the gulls for company.

✪ The little Musée de l'Huître et du Coquillage which tells the story of Cancale's oyster-growing and fishing industry (they have grounds off Newfoundland).

✪ A meal in any of the seafood restaurants that line the Quai Thomas or, if you can afford it, the 2-Michelin-starred Maisons de Bricourt in Rue Duguesclin.

✪ The breezy Pointe du Hock, and even breezier Pointe du Grouin with its lighthouse just out of town.

ⓘ 44 Rue du Port.

Somewhere to stay

➘ Le Continental, comfortable 3-star with a verandah restaurant facing the port – cosy on blustery days.
☎ 02 99 89 60 16.

➘ Hôtel de Bricourt-Richeux, an elegant 1920s villa in tranquil parkland overlooking the Bay of Mont-St-Michel.
☎ 02 99 89 64 76. (It's linked with the Maisons de Bricourt restaurant in Cancale.)

Rennes (Ille-et-Vilaine)
Saturday

The Marché des Lices, in the heart of old Rennes, is a fabulous market. On Saturday mornings, it clocks up the second highest attendance figures in the whole of France – well worth penetrating the outer flanks of the region's dynamic capital to reach (parking underground). Once you're in Place des Lices amid all the glorious sights, sounds and smells, you forget the traffic. This vast space, the site of tournaments in medieval times, is lined by some of the old quarter's finest half-timbered buildings.

Among the fray will almost certainly be some of the most celebrated local chefs. They come from miles around to buy for their restaurants, scrutinizing prime-quality *petit gris* melons, fat artichokes and silky green beans, as well as seeking out, as other discerning shoppers do, the small-time local producers who sell from their baskets: farm eggs, fresh herbs and delicately flavoured 'coucou' chickens.

Inside the two 19th-century Martenot food halls, all glass, steel and decorative brickwork, are the butchers, bakers and *traiteurs*, the special *pâtissiers* and *chocolatiers*. Outside again, the fish and shellfish market assails you with its seaweedy smells and silvery haul, and further on, in Place Saint-Michel, the scents become sweeter among the flowers and plants.

If you can't wait for lunch, try a popular Rennes filler, the *saucisse galette*. But do leave room for lunch. When the market ends at one o'clock, there are lots of jolly café terraces to sit on and some superb restaurants tucked away in the cobbled streets behind.

Flea market in Boulevard de la Liberté, Thursday morning.

Don't miss

✪ The Porte Mordelaise, remaining fragment of the city's ramparts.

✪ The Musée de Bretagne (a fascinating dip into the history of Brittany, its megaliths, rural life and crafts) and the Musée des Beaux Arts (lots of Breton paintings), both in the same building.

✪ The restored 17th-century law courts (seat of the Breton parliament until the Revolution), especially the coffered ceiling and gilded woodwork of the Grande Chambre.

✪ Escu de Runfao restaurant in Rue Chapître, with 17th-century beams, chimneys etc (closed most of August).

ⓘ 11 Rue St-Yves.

Somewhere to stay

↘ Le Coq-Gadby, exquisite small hotel with romantically clad rooms in a townhouse opening onto a secluded orangerie. Lovely cooking with inventive twists on the traditional.
☎ 02 99 38 05 55.

↘ Mercure Pré Botté, comfortable and spacious, no restaurant. Once the *Ouest-France* newspaper building, which explains 'the press' theme throughout. ☎ 02 99 78 82 20.

Pont-Aven (Finistère)
Tuesday

Even the publicity about Pont-Aven – 'artists' honeypot in the late 1800s' – didn't prepare me for its picture-book prettiness. Every corner is heavenly. Perhaps I've only seen it at its best, full of flowers but not an overload of tourists. It was on one of those breezeless, warm October days with tiny cottonwool clouds floating across a ceiling of hyacinth-blue – a painter's sky. There were still visitors peering in the galleries, shuffling across the cute bridge named after Paul Gauguin and wandering by the fast-flowing Aven river, but in high summer I'd guess it's impossible to move. This is somewhere to discover out of season if you can. Then, the Place de l'Hôtel de Ville is more than adequate for the Tuesday market. But between mid-June and the end of September it is removed to the port – an equally picturesque location with salty characters messing about in their assorted boats. Naturally the variety of merchandise increases in summer, with more crafts, novelties and knick-knacks like hand-painted slates and granite jewellery to sell to tourists, but the market still majors on local farm produce and fish, with lots to taste – tidbits of canned monkfish liver and cups of fish soup with seaweed, as well as the more familiar pancakes, cider and *chouchen* (mead).

Don't miss

- The little municipal museum.

- The walk (or drive) to the old stone chapel of Trémalo above town to see the primitive yellow-painted woodcarving of Jesus on the cross which inspired Gauguin to paint his famous 'Christ Jaune'.

- The Gauguin Trail.

- Boat trips on the Aven.

- Beaches galore nearby.

- The carved calvary at Nizon.

- Megaliths at Luzuen and Kerguillotu.

- Only a few miles away, Concarneau, France's foremost tuna-fishing port, where, Monday to Friday, there are 6am guided tours of the fish auction – '*crier à la voix*' (see Best of the Rest).

- ⓘ Place de l'Hôtel de Ville.

Somewhere to stay

- ⭲ Les Ajoncs d'Or, bang in the centre, occupies the house in which Gauguin lodged on his last visit to Pont-Aven. Charming restaurant inevitably packed in summer. Rooms double-glazed. ☎ 02 98 06 18 91.

- ⭲ The 18th-century Manoir de Kertaig, 10km hence near Moëlan-sur-Mer, soundproofed by 218 acres of parkland. A honey of a place. No restaurant. ☎ 02 98 39 77 77.

Josselin (Morbihan)

Saturday

The approach by the river Oust, part of the Canal Nantes-à-Brest, is the most charismatic, for the water washes the feet of Josselin's magical castle, and its three round towers, soaring sheer from the rock to their pencil-point conical roofs, are mirrored in the calm waters of the river. As you sweep round the bend in a barge or canal-cruiser, this mighty feudal seat of the Dukes of Rohan appears like an illustration from a fairy-tale. It is one of the most photographed sights in Brittany. This is how I first came here, as luck would have it in time for the last couple of hours of the Saturday morning market. But whichever way you get to Josselin you'll adore it. The small town huddles around its castle and the market place is right in front of the Basilica.

I remember buying cow's milk cheese marked 'pie-noire' and carefully wrapped farm butter, coarse bread to spread them on and a big bag of apples. There were also some beautiful as well as useful wooden accessories for home and kitchen on a stall set outside a permanent shop: bowls and boards, tongs for *cornichons* (gherkins), groovy spoons for scooping honey. Also wooden games and clogs, and very pretty pottery.

Don't miss

✪ The surprise of the château's living quarters – an early Renaissance extravaganza of flamboyant fretwork, dormer windows, gargoyles and stone balustrades built by Jean de Rohan around 1500. The Rohan family still live here. Ground-floor rooms are open to the public.

✪ The doll museum in one of the outbuildings.

✪ The lovely Gothic church, Notre Dame du Roncier – 'Our Lady of the Bramble Thicket'.

ⓘ Place de la Congrégation.

Somewhere to stay

↘ Hôtel du Château – not the feudal fortress but a comfortable roost on the opposite side of the riverbank with tasty, not overpriced menus. Medieval-style dining room with waterside terrace. ☎ 02 97 22 20 11.

↘ Le Cobh, a 2-chimney Logis described with justification as a 'détour gourmand', nestles in Ploërmel, next stop along the river. Fishing nearby. ☎ 02 97 74 00 49.

Roscoff (Finistère)

Wednesday morning

Resist the tendency to give ferry ports a miss. Next time you book a passage to this part of the Western Channel, whether you're coming or going, head for town. Away from the shipping terminal, Roscoff is a very cheery place, all speckled granite garnished with geraniums, and jolly seafood restaurants with sturdy tables balancing on the cobbles. Once, forced to overnight here when I missed the boat, I made so many pleasant discoveries I promised myself a return visit, and went back the following summer when a friend rented a summer house nearby.

The core town is the proverbial 'maze' of narrow streets with houses bunched together as if sheltering from Atlantic gales. Many of those around the main square and along the seafront were built by wealthy shipowners during the days of the corsairs. Centrepiece is the curious church of Notre-Dame-de-Kroaz-Baz with its tiered belltower and cannon poking threateningly from the walls – a relic of the days when the English were expected at any moment, and not carrying buckets and spades. The to-ing and fro-ing of trawlers and trippers, yachts and clippers keeps Roscoff constantly animated.

Every weekday afternoon you can buy fresh-caught fish by the harbour, and every Wednesday morning the bright canopies of a traditional market add colour to the Quai d'Auxerre near the lighthouse. Three-quarters of it is given over to food – the best of Brittany and elsewhere. The rest is a compulsive muddle of cheap underwear, cane chairs, sailor stripes, fishing smocks and clogs, with kitchen utensils clanging in the breeze in counterpoint to the tinkling of boat rigging. In summer, strolling minstrels play. There's nothing like the mellifluous sound of a bombarde, the Breton oboe, to oil the wheels of commerce.

Don't miss

✪ A spot of thalassotherapy – there are two spas specializing in salt water/seaweed treatments.

✪ The Charles Pérez Aquarium of sea creatures from the Channel.

✪ The vast rockeries of the Jardin Exotique.

✪ A boat trip out to the tiny Ile de Batz (pronounced 'Ba'), which has an even more stunning tropical garden, created by Georges Delaselle, as well as white beaches and rocky coves.

ⓘ Rue Gambetta.

Somewhere to stay

⭰ Le Brittany, an authentic Breton manor house fabulously sited looking out over the harbour to Batz island. On chillier days, a sauna, solarium and heated indoor pool cosset guests.
☎ 02 98 69 70 78.

⭰ Hôtel Talabardon, in the church square, run by the same family of chefs since 1890. Enjoy their fish expertise for dinner as you watch gulls wheeling to catch theirs. ☎ 02 98 61 24 95.

Dinan (Côtes d'Armor)
Thursday, Wednesday in summer for the flea market

Even if you just do a Brittany Ferries day trip or overnight in St-Malo, you can get to Dinan. It's barely a half-hour drive inland – if you don't have a car a boat trip up the river Rance will take you there. This marvellous medieval walled town was the first I ever visited in Brittany and however many times I see its towers and spires poking above the trees across the deep valley of the Rance I always catch my breath and smile.

The expression on the face of Bertrand Du Guesclin's statue is not so benign. He scowls menacingly as the weekly market gathers round his prancing horse's plinth. Since the great Breton hero of the Hundred Years' War was famous for trouncing Britain's Sir Thomas of Canterbury in single combat, one might have expected him to appear a little more pleased with himself, but it seems he was of notoriously gruff countenance.

This Thursday-morning market is sizeable and as complete as any in the region, with food from home and afar, flowers, fabrics, fashion, crafts – everything except *les puces*. For the flea market you must come on a Wednesday morning between the end of June and the beginning of September and head for Place St Sauveur. Stalls assemble at the west door of the basilica (which contains Du Guesclin's heart). Here, you'll find Breton dressers and old dresses, scraps of lace, milking stools, rusty farm implements, china chipped and perfect, and discarded fishing tackle. Afterwards, those who do not lunch in beamed and timbered style at Mère Pourcel in Place des Merciers, or go for grills in the 17th-century Cantorbery (sic), Rue Ste-Claire, will find the perfect picnic spot under a huge spreading cedar in the Jardin Anglais behind St Sauveur.

Don't miss

- ✪ A tour of the ramparts, keep, watchtowers and gateways (spectacular views).
- ✪ The medieval Château de la Duchesse Anne and its little history museum in the main tower.
- ✪ A climb up the 15th-century clocktower.
- ✪ Inside St Sauveur, with its many treasures.
- ✪ A wander down the steep and cobbled Rue du Jerzual to the tranquillity of the town's old port on the Rance (simple *moules-frites*-type cafés here).

ⓘ Place du Château.

Somewhere to stay

- ➘ Jerzual, charming new hotel by the port with courtyard pool and dining on outdoor terraces, one facing the river. Reasonably priced dining. ☎ 02 96 87 02 02.
- ➘ Avaugour, tucked into the ramparts, all ancient stone, polished wood and fabulous flower arrangements. Rooms freshly updated and small garden in which to *petit déjeuner*. No restaurant. ☎ 02 96 39 07 49

Best of the Rest

★ **Camaret** Laid-back small seaside town worth discovering at the end of the Crozon peninsula. Delightfully one-horse. Hikers who clamber over the 'Pile of Peas' rocks come to cool their feet in the shallows of its wide sandy bay. Daily market in July and August.

★ **Concarneau** The port not only offers the morning fish market but Monday and Friday food markets and a craft market in July and August on Wednesday evenings outside the Ville Close.

★ **Dinard** Famous resort, chic-to-chic with St-Malo, just the other side of the ferry port. Lively markets on Tuesday, Thursday and Saturday.

★ **Fougères** Location of a key livestock market since the 12th century (Friday, 5am to 9am, outside town – guided tours), this romantic old *ville* close to Normandy has a castle of many-towered splendour unusually nestling in a hollow. The upper town is 18th-century. Traditional markets take place on Thursdays and Saturdays.

★ **Lannion** Just inland from Perros-Guirrec on the Pink Granite Coast, a lovely small historic town with slate-faced gables, dormer windows and lots of half timbering. A sizeable Thursday market spreads along the Quai d'Aiguillon and around the central square and market hall. In summer, musicians rendezvous here and add an assortment of sound effects.

★ **Mur-de-Bretagne** This normally quiet place in the centre of Brittany, a favourite haunt of 19th-century painter Camille Corot, comes to life on Friday nights in July and August when it hosts an evening market from 18.00 to 20.00. A little night music adds to the fun and the *kan ha diskan* is sometimes performed – a song and dance with an irresistible rhythm. (Big *bio* food fair held here over a weekend each September.)

★ **Perros-Guirec** The main resort of the Côte de Granit Rose, with its big bay of firm sand sheltered by rugged rocks and pines, is especially fun on Friday when the market moves in. From the harbour, twitchers can catch boat trips to the bird colonies of the Sept Iles.

★ **Quiberon** One of southern Brittany's most attractive seaside resorts, with its indented coastline of pine-shaded bays, sandy creeks and sea bobbing with small craft. Saturday is market day.

★ **Quimper** Thoroughly relaxed old cathedral city with half-timbered nooks, crannies, *crêperies*, craft shops and a big covered market. Outdoor markets around this *halle* on Wednesday and Saturday morning; also an organic produce market in the Kerfeunteun on Fridays and Sunday food market in Le Braden.

★ **St-Malo** After World War Two damage, the reconstruction of this walled port was so effective it still looks every inch the city of corsairs. Every day except Sunday a market pulsates inside its walls, fish and shellfish dominating. There's also a fish auction Monday, Tuesday and Wednesday.

★ **Tréguier** I really like this fine old estuary town with its cloistered cathedral – a haven of peace inland when the Côte de Granit Rose resorts are chocka. Its Wednesday market is busy but relaxed and there are some good lunch places and shops among charming cobbled streets.

★ **Vannes** The biggest market in Morbihan takes place in the *département*'s capital every Wednesday and Saturday. Thousands flock to the market hall in Places des Lices (look for the *p'tites dames au beurre*, the butter ladies from nearby villages who sit on a bench selling from their wicker baskets). There's also a fish hall and a fruit and vegetable market in Place du Poids du Roi. The medieval Intra-Muros (within the walls) is full of interest. Check out the ancient market hall (La Cohue – 'the Hubbub') which has been brilliantly converted into a fine arts and folk museum.

Other significant flea markets

◎ **Brest**, Halle St Louis, second Saturday.

◎ **Douarnenez**, Quai du Port Musée, first and second Friday.

Christmas markets

◎ **Brest**, Place de la Liberté, whole of December.

◎ **Rennes**, Place du Parlement and Place Hoche, most of December.

🖱 www.tourismebretagne.com

Markets at a glance: Brittany

A

Acigné, *Wed*

Ambon, *Sun* (Jul/Aug)

Antrain, *Tue*

Argentré-du-Plessis, *Thu*

Arradon, *Tue*, *Fri*

Arzon, *Tue*

Audierne, *Sat*

Auray, *Mon*

B

Baden, *Sun*

Bain-de-Bretagne, *Mon*

Bannalec, 2nd and 4th *Wed*

Baud, 1st *Wed*, *Sat*

Bazouges-la-Pérouse, *Thu*

Beaucé, *Fri*

Bécherel, *Sat*

Bédée, *Sat*

Béganne, *Sun*

Bégard, *Fri*

Belle-Isle-en-Terre, *Wed*

Bénodet, *Mon*

Betton, *Sun*

Binic, *Thu* (+ *Fri* Jul/Aug)

Le Bono, *Sat*

La Bouexière, *Sat*

Bourbriac-Caulnes, *Tue*

Brasparts, 1st *Mon*

Bréal-sous-Montfort, *Sat*

Bréhat, daily (Jul/Aug)

Brest, daily

Briec, *Tue*, *Fri*

Brignogan-Plages, *Fri*
  (Jul/Aug)

Broons, *Wed*

Bruz, *Fri*

Bubry, 2nd and 4th *Wed*

C

Callac, *Wed*

Camaret-sur-Mer, 3rd *Tue*,
  daily Jul/Aug

Cancale, see Six of the Best

Carantec, *Thu*

Carentoir, 1st *Tue*

Carhaix, *Sat*

Carnac, *Wed*, *Sun*

Caudan, *Tue*

Caulnes, *Tue*

Cesson-Sévigné, *Sat*

La Chapelle-des-Fougeretz,
  Sat

Chartres-de-Bretagne, *Thu*

Châteaubourg, *Fri*

Châteaugiron, *Thu*

Châteaulin, *Thu* (+ *Sun*
  Jul/Aug)

Châteauneuf-du-Faou, 1st,
  3rd and 5th *Wed*

Châtelaudren, *Mon*

Chavagne, *Wed*

Cléden-Cap-Sizun, 4th *Thu*

Cléder, *Fri* (+ *Sun* Jul/Aug)

Cléguérec, *Wed* eve (Jul/Aug)

Clohars-Carnoët, *Sat*

Combourg, *Mon*

Combrit, *Wed*

Concarneau, *Mon*, *Fri*

Le Conquet, *Tue*

Corps-Nuds, *Wed*

Crac'h, *Thu*

Crozon, 2nd and 4th *Wed*

D

Damgan, *Tue* and *Sat*
  (Jul/Aug)

Daoulas, *Sun*

Dinan, see Six of the Best

Dinard, *Tue*, *Thu*, *Sat*

Dinéault, *Tue*, *Fri*

Dol-de-Bretagne, *Sat*

Douarnenez, *Mon*, *Wed*, *Sat*

E

Elven, *Fri*

Erdeven, *Mon* eve (Jul/Aug)

Ergué-Gabéric, 3rd *Tue*

Erguy, *Sat*

Etables-sur-Mer, *Tue* (+ *Sat*
  Jul/Aug)

Etel, *Tue*

F

Le Faou, *Tue*, last *Sat*

Le Faouët, 1st and 3rd *Wed*

La Forêt-Fouesnant, *Sun* (+
  Tue eve Jul/Aug)

Fouesnant-les-Glénan, *Fri*

Fougères, *Thu*, *Sat*

Fougeretz, *Sat*

Fréhel, *Tue*

G

La Gacilly, *Sat*

Gaël, *Fri*

Gourin, *Mon*

Goven, *Wed*

Grandchamp, 1st *Fri*

Le Grand-Fougeray, *Sat*

Guéméné-sur-Scorff, *Thu*

Guer, *Wed*

La Guerche-de-Bretagne,
  Tue

Guerlesquin, *Mon*

Guichen, *Tue*

Guidel, *Sun* (+ *Fri* eve
  Jul/Aug)

Guignen, *Wed*

Guilers, *Fri*

Guilliers, *Tue*

Le Guilvinec, *Tue*, *Sat* (+ *Sun*
  Jul/Aug)

Guingamp, *Fri*, *Sat*

Guipavas, *Fri*

Guipry, *Thu*

H

Hédé, *Tue*

Hennebont, *Thu*

L'Hermitage, *Sat*

L'Hôpital-Camfrout, *Fri*

Huelgoat, *Thu*

I

Iffendic, *Sat*

Ile-aux-Moines, *Fri*

Ile-d'Ouessant, *Wed*, *Sat*

Ile-Tudy, *Mon* (Jul/Aug)

Irodouer, *Fri*

J

Janzé, *Wed*

Josselin, see Six of the Best

Jugon-les-Lacs, *Fri*

K

Kerhuon, *Sat*

Kervoyal, *Wed* (Jul/Aug)

L

Lamballe, *Thu*

Lampaul-Plouarzel, *Thu*

Lancieux, *Tue* (Jul/Aug)

Landéda, *Tue*

Landerneau, *Tue*, *Fri*, *Sat*

Landivisiau, *Wed*

Lanester, *Tue*

Langouet, *Thu*

Languidic, *Fri*

Lanmeur, *Fri*

Lannilis, *Wed*

Lannion, *Thu*

Lanvollon, *Fri*

Markets at a glance: Brittany

Larmor-Plage, *Sun*
Larmour-Baden, *Sun*
Lécousse, *Sun*
Lesneven, *Mon*
Lézardrieux, *Fri*
Liffré, *Fri*
Locmaria, *Sun*
Locmaria-Plouzané, *Thu*
Locmariaquer, *Tue*, *Sat*
Locminé, *Thu*
Locmiquelic, *Fri*
Locquirec, *Wed*
Loctudy, *Tue*
Loguivy-Plougras, *Fri*
Lohéac, *Sat*
Lorient, *Wed*, *Sat*
Louargat, *Thu*
Loudéac, *Sat*
Louvigné-du-Désert, *Fri*
M
Malansac, *Tue*
Malestroit, *Thu*
Martigné-Ferchaud, *Fri*
Matignon, *Wed*
Maure-de-Bretagne, *Sun*
Mauron, *Fri*
Medrignac, *Wed*
Melesse, *Thu*
Melgven, *Sat*
La Mézière, *Sun*
Miniac-Morvan, *Fri*
Moëlan-sur-Mer, *Tue*
Moncontour, *Mon*
Monfort-sur-Meu, *Fri*
Montauban-de-Bretagne, *Wed*
Mordelles, *Tue*
Morlaix, *Wed*, *Sat*
Mûr-de-Bretagne, *Fri eve (Jul/Aug)*
Muzillac, *Fri*, *Sun*
N
Névez, *Sat*
Noyal, *Sun*
Noyal-Châtillon-sur-Seiche, *Sun*
Noyal-sur-Vilaine, *Tue*
P
Pacé, *Wed*
Paimpol, *Tue*
Le Palais, *Tue*, *Fri*

Pénestin, *Sun (+ Wed Jul/Aug)*
Penvenan, *Sat*
Perret, *Sun (Jul/Aug)*
Perros-Guirec, *Fri*
Le Pertre, *Wed*
Pipriac, *Tue*
Plancoët, *Sat*
Planguenoual, *Mon (Jul/Aug)*
Plédran, *Sat*
Pleine-Fougères, *Tue*
Plélan-le-Grand, *Sun*
Pléneuf, *Tue*
Pléneuf-Val-André, *Fri (Jul/Aug)*
Plerguer, *Wed*
Plérin, *Sun*
Plescop, *Sat*, *Sun*
Plestin-les-Grèves, *Sun (+ Tue eve Jul/Aug)*
Pleubian, *Sat*
Pleurtuit, *Fri*
Pleyben, *2nd Tue*, *Sat*
Plobannalec-Lesconil, *Wed*
Ploemeur, *Sun (+ Wed eve Jul/Aug)*
Ploeren, *Sun*
Ploërmel, *Mon*, *Fri*
Ploeuc-sur-Lié, *Thu*
Plogoff, *Fri*
Plogonnec, *Sat*
Plomodiern, *1st Fri*
Plonéour-Lanvern, *last Fri*
Plonévez-du-Faou, *2nd Fri*
Plouaret, *Tue*
Plouay, *Sat*
Ploubalay, *Fri*
Ploubazlanec, *daily (Jul/Aug)*
Ploudalmézeau, *Fri*
Plouescat, *Sat*
Plouezec, *Sat*
Ploufragan-Plurien, *Fri (Jul/Aug)*
Plougasnou, *Tue*
Plougastel-Daoulas, *Thu*
Plougonvelin, *Sun (Jul/Aug)*
Plougonven, *Tue*
Plougoumelen, *Fri*
Plouguerneau, *Thu*
Plouguerneau-Lilia, *Tue eve (Jul/Aug)*

Plouha, *Wed*
Plouhinec (Finistère), *Sun (Jul/Aug)*
Plouhinec (Morbihan), *Sun*
Plouigneau, *Sun*
Ploumilliau, *Sat*
Plounéour-Trez, *Thu (Jul/Aug)*
Plouzané, *Wed*
Plozévet, *1st Mon*
Pluvigner, *2nd Tue*
Pont-Aven, see Six of the Best
Pont-Croix, *Thu*
Pontivy, *Mon*
Pont-l'Abbé, *Thu*
Pontrieux, *Mon*
Pont-Scorff, *Sat*
Pordic, *Fri*
Port-Crouesty, *Mon (Jul/Aug)*
Port-Louis, *Sat (+ Tue eve Jul/Aug)*
Port-Navalo, *Fri (Jul/Aug)*
Primelin, *Thu (Jul/Aug)*
Q
Questembert, *Mon*
Quéven, *Sun*
Quiberon, *Sat*
Quimper, *Wed*, *Fri eve*, *Sat*, *Sun*
Quimperlé, *Fri*
Quintin, *Tue*
R
Redon, *Mon*
Le Relecq, *Sat*
Rennes, see Six of the Best
Retiers, *Sat*
Le Rheu, *Sat*
Riantec, *Wed*
La Richardais, *Sun*
Riec-sur-Belon, *Wed*, *Sat*
La Roche-Bernard, *Thu*
La Roche-Derrien, *Fri*
Le Roc-St-André, *Sun*
Roscoff, see Six of the Best
Rosporden, *Thu*
Rostrenen, *Tue*
S
Saint-Aubin-d'Aubigné, *Tue*
Saint-Aubin-du-Cormier, *Thu*
Saint-Ave, *Sun*

Saint-Briac, *Fri* (+ *Mon*, *Sat* Jul/Aug)

Saint-Brice-en-Coglès, 2nd *Sun*

Saint-Brieuc, *Wed*, *Sat*, *Sun*

Saint-Cast-le-Guildo, *Fri* (+ *Mon* Jul/Aug)

Saint-Domineuc, *Sat*

Sainte-Anne-d'Auray, *Wed*

Saint-Georges-de-Reintembault, *Thu*

Saint-Gildas-de-Rhuys, *Sun*

Saint-Gilles, *Sat*

Saint-Grégoire, *Wed*

Saint-Guénolé, *Fri*

Saint-Jacut-de-la-Mer, *Fri*

Saint-Jean-Brévelay, 1st and 3rd *Tue*

Saint-Lunaire, *Sun* (Jul/Aug)

Saint-Malo, daily (not *Sun*)

Saint-Martin-des-Champs, *Sun*

Saint-Médard-sur-Ille, *Sat*

Saint-Méen-le-Grand, *Sat*

Saint-Méloir-des-Ondes, *Thu*

Saint-Michel-en-Grève, *Mon*

Saint-Nic-sur-Pentrez, daily (Apr–Sep)

Saint-Ouen-des-Alleux, *Wed*

Saint-Philibert, *Fri*

Saint-Pierre-Quiberon, *Thu*

Saint-Pol-de-Léon, *Tue*

Saint-Quay-Portrieux, *Mon*, *Fri*

Saint-Renan, *Sat*

Saint-Servant-Surzur, *Sun*

Santec, *Sat* (+ *Sun* Jul/Aug)

Sarzeau, *Thu*

Sauzon, *Thu*

Scaër, *Sat*

Sené, *Fri*

Sens-de-Bretagne, *Mon*

Sérent, *Wed*

Servon-sur-Vilaine, *Sun*

Sizun, 1st *Fri*

Spézet, last *Fri*

T

Taden, *Fri* eve (Jul/Aug)

Telgruc-sur-Mer, *Tue*, *Fri*

Theix, *Sun*

Thorigné-Fouillard, *Sun*

Tinténiac, *Wed*

Trans, *Thu*

Trébeurden, *Tue*

Treffiagat, *Sat*

Trégastel, *Mon*

Trégourez, 3rd *Fri*

Trégueux, *Fri*

Tréguier, *Wed*

Trégunc, *Tue* eve, *Wed* (+ *Sun* Jul/Aug)

La Trinité-Porhoët, 2nd *Mon*

La Trinité-sur-Mer, *Tue*, *Fri*

V

Vannes, *Wed*, *Sat*, *Sun*

Vern-sur-Seiche, *Sat*

Vitré, *Mon*

WESTERN LOIRE

Meanders through Muscadet, eel appeal and a glazed look at pottery

The landscapes of Western Loire are soothing rather than spectacular. Farmed or filled with sunflowers, they ripple almost imperceptibly around the meander of the mighty Loire on its last lap from Saumur to St-Nazaire. Everywhere there is the rustic embroidery of wine growing, the junior vines like French knots, the more mature plants chain-stitching themselves together across expanses of gritty beige earth. Below ground, limestone caves provide champagne conditions for storing wines with a sparkle and for the cultivation of 75 per cent of the nation's button mushrooms. On the coast, pretty bays snuggle between wooded headlands or marathon sandy beaches run and run, and some of the most attractive family resorts in France boast some of the liveliest seaside markets. This is a land of quiet beauty and wide skies, where almost as many châteaux hold sway as do in the neighbouring Loire Valley region (the more high-profile tourist target), so there is no shortage of picturesque backdrops to the daily or weekly clusters of canopied stalls.

Still in my linen drawer are the table napkins I ran up from fine Boussac cotton bought in the market of old Le Mans thirty years ago. Tiny print patterns were just beginning to catch on in Britain and here were bales of them in fresh buy-me colourways. Micro white tulip heads on a bright red background leapt out at me from among a heap of remnants. I think the piece yielded six napkins for the equivalent of 50 pence each and they still haven't frayed at the edges. Together with Rosemary Milner, a colleague from my *Good Housekeeping* days, I had been let loose on Le Mans market as a reward for doing the flowers at the *manoir* where we were staying; not a hotel but the home of the de Galembert family, friends of Rosemary. Madame la Baronne, every centimetre the thoroughbred French aristocrat, with delicate bones and a halo of perfectly cut grey hair, ruled the household with the assurance of her breeding. Over a 'petit whisky' before dinner, she would quiz me about the day's doings and correct my faltering French, albeit with a twinkle in her intelligent brown eyes. 'Non, non, one must say *je fais la cuisine* not *je cuis* – you are not yourself too hot to the point of cooking!'

We did quite a bit of *la cuisine* as well as *les fleurs* when the cook/housekeeper went off duty and the whole family and their spouses were about to descend for the weekend. Friday's swan around the market was also to stock up the larder. Into our baskets went quantities of fat beefsteak tomatoes and anchovies from St-Gilles-Croix-de-Vie to make pasta sauces; also loads of the local *rillettes*, a pâté I once heard explained as 'the whole pig goes in at one end of the process and

Specialities

On the Atlantic coast of Loire-Atlantique and Vendée you can fish out to your heart's content. Markets are stacked with marvellous **seafood** – tuna from the Ile d'Yeu, sardines as well as anchovies from St-Gilles and La Turballe. Be brave and give the **eels** of the Loire estuary a go; *anguilles* – or when young *anguillettes*, *alevins* or *civelles* – are much sought after by the French yet seem to bother the British. Like most people, I thought eels would be slimy until I tried them. They are actually quite meaty, akin to monkfish in texture, and exceedingly good in a local dish called *bouilliture*, for which they are first grilled then lightly stewed in wine with onions, mushrooms and prunes. Superb *creuses* and *fines de claires* **oysters** are farmed in the Bay of Bourgneuf, and delectable *moules de bouchot* are raised in the waters of l'Aiguillon bay.

Inescapable is that other gift of the Atlantic: **sea salt**. The 'white gold' of Guérande, a handy souvenir packed in appealing bags and boxes.

Inland, the Loire and its tributaries in Mayenne, Sarthe and Maine-et-Loire teem with trout, zander, pike and perch. Delicately flavoured fish pâtés and terrines made from them crop up at markets.

Part of the great Loire **market garden**, Western Loire revels in its abundant supply of early vegetables. Thick, white asparagus, artichokes, crisp green beans and broad beans. Summer provides a feast of these and whereas in many other parts of France one can legitimately

comes out the other as *rillettes*'. It looks a bit stringy and fatty but is surprisingly good, especially spread on thick slices of crusty bread (no butter) and served with *cornichons*.

The same goodies are on offer in Le Mans' St Jacobins market today. Held in the lee of St Julien's cathedral, it is still one of the region's best, garnering prime produce from coast and countryside as well as bargain household novelties.

complain of the lack of vegetables served in restaurants, here they do make more of an appearance. And mounds of them make it to market, as well as mountains of the button mushrooms (*champignons de Paris*) which flourish in underground tunnels.

The soft red **fruits** of summer are also prolific, plus fruit jams and jellies from La Fraiseraie. In autumn come lovely rosy-cheeked apples and a glut of blackberries, particularly around Saumur. **Dessert** is never a problem. For added calories, keep an eye open for custard tarts called *fion* and *Plantagenets*, made with almond biscuits and cream laced with Cointreau and cherries; and a local coffee liqueur, Kamok, which adds a pleasant kick to a *crème brûlée* or *mousse au chocolat*.

Sooner or later, writers extolling the delights of fishy meals in Western Loire (or neighbouring Brittany) tend to toss in the words 'washed down with a bottle of Muscadet'. This always seems to me rather dismissive of one of France's crispest dry white wines, famously grown in this region and designed for drinking young. I admit that with the sheer volume of **Muscadet** produced (it runs a close second to Beaujolais), some of it can be knocked back without your palate really noticing. However, buy a better bottle and nothing is more refreshing or memorable. The words *sur-lie* added to the label is one guarantee of getting something a cut above the rest. Another is to go direct to the vineyards in the *pays Nantais* – around Le Pallet, Vallet and Clisson – and do a bit of tasting.

Sparkling Saumur is Western Loire's *pétillant* white made by the *méthode champenoise*. Look also for the dry white Jasnières, bone dry Savennières, sweet Bonnezeaux from Layon, quaffable Anjou reds and some good rosés – not so much the demi-sweet *rosés d'Anjou* but those termed *rosés de la Loire*. Angers is the place to buy **Cointreau**, especially on a visit to the distillery where the scent of oranges is almost as intoxicating as the finished liqueur.

Nowhere offers a chicer range of **resort wear** than the seaside towns of Pornic and Pornichet, St-Gilles and Les-Sables-d'Olonne. Even in the markets you can find beautifully cut shorts and chinos, striped cotton tops and classic navy jerseys. With Cholet, the country's textile capital, not far distant, lines from its cut-price designer outlets sometimes find their way to oceanside markets. This goes for household linens too.

Western Loire has about half a dozen significant regular **flea markets** – perhaps not as many as some regions, but there are lots of little ones. And there is as good a variety of **craftwork** as anywhere else. Malicorne's traditional glazed earthenware comes in vibrant colours and every shape from casseroles to cockerels, and there's plenty of choice in simpler sea-washed, biscuit-finish pottery.

Six of the Best

Le Mans (Sarthe)

Wednesday, Friday and Sunday mornings

At the confluence of the Huisne and Sarthe rivers, it's big, it's busy and it's famous for the Le Mans 24 Hours sports car race, a fact which has a certain irony when you get caught in a sluggish rush hour. Don't be put off. Within the walls of Vieux Mans, peace reigns. Houses the colour of old parchment flaunt timbers painted in the original medieval green, red or blue. Fine Renaissance facades and 18th-century mansions with wrought-iron balconies lean above the cobblestone lanes. Shops and restaurants are tucked in so discreetly that this remains one of the most complete medieval centres in the country, historically so perfect it's a movie-maker's dream. Give your imagination a twirl and it's not hard to summon up Gérard Depardieu cutting a swathe through the streets (Vieux Mans backgrounds were used in the film *Cyrano de Bergerac*).

There is a market somewhere around town every day except Monday, but the most atmospheric is the thrice-weekly Marché des Jacobins, centring on Place des Jacobins at the foot of the cathedral. A space developed over closed-in sections of the Jacobin and Cordelier convents, it has a lovely fountain and is edged by stands of fluttering lime trees.

Friday is the busiest day when food and flea market converge. Scales are heaped with the local Reinette and Chausson apples in season, and there is an apple liqueur called Pommeau. The *charcuterie* van trumpets the speciality pâté of potted pork, *rillettes*, some of which, in this its city of origin, is made with goose. There are rabbit terrines from Angers, buttery *sablé* biscuits from Sablé-sur-Sarthe and tin-glazed Malicorne earthenware. Meanwhile, ancient ironmongery is strewn on old dust sheets, motor-racing memorabilia gathers knots of enthusiasts, and a rumpled heap of lace and linen is rummaged through with feverish intent. The fabric stalls still thrive, with remnants of the classy *toiles de Mayenne*. Plenty of parking nearby.

A more focused antiques market takes place in Place Jet d'Eau on Friday mornings, and the Christmas Market in Place de la République is a major event, lasting a dozen consecutive days (usually from 12 to 24 December).

Don't miss

✪ The Roman walls and baths.

✪ St Julien's cathedral: a somewhat schizo mix of Romanesque and Gothic, it nevertheless boasts windows to rival those of Chartres.

✪ The *chocolatier* 'Béline', Place St Nicolas.

✪ *Crèperie* 'Les 3 Mats', 22 Rue Hippolyte Lecornué.

✪ The automobile museum next to the motor-racing circuit.

✪ Less than an hour's drive away: Malicorne's potteries and Espace Faïence museum; the Abbey of Solesmes (daily Gregorian chant); the tiny 'Venice' of La Ferté-Bernard, a little town laced with canals.

ⓘ Rue de l'Etoile.

Somewhere to stay

↘ La Perdrix, 2-star Logis in La Ferté-Bernard (about 40km away – Le Mans hotels are mostly rather businesslike and modern). ☎ 02 43 93 00 44.

↘ Also in La Ferté, the Hôtel du Stade, though it is closed all of August. ☎ 02 43 93 01 67.

peninsula, its eight-towered, four-gated fortified ramparts rising at the edge of the Marais Salants (salt marshes), just a few miles from the Atlantic. Impeccably restored, the town has a well-heeled veneer, as well it might since for centuries trade in sea salt has been the seasoning and sustenance of Guérande. As the 'white gold' crystallizes in the sun, it is still raked and collected by hand – a harvest which takes place twice a year in June and September, but you can visit the salt pans at any time to admire their graphic beauty. Like a huge expanse of

Guérande (Loire-Atlantique)
Wednesday and Saturday

This one is as much for the location as the market. Guérande is a splendid little citadel at the end of the Guérande

window panes, they reflect the intense light you get here from the great dome of sky that embraces the flatness of the coastal plain.

On market days in the town centre there is, needless to say, salt for sale.

Buy it in fine form as *fleur de sel* or *sel fin*, or as the coarser *gros sel* – even mixed with herbs and spices. I love the hand-carved pale wooden salt boxes and salt scoops used to store it. There is plenty else to sprinkle with salt – superb fish, local oysters and mussels, sardines from La Turballe and Le Croisic prawns, as well as all the usual *alimentation* and fripperies of a popular seaside market. Sweets for the sweet-toothed include St-Guénole biscuits, *niniches* – lollipops – made in nearby La Baule, and toffees flavoured with Guérande salt. Few with good taste will be able to resist the local craftwork – baskets, ceramics, paintings (this is something of an artistic enclave); some displayed outside the craft shops, which are a permanent fixture in the picturesque twisting streets. Seafood restaurants galore.

Don't miss

○ A breezy walk around the prom – once the moat.

○ The impressive ramparts built by the de Montforts.

○ St Aubin's abbey with its imposing granite west front and curious outdoor pulpit sprouting from one of the buttresses.

○ A trip in a flat-bottomed boat on the watery channels of the Brière nature park, home to thousands of water fowl. Or a bike ride through the traditional villages of reed-thatched cottages.

○ Scenic routes around the peninsula to

la Turballe, the Pointe du Castelli, or across to the fishing port of Le Croisic and bustling little Batz-sur-Mer.

ⓘ Place du Marché-au-Bois.

Somewhere to stay

↘ Les Voyageurs, if you book well in advance. It's the best of the few in town. ☎ 02 40 24 90 13.

↘ Les Nids in Le Croisic, a friendly, very comfortable 3-chimney Logis by the beach with a good restaurant. ☎ 02 40 23 00 63.

Saumur (Maine-et-Loire)
Several but Saturday is best

I find this one of the most civilised towns straddling the Loire. An ultra-romantic castle with sharp-edged towers commands it from a cliff above the river (photo tip: best shot is from the other side of the bridge down by the waterside). The outskirts flanking the historic centre don't sprawl endlessly. No violent traffic. And for wine-buffs or bibbers it's a must-stop for tasting and buying Saumur wines, not just the famous *crémant* and Champagne-style whites, but also some of the fruity light reds such as Saumur-Champigny.

The optimum day to go to market (as usual in a town of this size there is one practically every day) is Saturday when one sets up outside *les halles* in the most charming part of the old town, Place St Pierre. Observing the morning's comings and goings are a wonderful medieval church with 16th-century tapestries, and some striking medieval houses criss-crossed with timbers. The grand townhouses elsewhere are predominantly built of the local limestone, giving rise to Saumur being labelled 'the white town'.

Among specialities to look for in the market are delicious oils made from walnuts, hazelnuts and almonds (local label, Croix Verte), and *fouée*, a flat bread that puffs up in the oven to provide a pocket for *rillettes*, goat's cheese or whatever. This was a great favourite of Rabelais, one of the sons of Western Loire, and it is frequently served in the 'troglo' restaurants (see Don't miss). When I was here, Saumur market had a very jolly *fromagère* who stocked many of the region's indigenous cheeses such as Vieux Pané, Chaussée aux Moines, Rouy and Port Salut. But my prize purchase was a bottle of blackberry purée which has been the magic ingredient of my summer puddings ever since.

Don't miss

❂ Lunch (dish-of-the-day and gastronomic menu) under the exposed beams of the 15th-century Auberge St-Pierre in the market place.

❂ The Bar du Dolmen, where a massive prehistoric dolmen, one of the largest in France, looms in the back garden.

❂ The famous Cadre Noir riding school – dressage shows daily except Sunday – and the mushroom museum, both at St-Hilaire-St-Florent.

❂ The Abbey of Fontevraud, just to the south, where the painted effigies of the Plantagenet royals lie together in style (Henry II, Eleanor of Aquitaine and Richard Coeur de Lion).

❂ The troglodyte village of Rochemenier, inhabited until 50 years ago, complete with restaurant.

❂ The wine caves – Bouvet Ladubay, Ackerman, Vignerons de Saumur and several others.

ⓘ Place de la Bilange.

Somewhere to stay

❯ Hôtel St-Pierre, centuries-old haven with a touch of luxury near the St Pierre church. ☎ 02 41 50 33 00.

❯ Loire Hôtel, on an island in the Loire with fabulous views of the château. Peaceful location, regional cuisine. ☎ 02 41 67 22 42.

❯ Ile d'Offard, 4-star stunning campsite overlooking the river. ☎ 02 41 40 30 00.

Pornic (Loire-Atlantique)

Thursday and Sunday

Who isn't seduced by a working fishing port? Even if Pornic's fleet is small, its activities add to the pleasure of this very pretty resort, a gem on the Jade Coast. Beach-lovers are well supplied with a string of small sandy bays, mostly away from the town, which possibly saves Pornic from being totally overrun. A focal point is the 15th-century fort guarding the harbour, much photographed and painted. Another is the covered market which throbs with life each morning in summer and swells into an outdoor market on Thursday and Sunday mornings in Place des Halles.

Amateur artists who prop their easels around the quaint stone quays are frequently moved to record the activity of the market too. You name it, Pornic's has it all, from fish (ooh, the oysters, the glistening sardines!) to fishermen's sweaters, toy boats and seaweed cosmetics, teeny-weeny bikinis to sensible beach cover-ups for the less daring. If you want to take a picnic to one of the nearby beaches, grab some succulent Vendée ham or a ready-roasted free-range Challans chicken. For afters, there is *fion*, a light custard tart filled with cream and eggs flavoured with vanilla, cinnamon and orange water. Well, pretty light – just don't try to swim afterwards!

Don't miss

✪ Strolling along the wooden boardwalk to see the château's interior.

✪ Interesting bars, pulsating at night, tucked away among the town's alleyways.

✪ A walk along the undulating Custom's Path above little curving coves – marvellous sea views.

✪ A trip to the Ile de Noirmoutier across Bourgneuf Bay. You can drive across on the main causeway road or – better – brave the shorter route via the Passage du Gois when it is exposed at low tide. Noirmoutier is full of lush gardens, pinewoods and mimosa, watery dykes and windmills.

Somewhere to stay

↘ The Alliance, *very* comfortable, about a kilometre to the south of the port on the Plage de la Source. It has a thalassotherapy centre.
☎ 02 40 82 21 21.

↘ Les Sablons, an excellent Logis 3km away at Ste-Marie. ☎ 02 40 82 09 14.

Angers (Maine-et-Loire)

Saturday

The modern muddle of the approach to Angers, distinctly lacking in focal points, doesn't ignite one's enthusiasm. Not long ago, a film crew and I almost got lost trying to drive into the centre. Then we saw the massive glowering bastion of the château hedged in by its 17 uncompromising round towers. Unlike any others in France, they must have been as scary an objective as any medieval foe would ever have wished to see. For us, however, it was the perfect landmark. We soon found our way into the historic old town, which has much charm as well as unmissable treasures. Here, there is a choice of markets on Saturdays. I lingered over a small *bio* in rue St Laud, then found the *brocante* in Place Louis Imbach spread at the feet of Notre Dame church. An intriguing selection of little and large collectables included old petit point tapestry cushion covers that were a bargain.

Weekend food shoppers flock to the huge mixed market in Place Général Leclerc on Saturdays. This is a really big space – full of clothes and other stuff too – running alongside the Jardin de Mail with its splendid fountain and bandstand. I most remember the voluptuousness of the fruit. Here, in the heart of a big fruit-growing area, there was a mountain of it: the last strawberries meeting fabulous dark cherries and the first crops of autumn plums and pears. The Angers version of potted pork, *rillauds d'Anjou*, was also much in evidence – celebrated with much gusto at an annual fête.

Don't miss

✪ The château and the tapestry of the Apocalypse, a medieval masterpiece worked in the latter part of the 14th century. Originally 130 metres long, only some 75 sections remain but it is still enough to astound.

✪ For contrast, see another world's end in 'Le Chant du Monde', Jean Lurçat's prophetic vision displayed at the museum of contemporary tapestry, Boulevard Victor Hugo.

✪ The works of 19th-century sculptor David d'Angers, bathed in natural light under the new glass roof of the Toussaint abbey.

✪ Les Quernons d'Ardoise, 22 rue des Lices, for the greyish chocolate-nougat sweets named after the local slate.

✪ Maison du Vin de l'Anjou, Place Kennedy, close to the château.

✪ For local cuisine and a lively night out, L'Auberge Angevine in a former chapel, Rue Cordelle.

✪ At Saint-Barthélémy-d'Anjou, the Musée Cointreau, which tells you all about the versatile orange liqueur in its distinctive square bottle.

ⓘ 7 Place Kennedy.

Somewhere to stay

Both out of town.

↘ Château de Noirieux, Relais & Châteaux member in Briollay. Gorgeous place with rooms in the château itself or the 15th-century manor house. Swimming pool and tennis court. ☎ 02 41 42 50 05.

↘ Le Cavier, a charming 2-chimney Logis de France with a restaurant in an old windmill. Pool, and terrace for summer dining. ☎ 02 41 42 30 45.

Clisson (Loire-Atlantique)
Tuesday, Wednesday and Friday

At the joining of the rivers Moine and Sèvre lies one of the most attractive towns among the Muscadet vineyards. Something of a curiosity, it is unlike other Nantais wine towns such as Le Pallet and Vallet, for it was severely damaged during the Vendée wars in the latter stages of the Revolution. Its feudal lord, Olivier de Clisson, was a staunch royalist. The town was then redesigned by an architect from Lyon who gave it a distinctly southern air,

with russet-tiled roofs, arcades, umbrella pines and Italianate gardens. The ruined château looms romantically above the surviving medieval covered market, which is well filled with fresh local produce each Tuesday morning. There's also a lively market on Wednesday across the river (by La Trinité church and the old Benedictine abbey) and yet another on Friday in the quartier Notre Dame by the *halles*. As much as these are a pleasure, even without them Clisson would be an agreeable place to squander time and bone up on Muscadet.

Don't miss

✪ The Caveau des Vignerons where local winemakers offer tastings and sell.

✪ Maison du Pays, for guidance on touring the Muscadet wine route.

✪ The Château de Goulaine, about 24km away, the most rewarding domaine to visit. 15th-century, with exquisite painted ceilings, it has been in the same family for 1,000 years. The current English-speaking marquis not only nurtures delicious wines but a colony of tropical butterflies and the LU (of Petit LU biscuit fame) art collection.

✪ Cholet, less than half-an-hour's drive, the capital of cut-price fashion and home textiles, full of factory shops and bargain stores.

ⓘ Rue and Plage de Minage.

Somewhere to stay

↘ Don Quichotte, a reliable little Logis de France on the route de Clisson near Vallet. ☎ 02 40 33 99 67.

Best of the Rest

★ **Ancenis** Appealing old port on the Loire between Angers and Nantes. As little known as its fresh, fruity Coteaux d'Ancenis wines. Both are worth exploring. Market day is Thursday.

★ **Le Croisic** The Guérande peninsula's most attractive fishing-port-cum-resort with superb panoramic views from its Tréhic jetty. Thursday and Saturday markets are augmented by one on Tuesday in the summer.

★ **La Ferté-Bernard** With the most beautiful church in the Sarthe and a network of canals reflecting its old stones, La Ferté, not far from Le Mans, is a delight. Markets on Thursday and Saturday in the *centre ville*.

★ **La Haye-Fouassière** Serious territory for wine buffs in the Nantais vineyards. You can taste 140 local labels (in theory!) in the *vinothèque* of the Maison des Vins. Better do the shopping at the Wednesday market first.

★**Ile-d'Yeu** Port-Joinville, the tiny main town, is the market venue on this picturesque rocky island in the Atlantic. Cliffs one side, sheltered sandy bays the other. Markets Wednesdays, Saturdays and Sundays out of season, every day except Sunday in season.

★ **Laval** An arresting mix of dark granite and pale limestone, this medieval *ville* on the banks of the Mayenne deserves leisurely appraisal. Go on a Tuesday or Saturday and you'll catch its excellent market too. View the forbidding 11th-century castle from the river by taking a cruise on an old laundry-boat. Inside the castle is a collection of naïve paintings in homage to Henri 'Le Douanier' Rousseau, who was born here.

★ **Malicorne-sur-Sarthe** Old river port which is a particularly good place to stop when its Friday market is in full swing. There's a moated castle to explore and, of course, its famous glazed earthenware to buy. Nearby is the Sarthe's prettiest village, Asnières-sur-Vègre.

★ **Montreuil-Bellay** Everyone's idea of a fortified medieval stronghold, set high on an outcrop above a tributary of the Loire. Nice place to be at any time, and especially on Tuesday morning for the market.

★ **Montsoreau** Close to Saumur, Montsoreau's château scores just as high in the romance stakes as its Loire-side neighbour. Above the traffic, the core historic quarter is no bigger than a village and packed with elegant old houses. Sunday is market day and every second Sunday there's a flea market.

★ **Noirmoutier-en-l'Ile** Market days here (Friday and Monday plus Tuesday in summer) only serve to further enhance the pleasures of this little island capital.

★ **Pornichet** Really child-friendly resort with a great beach on the rocky coast west of St-Nazaire. Its Halle aux Poissons is open every day in the summer season, otherwise Wednesday and Saturday are market days.

★ **Les-Sables-d'Olonne** Home-port for the Vendée Globe yacht race, this huge resort has a big popular beach, a multitude of attractions and markets every day except Monday somewhere in town.

★ **Sablé-sur-Sarthe** Three rivers meet in this small town of immense charm with its Louis XlV architecture. Delicious buttery biscuits called *sablés* – rather like shortbread – were invented here and you'll probably come across them in the Monday, Friday or Saturday market.

★ **St-Gilles-Croix-de-Vie** Dunes, pine forest, caves and cliffs characterize this family favourite with one of the most significant fishing harbours in the Vendée. Markets every day except Monday and Friday. Fish out of this world.

★ **St-Jean-de-Monts** pleases both kids and grown-ups with its safely shelving

20km of beach, organized fun including an aerial tree-walk, plus thalassotherapy and golf. The market is every day throughout the summer and on Wednesdays and Saturdays out of season.

 www.westernloire.com

Markets at a glance: Western Loire

A
L'Aigullon-sur-Mer, *Tue*, *Fri*
Allonnes (Maine-et-Loire), *Sun*
Allonnes (Sarthe), *Tue*, *Sal*
Ambrières, *Sat*
Ancenis, *Thu*
Andouille, *Thu*
Angers, see Six of the Best
Arnage, *Sat*, *Wed*
Assérac, *Tue* (Jul/Aug)
Aubigné-Racan, *Sat*

Avrillé, *Tue*, *Fri*
B
Babatre, *Wed* (mid-Jun–mid-Sep)
Ballon, *Wed*
Basse-Goulaine, *Wed*
Batz-sur-Mer, *Mon* (+ *Fri* in Jul/Aug)
Baugé, *Mon*
La Barre-de-Monts, *Sat* (mid-Jun–end Aug)
La Baule, daily (closed *Mon*

Oct–Mar, except school hols)
La Baule-les-Pins, *Tue*, *Sat* (+ *Thu* May–Sep)
Bauné, *Fri*
Bazouges, *Sun*
Beaucouzé, *Sat*, *Sun*
Beaufay, *Fri*
Beaufort-en-Valée, *Wed*, *Sun*
Beaumont-sur-Sarthe, *Tue*
Beaupréau, *Mon*
Beauvoir-sur-Mer, *Thu*
Belleville-sur-Vie, *Wed*, *Sat*
Benet, *Mon*
Le Bernard, *Wed*
La Berniere-en-Retz, *Fri* (+ *Tue* mid-Jun–mid-Sep)
Bessé-sur-Braye, *Sat*
Bonnétable, *Tue*, *Fri*
Le Borgneuf, *Sun*
Bouaye, *Thu*, *Sun*
Bouguenais, *Thu*, *Fri*
Bouin, *Sat*
Bouloire, *Sat*
Le Boupère, *Tue*
Bourgneuf-en-Retz, *Tue*, *Sat*
Bournezeau, *Fri*
Brem-sur-Mer, *Tue* (+ *Fri* in summer)
Bretignolles-sur-Mer, *Thu*, *Sun*
Brissac-Quincé, *Thu*
Brulon, *Sat*
C
Campbon, *Sat*
Candé, *Mon*
Carquefou, *Thu*, *Fri*
Cérans-Foulletourte, *Tue*
Challans, *Tue*, *Fri*
Challonnes-sur-Loire, *Tue*, *Sat*
Chambretaud, *Mon*
Champagné, *Fri*
Champagne-les-Marais, *Wed*
Champigné, *Tue*
Champ-Saint-Pere, *Thu*
Changé, *Thu*, *Sat*
Chantonnay, *Tue*, *Thu*, *Sat*
La Chapelle-D'Aigné, *Fri*
La Chapelle-sur-Erdre, *Fri*, *Sun*
La-Chartre-sur-Loir, *Thu*, *Sun*
La Châtagneraie, *Sat*

Markets at a glance: Western Loire

Chateaubriant, *Wed*
Château-du-Loir, *Sat*
Château-Gontier, *Thu*
Châteauneuf-sur-Sarthe, *Fri*
Chavagnes-en-Paillers, *Wed*, *Sat*
Chemillé, *Thu*
Cheviviré-le-Rouge, *Thu*
La Chevrolière, *Wed*
Cholet, *Tue*, *Wed*, *Thu*, *Sat*
Le Clion-sur-Mer, *Wed*, *Sat*
Clisson, see Six of the Best
Coex, *Sat*
Combrée, *Fri*, *Sat*
Commequiers, *Wed*
Conlie, *Thu*
Connerré, *Wed*
Corné, *Tue*
Cossé-le-Vivien, *Wed*
Couëron Bourg, *Thu*
Couëron La Chabossière, *Sat*
Coulaines, *Tue*, *Sat*
Coulongé, *Tue*
Courdemanche, *Sat*
Craon, *Mon*
Cré-sur-Loir, *Fri*
Le Croisic, *Thu*, *Sat* (+*Tue* Jul/Aug)
D
Dollon, *Wed*
Doué-la-Fontaine, *Mon*
Durtal, *Tue*
E
Ecommoy, *Tue*
L'Epine, *Sat*
Ernée, *Tue*
Les Essarts, *Wed*, *Sat*
Evron, *Thur*
F
La Faute-sur-Mer, *Thu*, *Sun*
La Ferté-Bernard, *Thu*, *Sat*
La Flèche, *Wed*, *Sun*
Fontenay-le-Comte, *Sat*
Fontevraud l'Abbaye, *Wed*
Fougerolles, *Fri*
Foussais Payre, *Wed*
Fresnay-sur-Sarthe, *Sat*
Frossay, *Thu*
G
La Gaubrètiere, 1st *Wed*
Gennes, *Tue*
Gesté, *Tue*
Gorron, *Wed*
Grandchamp-des-Fontaines, *Sat*

Le Grand-Lucé, *Wed*
Grez-en-Bouère, *Tue*
Grosbreuil, *Tue*
Guécélard, *Sun*
Guérande, see Six of the Best
La Guerinière, *Thu* (mid-Jun–mid-Sep), *Sun*
H
Haute-Goulaine, *Tue*s
La Haye-Fouassière, *Wed*
Les Herbiers, *Thu*, *Sat*
Herbignac, *Wed*
L'Hermenault, *Wed*
I
Indre, *Thu*, *Sat*, *Sun*
Ingrandes-sur-Loire, *Fri*
Ile-d'Elle, *Fri*
Ile d'Yeu (Port-Joinville), *Wed*, *Sat*, *Sun* (+ daily except *Sun* in summer)
J
Jallais, *Fri*
Jard-sur-Mer, *Mon*
Javron, *Fri*
Jupilles, *Sun*
L
Laigné-en-Belin, *Thu*
Le Langon, *Mon*
Lassay, *Wed*
Laval, *Tue*, *Sat*
Legé, 1st and 3rd *Tue*
Le-Lion-d'Angers, *Fri*
Longue-Jumelles, *Thu*
Le Loroux-Bottereau, *Sun*
Loué, *Tue*
Le-Louroux-Béconnais, *Thu*
Le Luart, *Fri*, *Sun*
Luch-Pringé, *Tue*
Luçon, *Wed*, *Sat*
Le Lude, *Thu*
M
Le Mans, see Six of the Best
Le May-sur-Evre, *Wed*
Les Moutiers-en-Retz, *Sat* (+ *Thu* mid-Jun–mid-Sep)
Machecoul, *Wed*
Maillezais, *Wed*
Malicorne-sur-Sarthe, *Fri*
Mamers, *Mon*, *Fri*
Mansigné, *Mon*
Mareuil-sur-Lay, *Thu*
Marolles-les-Braults, *Thu*
Martigné-Briand, *Sat*

Mayenne, *Mon*, *Sat*
Mayet, *Sun*
Mazé, *Fri*
La Ménitré, *Fri*
Meslay-du-Maine, *Fri*
Mesquer-Quimiac, *Fri* (+*Tue* mid-Jun–mid-Sep)
Missillac, *Wed*
La Montagne, *Wed*
Montaigu, *Sat*
Montfaucon-sur-Moine, *Tue*
Montfort-le-Gesnois, *Sat*
Mont-Jean-sur-Loire, *Thu*
Montoir-de-Bretagne, *Mon*
Montreuil Bellay, *Tue*
Montreuil-Juigné, *Fri*
Montreuil-le-Henri, *Wed*
Montrevault, *Wed*
Montsoreau, *Sun*
Montsurs, *Tue*
Morannes, *Thu*
Mortagne-sur-Sèvre, *Tue*, *Fri*
La Mothe Achard, *Fri*
Mouchamps, *Fri*
Moutiers-les-Mauxfaits, *Fri* (+ *Wed* Jul/Aug)
Mulsanne, *Sat*
N
Nantes, daily except *Mon*
Nieul-sur-l'Autise, 1st *Wed*
Nogent-le-Bernard, *Thu*, *Sun*
Noirmoutier-en-L'ile, *Fri* (+ *Mon*, *Tue* mid-Jun–mid-Sep)
Nort-sur-Erdre, *Fri*
Notre-Dame-de-Monts, *Sun*
Notre-Dame-de-Riez, *Sun*
Noyant, *Fri*
Noyen-sur-Sarthe, *Sat*
O
Orvault, *Fri* eve
P
Paimboeuf, *Tue*, *Fri*
Parçay-les-Pins, *Sat*
Parcé-sur-Sarthe, *Thu*
Parigné-l'Evèque, *Thu*
Le Pellerin, *Sat*
Le Perrier, *Mon*, *Thu* (Jul–Sep)
Petosse, *Wed*
Pirlac-sur-Mer, *Tue* (+ *Mon*, *Wed*, *Sat* mid-Jun–mid-Sep)
La Plaine-sur-Mer, *Sun* (mid-Jun–mid-Sep)

Le Poire-sur-Velluire, *Thu* eve
Le Poire-sur-Vie, *Thu*, *Sat*, *Sun*
La-Pommeraye, *Sat*
Pontchâteau, *Mon*
Pont-Saint-Martin, *Sat*
Les Ponts-de-Cé, *Fri*, *Sun*
Pontvallan, *Fri*
La Poueze, *Tue*
Le Pouliguen, *Tue*, *Wed*, *Sun*
Pornic, see Six of the Best
Pornichet, *Wed*, *Sat* (+ fish market daily in summer)
Port-Brillet, *Tue*
Pouancé, *Thu*
Pouille, *Fri*
Précigné, *Sat*
Pré-en-Pail, *Sat*
Préfailles, *Sat* (+*Wed* mid-Jun–mid-Sep)
R
Renazé, *Fri*
Requeil, *Sat*
Rezé, *Tue*, *Fri*, *Sat*, *Sun*
Rochefort-sur-Loire, *Wed*
La Roche-sur-Yon, *Tue*, *Wed*, *Thu*, *Sat*
Les Rosiers-sur-Loire, *Mon*
S
Les Sables-d'Olonne, daily except *Mon*
Sablé-sur-Sarthe, *Mon*, *Fri*, *Sat*
Saint-Aignan-de-Grandlieu, *Tue*
Saint-Barthélémy d'Anjou, *Tue*
Saint-Berthevin, *Wed*
Saint-Brévin-les-Pins, *Thu*, *Sun*
Saint-Brévin-l'Océan *Sat*
Saint-Calais, *Sun*,*Thu*
Saint-Christophe-du-Bois, *Fri*, *Sun*
Saint-Cosme-en-Vairais, *Sat*
Saint-Crespin-sur-Moine, *Wed*
Saint-Etienne-de-Montluc, *Fri*
Saint-Etienne-du-Bois, *Thu*, *Sun*
Sainte-Flaive-des-Loups, *Tue*
Saint-Florent-des-Bois, *Fri*

Saint-Florent-le-Vieil, 2nd and 4th *Fri*
Saint Fulgent, *Fri*
Saint-Georges-le-Gaultier, *Tue*
Saint-Georges-sur-Loire, *Thu*
Saint-Germain-sur-Moine, *Sat*
Saint-Gilles-Croix-de-Vie, *Tue*, *Wed*, *Thu*, *Sat*, *Sun*
Saint-Herblain, *Tue*, *Wed*, *Fri*, *Sat*
Saint Hermine, *Fri*
Saint-Hilaire-de-Riez, *Thu*, *Sun*
Saint-Hilaire-des-Loges, *Fri*
Saint-Jean-de-Boiseau, *Sat*
Saint-Jean-de-Monts, *Wed*, *Sat* (+ daily Jun–Sep)
Saint-Joachim, *Sat*
Saint-Julien-de-Concelles, *Sat*
Saint-Lambert-du-Lattay, *Wed*
Saint-Laurent-sur-Sèvre, *Thu*
Sainte-Luce-sur-Loire, *Sat*
Saint-Macaire-en-Mauges, *Fri*
Saint-Maixent, *Tue*
Saint-Malo-de-Guersac, *Sun*
Sainte-Marie-sur-Mer, *Wed*, *Sat*
Saint-Mars d'Outillé, *Thu*
Saint-Mars-du-Désert, 1st and 3rd *Sun*
Saint-Mars-la-Brière, *Fri*
Saint-Martin-des-noyers, *Thu*, *Sat*
Saint-Mathurin-sur-Loire, *Tue*
Saint-Michel-en-l'Herm, *Thu*
Saint-Nazaire, *Tue*, *Wed*, *Sun*
Saint-Osmane, *Fri*
Saint-Pazanne, *Fri*
Saint-Père-en-Retz, *Tue*
Saint Philbert-de-Grand-Lieu, *Sun*
Saint-Pierre-du-Lorouer, *Fri*
Saint-Pierre-Montlimart, *Sat*
Saint-Remy la-Varenne, *Sun*
Saint-Sébastien, *Tue*, *Thu*
Saint-Sylvain-d'Anjou, *Fri*, *Sat*, *Sun*

Saint-Vincent-du-Lorouer, *Sat*
Saint-Vincent-Sterlanges, *Fri*
Sargé-lès-le-Mans, *Tue*
Saumur, see Six of the Best
Sautron, *Sun*
Savenay, *Wed*
Savigné-l'Evêque, *Sat*
Segré, *Wed*
Seiches-sur-le-Loir, *Thu*
Sillé-le Guillaume, *Wed*
Les Sorinères, *Thu*
Soullans, *Fri*
Spay, *Sun*
La Suze-sur-Sarthe, *Thu*
T
Teloché, *Thu*
Le Temple-de-Bretagne, *Tue*
Thorigny, *Fri*
Thouarcé, *Tue*
Thouaré-sur-Loire, *Sat*
Tiercé, *Wed*
Torfou, *Fri*
Touvols, 2nd and 4th *Mon*
La-Tranche-sur-Mer, *Tue*, *Wed*, *Fri*, *Sat*
Treillières, *Thu*
Treize Septiers, *Tue*
Trélazé, *Thu*, *Sun*
Tresson, *Sat*
Triaize, *Wed*
Tuffé, *Thu*
La Turballe, *Wed*, *Sat*
V
Vaas, *Tue*
Vallet, *Sun*
Vancé, *Tue*
Varennes-sur-Loire, *Sat*
Vernantes, *Wed*
La Verrie, *Sat*
Vertou, *Sat*, *Sun*
Vibraye, *Fri*
Vigneux-de-Bretagne, *Sat*
Vihiers, *Wed*
Villaines-la-Juhel, *Mon*
Villedieu-la-Blouère, *Thu*
Vix, *Fri*
Vue, *Sun*
Y
Yvré-le-Polin, *Fri*
Yvré-l'Evêque, *Sat*

The accidental nectar, marvellous melons and marine memorabilia

Once upon a time in Poitou-Charentes, I proved – if proof were needed – that markets can be therapeutic. In the course of recording a radio programme for the BBC about Futuroscope – no mean feat in a theme park devoted to the moving *image* – I was bidden to strap myself into the passenger seat of a Formula One car to be driven at eyeball-jiggling speed round a racing circuit. The producer, Dave Harvey, was such a charmer I didn't argue. He said he thought it would make 'good listening' to reflect the true thrills of the Vienne countryside in counterpoint to the virtual excitements offered by Futuroscope's dynamic cinemas. Thrilling it was not. Terrifying, yes. After four minutes of G-force torture, taking corners at 100mph, I screamed '*J'en ai assez!*' (I've had enough) above the roar of the engine and Didier the driver swiftly brought us to a stop. I felt sick but smiled through gritted teeth as we headed for the medieval towers of Chauvigny – which was to be another aspect of 'the real Vienne'. Someone mentioned lunch. That did it. 'Could I just walk about for a bit?'

The Saturday morning market was still in progress in Chauvigny's lower town so, breathing deeply, I staggered round the stalls until my dislodged eyeballs began to return to their sockets and my stomach subsided. Focusing on the cheerful displays of vegetables and fruit and trying to catch little interchanges between customers and traders – the frosty and the chatty always met with equal brisk *politesse* – took my mind off the problem. In no time, I was back to normal and trotting happily in the direction of the shoe stall when a forceful arm guided me away. 'No shopping! If you're better, we'll crack on.'

When I think of Poitou-Charentes, I don't always remember that little whizz. I think of hollyhocks trimming the whitewashed houses of the Ile de Ré. I think of sunflowers patching a landscape of unruffled calm, except where strategic outcrops still hold aloft ancient fortresses that have survived since the Hundred Years War. I think of flat-bottomed boats gliding through the dappled channels of the 'Green Venice', the Marais Poitevin; of small cruisers puttering on indolent rivers; and of sailing dinghies spinning past creamy dunes anchored by esparto grass.

Brochure images? To be sure, yet these aspects of Poitou-Charentes do exist. It is a region where there are real tourist honeypots – like the islands, La Rochelle and Cognac – as well as beautiful unspoilt backwaters, but there's no denying there are other areas, particularly the Vienne, which have had to struggle in recent years to reverse a long economic decline. Futuroscope has been just one of many imaginative ploys used to turn things around.

Poitou-Charentes tries harder than most to provide entertaining attractions for visitors, especially families. And since many of them are self-catering, markets also pull out all the stops – often three times a week in Atlantic resorts like Fouras and Royan or in the islands' fishing villages. 'Bienvenue à la Ferme' signs point to produce markets on farm premises. Tiny floating markets lie in wait to sell local goat's cheeses to Green Venice traffic. And historic towns rifle their attics to keep abreast of the demand for bric-a-brac.

Specialities

The strip of Atlantic coast edging the *département* of Charente-Maritime means superb **seafood** and in particular **oysters**. A benign climate plus the blend of fresh and salt water makes the Marennes-Oléron Bassin France's largest oyster-producing area. The *fines de claires* are refined for a month at twenty or so to the square metre. The *spéciales de claires* are given more space and time, while the absolute bee's knees are the mature *pousses en claires*, raised in even smaller groups for up to eight months – these have the most distinctive flavour and should be eaten in situ. There are also marvellous mussels – look out for them cooked in big pans as *mouclade charentaise*, a richer take on *moules marinière*, with egg yolks, butter, crème fraîche, saffron and herbs added. Inland, small snails of the *petis gris* variety are much extolled by *escargot* connoisseurs.

Large white dried **beans** called *mojhettes* are a familiar sight at markets. For an old-fashioned feast-day treat these are casseroled with kid, and they go tremendously well with the highly rated local lamb – from flocks that feed on lush spring grass buffed by salty Atlantic breezes and often seen attended by a flat-capped shepherd. **Beef** is excellent here too – you have the choice of cattle bred around Parthenay or in neighbouring Limousin. Rabbit, another favourite main course, is great cooked with prunes and Pineau des Charentes, the apéritif derived from cognac.

Cognac, like champagne, was discovered by accident when the wines of the Charente failed to travel well (they still don't). In the 13th century, when they were shipped round the Bay of Biscay to other countries in northern Europe, they arrived shaken if not stirred. Traders began to distil to stabilize them. That was the beginning. Several hundred years and much experimentation later, cognac was born. Victor Hugo considered it the 'liqueur of the gods' and the place to see how they achieve it is the town of Cognac. It may be on sale at markets where vintners display a few bottles outside in the shade, along with Pineau des Charentes, which comes in white or deep rosé. Both cognac and this sherry-like drink (made from grape must and brandy – another accident) tend to overshadow the **wines** of the region. Those of Haut-Poitou, the Thouarsais and Charentes are perfectly palatable but fairly ordinary. The vivid green liqueur you may spot around Niort is made from angelica, the plant culled from the Marais Poitevin which is also crystallized for cakes and confectionery.

Poitou-Charentes claims to provide two thirds of France's **goat's cheese**. Since I've seen lots of distinctly labelled local *chèvre* in almost every region – Provence has loads – I find this statistic a little surprising. But there's no doubt goat's rather than cow's cheeses dominate the *fromagerie* stands and vans in every market. Flat rounds, little lopped-off pyramids, small cylinders and square logs dusted with ash – it comes in myriad shapes and degrees of ripeness. The AOC, with its grey-blue tinted crust, is Chabichou du Poitou. This is extra good served warm on a slice of walnut bread with some dressed salad leaves. The region also produces AOC **butter** which is used liberally in cooking, in preference to oil. Along with fresh, drained curd cheese, it goes into the signature cheesecake, *tourteau fromagé*.

The historic naval ports of La Rochelle and Rochefort guarantee a plethora of **marine antiques**, while the presence of busy marinas full of gung-ho sailors and chic yachting types creates a market for all kinds of ship's chandlery, model boats, rope lamp-bases, brass lanterns etc. And if you're anywhere within ozone-sniffing distance of the nautical scene, you need to look the part. Markets as well as local shops carry the full gamut of **seagoing** and **resort gear**.

Six of the Best

La Rochelle (Charente-Maritime)

Daily; antiques on Saturday

It was November, but a wide blue dome of sky was filled with Atlantic light. I ordered a Pineau in one of the cafés by the *vieux port* and sat blinking at the dazzle of fishing boats and the not-quite-matching towers at the harbour entrance. La Rochelle is stiff with people in August – it has always been a favourite with the British – but it's so much better off-season when you can more easily see the bones of its wonderful architecture.

Despite Cardinal Richelieu's efforts to destroy La Rochelle after the English tried unsuccessfully to support its Calvinist residents in the terrible siege of 1627, there are still 9 kilometres of arcades in the old town dating from the 14th century. In the middle of this warren, beyond the handsome Big Clock, stands the covered market which busies itself daily until 1pm. The best day is Friday, when in the afternoon a fresh produce market takes over Rue Gargoulleau just outside. Here, the chalky coats of the local goat's cheeses are shown off to advantage in teak wooden trays. You can buy home-made *tourteaux fromagés*, the cheesecakes that look like legless crabs with their dark pastry 'shell', as well as real crabs and lobsters straight out of the tank, and *grillons*, small spicy sausages that are eaten hot with cold oysters.

A *marché aux puces* arrives on Saturday, occupying Rue St Nicolas which runs behind Quai Valin. Lots of marine memorabilia such as sextants and ship's bells, sailors' embroidery, tantaluses and tarnished compasses in worn leather cases can be trawled from among its shoal of small treasures. There are some larger collectables too. Sea chests, quilts, cutlery and huge salt jars – a reminder that trading salt, along with wine, once made La Rochelle's fat cats plumper. Their graceful mansions, built on the profits, are still hot property in the *vieille ville*.

Don't miss

✪ In summer, on Thursday evenings, a town tour in the footsteps of a night watchman (advance booking at tourist information).

✪ The 'Canadian' cobbles, brought back as ballast when ships had taken emigrants to North America.

✪ A stroll along the pontoons of the vast new Port des Minimes marina.

✪ The Chain and St Nicolas harbour towers.

✪ The aquarium, everything from shrimps to sharks.

✪ The museums, especially the New World in its 18th-century mansion and the unusual perfume bottle museum and its shop La Saponaire.

✪ Chicest resort wear at Bleu Marine, Cour des Dames, and chicest home accessories at H de B Marine, Quartier St-Nicolas.

ⓘ Quai du Gabut.

Somewhere to stay

↘ La Monnaie. Only the odd seagull's cry gives away the closeness of the Lantern Tower when you're ensconced in this sybaritic 17th-century merchant's house. Sun-trap inner-courtyard garden of box and rose bushes. No restaurant.
☎ 05 46 50 65 65.

↘ Trianon et Plage in the same street is less luxurious but very nice. 19th-century building, calm rooms at the back, breakfast in the little winter garden. Small restaurant.
☎ 05 46 41 21 35.

Angoulême (Charente)
Daily

Never mind its undisciplined suburbs, engineering works and paper mills, Angoulême's medieval town is delightful. Encircled by ramparts, it rises steeply above the river Charente. The way to the top is like following a maze but at the upper level streets are pedestrian and full of distractions – gorgeous *pâtisseries*, galleries and cafés. Dignified on the surface, Angoulême has a lighter side, for it revels in the role of strip-cartoon centre of the earth. Its Festival International de la Bande Dessinée draws thousands every last weekend of January and its permanent comic-strip centre will raise a smile. So too will the story of the retired general who in 1806 launched himself from the ramparts in a home-made flying-machine. The test-flight aborted, putting paid to one of his legs and his plans to invade England by air.

The recently restored 1850s covered market (Place des Halles) snuggles close to the walls in the *ville haute*, on the opposite side from the cathedral. From 7.30 to 12.30, every day, it presents a feast of food from the Charente and beyond. The *traiteur* counters offer some unusual ready-to-heat combinations – snails in red wine and eels with leeks; if you come across green garlic, give it a try – it imparts a subtly different taste; and don't forget the Pineau des Charentes to give your sauces a kick.

Outside the *halles* on Wednesdays and Saturdays, an open-air fresh produce market extends possibilities. Look for the tasty but filling f*arci Poitevin*, a baked mélange of vegetables, eggs and breadcrumbs. The Tuesday to Sunday food market in Place Victor Hugo in the lower town (where the Boulevard de la République meets the D699) becomes a big all-sorts market on Sundays.

Don't miss

❂ Centre National de la Bande Dessinée et de l'Image.

❂ The 12th-century stone-carved figures on the cathedral's west front.

❂ A wonderful Celtic gold helmet in the Musée des Beaux Arts.

❂ A meal at Les Gourmandines, a 2-tiered restaurant near Les Halles which captures the flavours of the day.

❂ The Musée du Papier in the Moulin de Fleurac (at nearby Nersac) which shows luxury paper being made out of rags.

✪ Tours of the ramparts.

✪ A river cruise to Cognac to see the distilleries. The *Angoumois* departs on themed trips day and evening from Port l'Houmeau.

ⓘ Place des Halles.

Somewhere to stay

➘ Mercure-Hôtel de France, Place des Halles. Rather swish extended 16th-century *maison* where Guez de Balzac, one of the original members of the Académie Française, was born. Pretty garden with glimpse of the Charente. ☎ 05 45 95 47 95.

➘ 29 Rue du Sauvage, a modest 2-star pension within the pedestrian area. ☎ 05 45 94 04 62.

St-Martin-de-Ré (Charente-Maritime)
Tuesday, Thursday, Saturday

The roughly 30-by-50-kilometre sliver of the Ile-de-Ré, linked to the mainland by a curving concrete toll bridge, maintains a sleepy, watery stillness, gentle tides lapping white beaches, fishing harbours and oyster beds. In St-Martin-de-Ré, its main port, picturesque red-roofed whitewashed houses sport green and blue shutters to match the boats in the harbour, and hollyhocks in assorted pinks nod around their doors.

St-Martin is laid back despite the influx of daytrippers, but three times a week the market quickens the pace. The oysters, straight from the *parcs*, could hardly be

fresher – you can enjoy them year round. There are crates of beautiful mussels, scallops, and pink and grey shrimps (*chevrettes* and *boucs*) and bags of Sel de Ré sea salt. In early summer, the new potatoes still have the island's sandy soil clinging to their skins and other fresh vegetables are delivered from Ré's own market gardens. Specialities of the region come from the mainland: cheese and butter and buttery caramels; biscuits and pastries such as *tourtisseaux* – related to doughnuts – and *broyés*, a kind of shortbread. Pineau des Charentes is there, and chocolates filled with cognac. Significantly, none of this stuff draws a glance from the bronzed nymphets inspecting midriff-baring tops and bright straw baskets. They must live on oysters. Country crafts in wood – tiny carved and painted lighthouses, boats, seabirds and deckchairs – are just asking to be taken home to bring a breath of the islands to some dull bathroom in Manchester or Minneapolis.

Don't miss

✪ The numerous quaint antique shops hiding in the citadel.

✪ The ramparts and the panoramic view from the church tower.

✪ A bike ride – there are 90 kilometres of easy-going flat tracks through the salt marshes, vineyards and woods. Bicycles are for hire.

✪ The other island villages, especially La Flotte, Ars and Sainte-Marie, which have markets too.

○ A tour of the oyster *parcs*.

○ Boat trips to La Rochelle and the other islands of Oléron and little traffic-free Aix where Napoleon was held before being taken to St Helena.

○ Lilleau des Niges bird sanctuary. At migration periods and in winter, flocks of barnacle geese, shelducks, redshanks and oystercatchers can be seen.

ⓘ Place Carnot, Ars-en-Ré.

Somewhere to stay

⬃ Maison Douce *is* sweet. No restaurant, but a charming old house within the citadel. Pastel rooms have retro bathrooms and there's a courtyard garden for breakfast. ☎ 05 46 09 90 90.

⬃ In Le Bois-Plage-en-Ré, there's L'Océan, a charming hotel-restaurant full of lessons on how to decorate a seaside home. Lots of pale tongue-and-groove, Lloyd loom chairs and sails for shade in the interior courtyard where you dine. ☎ 05 46 09 23 07.

Chauvigny (Vienne)
Tuesday, Thursday, Saturday

Bouquets of purple-tipped artichokes lean on bundles of white asparagus tied like sticks of dynamite. Crates of striped Charentais melons support a few of their juiciest split in half to reveal appealing peachy interiors. A thin girl with luminous brown eyes and a litter of mongrel puppies collects 'oohs' and 'aahs' and money for animal rights. There are bedsteads and broomsticks, glazed earthenware pottery, clothes, bargain underwear, herbal remedies . . .

The Saturday market in Chauvigny – the one that cured my Formula One reaction (see intro) – is one of the biggest and best in the Vienne *département*. The Tuesday and Thursday events are smaller and sell food only. All three set up within the ample dimensions of the Place du Marché in the lower part of town. This lies underneath a rocky ridge encrusted with no fewer than five ruined turreted castles and four churches – Chauvigny the elder. Here, you get a double whammy: an incredibly picturesque location and a great market.

The ancient top town is quite small, with steep cobbled streets and sloping squares. Its fairytale fortresses, one of which belonged to the Bishops of Poitiers, are watched over by the belltower of the Eglise St Pierre, a Romanesque jewel. Fascinating fact: Chauvigny's limestone is much prized. It was used for the base of Manhattan's Statue of Liberty and some helped to build the Cubitt terraces of London's Pimlico grid.

Have lunch after the market at the welcoming Lion d'Or (Rue du Marché), and lose the afternoon exploring this charming place on the banks of the Vienne near Poitiers.

Don't miss

○ St Pierre's inner glories – especially the monsters, birds of prey, angels and shepherds on the capitals in the chancel.

- ☉ The museum of popular traditions.

- ☉ The Géants du Ciel show at the Château des Aigles in which eagles, vultures, marabou storks and brightly coloured parrots fly among the audience by some technological wizardry.

- ☉ Porcelain in the shops from the local company that makes tableware collections for Kenzo and Inès de la Fressange.

- ☉ Futuroscope, about 40 minutes away.

- ☉ Poitiers, 30 minutes.

- ⓘ In the high town.

Somewhere to stay

- ↘ Lion d'Or, close to the market. A cheerful well-managed 2-star Logis de France whose chef uses market produce in regional dishes served in generous portions. ☎ 05 49 46 30 28.

- ↘ The businesslike little Hôtel de France in St-Savin, about 16km away, also a 2-star Logis. ☎ 05 49 48 19 03.

Rouillac (Charente)

Wednesday, Saturday and every 27th of the month

At the crossing of antique Roman roads in the midst of the Cognac vineyards, this pleasant village bunches up around its beautifully proportioned Romanesque church. Nothing much happens in Rouillac – small food markets materialize twice a week – but on the 27th of each month, everything happens. Then, if you're anywhere near it, get there fast, for it holds a corker of a fair: a bumper market that is actually bigger than Rouillac itself. There are cows and sheep and chickens for sale. Tractors, motorbikes and cars. Lawnmowers, rolls of wire, bolts of furnishing fabric. Sewing machines. Trinkets. Furniture. Food. Wines to taste. Cognac and Pineau are sold from the *chais* and braziers flare under pans of moules, chips and other inviting take-aways. Musicians strum and cheeses hum.

The 'Vingt Sept', which lasts all day from 8.30 until 17.00, is a tradition that goes back centuries and draws massive crowds – people come from as far away as Paris. The streets are crammed from one end of the village to the other and the cars are parked halfway to Cognac.

Don't miss

- ☉ The village's open-air swimming pool.

- ☉ Rouillac's harmonious Eglise St Pierre plus a trail to follow of twenty other 12th-century churches that seem to peg their villages in place on the surrounding carpet of vineyards.

- ☉ At Les Bouchards: vestiges of a Roman theatre, the biggest in a rural site in former Gaul; and at Saint-Cybardeaux, ruins of Celtic temples.

- ☉ A visit to a local brandy distillery.

- ☉ Cognac itself, about 24km away.

- ⓘ Place Gambetta.

Somewhere to stay

⬊Hostellerie du Maine Brun, at Asnières-sur-Nouère (12km). An appealing member of both Relais du Silence and Châteaux & Hôtels de France. Pool, riverside dining. ☎ 05 45 90 83 00.

⬊The Karina at Jarnac (16km) is a pleasant, unassuming little Logis; normally demi-pension only (if not, eat at La Ribaudière in Bourg-Charente). ☎ 05 45 36 26 26.

Confolens (Charente)

Wednesday, Saturday and every 12th of the month

At the meeting of the rivers Vienne and Goire, Confolens is one of the loveliest medieval towns in Poitou-Charentes. Trading in salt, wood and skins made it rich in the Middle Ages and its timber-framed houses and gateways were built on the proceeds. Today its lack of noisy industry – and traffic – makes it the perfect rallying point for a ten-day international folk festival in mid-August, Danses et Musique du Monde.

Come upon Confolens on a still sunny morning when its weathered rust-roofed houses and sturdy 15th-century bridge seem idly content simply to admire their reflections in the river, and you might assume it's something of a backwater. Arrive on Wednesday or Saturday morning and the place is alive. Centred on the Place de l'Hôtel de Ville, this is the sort of country market that sells freshwater fish and, depending on the season, hare, rabbit, quail or even thrush.

Home-baked macaroons and *merveilles* biscuits are set out in pretty boxes and the dewy local fruit and perfect vegetables have that just-picked look.

On the 12th of each month, there's a fair which is really an enlarged market (not as important as Rouillac's). Then, merchants manoeuvre their vans into the narrow streets to sell clothes, shoes and fabrics as well as food around and under the *halles*.

Don't miss

❍ St Barthélémy's – it is 12th century.

❍ Château de St Germain.

❍ The Maison de la Résistance.

❍ Canoeing, rafting or kayaking on the Vienne.

❍ Oradour-sur-Glâne in Limousin (just 20km away), the village whose 600 inhabitants were annihilated by the Nazis in a single afternoon. It remains frozen in time as an incredibly moving memorial.

ⓘPlace des Marronniers.

Somewhere to stay

⬊Mère Michelet, a modest but cosy 2-chimney Logis. ☎ 05 45 84 04 11.

⬊Château de Nieuil, about 24km away. Delicious Renaissance hunting lodge used by Francis I surrounded by a park. ☎ 05 45 71 36 38. A charming restaurant, La Grange aux Oies (separate management), occupies the old stables. ☎ 05 45 71 81 24.

Best of the Rest

★ **Angles-sur-l'Anglin** A 'plus beaux' village whose old streets and houses are still commanded by a ruined fortress. Quiet save for the bustle engendered at weekends by the Saturday and Sunday markets. Jours d'Angles workshops tell the story of the village's distinctive drawn-thread work. Angles-sur-Anglin once furnished the linens for great ocean liners like the *Normandie* and the *QE2*, and a black satin trousseau for the cabaret queen Josephine Baker.

★ **Aubeterre-sur-Dronne** Tipping the border with Aquitaine, another of France's 'most beautiful' villages, built in a half-circle on a cliff looking down on the river Dronne. Its wooden balconies and rounded roof tiles hint at the south. Fabulous west front on the Romanesque church. Small market on Sunday.

★ **Cognac** Connoisseurs of the world's finest amber liquid will want to sniff what's known as the angel's share at the distilleries of Hennessy, Martell, Courvoisier or Rémy-Martin. The whole town is bound up with the production of brandy, the coopering of barrels, blowing glass for bottles and selling the finished product. Otherwise, Cognac doesn't really invite you to linger, but there are nice bits by the river Charente and there's a superb covered market that's open every day.

★ **Châtelaillon** There are echoes of Deauville about this big family resort with its safe beach and long straight promenade dominated by an elegant old casino. Endless fun laid on – water park, kids clubs, sailing school etc. Daily market.

★ **Fouras** Facing the island of Aix and Fort Boyard, another jolly family resort with an old castle and four of the best pine-backed beaches on the coast of Poitou-Charentes. Daily market.

★ **Montmorillon** Delightful small town on the banks of the river Gartempe with Romanesque churches, frescoes, a curious funeral monument and 11th-century hospice. Two markets: Wednesday and Saturday.

★ **Niort** Along with a double Romanesque keep and pillory, Niort's venerable covered market is one of the town's 'sights'. It's in action on Tuesday, Thursday and Saturday. Since the town is only a few miles from the Marais Poitevin, this is a good place to enjoy the urban scene before or after drifting through the rural waterways of this 'Green Venice'.

★ **Parthenay** Picturesque medieval bastion on the banks of the Thouet: a famous stop for pilgrims on the way to Compostela. Its Wednesday market has livestock.

★ **Poitiers**, capital of Poitou-Charentes. Daunting to get into – visitors going to Futuroscope via the TGV station usually leave without exploring. But the centre has one of the most impressive sets of Romanesque buildings in France and the covered market nestles right in the thick of things beside the great Notre-Dame-la-Grande church. Markets every day except Monday and Wednesday. Flea market on Friday, Place Charles de Gaulle.

★ **Rochefort** The fortifications and arsenal of this historic naval port on the Charente estuary give it a unique character. You can see the frigate *Hermione* on which General Lafayette sailed for America, and travel writer Pierre Loti's house full of exotic treasures. Tuesday, Thursday and Saturday are market days.

★ **La Rochefoucauld** Known mainly for its 12th-century château, this is the home of the famous writer, de la Rochefoucauld. Nice town. Market on Wednesday and Saturday.

★ **Saintes** was, in the first century AD, the Roman capital of Aquitaine. Reminders can still be seen: a ruined amphitheatre and portions of columns, capitals and reliefs in the Musée Archéologique. Aside from this, Saintes is an appealing and cultured city. There's excellent shopping in the centre and a Tuesday to Sunday market in *les halles* by the river Charente next to the cathedral.

★ **St-Georges-de-Didonne** Nicer than Royan and just south of it, a resort with a good beach and small town cosied in by pinewoods. Daily market in summer and winter except Monday from October to May.

★ **St-Trojan les Bains** Bustling main port and resort on Oléron, France's largest island after Corsica. Markets are daily in summer, Tuesday, Thursday and Saturday out of season.

★ **Thouars** Built on a spur above the River Thouet, another historic, flower-filled town. Markets on Tuesday and Friday.

🖰 www.poitou-charentes-vacances.com

Markets at a glance: Poitou-Charentes

A
Aigre, *Thu, Sat, Sun*
Aigrefeuille-d'Aunis, *Sat*
Airvault, *Sat*
Angles-sur-l'Anglin, *Sat, Sun*
Angoulême, see Six of the Best
Angoulins, *Sat*
Archiac, *Sat*
Argenton-Château, *Thu*
Ars-en-Ré, *Tue, Fri* (daily mid-Jun–mid-Sep)
Aubeterre, *Sun*
Les Aubiers, *Fri*
Aulnay, *Sun*
Availles-en-Châtellerault, *Sat*
Availles-Limouzine, *Thu*
Aytré, *Fri*
B
Baignes-Ste-Radegonde, 4th *Wed*
Barbezieux, *Tue, Fri, Sat*
Beaumont, *Sat*
Beauvais-sur-Matha, *Tue, Thu*
Bignoux, *Sat*
Blanzac, *Sat*
Le Bois-Plage-en-Ré, *Tue, Thu, Sat* (+ daily mid-Jun–mid-Sep)
Bonneuil-Matours, *Sat*
Bourcefranc-le-Chapus, *Sun*
Brée-les-Bains, *Wed, Fri, Sun* (+ daily mid-Jun–mid-Sep)
Bressuire, *Tue, Sat*
Brioux-sur-Boutonne, 2nd and 4th *Thu*
Brossac, *Sat*
Buxerolles, *Thu*
C
Celles-sur-Belle, *Wed*
Cérizay, *Sat*
Chabanais, *Thu*
Chalais, *Mon*
Champagne-Mouton, *Tue, Fri*
Champdeniers, *Sat*
Chaniers, *Wed, Sat*
Chârellerault, *Tue, Wed, Thu, Sat*
Charroux, *Thu*

Chasseneuil-du-Poitou, *Thu*
Le Château-d'Oléron, *Sun*
Châteauneuf, *Tue, Thu, Sat*
Chatelaillon, daily
Chauvigny, see Six of the Best
Chef-Boutonne, *Sat*
Chevanceaux, *Sat*
Civaux, *Thu, Sat*
Civray, *Tue, Fri*
Cognac, daily
Confolens, see Six of the Best
La Couarde-sur-Mer, *Wed* (+ daily Jul/Aug)
Couhé, 2nd and 4th *Thu, Sat*
Coulon, *Fri, Sun*
Coulonges-sur-l'Autize, *Tue, Sat*
Courçon, *Wed*
La Couronne, *Wed, Sat*
Cozes, *Wed*
La Crèche, *Tue*
D
Dangé-Saint Romain, *Tue, Sat*
Dissay, *Fri, Sat*
Dolus-d'Oléron, (daily mid-Jun–end Sep)
E
Echillais, *Wed*
F
La Flotte-en-Ré, daily
Fontaine-le-Comte, *Sun*
Fouras, daily
G
Gémozac, *Tue, Fri*
Gençay, *Thu, Sat*
Gond-Pontouvre, *Thu, Sun*
H
Hiersac, *Sun*
I
Isle-Jourdain, *Tue, Fri, Sat*
Iteuil, *Sat*
J
Jarnac, daily (not *Mon*)
La Jarrie, *Thu*
Jaunay-Clan, *Fri*
Jonzac, *Tue, Fri*
L
Latillé, *Mon*

Leignes-sur-Fontaine, *Wed*
Lencloître, *Sat*
Leugny, *Tue*
Lezay, *Tue*
Loix, *Tue, Fri* (daily Jul–mid Sep)
Loudin, *Tue*
Loulay, *Fri*
Lugugé, *Fri*
Lusignan, *Wed*
Lussac-les-Château, *Fri*
M
Mansle, *Tue, Fri*
Marans, *Tue, Sat*
Marennes, *Tue, Thu, Sat*
Matha, *Tue, Fri, Sat, Sun*
Les Mathes, *Fri*
Mauléon, *Fri*
Mauze-sur-le-Mignon, *Wed, Sat*
Melle, *Fri*
Meschers-sur-Gironde, daily
Migné-Auxances, *Sat*
Mirambeau, every other *Sat*
Mirebeau, *Wed, Sat*
Moncontour, 3rd *Sat, Sun*
Moncoutant, *Sat*
Montbron, *Tue, Fri, Sat*
Montemboeuf, *Thu*
Montendre, *Thu*
Montguyon, *Sat*, 3rd *Wed*
Montignac, daily (not *Mon*)
Montmoreau-Saint-Cybard, *Wed, Sat*
Montmorillon, *Wed, Sat*
Monts-sur-Guesnes, *Sat*
Mornac-sur-Seudre, *Wed*
La Mothe-Saint-Héray, *Thu*
N
Naintré, *Sun*
Neiville-de-Poitou, *Thu*
Neuville, *Sun*
Nieulle-sur-Seudre, *Fri*
Nieul-sur-Mer, *Sun*
Niort, *Tue, Thu, Sat*
Nouaille, *Fri*
Nueil-sur-Argent, *Sat*
O
Oyré, 1st *Wed*
P
Parthenay, *Wed*, livestock

Persac, 2nd *Wed*
Poitiers, *Tue*, *Thu*, *Fri*, *Sat*,
  Sun
Poitiers-Zup-des-
  Couronneries, *Wed*
Pons, *Wed*, *Sat*, *Sun*
Pont-l'Abbé-d'Arnoult, *Fri*
Port-d'Envaux, *Thu*
Port-des-Barques, *Wed*, *Sun*
Les Portes-en-Ré, *Wed*, *Sun*
  (+ daily Jul/Aug)
Pressac, 1st *Wed*
R
Rivedoux-Plage, *Mon*, *Tue*,
  Wed, *Sat* (Jun–Sep)
Rochefort, *Tue*, *Thu*, *Sat*
La Rouchefoucauld, *Wed*, *Sat*
**La Rochelle, see Six of the
  Best**
La Roche-Posay, *Tue*, *Wed*,
  Fri, *Sat*
Roches-Prémarie, *Sat*
Rouillac, see Six of the Best
Rouillé, *Fri*
Royan, daily
Ruelle, *Thu*, *Sun*
Ruffec, *Wed*, *Sat*
S
Saint Loup Lamairé, *Sun*
Saint Palais-sur-Mer, *Tue*,
  Thu, *Sat*
Saint-Benoit, *Sat*
Saint-Claud, *Fri*
Saint-Clément-des-Baleines,
  daily (Jul/Aug)
Saint-Denis-d'Oléron, *Tue*,
  Thu, *Sat* (daily Jul/Aug)
Sainte-Marie-de-Ré, (daily
  mid-Jul–Aug)
Saintes, daily (not Mon)
Saint-Fort-sur-Gironde, *Tue*,
  Sat, *Sun*
Saint-Genis-de-Saintonge,
  1st, 3rd and 4th *Thu*
Saint-Georges-de-Didonne,
  daily (not *Mon* Oct–May)
Saint-Georges-des-Coteaux,
  Wed
Saint-Georges-d'Oléron,
  (daily mid-Jun–mid-Sep)

Saint-Gervais-les-Trois-
  Clochers, *Sat*
Saint-Jean-d'Angély, *Wed*,
  Sat
Saint-Jean-de-Sauves, *Fri*
Saint-Jouin-de-Marnes, 1st
  Sat
Saint-Julien-l'Ars, *Thu*
Saint-Loup-Lamairé, *Sun*
Saint-Maixent, *Wed*, *Sat*
**Saint-Martin-de-Ré, see Six
  of the Best**
Saint-Palais-sur-Mer, *Tue*,
  Fri, *Sat*
Saint-Pierre-d'Oléron, *Tue*,
  Thu, *Sat*, *Sun* (daily in
  summer)
Saint-Porchaire, *Wed*
Saint-Savinien, *Sat*
Saint-Sulpice-de-Royan, *Wed*
Saint-Trojan-les-Bains, *Tue*,
  Thu, *Sat* (daily in summer)
Saint-Xandre, *Tue*, *Sun*
Saires, *Sat*, *Sun*
Saujon, *Tue*, *Thu*, *Sat*
Sauzé-Vaussais, *Thu*
Secondigny, *Tue*
Segonzac, *Tue*, *Fri*, *Sun*
Smarves, *Sat*
Sossay, *Sun*
Soyaux, *Tue*, *Sun*
Surgères, *Tue*, *Thu*, *Sat*
T
Thénezay, *Sun*
Thouars, *Tue*, *Fri*
Tonnay-Charente, *Sat*, *Sun*
La Tremblade, *Sat* (daily in
  summer)
V
Vasles, *Tue* (+ sheep mkt)
Vaux-sur-Mer, *Tue*, *Sat* (daily
  in summer)
Vendeuvre-du-Poitou, *Tue*
Vicq-sur-Gartempe, *Sat*
Villebois-Lavalette, *Sat*
La Villedieu-du-Clain, *Tue*
Villefagnan, *Tue*, *Fri*
Vivonne, *Tue*, *Sat*
Vouillé, *Sat*
Vouneuil-sur-Vienne, *Thu*

AQUITAINE

The south-west's oyster worlds, red pepper obsession and Dordogne ducks

The 10th of September 2001. The day before 9/11. Scene: a waterside table at
L'Escale restaurant on Cap Ferret, looking out on the oyster bed stakes spiking
the glittering Bay of Arcachon. It was one of those intensely lit, deeply happy days
when the company was good, the wine perfectly chilled and all seemed right with
the world. Ever since, the world has felt distinctly skewed. Some months later, I
caught up with Jacqueline, who'd hosted that lunch, and discovered she felt
exactly the same. Happily, I've since been back to L'Escale, and it was just as
wonderful, as well as to the resort of Arcachon itself, where the bumper daily
market is one of the best in the west. Cap Ferret's is pretty good too.

Both are in Gironde, a vast swathe of land around the Gironde estuary on
France's Atlantic coast, where pinewoods anchor non-stop sandy beaches and
pretty weatherboarded buildings hint at the Caribbean. Inland is golf heaven;
leisure lakes are flecked with sails; the Médoc vineyards roll; and the Dordogne
meets the Garonne north of Bordeaux. The legend goes that when the two rivers
met, they said, '*J'irons deux*' (as in '*nous irons à deux*' – let's go together) which just
happens to sound like Gironde.

Gironde, the *département*, is not typical of the whole of Aquitaine, but it is
fairly similar to neighbouring Landes, which is also pine-wooded and beach-
edged. The long ribbon of the Silver Coast runs almost in a straight line to
Biarritz. Then there is Dordogne – not quite as all-embracing a space as 'the
Dordogne' referred to by so many British visitors (who locate it vaguely
anywhere that abuts the rivers Dordogne or Lot), but a big *département*
nevertheless, where Périgord truffles lurk in oak woods, dovecotes punctuate
rural idylls and storybook castles like Beynac teeter above the snaking river.
Imperceptibly, Dordogne blends into Lot-et-Garonne, but in the south comes the
major gear-change: as the coast wiggles towards Spain and the Pyrenean foothills
rise, we're in Basque country, so different in character it is hardly like France at all.

No wonder the English found it so hard to loosen their grip on Aquitaine.
They held it for three hundred years, calling it Gascony, built half the *bastides* –
the fortified towns – and developed the wine trade. Today, the vineyards still
produce A-list AOC labels and hundreds of scrumptious dishes have been devised
to go with both the great and good: often filling – and usually fattening – recipes
with strong flavours, for Gascons and Basques are hearty eaters. Pungent
casseroles like *cassoulet* and thick soups called *garbure*, a meal in themselves, are
often sold at markets pre-prepared.

Specialities

A glance at the length of that strip of coast on the map and you know **fish** is going to tip the scales (sorry!) from Bordeaux to St-Jean-de-Luz and beyond. At the *poissonneries* in covered markets, vast piles of silver sardines and muscular sea bass shine like treasure, while massive chunks of tuna are sawn like logs. But size doesn't matter – large or small, everything found on this Atlantic seaboard is top quality. Arcachon's **oysters** are the creamiest, most delectable in existence. To eat them the Gascon way, you must sample spicy little sausages called *crépinettes*. Bite a piece of hot sausage after swallowing each cold oyster, down it with a mouthful of flinty white Médoc – and dissolve with pleasure.

Mussels are excellent too, sometimes ready-cooked in the markets *à la Bordelaise* – in a red wine sauce with tomatoes and herbs. And look for portions of *ttoro*, tuna fish stew. Wonderful freshwater fish are available in Dordogne and Lot-et-Garonne, and from the fast-flowing rivers of the Pyrenees come trout, salmon and, in the spring, young eels – *piballes* – sold fresh or crisply fried.

They are **pepper** crazy in the deep south-west. Large sweet peppers, red and green, are heaped on market carts, also sold cooked – stuffed with cod, stewed with veal and, of course, added to eggs for *piperade*, a tasty scramble that is especially good with the famous *jambon de Bayonne*. Perversely, Bayonne ham mostly comes from Orthez but the salt used for curing it is from Bayonne. Sliced wafer thin and served with wedges of juicy melon, it is every bit as good as Parma ham.

Small hot chilli peppers spice up a whole raft of produce and dishes. Look for *saucissons* like the Spanish-style chorizo, and for *tripotchpa*, a fiery *boudin blanc*. You can buy chillis powdered, puréed or dried. *Piments d'Espelette* are the best. In late summer and autumn, the little town of Espelette above St-Jean-de-Luz is festooned with drying chillies, and at any time of year is still decorated with a few. They look stunning against the white chalet-style houses with their red roofs and shutters to match.

Pepper red is also one of the colours used in the lovely traditional Basque tablecloths made of heavy cotton. On a cream background, the red, green or navy stripes represent the seven cantons of Basque country.

Basque country can also lay claim to some very pleasant if not great wines: Irouléguy and Jurançon the most memorable.

Like the Midi, Aquitaine is in love with

foie gras and all the attending **duck** and **goose** goodies – *confit*, smoked *magret* et al. The Landes area is a big producer, also Dordogne. The local slant on serving it when you get it fresh (*gras* markets are held from October to April) is to fry it lightly and serve it with a glass of Monbazillac dessert wine, or with Chasselas grapes macerated in Sauternes.

The **truffles** of the Périgord are world renowned but, let's face it, few of us are likely to trip over them – certainly not in summer markets, unless you see micro chips of them speckling a pâté. December to March is truffle time. If you want to buy a 'black diamond', bring one to pay for it. *Cèpes*, the fleshy autumn mushrooms, are more within reach, extra special when freshly gathered, but also good preserved in oil or dried.

Although Aquitaine is not a big **cheese-** producing region, there's creamy *cabécou* goat's cheese, trimmed with Périgord walnuts, and any number of assorted Pyrenean ewe's milk cheeses – *ardi gasna*, *mamia*, *etoki*. Hard, sharp and slightly salty, these are excellent eaten with something sweet, like honey, jam or fruit compote. For the **dessert course** proper, try walnut cakes; *gâteau basque* filled with almond cream, cherries or prunes; *canelés* from Bordeaux; and the divine *tourtière*, a layered flaky pastry cake filled with apples or prunes and flavoured with armagnac. If not an armagnac to follow, go for Izarra, a Basque herb liqueur, or Patxaran made from sloes – plus some luscious chocolates from Bayonne.

Six of the Best

St-Jean-de-Luz (Pyrénées-Atlantique)

Tuesday and Friday

This penultimate resort on France's Atlantic coast has charm in spades. Fifteen kilometres hence is Spain, but don't expect to hear the rattle of castanets. St-Jean-de-Luz is an individual: Basque to the core and a major tuna-fishing port. Behind the bay-view hotels and apartments, built mostly between the 20th-century world wars, a cat's cradle of narrow lanes throngs with holidaymakers in season. Picturesque, whitewashed and low-rise, this hub of restaurants, boutiques and art galleries contains the daily covered market on Boulevard Victor Hugo.

Twice a week, open-air stalls mass around the back of the old *halles*, bringing the distinctive wares of small producers to town. Friday is the busiest morning. From the mountains come thickets of bouncy thyme and from the market gardens tarragon and basil; from the Vallée d'Aspe, hand-made cheeses such as *xokoa*, a pure *brebis* from Ossau; and, to partner the cheeses, quince pâté and cherry sauce. If you're self-catering there's a huge choice of ready-to-heat specialities: stuffed peppers, *piperade* (pepper omelette) and *truooxa* (black pudding in a pepper and tomato sauce); bag some cider to drink with it, as well as assorted Basque cakes, oozing rum, for afters.

Local flavours are well to the fore in St-Jean-de-Luz; this could not be a market anywhere else but Basque country. Even the seller of Guérande sea salt, that prized seasoning from Western Loire, adapts his offerings to engage local palates with packs of salt laced with chilli pepper from Espelette.

Don't miss

- The 13th-century church where the young Louis XlV married the Spanish Infanta Marie-Thérèse, and the Lohobiague mansion, where the royal couple later coupled.

- Classic Basque eating at Kaïku or L'Alcalde in Rue de la République.

- Iban, a souvenir-hunter's dream shop stacked with red Basque berets, Poire William liqueurs, little wooden saws for *saucisson* and striped table linen.

✪ Pierre Oteiza for Basque charcuterie.

✪ Espelette, the pepper capital, half-an-hour's drive away, where there's a live sheep market on Wednesdays.

ⓘ Rue Mazarin.

Somewhere to stay

↘ Le Parc Victoria, 18th-century Relais & Château, a step from the beach. Pool. Gastronomic restaurant with astronomic prices but gorgeous for a special treat. ☎ 05 59 26 78 78.

↘ The delightful Hôtel Euzkadi in Espelette (half-an-hour's drive from St-Jean-de-Luz): old Basque auberge whose facade is covered in creeper and chillies. Simple but stylish interior. Good restaurant. Pool.
☎ 05 59 93 91 88.

St-Emilion (Gironde)
Sunday morning

The setting is perfection – steep medieval streets of biscuit-coloured houses twisting up to the Hostellerie de Plaisance, from whose terrace the view across tweedy tiled rooftops to a sea of vines is sublime. Inevitably this premier-cru walled wine town swarms with tourists in season, but they don't dent its appeal. Since 1199, when King John of England founded St-Emilion's *Jurade* to control the quality of the famous Bordeaux red, the town has been devoted to the cult of the vine: at every step, you pass a *cave*, with bottles displayed outside; a wine school and *dégustations* are flagged up; souvenir shops sell decorative corkscrews and fridge sticker 'bottles'; wine merchants are poised to ship cases home.

When wine was first exported to England, the stones returned as ships' ballast were used to pave some of St-Emilion's streets; so you may well be walking on a little bit of Bristol.

The small Sunday morning market, which offers a bit of everything – even baby vines in pots, in case you want to grow your own – nestles at the foot of the hill in Place Bouqueyre just outside the walls. Get there early for, as with most Sunday morning markets, the end time is imprecise – '*ça dépend*', as the locals say, meaning stallholders can pack up on a whim if they get bored or have something better to do – like slope off for a glass of St-Emilion.

Don't miss

✪ The Maison du Vin.

✪ 14th-century cloisters of the Eglise Collégiale.

✪ The old Place du Marché, where café tables are shaded by an arthritic acacia tree and there is a church carved out of the underlying rock by Benedictine monks.

✪ In the charming little Place du Clocher, the Union des Producteurs de St-Emilion for tastings and sales.

ⓘ Rue du Clocher.

Somewhere to stay

↘ Hostellerie de Plaisance in Place Clocher. Nice hotel in a prime position at the top of town. Expensive but worth it. ☎ 05 57 55 07 55.

↘ Auberge de la Commanderie snuggles in Rue Cordeliers, a lovely old house beautifully updated. No restaurant. ☎ 05 57 24 70 19.

Brantôme (Dordogne)

Friday

My heart missed a beat the October night I arrived some years ago in this gorgeous little town to the north of Périgord truffle country. Enclosed on an islet by a split in the river Dronne, Brantôme is full of nooks and crannies, willow-draped bridges and medieval and Renaissance buildings. Softly lit corners came and went as I drove through in search of the Moulin de l'Abbaye, where I dined in fine style in its cellar restaurant and was shushed to sleep by the mill's still-turning water wheel. Next morning, ducks cackled indignantly as they slid sideways on the wide weir, unable to paddle in a straight line.

In Brantôme's Friday food market, which spreads hither and thither through the narrow streets, ducks and geese are transformed into Périgourdian delicacies – *confit*, *foie gras* and *pâté*: available both from surrounding shops as well as the street stalls. In autumn – when, as in spring, it's mainly a farmers' market – there are huge baskets of fresh walnuts and walnut conserves, cèpes, chanterelles and morilles mushrooms.

One of the most enchanting French towns to kill time in – though a lot busier now. Perfect, though, either side of summer.

Don't miss

✪ The abbey of abbot Pierre de Bourdeille, known as 'Brantôme', a 16th-century gossip writer at the court of Henry II who never actually took Holy Orders – his title was commendatory. His former home is worth a look (open to the public 1 June to mid-September). The rose garden and pavilion, reached across a curious 16th-century crooked bridge, are particularly lovely.

✪ The church and its 11th-century bell tower perched on a rock above the river.

✪ Au Fil de l'Eau restaurant with its waterside terrace.

✪ The Château de Bourdeilles and the Château de Puyguilhem, both about 10km away.

ⓘApril to mid-October, Renaissance Pavilion.

Somewhere to stay

↘Moulin de l'Abbaye, a heavenly hotel in a heavenly location. One-Michelin-star restaurant.
☎ 05 53 05 80 22.

↘Hôtel Chabrol, by the bridge. Restaurant a local favourite. Good wine list. ☎ 05 53 05 70 15.

Arcachon (Gironde)

Every day

A pilgrimage for oyster lovers, Arcachon is as Arcadian as it sounds. Studded with pines and fanciful winter villas, it stretches languorously around a southern curve of the Bay of Arcachon, boasting a huge blond beach, a sky full of light and boat trips in all directions. A few streets back from the restaurant-lined prom, the covered market at the elegant 19th-century Mairie in Place Lucien de Gracia is open every day, year round. Traders also pack the surrounding streets during the season (otherwise Wednesday, Saturday and Sunday mornings).

On a Saturday in July, the market was massive and full of sales people with fixed smiles pressing wispy sundresses and leopard pants on women who should not have attempted wearing them. Tattoo and henna experts invited the willing-to-experiment; paintings of the bay, local pottery, bright totes and fun novelties for children were going like hot cakes. And there were cool cakes too: wonderful tarts – *croustades*, combining pear and chocolate, plum and apple – and buttery biscuits topped with praline (Palets d'Arcachon).

Any lazy cook could have taken home a gourmet lunch, so compelling were the aromas from vast pans of mussels à la Bordelaise (tomato, garlic and red wine) and ham casseroled in white wine with pimento butter from Espelette. Under cover were the sublime oysters. Arcachon supplies them in embryo to be raised around other French shores.

Don't miss

○ A walk round the villas of the Ville d'Hiver (map from the tourist office).

○ A boat trip to the Ile aux Oiseaux or across to Cap Ferret (market daily in season). Book a table at L'Escale – just by the jetty – then get an appetite by climbing the old lighthouse or shopping in the boutiques. For a cheaper lunch, hire a bike and follow the *Route des Huitres* where you can stop at shacks on the beach and have six *claires*, chunks of bread and a glass of white Médoc for a handful of euros.

○ The Pyla dune, a mountain of sand to ascend, if your calf muscles can stand it.

○ L'Herbe – a fisherman's village of adorable white cottages wreathed in flowers.

ⓘ Esplanade Georges Pompidou.

Somewhere to stay

↘ Hôtel les Vagues. Nautically themed, modern 2-chimney Logis de France by the sea where the beach narrows along the Boulevard de l'Océan. A bit of a hike from the centre but it has car parking and a good restaurant. ☎ 05 56 83 03 75.

↘ Hôtel de la Plage, with its seafood restaurant Chez Magne, in the village of L'Herbe, on Cap Ferret. Very picturesque and right by the sea. ☎ 05 56 60 50 15.

Bordeaux (Gironde)

Daily, but best on Sunday for brie, bio and bygones

The Médoc wine port that was once the English capital of Aquitaine is, at the time of writing, like a building site. New tramlines, telephone and TV cables are being laid all at once. That said, work should be completed by 2006 and the city's elegant 19th-century architecture (the Marquis de Tourny did for Bordeaux what Haussmann did for Paris) undisturbed by the judder of the pneumatic drill.

Even now, Sunday morning is peaceful. In the park, you can hear only the fizz of the spectacular fountain dedicated to the Girondins (fated liberals of the Révolution) and a walk along the banks of the Garonne river leads to a lively food market in the shadow of the ex-World War Two battleship *Colbert* on Quai des Chartrons. Here, you can sample cheeses from the country, fruit, vegetables and oysters, before heading up river – past the splendid old Exchange, the Custom House, a *marché bio*, and the impressive Portes de Cailhau and de Bourgogne – to the flea market in Saint-Michel.

This is not Paris *puces*. It's a scrabble for bargains among junk spread out under the pinnacles of the Saint Michel Basilica. Flanked by cafés and restaurants with a North African flavour, the space swirls with the mixed aromas of Arab coffee and dusty attics. People-watching is compulsive. Well-heeled

Great museums – Maison du Vin, Beaux Arts, Arts Décoratifs (in a delightful mansion) and the Centre Jean Moulin (Resistance memorabilia).

The plane-shaded Allées de Tourny with their graceful wrought-iron balconied houses and the friendly café-brasserie, Le Noailles.

ⓘ Cours du 30-Juillet.

Somewhere to stay

↘ Hôtel de Normandie, a really good address in Cours du 30-Juillet just off the Allées de Tourny. Well-placed, efficient, comfortable, welcoming. No restaurant, but several nearby. Public parking underground in the *allées*.
☎ 05 56 52 16 80.

women forage in cardboard boxes for china dinner service spares. Water buffalo heads nudge bronze Christs and frilly glass decanters. Tatty sofas ooze stuffing, fire dogs lie in tangled heaps and hot dogs strain on their leads, while the market's regular loony shouts '*Donnez-moi un euro!*' at the top of his voice.

Good second-hand furniture and better collectibles are stashed away indoors in cavernous Le Passage (40 dealers), which also hides a lively café-restaurant.

Don't miss

The beautiful 18th-century Grand Théâtre, as jaw-dropping as the Opéra Garnier in Paris.

Vieux Bordeaux's intrigue of lean streets around the cathedral of Saint André.

Monpazier (Dordogne)
Thursday and Saturday

This, for me, is *the* Dordogne gem. Sturdy arcades stride around its mellow square in which markets have been held for over 700 years. Equidistant from bigger and better-known Bergerac and Sarlat, Monpazier was a *bastide* built for Edward 1 of England as part of the defences of Périgord. There's a wonderful story of how its citizens set out one dark night to loot and pillage the rival French *bastide* of Villefranche down the road. When they returned they discovered Monpazier itself had been done over by Villefranche. Here, history seeps out of every pore – medieval town gates still stand, old grain measures survive in the covered market hall, honeyed stone houses line offshoot streets. It is absolutely beautiful.

Get to market early as shafts of morning sunlight slant under the arcades. Buy an heirloom chestnut-wood basket and in ten minutes I guarantee you will have filled it – with truffled pâté, plum liqueur and jars of walnut pesto (*'Bon pour les grillades de poisson,'* suggests the lady who makes it in nearby Molières).

Monpazier also holds a fair on the third Thursday of the month and special *cèpes* markets in autumn when the fleshy fungus arrives in assorted baskets, paper bags and cardboard boxes to be bargained for with almost as much fervour as truffles.

Don't miss

✪ The fortified church with its lovely rose window.

✪ The chapter house in the square, once used as a tithe barn.

✪ The formidable Château Biron towering a few kilometres to the south.

ⓘ Place des Cornières.

Somewhere to stay

↘ La France, 13th-century auberge offering simple rooms, rich Périgourdine cooking.
☎ 05 53 22 68 59.

↘ Edward 1er, pleasant 19th-century converted townhouse, dinner only.
☎ 05 53 22 44 00.

★ **Bayonne** A must for the experience of the moonlit markets on the Pannecau and Marengo bridges. Starting at 2.30am, Tuesday, Thursday and Saturday, farmers sell direct at lower prices until 8.30am when they transfer to stalls in the covered market (Monday to Saturday).

★ **Bergerac** Wednesday and Saturday mornings. It may be the biggest river port straddling the Dordogne river, but when the farmers come to town its old heart is in the country. The cobbles around the Eglise Notre Dame – in Place Gambetta, Place du Marché and Rue de la Résistance – almost vibrate under the impact. On the first Sunday in the month, a huge flea market fills Place Dr Cayla.

★ **Domme** Thursday morning: another golden *bastide* on the Dordogne in an arresting setting. A huge tourist favourite.

★ **Labastide d'Armagnac** Monday morning in July and August. Charming *bastide*.

★ **Montfort-en-Chalosse** Wednesday morning sees one of the most important duck and geese (and related products) markets in the country. An English *bastide* with stepped alleyways and old Gascon houses.

★ **Périgueux** Wednesday and Saturday mornings.The outskirts are offputting and congested with traffic, but the truffle markets (September to March, place de la Clautre) are fascinating. The

old town is full of Renaissance curiosities and a Sacré Coeur look-alike cathedral.

★ **Pau** Daily (except Sunday) markets in this airy city in the mountains overflow with Pyrenean specialities. Weekends are for serious antique-hunters with *les puces* running through Saturday, Sunday morning and all day Monday (Place du Forail).

★ **Sarlat** Wednesday and Saturday, the entire centre is filled with market. Now a mecca for British visitors, Sarlat was in a sorry state after World War Two. Its unique medieval architecture was restored after a crusade by French culture minister André Malraux.

★ **St-Jean-Pied-de-Port**. There's a Monday morning market, *centre ville*, in this tourist honeypot with its commanding old citadel perched on the river Nive. Crammed in season, but very attractive.

★ **Villeneuve-sur-Lot** Another full of medieval charm. The Tuesday or Saturday morning traditional markets are *the* place to pick plums in season as this is one of the main centres for the famous grafted Agen *prune* (delicious preserved in Armagnac). Saturday afternoons are reserved for an eclectic and popular flea market. There's also a market of organic produce on Wednesday, and a Friday evening market in summer.

Other significant flea markets

◎ **Fronsac**, Plaisance, first Sunday.

◎ **Mérignac**, Rocade, sortie 9, second Saturday.

◎ **Marmande**, esplanade de Mare, second Sunday.

◎ **Dax**, Place Camille Bouvet, first Thursday.

◎ **La Bastide d'Armagnac**, Place Royale, fourth Sunday.

◎ **Mont-de-Marsan**, Place St Roch, first Wednesday.

◎ **Bayonne**, Place St-André, Friday.

◎ **Ciboure**, quartier Socoa-Untzin, first Sunday.

Christmas markets

In Bordeaux, Saint Sever, Pau, Libourne.

🖱 www.tourisme-aquitaine.fr

Markets at a glance: Aquitaine

A

Abjat, last *Tue*
Agen, *Wed, Sat, Sun*
Aiguillon, *Tue, Fri*
Aire-sur-l'Adour, *Tue, Sat*
Amou, *Sun*
Andernos, *Tue, Thu, Fri, Sat*
Aramits, *Sun*
Arcachon, see Six of the Best
Arcs, *Tue*
Arthez-de-Béarne, *Sat*
Artix, *Wed*
Arudy, *Tue, Sat*
Arzacq-Arraziguet, *Sat*
Astaffort, *Mon, Sat*
Audenge, *Tue*
Azur, *Tue*

B

Bayonne, daily
Bazas, *Sat*
Beaumont, *Sat*
Beauville, *Sun*
Bedous, *Thu*
Belvès, *Sat*
Bergerac, *Wed, Sat*

Biarritz, daily
Billère, *Sat*
Biscarrosse, *Fri, Sun* (daily in summer)
Blaye, *Wed, Sat, Sun*
Bordeaux, see Six of the Best
Bourg-sur-Gironde, *Sun*
Brantôme, see Six of the Best
Le Bugue, *Tue, Sat*

Le Buisson-de-Cadouin, *Fri*
Bussière-Badil, 2nd and 4th *Wed*

C

Cadouin, *Wed*
Cancon, *Mon*
Cap Ferrat, *Wed* (daily in summer)
Capbreton, *Tue, Thu, Sat* (daily in summer)
Captieux, *Mon*
Castets, *Thu*
Castillon-la-Bataille, *Mon*
Castillonnès, *Tue, Fri* (Jul/Aug)
Cauderan, *Wed, Sat* (organic food)
Champagnac-de-Belair, 1st *Mon*
Clairac, *Thu* (summer)
Claouey, daily (summer)
La Coquille, *Thu*
Coulounieix-Chamiers, *Tue, Fri, Sat*
Coutras, *Wed, Sat*
Couze-et-Saint-Front, *Sun*
Créon, *Wed*
Creysse, *Sun*

D

Dax, *Sat*
Domme, *Thu*
Duras, *Mon* (all year), *Thu* and *Sat* (Jun–Sep)

E

Eaux-Bonnes, *Wed* (Jul/Aug)
Etsaut, *Sun* (Jul/Aug)
Eugénie-les-Bains, *Wed* (summer)
Excideuil, *Thu*
Eymet, *Thu, Sun* (summer)
Eysines, *Sat, Sun*
Les Eyzies-de-Tayac, *Mon*

F

Le Fleix, *Mon*
La Force, *Thu*
Frespech, *Fri* (Jul/Aug)
Fumel, *Sun*

G

Gabarret, *Wed* eve
Gan, *Wed*
Gardonne, *Sun, Wed*

Garlin, alternate *Wed*
Geaune, alternate *Thu*
Génis, 2nd *Mon*
Grenade-sur-l'Adour, *Mon*
Gujan-Mestras, *Wed*

H

Habas, *Fri*
Hagetmau, *Wed*
Hautefort, 1st *Mon, Wed*
Hendaye, *Wed, Sat*
Hourtin, *Tue, Wed* (summer), *Thu, Sat, Sun*

I

Issigeac, *Sun*

J

Jumilhac-le-Grand, 2nd and 4th *Wed*

L

Labastide d'Armagnac, *Mon* (Jul/Aug)
Labenne, *Tue, Sat*
Labouheyre, *Thu*
Lacapelle-Biron, *Mon*
Lalinde, *Thu*
Lacanau, *Tue, Wed*
Lanouaille, 2nd and 4th *Tue*
Le Lardin-St-Lazare, *Fri*
Laruns, *Sat*
Lasseube, *Sat*
Lavardac, *Wed* (Jun–Sep)
Lembeye, *Thu*
Léon, *Tue* (+ daily in summer)
Lesparre, *Tue, Fri, Sat*
Libourne, *Tue, Fri, Sun*
Linxe, *Tue, Fri*
Lisle, *Tue* (+ walnuts Oct/Nov)
Lit-et-Mixe, 1st and 3rd *Tue* (+ daily in summer)
Luxey, 2nd *Thu*

M

Magescq, *Thu*
Mauléon, *Tue, Sat*
Merignac, *Wed, Sat, Sun*
Messanges, *Wed* and *Sat* (summer)
Mézin, *Thu, Sun*
Miallet, 3rd *Mon*
Mimizan, *Thu* (summer), *Fri*
Miramont, *Mon, Fri*

Moliets-et-Maa, *Tue*, *Thu*, *Sat* (summer)
Monein, *Mon*
Monflanquin, *Tue* and *Thu* and *Sat* (summer)
Monpazier, see Six of the Best
Monségur, *Tue*, *Fri* (+ *Mon* Jun–Sep)
Monsempron, *Thu*
Montardon, *Sat*
Mont-de-Marsan, *Tue*, 1st *Wed*, *Sat*
Montfort-en-Chalosse, *Wed*
Montignac, *Wed* (+ walnuts Oct/Nov), *Sat*
Montpon-Ménestérol, *Wed*
Morcenx, *Wed*, *Sat*
Moriaàs, *Fri*, *Sat*
Mouleydier, *Thu*
Mourenx, *Wed*, *Sat*
Mugron, *Thu*
Mussidan, *Sat*
N
Navarrenx, *Wed*
Nay, *Tue*
Nerac, *Sat* (+ *Tue* eve Jun–Sep)
Neuvic, *Tue*, *Sat*
O
Oeyreluy, *Tue*, *Fri*
Oloron-Ste-Marie, *Fri*
Orthez, *Tue*, *Sat*
P
Parentis-en-Born, *Tue*, *Thu*, *Fri* (+ *Tue* eve and *Sat* in summer)
Pau, daily (not *Sun*)
Pauillac, *Sat*
Payzac, 1st and 3rd *Tue*
Penne-d'Agenais, *Sun*
Périgueux, *Wed*, *Sat* (+ truffles Nov–Feb)
Pessac, *Wed*, *Sat*, *Sun*
Peyrehorade, *Wed*, *Sat*
Piégut-Pluviers, *Wed*
Podensac, *Tue*, *Fri*
Pomarez, *Mon*, *Wed*
Pontacq, *Sat*
Pontenx-les-Forges, *Sat*
Pontonx, *Tue*

Port-Ste-Foy-Ponchapt, *Tue*
Pressignac-Vicq, *Sun* (summer)
Prigonrieux, *Tue*, *Sun*
Pujols, *Sun*
R
Ribérac, *Wed*, *Fri* (walnuts Nov–Feb)
Rion-des-Landes, *Thu*
La Rochebeaucourt, 1st *Thu*
La Roche-Chalais, 1st *Thu*, *Sat*
Roquefort, *Sat*
Rouffignac, *Sun*
S
Sabres, *Thu*
Saint-André-de-Cubzac, *Thu*, *Sat*
Saint-Astier, *Thu*
Saint-Aulaye, last *Tue*, *Sat*
Saint-Cyprien, *Wed*, *Sun*
Sainte-Alvère, *Mon* (+ truffles Dec–Mar)
Sainte-Foy-la-Grande, Daily
Saint-Emilion, see Six of the Best
Saint-Jean-de-Luz, see Six of the Best
Saint-Jean-Pied-de-Port, *Mon*
Saint-Julien-en-Born, daily (Jul/Aug)
Saint-Léon-sur-l'Isle, *Sat* eve
Saint Martin-de-Seignanx, *Sat*
Saint-Palais, *Fri*
Saint-Pardoux-la-Rivière, 2nd *Tue*, *Sat*, *Sun*
Saint-Paul-les-Dax, *Thu*
Saint-Saud-Lacoussière, last *Mon*
Saint-Savin, *Mon*
Saint-Sever, *Sat*
Saint-Vincent-de-Tyrosse, *Fri*
Salies-de-Béarn, *Thu*, *Sat*
Salignac-Eyvigues, last *Fri*
Sanguinet, *Wed* (summer), *Sat*
Sarlat-la-Canéda, *Wed*, *Sat*
Sauvagnon, *Sun*
Sauveterre, *Wed*, *Sat*

Sauveterre-de-Guyenne, *Tue*
Seignosse, *Tue*
Sigoules, *Fri*
Singleyrac, *Sun* (summer)
Siorac-en-Périgord, *Wed*
Soorts-Hossegor, *Sun* (+ *Mon*, *Wed*, *Fri* in summer)
Sore, *Thu*
Sorges, *Fri*
Soulac-sur-Mer, daily
Soumoulou, alternate *Fri*
Soustons, *Mon*, *Thu* (summer)
T
Talence, *Sat*
Talence-Thouars, *Sun*
Tardets-Sorholus, alternate *Mon*
Targon, *Mon*, *Fri*
Tarnos, *Sat*
Tartas, *Mon*, *Sat* (summer)
Terrasson-la-Villedieu, *Thu*
La Teste-de-Buch, daily
Thenon, *Tue* (+ truffles Nov–Feb)
Thiviers, *Sat*
Tocane-St-Apre, *Mon* (+ walnuts Oct/Nov)
Tournon-d'Agenais, *Fri* (+ *Thu* in summer)
Trémolat, *Tue*
U
Urrugne, *Wed*, *Fri*
V
Vélines, *Wed*
Vendays-Montalivet, daily mid-Jun–mid-Sep
Vergt, *Fri*
Verteillac, *Sat* eve
Vielle-Saint-Girons, *Sun*
Vieux-Boucau, *Tue*, *Sat* (+ daily in summer)
Villamblard, *Mon*
Villandraut, *Thu*
Villefranche-de-Lonchat, *Tue*
Villeneuve-de-Marsan, *Tue*
Villeneuve-sur-Lot, *Tue*, *Wed*, *Fri* eve, *Sat*
Y
Ychoux, *Sat*
Ygos, *Sun*

MIDI-PYRÉNÉES

Foie gras *forever, black diamonds and floaty summer dresses*

One can get too much of a good thing. With a group of other journalists, I once went on a fact-finding jaunt around the Lot Valley during which we were smothered with kindness and a surfeit of *foie gras*. Leaving aside the morality – or otherwise – of force-feeding ducks and geese to achieve this highly-regarded delicacy of super-fattened liver, even if you love the stuff there are limits to how much of it you can take. As we lurched from rustic auberge to civic reception, our hosts naturally considered they were spoiling us by serving *foie gras* every time we slid our knees under a table. By the final evening's banquet, only the truly greedy could cope with another morsel. Polite refusals of the inevitable first course were met with outrage by the waiters, who flung semi-grilled *foies* oozing blood onto our plates with cries of 'Eat! Eez good!' The brave held their ground. The rest of us pushed it around our plates lest we in turn might be force-fed. If *une crise de foie* – a liver crisis – is French for the effects of overindulgence, we were clearly suffering *une crise de foie gras*.

There is certainly a lot of it about in the Lot, as well as in the other seven *départements* of Midi-Pyrénées, a big, bountiful and beautiful region which sprawls from the Massif Central in the north-east to the Pyrenees in the south-west. In between is a kaleidoscope of landscapes veined by the rivers Dordogne, Lot, Gers, Ariège and Garonne as well as umpteen lesser streams and half the Canal-du-Midi. Basking in southern warmth, with an average temperature that rarely drops below 20 degrees from May to the beginning of October, everything grows apace and the artisan farmer rules.

Markets in Midi-Pyrénées are wonderful affairs. Not only are they a gastronomic *tour de force* with small family businesses bringing their lovingly produced wares to town, but the settings can be unbelievably picturesque. In mellow, medieval *bastides* with arcaded squares and fortified churches, the fruits of the earth and of men's and women's labours have been bought and sold for a thousand years or more.

In summer, evening markets bring added excitement, the lights from the stalls softly caressing distressed stonework as the sounds of jazz or modern rock endeavour to split it. Sometimes musicians with lutes, pipes and drums become *troubadours*, recreating traditional folk music. Then, you only have to half close your eyes to melt back into the Middle Ages.

Night markets are sporadic. Some are regular during July and August, others occur perhaps once a month. Small local tourist information offices will soon direct you to where and when they're likely to crop up in the vicinity.

Specialities

From October to April, fresh **foies gras** and poultry are sold almost every day at special weekly *gras* markets. These are something else. Serried ranks of ducks and geese are ranged neatly on racks while the plump, newly, er, harvested livers are sold both separately and 'on the bird': that is to say, still in place but exposed by a delicate bit of nipping and tucking. To a *foie-gras* connoisseur this has a strange beauty. To the rest of us, it may be a touch too Damien Hirst.

Summer markets sell the livers canned, in jars, as pâté and even dried. Also preserved duck and goose, or *confit*, the essential ingredient of **cassoulet**. This robust garlicky, beany casserole from Castelnaudary is a Midi-Pyrénéenne favourite that has always scored highly with British visitors. I love it, but you need to be ravenously hungry. For something lighter, look out for *jambon de magret*, duck breast dry-cured like ham. This is delectable sliced wafer thin with a smidgin of fruit compote accompaniment.

Unless you're here in wintertime, you won't see much of *tuber melanosporum.* December to March is the optimum time for the **truffle** markets, the key ones taking place at Lalbenque and Limogne. Colloquially known as the 'black diamond' or 'black pearl', the precious black truffle finds all it needs here to thrive – limestone soil, the roots of oak and hazelnut trees, and a near-Mediterranean climate. It's fascinating to see these misshapen lumps of fungus being weighed, auctioned and priced out of sight. The buyers are mostly restaurateurs – otherwise it's a spectator sport for all but the exceedingly flush. Size matters. Sometimes a crusty old farmer selling out of the back of his beaten-up Peugeot will laugh all the way to the Crédit Agricole following the sale of one huge truffle.

For picnics, you'll need a sleek Laguiole **knife** to slice your *saucisson*. Traditionally used by the cattle men of the Aubrac, this handy blade was given a new lease of life after cutting-edge designers like Philippe Starck were drafted in to update its looks. Now the Laguiole with its one blade and corkscrew has almost upstaged the multi-skilled Swiss Army knife. Beautifully balanced, it comes in different sizes and trims with horn, ebony or boxwood handles in the form of a bird's wing or shapely leg. Markets nearly always have a selection, but local *quincailleries* stock them too.

There's also Laguiole **cheese**, mild with a hard rind, one of three cow's milk cheeses that come from the high pastures. The others are Bleu des Causses and Aligot, which, with garlic and potatoes, makes a moreish dish of the same name. But the big cheese is, of course, Roquefort, the king of the blues, made from ewe's milk. Production is primarily at Roquefort-sur-Soulzon, where you can see it being matured in natural caves below ground. No market *fromagerie* throughout the region fails to carry a ready supply. With a chunk of *croustillot*, the 100-per-cent-wheat country bread from Lot, and a bag of juicy peaches or greengages (*reine-claudes*), what more do you need for a riverbank lunch?

Ah, the **wine**. Gaillac, Cahors, Madiran, Fronton and Marcillac are the region's AOC labels, followed by a series of VDQS worth remembering: Côtes de St-Mont, Côtes de Brulhois, Entraygues, Fel, Estaing and Côtes de Millau. Neither would you sniff at – or rather you *would*, with pleasure – *vin de pays* such as Côtes du Tarn, Comté Tolosan, Côtes de Gascogne and Côteaux de Glanes.

How have I got thus far without mentioning **armagnac** – the 'best grape spirit in the world'? A glass of Midi-Pyrénées's amber nectar is not only the perfect end to a meal but a sublime marinade for preserving fruit, especially Agen prunes. Young armagnac also gets added to fresh grape juice to produce the sensual and sweet Floc de Gascogne, which comes in both red and white – a before or after drink, to be served fresh with *foie gras*, fruit or chocolates.

Significant **liqueurs** to savour or bring back as souvenirs? *Eaux de vie* distilled from Périgord walnuts or chestnuts from the Ségala are good, and you've got to try a Pousse Rapière ('rapier thrust'). Also based on armagnac, this lethal weapon hits several spots from somewhere just below the heart to the solar plexus. Mixed in a cocktail, however, it's delicious. One part Pousse Rapière, six parts dry champagne, one ice cube and half a slice of orange – guaranteed to kick-start any evening. *Santé!*

Cordes-sur-Ciel (Tarn)

Saturday morning

On a hot August afternoon, Cordes shimmers like a mirage above the flat expanse of the Cérou valley's shorn wheatfields. Early on an autumn morning, chiffony mists detach it from reality. It is well described as 'sur ciel'.

A very old hilltop *bastide*, packed with ornate Gothic houses immaculately restored by those with *beaucoup de goût* as well as money, Cordes has always harboured artists and craftspeople. It is one of the most picturesque market towns of the region, today dependent on the flocks of summer visitors who comb its classy interiors boutiques and souvenir shops, then order drinks and meals in the shade of dove-white canvas parasols. But the dignified old stones rise above the onslaught – in every sense.

One could be forgiven for expecting the Saturday market to be held in the much-restored *halle* with its octagonal pillars and chestnut roof timbers. No doubt markets were held here back in the 14th century, but this is nowadays reserved for special fêtes and medieval fairs. The weekly market proper spreads itself at the bottom of the hill, creating havoc for traffic determined to drive up into the centre. Much better to leave your car below when you want to sightsee. Cordes is not very big.

Market produce is superb and there are all the usual Gascon specialities: from neighbouring Aveyron the splendid blue cheeses of Roquefort and Bleu des Causses; *foie gras* in various guises, if not actually geese – sometimes as pâté speckled with truffles. 'Medieval' crafts abound and in summer there's a distinct Maid Marian touch to the floaty numbers on the women's fashion stalls.

Don't miss

✪ The Maison du Grand Fauconnier, one of the star Gothic houses – filigree stonework, huge arcades. On the first floor, the Yves Brayer Museum with paintings donated by the artist.

✪ The Musée de l'Outil et des Métiers Anciens, which shows how Cordes used to occupy itself before it became a tourist attraction – by producing linen, blue dye and leatherwork.

✪ If you have euros to spare, Yves Thuriès' Michelin-star restaurant in the Maison du Grand Ecuyer (equerry).

✪ 15km away, the Château du Bosc, childhood home of painter Henri de Toulouse-Lautrec.

✪ The Gorges of the Tarn, a lovely scenic route.

ⓘ Maison Fonpeyrouse.

Somewhere to stay

↘ If the Grand Ecuyer (☎ 05 63 53 79 50) is out of the question, the more reasonably priced and pleasant Annexe La Cité (☎ 05 63 56 03 53) is still within Vieux Cordes.

Cahors (Lot)
Saturday morning

I first went to Cahors back in the 1980s when staying with friends on the way to a wedding. My hosts, Patrick and Maryse Goyet, promptly armed me with a basket and propelled me to market in front of its magnificent old cathedral. Ever since, this has been my yardstick for market charm.

Patrick, who faintly resembles the French writer/aviator St-Exupéry, has been, in his own way, a pretty high flyer. Then director of the French Tourist Office in London, he was still hyperactive at his family home in the Lot. Before I could open one ear the first morning, I could hear his brushstrokes painting the walls of the corridor outside my bedroom. Then it was 'Anne, *venez ici, coupez la lavande*', and 'Anne, come, now we go to shop in Cahors.'

So we went to Cahors market and I dutifully held the basket while peaches and pink garlic were loaded in with crisp lettuces and a carton of *museaux* salad for lunch (only after I'd appreciatively crunched a mouthful of these gristly slivers did I discover *museaux* were pig's snouts).

Cahors' is an excellent open-air market (on Wednesdays too but best on Saturdays) with a melange of everything from food to crafts and sometimes a bit of bric-a-brac as well. Look for local goodies: Cabécou cheese, stuffed prunes and chocolate-covered walnuts. The location in Place Chapou is beautiful and surrounded by cobbled medieval streets. There's also a daily covered market in the 19th-century *halle*.

What I like about this mellow wine capital contained within a loop of the river Lot is that the usual sprawl of supermarkets, do-it-yourself and home-equipment stores is kept well out of town, leaving the relatively small centre happily blending its historic past with present elegance.

Don't miss

✪ Saint Etienne's cathedral, begun around 1109, with its vast nave and painted cupolas, and the archdeacon's house set around a Renaissance courtyard.

✪ The stunning, honey-coloured Pont Valentré, begun in 1308, which spans the Lot. Best first impression is early in the morning from the Quai Cavaignac on the river's opposite bank.

○ In the main town square, the statue of Léon Gambetta, after whom all Boulevards (Rues, Avenues) Gambetta are named, including Cahors'. The distinguished French statesman was born here in 1838.

○ The Maison du Vin for information on growers of Cahors wine.

○ A meal at Balandre (Michelin-starred) in the Hotel Terminus (see below) – good food to do justice to a bottle of Cahors wine.

ⓘ Place Aristide Briand.

Somewhere to stay

○ In town, the fresh and inviting Hôtel Terminus, Avenue Charles de Freycinet. ☎ 05 65 53 32 00.

○ Just outside, the wine-producing Château de Mercuès, a Relais & Châteaux hotel splendidly sited on a spur overlooking the Lot. Ancient cedars of Lebanon in the garden and a cellar stocked with its own label. ☎ 05 65 20 00 01.

Toulouse (Haute-Garonne)
Every day

It may be a bit like a multi-storey car park, but the big indoor produce market in this lively university city's Place Victor Hugo is a must for serious foodies. Not only does it sell everything edible from all over France and beyond, but when the market finishes at noon the restaurants above on the next floor go into overdrive

for lunch. Small, jam-packed and noisy, they're an experience not to be missed. Here, you're as likely to rub shoulders with businesswomen in Chanel suits as with plumbers in *bleu de travail*. The market and restaurants operate every day except Monday.

Most of Toulouse's open-air markets also close on Mondays. The exception is Boulevard de Strasbourg, which as well as having a morning market Tuesday to Sunday has an all-day market on Mondays. For atmospheric surroundings, however, Place du Capitole wins. It has flowers every morning (except Monday), *bio*-grown stuff on Tuesday and Friday and a big traditional market plus old books on Wednesday. This is one of Europe's most splendid squares, its style reminiscent of a Spanish *plaza*. You'd never know there was a car park underneath. The enormous 18th-century Hôtel de Ville, or Capitole, is quite opulent inside (visitable) with glittering chandeliers and massive paintings of the city's defining moments.

Another delightful market to earmark is the *brocante* on Saturdays and Sundays in Place Saint Sernin, in the lee of the glorious basilica whose russet bricks, along with those of other historic landmarks, have earned Toulouse the soubriquet of 'pink city'.

Don't miss

○ Top sights: the Opéra, the Basilica of St Sernin and its tiered 12th-century belfry, the palm vaulting in Les Jacobins convent and the sublime cloister of the Musée des Augustins.

- ✪ Bibent, *the* grand café to be seen in – Belle Epoque decor, nattily turned-out waiters and comfy cane chairs from which to gaze out on Place du Capitole.

- ✪ Mini-cruises on the Garonne and the Canal-du-Midi.

- ✪ Hélène Vie's enchanting Maison de la Violette barge on the Canal-du-Midi for everything violets from crystallized bonbons to soap, scent and liqueurs.

- ✪ Space City just outside town, with interactive exhibits, a planetarium and mock-up of the Mir space station.

ⓘ Donjon du Capitole.

Somewhere to stay

- ⬗ Grand Hôtel de l'Opéra on Place du Capitole. Despite its grandeur, staff are unstuffy and friendly. I once arrived in a parlous state after a long, dusty drive and was greeted like a long-lost relative. ☎ 05 61 21 82 66.

- ⬗ The small but charming Beaux Arts near the Pont Neuf (interior full of antiques). No restaurant.
☎ 05 34 45 42 42.

Mirepoix (Ariège)
Monday, Thursday

I was nagged into visiting Mirepoix by a friend living in neighbouring Languedoc-Roussillon who kept extolling its glories. As it happened, the only way I could fit it in was on a market-less day, but I saw enough to confirm it a potential corker. In the heart of Cathar country, south-west of Carcassonne, Mirepoix is a creakingly lovely *bastide* (first stone laid 1289). Its timbered houses, painted in pastel blues, greens and ochres, lean their elbows upon sturdy oak arcades worn to the shade and texture of old garden benches. The remains of carved birds, beasts and human heads peer from lintels – the best above the Maison des Consuls café.

The once-fortified enclosure is the market square. Here, roses grow, and a patch of grass. A pretty carousel turns. But pride of place is taken by a lofty open wrought-iron *halle* with polished floor tiles.

On the south side of the square looms the amazing early-Gothic cathedral of Saint Maurice which, although sadly in need of repair – indeed almost because of it – exudes the breath of the 13th century. Faded decorative strips, patterned like country cottons, outline the vaulting of the vast nave, the second widest of its kind in Europe.

Everything else in Mirepoix has a hint of luxury about it. There are lovely shops and the surrounding café terraces are equipped with remarkably chic cane and canvas chairs – the kind you hog long after the dregs of your coffee have dried up.

I asked a man which streets as well as the square were occupied by the Monday market. '*C'est partout*,' came the answer with an expansive wave of both arms, and I could imagine it brimming over. There's also a small farmers' market on Thursday mornings, a huge *brocante* fair over Whit weekend, night markets and pottery markets in July and August and in the winter the biggest cattle market in the region on the second and fourth Mondays of the month. What a backdrop.

Don't miss

✪ As well as the cathedral – which you can't miss – the Porte d'Aval, the only remaining gate of the town's original four.

✪ Pony rides for children from noon outside the cathedral.

✪ Tempting pottery and ceramics shops.

✪ Gems in the immediate environs: the fortified village of Camon and Vals church with its Romanesque frescoes. Forty minutes' drive to the south, the spectacular hilltop ruins of Montségur, once HQ of the Cathars, whose last defence against the Catholic armies was commanded by local hero Pierre Roger de Mirepoix.

ⓘ Place du Marché.

Somewhere to stay

↘ Maison des Consuls, main square – quaint, a true *hôtel de charme* with 8 rooms but no restaurant.
☎ 05 61 68 81 81.

↘ Le Commerce, Cours du Docteur Chabaud. A family-run Logis in a former coaching inn with a charming restaurant in the courtyard garden.
☎ 05 61 68 10 29.

Albi (Tarn)
Saturday morning, Thursday nights in summer

Fabulous Albi. I remember approaching it from the west on a day when the sky was a hot blue and the whole sunset-coloured mass of it towering above the river Tarn made me stop in my tracks, get out of the car and stare. The traffic behind wasn't amused.

There's a small Saturday morning open-air food market, but the main focus is on the flea market in the Halle de Casteviel, quite near to, and signposted from, the bishop's palace and fortress-like cathedral of Ste-Cécile – the core of the historic town. A sophisticated clientele flocks to this from miles around to buy country furniture and candelabra, fine china, old ashtrays and mournful religious paintings. The market gets bigger on the first weekend in June when it becomes *Les Puces Géantes*, with more dealers and lots of additional fun.

Just recently started are the night markets on Thursday evenings held in the Jardin National throughout July and August. Expect to see *charcuterie* from Lacaune, mountains of ripe, juice-heavy melons from Quercy and Lectoure, and the renowned Chasselas table grapes from Moissac. Local wine and honey are also for sale, as well as arts and crafts. Much is eaten and drunk on the sidelines and a bit of music keeps things rolling from 18.00 to almost midnight.

Don't miss

✪ Henri de Toulouse-Lautrec's birthplace in Rue Toulouse-Lautrec. More importantly, the museum devoted to his

work in the bishop's palace. The celebrated posters are on the second floor but especially poignant are his early drawings of horses – his great passion until he broke his legs, which failed to mend properly.

✪ Sainte Cécile, a whopper of a cathedral built to flaunt the power of the Church in the wake of the Albigensian crusade. Inside, several wonders, including the mammoth and rather gory 'Last Judgement' and a superlative Baroque organ.

✪ The restaurants along the banks of the Tarn – easy to miss as there are plenty of temptations in the historic quarter.

ⓘ By the cathedral.

Somewhere to stay

⬃ Hostellerie St-Antoine, in the Rue St Antoine on the edge of the old centre, offers breathing space in its small garden and antique furnishings within. ☎ 05 63 54 04 04.

⬃ La Réserve, a special place a couple of miles out of town in a park along the banks of the Tarn. Colonial-style dining room (expensive). ☎ 05 63 60 80 80.

Auch (Gers)
Thursday, Saturday

Amid serried hills patched with sunflowers in the fertile land of the Gers stands the Fourth Musketeer's home town of Auch. You can't miss the statue of d'Artagnan, born Charles de Batz, the

only one of Alexandre Dumas's swashbuckling quartet to have really lived. There he is – big hair, big hat and big boots – at the top of the Monumental Stairway, a calf-stretching cascade of steps (230) connecting the ancient *ville haute* with the newer lower town. I viewed him from all angles on a very hot morning when, acting upon faulty information, I parked my car in Place de la République, where the market wasn't, and had to leg it down the stairway to where the market was – on the other side of the river Gers (Avenue Hoche and around). But the effort was worth it.

Auch market offers big bargains in leisure wear (certainly in summer – only in the south do they understand about really *thin* cotton tees and loose, light, trousers). Beyond a mass of flowers, a rich menu of produce from near and far spills beyond the boundaries of the open *halle*: bumper boxes of local *haricots* in green, white and speckled pink, slivers of

jambon de Bayonne and fist-sized frilly *mousserons*, the wild mushrooms from the Pyrenees still with mountain earth clinging to their wavy edges. Lots to taste – different varieties of *fromage de brebis*, ewe's cheese, sweet and milky, salty and hard, and *rillettes de canard*, a fatty pâté made from what's left of the duck after the *foie* is removed. Small producers hand out leaflets inviting you to buy direct from their farms. I took away some *bière blonde du Gers* which turned out to be strong rather than thirst-quenching, but went down a treat with charcuterie.

Auch was capital of the old province of Gascony, a land with a turbulent history, past and recent. During World War Two, many Gascons joined the Resistance and, aided by Spanish Republicans, fought courageously to drive out the Nazis. Today, Auch is a relaxed, easygoing town with an intriguing old quarter which contains a gastronomic beacon, the restaurant of André Daguin, master of *confit d'oie*.

Don't miss

○ The carved choir stalls of the Cathedrale de la Sainte Marie, with over a thousand figures and some curiously erotic misericords.

○ The warren of alleys and stairways around medieval and Renaissance houses.

○ The Musée de la Résistance, a salutary look at Gers's more recent history.

○ André Daguin's restaurant at the Hôtel de France, Place de la Libération (see right).

○ And, in the village of Lannepax (about 20 minutes away), the Hostellerie Gasconne, where a jovial retired carpenter demonstrates his natural flair for cooking. ☎ 05 62 58 02 00.

ⓘ1 Rue Dessoles.

Somewhere to stay

↘Hôtel de France, charming 3-star with no fewer than three restaurants, of which André Daguin's is one.
☎ 05 62 61 71 71.

↘In the tiny medieval village of Jegun, Mme Rolande Mengelle's spacious chambres d'hôtes in a restored town house. I slept in a vast room with high beamed ceiling and shuttered windows, wakening to the burble of wood pigeons and the 7am bong of the church clock (it stops at night). Luxury at a reasonable price. ☎ 05 62 64 55 03.

Best of the Rest

★ **Bassoues** One of the prettiest small *bastides*. Market on Sunday morning.

★ **Condom** Leaving aside its silly-postcard potential, this rather elegant *ville* of 17th- and 18th-century townhouses in the heart of *armagnac* country is one of the main *foie gras* sales locations from October to April. Market Wednesday.

★ **Espalion** Just below the Aubrac plateau, a picturesque little Aveyronnais town with severe, slate-roofed houses and a bridge spanning the Lot. The Tuesday and Friday markets are declared best in the area – even by people from the Cantal in neighbouring Auvergne.

★ **Fleurance** *Bastide* town where an unusual two-storey market hall operates on Tuesdays. Beautiful cathedral.

★ **Gimont** Pleasant little town where the road runs underneath the covered market. Wednesday.

★ **Lalbenque** The town for serious truffle connoisseurs during the winter months. From December to March, markets dedicated to the fungus are on Tuesdays in the afternoons (from 14.00). I presumed, wrongly, that the timing was because the gatherers were out with their dogs and pigs till all hours – Limogne's truffle market (see below) is in the mornings.

★ **Lézat-sur-Lèze** Lovely small town with a brick covered market hall and timber-framed houses. Market on Saturday morning. Just south of Toulouse, the Lèze valley has a lot of charm.

★ **Limogne** Truffles rule here on Friday mornings, December to March, starting at 10am. Even if you can't afford to pay for a minuscule gnarled lump, the sheer theatre of sniffing and selecting, bargaining and weighing is a spectacle worth witnessing.

★ **Marcilhac-sur-Célé** Its Sunday morning market is the perfect objective on a tour of the Célé, a leafy tributary of the Lot (the Pech-Merle prehistoric caves are nearby). There's also a Tuesday afternoon market in summer. Outstanding site.

★ **Mauvézin** A particularly charming *bastide* with arcades all round the square, gîtes in old buildings and a 13th-century covered market. Monday is the day.

★ **Montauban** City with a *bastide* at its core and the incomparable Ingres museum. Wednesday and Saturday morning markets, also regular flea market Saturday morning in Place Lalaque. Night markets in summer.

★ **Rabastens** Genteel small town on the River Tarn halfway between Toulouse and Albi. Ticks over quietly until the Saturday morning market. Swings into major action in August for a national *brocante*.

★ **Rodez** Business is brisk on Wednesday and Saturday mornings in Place de la Cité, near the immense Gothic cathedral which turns otherwise not-so-remarkable Rodez into a town worth seeing. There's also a market on Friday night in summer.

★ **St-Antonin-Noble-Val** Also on the Aveyron. Untouristy town of crumbly medieval houses under the towering Roc d'Anglars. Contains one of the oldest town halls in the country. Sparky Sunday market.

★ **St-Céré** Market town and walking centre on the River Bave with flower-garnished houses and nice upbeat atmosphere. Saturday market. Night markets in summer. Cattle market in October.

★ **Vicdessos** Mountain village with an old castle and 13th-century belfry en route to the lake district of Hautes-Pyrénées. Thursday market of Pyrenean specialities.

★ **Vic-Fezensac** Small market town near Auch which is one of the venues for French bullfighting. It boasts one of the liveliest – and noisiest – night markets in the Gers. Held on Wednesdays once a fortnight in July and August. Normal market day Friday.

★ **Villefranche-de-Rouergue** I love this charming *bastide* on the Aveyron. The arcaded market place fairly throbs on Thursday mornings, especially from November to January when each week it is augmented by a *foire au gras* (foie gras and poultry sale) under the covered market.

www.tourisme-midi-pyrenees.org (English-language website)

Markets at a glance: Midi-Pyrénées

A
Aignan, *Mon*
Alban, *Fri* 5–8pm (Jul/Aug)
Albas, *Sun*
Albi, see Six of the Best
Albias, *Fri*
Angles, last *Thu*
Arcambal, *Sun*
Arreau, *Thu*
Arrens Marsous, *Sun* (Jul/Aug)
Argelès-Gazost, *Tue, Sat*
Aspet, *Weds, Sat*
Assier, *Mon* (sheep mkt)
Aubin, *Wed, Fri*
Auch, see Six of the Best
Aulus-les-Bains, *Sun*
Aurignac, *Tue*
Aussillon, *Thu*
Auvillar, *Sun*
Ax-les-Thermes, *Tue, Thu, Sat,* mid-Jun–mid Sep

B
Bagnac-sur-Célé, *Wed*
Bagnères-de-Bigorre, *Sat*
Bagnères-de-Luchon, *Wed, Sat*
Barbaton-les-Thermes, *Wed*
Barèges, *Wed*
La Barthe-de-Neste, *Sun* (May–Oct)
Bassoues, *Sun*
La Bastide-de-Serou, *Thu*
La Bastide-Murat, *Sun* in summer
La Bastide-sur-l'Hers, *Sat*
Beaumont-de-Lomagne, *Sat*
Beauregard, *Tue, Thu, Sat*
Belesta, *Tue, Thu*
Belmont, *Sun*
Bessières, *Mon*
Biars-sur-Céré, *Sun*
Blaye-les-Mines, *Tue, Thu*
Bordères-Louron, *Sun* in summer
Boulogne-sur-Gesse, *Wed*
Bozouls, *Thu*
Brassac, 1st *Mon*
Brentenoux, *Mon, Sat*

C
Les-Cabanes, *Sun*
Cagnac-les-Mines, *Wed*
Cahors, see Six of the Best
Cahuzac-sur-Vère, *Wed*
Cajars, *Sat*
Capdenac-Gare, *Tue, Sat*
Caraman, *Thu*
Carbonne, *Thu*
Carmaux, *Fri*
Cassagnes-Béghones, *Fri*
Castelnau-Magnoac, *Sat*
Castelnau-Montratier, *Sun*
Castelsarrasin, *Thu* (+ night mkt Jul/Aug)
Castelsagrat, *Sun*
Castillon, 3rd *Thu* (every *Thu* in summer)
Castres, *Tue, Thu, Fri, Sat*
Catus, *Tue* (+ night mkt in summer)
Caussade, *Mon* (+ night mkt Jul)
Cauterets, *Thu* (Jun–Sep)
Caylus, *Tue*
Cazaubon, *Fri*
Cazères, *Sat*
Cazuls, *Sun*
Cintegabelle, *Wed*
Cologne, *Thu*
Concots, *Sun*
Condom, *Wed*
Cordes-sur-Ciel, see Six of the Best
La Couvertoirade, *Wed, Sun* (mid-Mar–mid-Sep)

D
Daumazan-sur-Arize, *Sat*
Douelle, *Sun*
Duravel, *Sat* (+ night mkt in summer)
Durenque, *Wed*

E
Eauze, *Thu*
Entraygues, *Fri*
Espalion, *Tue, Fri*
Espère, *Sun*

F
Figeac, *Sat* (+ night mkt in summer)
Finhan, *Wed*
Firmi, *Sat*
Fleurance, *Tue*
Floirac, *Mon, Fri*
Foix, *Wed, Fri*
Le Fossat, 3rd and 5th *Thu*

G
Gaillac, *Tues, Fri, Sat*
Gimont, *Wed*
Gondrin, *Sun*
Gourdon, *Tue, Sat* (+ *Thu* Jul/Aug)
Graulhet, *Tue, Thu, Sun*
Grenade, *Sat*
Grisolles, *Wed*

I
Isle-en-Dodon, *Sat*
L'Isle Jourdain, *Sat*

L
Labastide-Rourairoux, *Thu, Sat*
Labastide-Saint-Pierre, *Wed*
Labruguière, *Fri*
Lacapelle-Marival, *Tue, Sun*
Lacaune, *Sun*
Lafrançaise, *Wed* (+ night mkt Jul)
Laguepie, *Wed* (+ night mkt Jul)
Laguiole, *Sat* (Jun–Aug)
Laissac, *Tue*
Lalbenque, truffle mkt, *Tue* (Dec–Mar)
Lamagistère, *Wed*
Lannemezan, *Wed*
Lanuejouls, *Sun*
Laroque-d'Omes, *Thu, Sat*
Lautrec, *Fri*
Lauzerte, *Wed, Sat*
Lavaur, *Sat*
Lavit-de-Lomagne, *Fri*
Lectoure, *Fri*
Leyme, *Tue* (Jul–Sep), 2nd and 4th *Tue* (Oct–Jun)
Lézat-sur-Lèze, *Sat* + 2nd *Wed*
Limogne-en-Quercy, *Sun* (truffles, *Fri*, Dec–Mar)
Lisle-sur-Tarn, *Sun*
Livernon, *Wed* (Jun–Sep)
Lourdes, daily
Loures-Barousse, *Fri*
Luzech, *Wed*

M
Marcilhac-sur-Célé, *Sun*
Marcillac, *Sun*
Marsac, *Fri*
Martel, *Wed, Sat*
Massat, 2nd and 4th *Thu*
Masseube, *Sat* (mid Jun–mid-Sep)
Le-Mas-d'Azil, *Wed*, farmers' *Sat*

Mauvézin, *Mon*
Mazamet, *Tue*, *Sat*
Mazères, *Thu*
Mercuès, *Thu*
Mielan, *Thu*
Miers, *Fri* in summer
Millau, *Wed*, *Fri* (+ night mkt
    Mon Jul/Aug)
Mirande, *Mon*, 1 Oct–30 Apr
Mirepoix, see Six of the Best
Moissac, *Sat*, *Sun* (+ night
    mkt Jul/Aug)
Molières, *Fri*
Monclar-de-Quercy, *Sat*
Monesties, *Sun*, in summer
Montaigu-de-Quercy, *Sat*
Montauban, *Wed*, *Sat* (+ night
    mkt Jul/Aug)
Montbazens, *Wed*
Montbeton, *Sun*
Montcuq, *Sun* (+ *Thu* in
    summer)
Montech, *Tue*
Montesquieu-Volvestre, *Sat*
Montréal, *Fri*
Montricoux, *Fri* (+ night mkt
    Aug)
Montredon, *Sun*, in summer
Murat-sur-Vèbre, *Sat*
Mur-de-Barrez, *Thu*
Muret, *Tue*, *Sat*
N
Nailloux, *Wed*
Najac, *Sun* (mid-Jun–mid-
    Sep)
Negrepelisse, *Tue*
Nogaro, *Wed*, *Sat*
O
Onet-le-Château, *Fri*
P
Pamiers, *Thu*, *Sat*
Pampelonne, *Sun*
Payrac, *Wed*
Pierrefitte-Nestalas, *Sat*
Plaisance, *Thu*
Prayssac, *Fri* (+ *Sun* in
    summer)
La Primaube, *Sun*
Puybrun, *Sun*
Puylaurens, *Wed*
Puy-l'Evêque, *Tue*, *Sat* (+
    night mkt in summer)
Q
Les-Quatre-Routes, *Sun*

R
Rabastens, *Sat*
Rabastens-de-Bigorre, *Mon*
Réalmont, *Wed*
Realville, *Sun*
Requista, *Mon*
Revel, *Sat* (+ foie gras
    Nov–Mar)
Rieumes, *Thu*
Rignac, *Tue*
Riscle, *Fri*
Rocamadour, nights in
    summer
Rodez, *Wed*, *Sat* (+ *Fri* nights
    in summer)
Roquecor, *Sun*
Roquecourbe, *Fri*
S
Saint-Affrique, *Sat* (+ *Thu*
    Jul/Aug)
Saint-Antonin-Noble-Val, *Sun*
Saint-Béat, *Tue*
Saint-Céré, *Sat*
Saint-Chély-d'Aubrac, *Sun*,
    Wed
Saint-Cirq-Lapopie, *Wed* in
    summer
Saint-Clar, *Thu*
Sainte-Marie-de-Campan,
    Wed
Saint-Geneviève, *Wed*
Saint-Geniez-d'Olt, *Wed*, *Sat*
Saint-Géry, *Sun*
Saint-Girons, *Sat*
Saint-Germain-du-Bel-Air,
    Fri
Saint-Jean-de-Bruel, *Thu*
Saint-Jean-du-Falga, *Wed*
Saint-Juery, *Thu*
Saint-Martory, *Fri*
Saint-Nicolas-de-la-Grave,
    Sun
Saint-Paul-Cap-de-Joux, *Tue*
Saint-Pé-de-Bigorre, *Wed*
Saint-Sernin-sur-Rance, *Wed*
Saint-Sulpice, *Wed*
Salies-du-Salat, *Mon*
Salles-Curan, *Sat* (+ *Tue* night
    Jul/Aug)
Salvagnac, *Wed*
Sauveterre-de-Rouergue,
    night mkt *Fri* (Jul/Aug)
Le-Salvetat-Péyrales, 1st *Wed*
Salviac, *Tue*, *Fri*

Saramon, *Tue*
Sarrancolin, *Tue*, *Sat*
Sauzet, *Thu*
Saverdun, *Sun*
Seissan, *Fri*
Septfonds, *Wed*
Senegas, *Sat*, in summer
Sévérac-le-Château, *Thu* (+
    night mkt, *Fri*, Jul/Aug)
Seysses, *Fri*
Souillac, *Fri*
Sousceyrac, *Thu*
T
Tarascon-sur-Ariège, *Wed*,
    Sat
Tarbes, *Thu*
Tauriac, *Wed* (late) in
    summer
Teillet, 3rd *Thu*
Trébas, *Sun*, in summer
Trie-sur-Baïse, *Tue*
Toulouse, see Six of the Best
La Tour du Crieu, *Wed*
Tournay, *Tue*
La Tronquière, *Tue*, *Fri*
U
Ussat-les-Bains, *Thu*, in
    summer
V
Vabre, *Thu*
Valence-d'Agen, *Tue* (+ night
    mkt in Aug)
Valence-sur-Baïse, *Wed*
Vaour, *Thu*
Varilhes, 2nd and 4th *Tue*
Vatrac, *Thu*, *Sat*
La Velanet, *Wed*, *Fri*
Verfeil, *Tue*
Verniolle, *Sun*
Viare, 3rd *Mon*
Vicdessos, *Thu*
Vic-Fezensac, *Fri* (+ *Wed*
    Jul/Aug)
Le Vignan, *Sun*
Vielle-Aure, *Tue*, Jul/Aug
Villefranche-de-Lauragais,
    Fri
Villefranche-de-Rouergue,
    Thu
Villemur, *Sat*, *Sun*
Villeneuve-d'Aveyron, *Sun*
Villeneuve-sur-Tarn, *Wed*, in
    summer
Viviez, *Sat*

LANGUEDOC-ROUSSILLON

The seductions of the Med's west end, espadrilles,
sunny wines and rainbow bikinis

Pépieux is a lovely sleepy little town on the edge of the Corbières vineyards, but I remember it as sleepless. It used to (and probably still does) have an amnesic church clock that repeated each hourly strike about five minutes after the first. This, as you can imagine, was a bit of a pain if you went to bed before midnight, for twenty-four resounding bongs would surely awaken even the most befuddled-by-Corbières-wine. Staying at the Hôtel du Minervois during a film shoot I, like the rest of the crew, postponed getting my head down until 00.05am. As the small hours increased, I slept more and more fitfully, only to fall deeply unconscious with exhaustion after the seven o'clock double. Suddenly, at eight, I shot bolt upright as a hooter like an aircraft-carrier's scramble alert pierced the morning. I stuck my head through the shutters. There, in the square below, was a man in a van. Pépieux's mobile market had arrived.

As we loitered, hollow-eyed, over breakfast out of doors, the van was attended by a scattering of customers. It had all the basics and some fresh farm produce – a boon for anyone living in Pépieux, but it hasn't made my 'six of the best' list for Languedoc-Roussillon. There's just too much competition.

This is the west end of the Mediterranean. Some might say the less smart end, but the smart money these days is being invested in property in the region's relatively under-developed back country where jaw-dropping Roman relics, winsome villages and historic *villes* packed with architectural treasures preside over what is now the world's largest vineyard.

Rabelais, who took a medical degree at Montpellier in 1532, wrote of the Languedoc capital's 'excellent wines and company' in his first novel. After a prolonged decline because of blight, the wines of Languedoc-Roussillon have over the last twenty years been elevated again to a state of excellence. Labels from the Corbières, the Minervois, Banyuls, Rivesaltes and Côtes du Roussillon are littered with AOCs. There are superb wines to buy and lay down, a wonderful range of sunny *vin de pays* to enjoy on the spot and the deep golden dessert wine, Muscat de St Jean, to savour or take home as a souvenir. Rarely is a display of bottles from local domaines missing from the markets.

Rabelais would be pleased – as well as delighted by the quality of the produce on offer. The coast hugs almost as much of the Mediterranean as the Riviera does and you get the same superabundance from both *mer* and *terre*; the same limitless variety of terrain, snow-dusted Pyrenees replacing the Alps. There are the rugged

peaks and pastures of the Cévennes and the high forested hills of Lozère. The blond wheatlands of Gard. The spectacular Tarn Gorges cutting through the limestone plateaux known as Causses. Dry wastes of gorse- and herb-strewn *garrigues* – rocky moorlands – descending to the Canal-du-Midi, Paul Riquet's 17th-century masterpiece of engineering. Then the undulating sea of vineyards, sometimes reaching almost to the sea itself. And, just as neighbouring Italy has influenced the Côte d'Azur, the rattle of castanets grows metaphorically louder as Languedoc-Roussillon stretches towards the Spanish border. It all dictates the cuisine, the crafts and the customs of the ancient land of Oc and the Vermilion Coast.

Specialities

Although the flat Languedoc coastal plain is less scenic than the Riviera, it has its compensations – some terrific uncrowded beaches and, of course, wonderful **seafood**. Sète operates the largest fishing fleet in the Mediterranean. Red mullet (*rouget*), tuna (*thon*) and sea bream (*daurade*) caught locally are plentiful in the cool covered markets. Superb mussels and oysters are raised in the

saltwater lagoon of Etang de Thau (Bouzigues is the name to look for, and they're best when there's an R in the month), while the **anchovies** of Collioure are rightly raved about. Try *anchoïade*, the creamy paste made from them.

You'll also see dried **salt cod** (*morue*) and, if you're lucky, *brandade de morue*,

another lovely garlicky purée redolent of the golden olive oil of Hérault. Another speciality is *La Tielle Sétoise*, a kind of sailor's Cornish pasty containing mashed octopus (or more usually mixed fish) which is for sale well beyond Sète. It's best eaten hot.

From the mountains come fine air-dried **hams** and herb-flavoured *saucissons*, also sheep's and goat's **cheeses** (*bleu du berger*, *fedou*, *pérail de brebis*) and goat's milk curd (*caille de chèvre*). Don't miss ready-made *aligot*, a moreish potato mash with cheese and garlic. In the Aude *département* they do a rather tasty black pudding and an even tastier maize-flour pancake called *millas*, which is fried then sprinkled with sugar or spread with jam. The *garrigue* produces herbs and a distinctly different honey, quite strong and smoky, while the Camargue contributes two staples no gourmet store cupboard should be without: coarse **sea salt** and Camargue **red rice**.

They make a fuss of their **sweet onions** here, and they are exceptionally good. If you see onion jam, or *confit*, pounce on it. Usually in little glass jars, this has no end of uses, not least to pep up a sandwich.

Spanish flavours become more evident the further west you go. For sweet tooths, *coupetado*, a plum and baked-custard tart, and yummy *touron*, a Basque speciality made of almond paste with pistachios, hazlenuts and fruit. The most ubiquitous savoury is undoubtedly **paella**. The best that ever rattled onto my plate was guzzled on the banks of the Canal-du-Midi near Narbonne. Making a paella is a regular star turn in markets all over the south. If you get there early, you can watch the process from the beginning: the chicken pieces being browned, then propped against the side of a vast pan. Next, leeks, onions and garlic sizzle in the middle while mussels and prawns steam in a separate casserole. The aromas are intoxicating. Is your mouth watering? That's the general idea – it's a great draw to make customers hungry and buy lots of produce and, of course, a portion of *paella*.

I've often wished I'd just brought an empty suitcase when in the south of France in summer. The bigger markets are such a good source of hot-weather clothes, shoes, espadrilles and panama hats. Also of lovely furnishings – quilts, cushion covers, curtains. Tablecloths and other accessories are often made from traditional coarse grey linen, trimmed in cream or white, and/or with subtle touches of embroidery: a wheatsheaf, an olive twig, a sprig of thyme. Provençal cottons are here too but tend to peter out as you go west where the Sardane cottons inspired by the *sardana* dance offer competition; their patterns, though also small, are in slightly more subdued shades. There's beautiful pottery, too, from plain white faïence to vibrant arty pieces and rough-hewn terracotta. And the work of local painters even reaches the markets along the Côte Vermeille where the Fauvists – Picasso, Derain and Dufy – used to prop up their easels.

Uzès (Gard)
Saturday and Sunday

Years ago, driving across the Gard towards Avignon on a chilly March evening, I arrived in Uzès at sunset when its Renaissance mansions and medieval walls were glowing like embers. I did three circuits of the town centre just to admire it. One of the first dukedoms of France, Uzès has been around since Roman times but its heyday was in the 18th century, when many fine Baroque buildings like the Eglise St Etienne were added.

I knew Uzès would have a fabulous market and it does – every Saturday morning. In full summer, it blankets the entire town. Racks of whisper-light trousers line the outer boulevards. Canopied stalls draped with soft furnishings camp like Bedouin tents. There are demos of never-stick pans and unbelievably versatile secateurs. Then the crowds thicken along the pedestrian Rue de la République, pausing at dumper displays of honey, mustard and Marseille soap, before the food stalls appear in the big arcaded square, Place aux Herbes. Here, a vendor proclaims, *'Toute la fraîcheur du sud!'* – which is what it is. A garden of vegetables, an orchard of fruit, oysters from the coast and olives from the Gard – small green *picholines* and elongated *lucques*. When I was there, the spice lady had a ready-mix (chilli, paprika, coriander, garlic) for *rouille*, the hot mayonnaise served with *soupe de poissons*. A nun in her black habit was selling wine made from *bio* grapes. And a magical clown in pointed hat was doing a graceful slow-mo turn as euros were dropped, with amazing regularity, at his pointed feet. Later, from my table at the Lou Mazet *brasserie* under the arcades, I spotted him still in costume but out of character, plodding off with a cigarette glued to his bottom lip.

Bonus, there's a big *brocante* on Sunday mornings in Boulevard Gambetta.

Don't miss

✪ Jars of honey packed with nuts.

✪ Rue de la République's wine and craft shops.

✪ Le Duché, the ducal château, behind the Hôtel de Ville, and the lofty 12th-century Tour Fenestrelle, a round belfry 42 metres high.

✪ Half-an-hour's drive away, the astonishing 48-metre high Pont du Gard, the tallest aqueduct the Romans ever built, which once channelled water from the springs at Uzès to Nîmes, 48km away. Great views from the topmost gallery or from the river looking up – especially when the Pont is floodlit.

ⓘ Chapelle des Capucins.

Somewhere to stay

↘ The comfortable Hôtel du Général d'Entraigues, a 15th-century townhouse with a small pool and outdoor dining. ☎ 04 66 22 32 68.

↘ Out of town, La Bégude, a delightful B&B in an old family house less than a mile from the Pont du Gard. ☎ 04 66 37 16 25 and 06 86 90 44 84.

Montpellier (Hérault)
Daily

The university city of Montpellier has a chemistry of its own. Although well hidden by heavy-duty commercial outskirts, the inner core's pedestrian lanes and little squares are full of architectural curiosities, classy shops and relaxed restaurants. Ricardo Bofill's neo-classical Antigone development may be of interest to design students, but traditionalists will want to stick to the area west of Place de la Comédie. In front of the opera, this airy oval is known affectionately as l'Oeuf. I sat for ages one evening on the terrace of the Café Riche, enjoying the balmy air as students argued, lovers met and the fountain played. There are at least nine different markets in Montpellier. These include a daily one in the newly restored 19th-century *halle*, a regular bargain clothes and accessories one on Place de la Comédie and another for fruit, veg and crafts on the elegant Promenade du Peyrou. But the best traditional morning food market by popular consent operates at Les Arceaux from Tuesday to Saturday. This is an 18th-century aqueduct on the west side of town, which has space to spare under its monumental arches for a mass of stalls. Montpellierain gourmets come to buy seafood from the Mediterranean (11km away), olive oil from Clermont-l'Hérault and *pélardons* and *pérails* – little goat's and sheep's cheeses – from the *garrigues*. On a July morning the air is filled with the scent of ripe melons, peaches and apricots; in autumn with the musty odour of wild mushrooms from the Cévennes or the Causses. Miss breakfast. Get there early and pick up a slice of *fougasse* or crisp *oreillettes* fritters to dip in your coffee as the locals do at one of the nearby cafés.

On Saturday mornings, Place des Arceaux incorporates a big bric-a-brac and *brocante* section.

Don't miss

✪ On Sunday mornings, La Paillade flea market next to the La Mosson stadium. Pickings are encyclopaedic and you can get there by smart blue tram.

✪ The ancient Saint Anne quarter (small antique markets here on the third and last Saturdays of the month).

✪ Beautiful 17th- and 18th-century mansions (courtyards and stairways accessible).

✪ Saint Pierre cathedral.

✪ The Mikve, ancient Jewish ritual baths.

✪ The Fabre Museum's art collection, including Dufy's inimitable sketches of the region.

✪ Les Grès de Montpellier, the local red wines.

ⓘ30 Allée Jean-de-Lattre-de-Tassigny.

Somewhere to stay

➘ Hôtel des Arceaux, friendly 2-star in a villa looking out on the Arceaux market. Quiet at night. Shady garden for breakfast. ☎ 04 67 92 03 03.

➘ Hôtel du Palais, a 2-star boutique hotel just off the tranquil Place de la Canourgue in the Sainte-Croix quarter. Good restaurant opposite – La Coquille. ☎ 04 67 60 47 38.

Sète (Hérault)

Daily except Monday

Recceing the market square in Sète before dinner, I fell in with a staffer from the local hospital eager to practise his English. 'Where's a good place to eat?' I asked. 'Follow me,' said he. On the night of a water-jousting contest (Sète is to water jousting what Wimbledon is to tennis), restaurants were filling up fast. We stopped at Chez Fanny on Quai Général Durand. Here, young Jean-Louis Magliocca had taken over where Fanny, recently retired, left off. He was offering simple *dégustations* of the freshest shellfish, homemade *aïoli*, bread and a glass of wine for a third of what you'd pay in a more formal restaurant. And it was superb – as you would expect in one of the country's biggest fishing ports. The boats come in around four or five in the afternoon and the catch of the day swiftly makes its way to the covered market (Tuesday to Saturday) on the Rue Jean-Jaurès. Here, you can have squid in pink (*encornets*) or white (*blancs de Sièche*), sardines, anchovies and mackerel from the Golfe du Lion and the freshest oysters and mussels from nearby Bouzigues (or the Atlantic in summer). On Wednesdays and Saturdays, a traditional street market surrounds the Halles. Flowers mass in Place Léon Blum, a nicely faded, plane-shaded square with a super snack/ice-cream parlour, Le Galoubet. And on Sunday mornings, there's bric-a-brac in Place de la République.

Sète has a raffish, Neapolitan air. Bisected by canals and with cargo boats, pleasure craft and trawlers at anchor, it is businesslike and even a bit scruffy. Despite this and its outlying oil refineries, I like it enormously. If you hit a night when the water jousting is on, the port atmosphere is electric.

Don't miss

○ Bouzigues. Twenty minutes away, this gem of a fishing village in golden stone has the Picpoul de Pinet vineyards rippling up behind it and the calm salt water lagoon of the Etang de Thau lapping its toes. Here, suspended from wooden frames in the shallows grow the renowned mussels and oysters of Bouzigues. They used to be bred here from embryo until hit by a blight. Now the baby oysters are transported from the west coast and farmed from September to April. Sample them in Chez Tcheppe or Chez Francine's jolly turquoise and terracotta interior.

Somewhere to stay

↘Although in a rather impersonal area a couple of miles out of town, Les Terrasses du Lido is a little oasis of tranquillity, well-run (3-chimney Logis de France) and with a pool in a walled garden. ☎ 04 67 51 39 60.

↘In Bouzigues, La Côte Bleue. Small, unassuming, modern hotel whose balconies and pine-shaded dining terrace overlook the oyster beds. ☎ 04 67 78 31 42.

Narbonne (Aude)
Daily but Sunday mornings best

The nicest way to arrive in this leafy, laid-back southern city is by water. The Canal de la Robine, an offshoot of the Canal-du-Midi, takes you through the centre and straight to market. There's a mooring actually called 'Halles' at the Pont des Marchands. Climb the steps and you're there, in front of the mammoth 19th-century glass and steel market hall whose facade sports huge sepia photographs of latterday traders. For motorists, there's underground parking at the entrance.

Narbonne's Sunday vendors line both sides of the Canal. Many seem to specialize in vividly coloured lingerie – stall after stall festooned with itsy-bitsy bras and briefs in lavender purple, fuchsia pink and citrus yellow. Chaps in charge of the minimalist stuff stand mindlessly twanging thongs in time to jangly North African music, while ample-bosomed ladies of a certain age rummage through piles of cut-price bras in double D and E. They then try cups against themselves or burrow up the back of each other's T-shirts to check sizes.

The range and quality of outerwear for sale is exceptional too – chic, cool style for both sexes. Not designer labels but unusual lines by clever fashion entrepreneurs. Soft linen shirts. Well-cut dresses. Exotic costume jewellery. Embroidered bags and Moroccan slippers. Plus lots of household items from knobbly cotton rugs to smooth white *faïence* porcelain.

Edibles, aside from things like herbs, *tisanes*, spices and pale local honey, are mostly indoors in the *halles*.

Don't miss

❂ The Roman Horreum, a 1st-century underground grain store with a mesmerizing cat's cradle of chutes.

❂ The former archbishop's palace which contains the museum of art and prehistory and the Hôtel de Ville – view it from the terrace of the cheerful Brasserie l'Agora just across the square.

❂ The city's half-finished cathedral shared by two saints, Saint Just et Saint Pasteur.

❂ 14km to the south-west, the 11th-century Cistercian Abbaye de Fontfroide in its tranquil valley.

Somewhere to stay

↘ If not waterborne, *installez-vous* 10km to the south amid the vineyards at the wine-producing Domaine de l'Hospitalet, Auberge des Vignes. ☎ 04 68 45 28 50. Good regional food to go with the house labels.

↘ The Residence, in town, offers traditional atmosphere in a 19th-century town house. ☎ 04 68 32 19 41.

Pézenas (Hérault)
Saturday

If a market looks good in winter, you can bet it will be brilliant at the height of the season. In the case of Pézenas, I have to

admit that seeing it in the company of a Renaissance man helped. Peter Glynn-Smith is not only a top interior designer, but a gifted musician, composer and painter as well as historian and bon viveur; a man of inspirational taste who, with his French wife Dominique and their children, lives just outside Pézenas. On a sharp February morning, we set out muffled in sweaters, but the warmth of their enthusiam soon made it seem like August.

Pézenas's mellow *centre historique* is full of treasures. In the 17th century, it was the winter retreat of the Barons of Lacoste. Later, the playwright Molière, failing to make his mark in Paris, came and stayed on. His first plays were performed here, and some still are on summer nights in Place Gambetta.

The Saturday market, unusually, lasts all day – 9.00 to 18.00. It stretches from one end of town to the other, filling the entire Cours Jean-Jaurès and curling round a charming fountain in the Place de la République. Even in February Pézenas's offerings were eclectic: gleaming fresh fish from Sète, crusty air-dried hams and *saucissons* from the Cévennes. Fresh oysters from Bouzigues lay in blue plastic crates, walnuts from the Lot in wicker baskets, bitter purple Calamata olives in terracotta bowls (how important the *right* container). As tantalizing aromas began to waft from a vast *paella* being cooked in situ, we moved on to the fashion department. Puffas and anoraks as far as the eye could see! In summer, said Dominique, there would be masses of expertly cut light linen outfits. Also elegant tablewear made from traditional heavy grey-beige linen.

Don't miss

○ Petits Pâtés de Pézenas, legacy of Clive of India's visit when his cooks introduced these little cotton-reel-shaped pies filled with sweet, spiced mutton – the *pâtisseries* and *boulangeries* sell them.

○ A feast of architectural detail: Gothic, Renaissance, Classical; mullioned windows, watchturrets, sinuous ironwork balconies; the cross-ribbed vaulting of the Hôtel de Lacoste's entrance courtyard and its monumental stone staircase open to the sky.

○ Favourite rendezvous, L'Anatole and the Café des Arts.

○ Les Marronniers, Avenue de Verdun, for good inexpensive food.

ⓘ Place Gambetta, the former workshop of Barber Gély with whom Molière lodged.

Somewhere to stay

○ Le Molière, a lively 2-star hotel and brasserie in Place du 14 Juillet. ☎ 04 67 98 14 00.

Collioure (Pyrénées-Orientales)

Wednesday and Sunday mornings

The French cannot quite understand the English love affair with Collioure. Perhaps because its beach is stony (like Brighton's). Perhaps because they don't consider it truly Gallic. But the raw light of this picturesque little Catalan port half an hour from the Spanish border seduced Picasso, Matisse, Derain, Dufy and Chagall. Their vivid, clashing colour palettes gave them the collective term of Fauvists, and ever since Collioure has been the haunt of artists.

The stonework of its much-painted watchtower and castle (once occupied by the Majorcan kings) is mottled like the bark of plane trees, a foil for the warm ochres of the houses in their neat streets and dappled patios. Bright primaries daub the two bays with fishing boats, yachts and pleasure cruisers. And the background is an armchair of green-fleeced Pyrenean foothills.

I love Collioure. It doesn't have an enormous market, but a selective one twice a week in a setting near the port which is as photogenic as everywhere else – Place Général Leclerc. Among local goodies, I found *panellets* (pastries made with smashed nuts and honey); mild and sharp mountain cheeses; and Les Fabuleuses Terrines d'Amélie-les-Bains – made of duck speckled with *girolles* mushrooms; quail with grapes; wild boar with cèpes; rabbit with onion *confit*.

No sign of the anchovies that earn Collioure the accolade of *site remarkable du goût* (see Don't miss), but there was a fabulous fish stall nevertheless. The *chouchou* man with his yellow cart piled with hot sugared peanuts was at the beginning of a very long day. At nearly midnight, I saw him by the beach still wearing his battered panama hat, still shovelling nuts into bags, as a Latin-American jazz group held the crowds enthralled on the terraces of the Bar Ambiance and Copacabana.

Don't miss

❂ Ets Roque, the little anchovy packing depot where four women do all the salting, filleting and conserving by hand of the tiny silvery blue fishes so intrinsic to the flavours of Catalan cooking.

❂ Les Caves du Roussillon, by the market place, for Collioure AOC labels and Banyuls apéritifs.

○ Atelier Sardane, Rue de la République, for Catalan cottons.

○ La Trémail restaurant, Rue Arago, for local specialities and fish *à la planxa* – on boards.

○ Les Templiers hotel where the Fauvists used to hang out – walls thick with paintings and ceramics.

○ Prints of Fauvist pictures outdoors where the originals were painted.

ⓘ Boulevard du Boramar.

Somewhere to stay

⭲ Le Mas des Citronniers, a modest but charming small hotel with air conditioning, on Rue de la République. ☎ 04 68 82 04 82. The only problem is parking. If the pay car parks are full, it's pot luck.

⭲ Les Templiers (see above). ☎ 04 68 98 31 10.

★ **Amélie-les-Bains** Delightful small spa in the Pyrenees known as 'Petite Provence'. Morning market on Thursdays.

★ **Béziers** To get in and out by car is tortuous, but the old centre has a lot of character and some wonderful old buildings, like the theatre at the end of the enormous tree-lined Allées Paul-Riquet. Filling this space on Friday mornings is a spectacular flower market and every first Saturday a *brocante*. Another *brocante* on Friday mornings in Place du Temple.

★ **Carcassonne** One of the signature images of the region, a fairytale almost-too-impeccably-restored walled citadel, but people do love it. In the lower town, the covered market is open daily except Monday and outdoor markets are on Tuesday, Thursday and Saturday mornings. Place Carnot for food; Boulevard Barbès for clothes, local crafts etc.

★ **Céret** Half-an-hour's drive inland from Collioure, a cheery little town famous for cherries. Has live chickens at the Saturday market and a museum with a collection of Fauvist, Surrealist and Cubist paintings. *Brocante* on Wednesday morning.

★ **Chanac** Ramparts, the King of Aragon's ruined castle, a 12th-century church and higgledy-piggledy old houses – you get the picture? Renowned for its markets on Thursday and Sunday. Don't miss the reproduction of a medieval farm – the Domaine des Champs.

★ **Langogne** On the river Allier, almost on the borders of Auvergne, this historic town has one of Lozère's best markets on Saturday mornings in and around a marvellous 18th-century market hall.

★ **Limoux** Famous for its sparkling white wine, Blanquette, and the Fécos, a carnival held since the Middle Ages which runs January to March. Limoux has a terrific flea market every first Sunday in the month except September. Weekly market Friday.

★ **Marvejols** Ancient fortified town in Lozère with spectacular gates and Renaissance houses with 17th-century wrought-iron balconies. Look out for the Beast of Gévaudan (the statue!). Saturday market offers superb work by local artisans.

★ **Nîmes** Here, an architectural bonanza awaits, from the Roman amphitheatre to a controversial Philippe Starck bus stop, from cutting-edge arts complex to old-town charm. The *halles* are open daily except Monday and there are open-air markets on Monday and Friday. Flea markets on Boulevard Jean Jaurès, Monday, and in the Parking du Stade, Sunday.

★ **Perpignan** Big city but very attractive old centre with the massive palace of the Majorcan Kings, an atmospheric Arab quarter, painted houses and palm-lined river promenades. The daily markets are good for a last minute stock-up with goodies if you're flying out of the airport here. Flea markets on Promenade des Platanes, Saturday;

Ave Palais des Expositions, Sunday morning.

★ **Port-Vendres** Markets on Place de l'Obélisque on Saturday morning all year plus farmer's market Thursdays, mid-June to mid-September. Direct-sell fish when the boats arrive.

★ **Pradès** A must if nothing else to see the beautifully preserved cloistered abbey of St-Michel-de-Cuxa, founded over a thousand years ago by Benedictine monks. It stands a little further up the Têt valley from the pink marble town, which has picturesque markets on Tuesday and Saturday.

★ **St-Eminie** In the heart of the Gorges of the Tarn, this beautiful, medieval little town with its 12-century abbey is not surprisingly on the *plus beaux villages* list. It only has a market on Thursday evenings in July and August, but the setting is all.

★ **St-Jean-du-Gard** The town where RL Stevenson finally fetched up with Modestine after his *Travels with a Donkey* through the Cévennes. It holds one of the liveliest markets in the Gard on Tuesday mornings and a *brocante* every Monday in July and August.

★ **Sommières** Small medieval town with two Romanesque churches and old-fashioned allure. Holds a great flea market every Saturday morning on the shady Esplanade by the river and fabulous night markets in summer.

★ **Villeneuve-les-Béziers** Right on the Canal-du-Midi, a perfect little town that nearly made it into the best six. Architecturally all of a piece – entirely rebuilt in the 15th century after Simon de Montfort had razed it so often it was branded 'la Crémade', 'the burnt one' (a name now appropriated by the excellent waterside pizzeria-grill, which doesn't burn anything). Villeneuve's thrice-weekly food market is minute, but its major attraction is the *marché aux puces* held in Place Farenc every Saturday and Sunday morning year round and on public holidays too.

Other significant flea markets

◎ **Alès**, Ave Carnot, Sunday morning.

◎ **Castries**, Parc du Guesse, first Sunday.

◎ **Cers**, Parking Champion, Saturday and Sunday.

◎ **L'Ille-sur-Têt**, Cours de la Gare, Sunday morning.

◎ **Lunel**, Ave des Abrivados, Saturday morning.

◎ **Méjannes-les-Alès**, Saturday.

◎ **Palavas**, Parking des Arènes, Saturday morning.

◎ **Portiragnes**, Puces de la Vitarelle, Wednesday, Thursday and Saturday.

◎ **St-Christol-les-Alès**, Place de la Mairie, Saturday morning.

◎ **Villeneuve-lès-Avignon**, Place du Marché, Saturday.

🖱 www.sunfrance.com

Markets at a glance: Languedoc-Roussillon

A

Agde, *Tue*, *Wed*, *Thu*, *Sat*, *Sun*
Aigues-Mortes, *Sun*, *Wed*
Aigues-Vives, *Mon*, *Wed*, *Sat*
Aimargues, *Sun*, *Tue*, *Fri*
Alès, daily (except *Sun*)
Alignan-du-Vent, *Wed*, *Sat*
Amélie-les-Bains, daily
Anduze, *Thu*
Aniane, *Thu*
Aramon, *Wed*
Argelès, *Wed*, *Sat* (+ daily Jul/Aug)
Argeliers, *Tue*, *Fri*
Arles-sur-Tech, *Wed*
Armissan, *Fri*
Aspiran, *Mon*, *Thu*
Aulas, *Thu* (May–Oct)
Aumont-Aubrac, *Fri*
Axat, *Thu*
Azille, *Sat*

B

Bages, *Tue*, *Fri*
Bagnols-sur-Cèze, *Wed*, *Sat*
Baillargues, *Tue*, *Fri*
Baixas, *Wed*
Balaruc-les-Bains, *Tue*, *Fri*
Banyuls-sur-Mer, *Thu*, *Sun*
Barcarès, *Wed*, *Fri*, *Sun* (+ *Mon*, *Tue*, *Thu* in summer)
Barjac, *Fri*
Bassan, *Tue*, *Fri*
Baulieu, *Wed*, *Sat*
Beaucaire, *Sun*, *Thu*
Beauvoisin, *Thu*
Bédarieux, *Mon*, *Fri*, *Sat*
Bellegarde, *Fri*
Bellpech, *Wed*
Bessan, *Tue*, *Sun*
Bessèges, *Thu*
Béziers, daily
Bezouce, *Fri*
Bizanet, *Mon*
Bolquère, *Mon*
Bompas, *Thu*
Bouillargues, *Tue*
Boujan-sur-Libron, *Thu*
Bouleternère, *Wed*
Le Boulou, *Thu*
Bourg-Madame, *Sat* (Jun–Sep)
Le Bousquet-d'Orb, *Sat*

Bouzigues, *Tue*, *Fri*
Bram, *Wed*
Breau-et-Salagosse, *Sun* (Jul/Aug)
Brouilla, *Mon–Fri*

C

Cabestany, *Thu*
Cadognan, *Tue*
Cahmborigaud, *Sat* (+ *Sun* in summer)
Calvisson, *Sun*
Candillargues, *Sat*
Canet (Herault), *Tue*, *Thu*
Canet (Pyrénées Orientales), *Tue*, *Sun*
Canohes, *Tue*, *Thu*
Cap d'Agde, *Tue*, *Wed*, *Thu*, *Sat*, *Sun*
Capestang, *Wed*, *Sun*
Caraman, *Thu*
Carcassonne, *Tue*, *Thu*, *Sat*
Carnon-Plage, *Sat* (+ *Tue*, *Thu* in season)
Castelnaudary, *Mon*
Castelnau-les-Lez, *Tue–Sat*
Castries, *Tue*, *Fri*
Caux, *Fri*
Cendras, *Tue*, *Fri*
Cerbère, *Tue*, *Fri*
Céret, *Sat*
Cers-sur-Orb, *Tue*, *Thu*, *Fri*
Cessenon, *Tue*, *Sat*
Chalabre, *Tue*, *Thu*, *Sat*
Chanac, *Thu*, *Sun*
Claira, *Wed*, *Fri*
Clermont-l'Hérault, *Wed*
Collias, *Wed*
Collioure, see Six of the Best
Colognac, *Sat* in summer
Colombières, *Wed*
Comps, *Thu*
Corconne, *Sun*
Corneilla-la-Rivière, *Wed*, *Fri*
Couiza, *Tue*, *Sat*
Cournonterral, *Wed*, *Sat*
Coursan, *Sat*
Creissan, *Tue*
Cruzy, *Tue*, *Fri*
Cuxac-d'Aude, *Tue*, *Wed*, *Thu*, *Fri*
La Canourgue, *Tue*

Le Cailar, *Fri*
Le Crès, *Sun*, *Wed*
Le Caylar-en-Larzac, *Sun*

E

Elne, *Mon*, *Wed*, *Fri*, *Sun*
Espéraza, *Thu*
Espira-de-l'Agly, *Mon*, *Thu*
Estagel, *Mon*, *Fri*

F

Fabrègues, daily except *Sun*
Fabrezan, *Tue*, *Thu*, *Fri*
Ferrals-les-Corbières, *Tue*, *Fri*
Fitou, *Wed*
Fleury-d'Aude, daily except *Sun*
Florac, *Thu*
Florensac, *Tue*, *Sat*
Font-Romeu, *Wed* (in summer/winter season)
Formiguères, *Sat*
Fourques, *Thu*
Frontignan, *Thu*, *Sat*

G

Gagnières, *Wed*
Gallargue-le-Montueux, *Tue*
Ganges, *Tue*, *Sat*
Générac, *Fri*
Générargues, *Fri*
Génolhac, *Tue*, *Sat*
Gigean, *Tue*
Gignac, *Sat*
Goudargues, *Wed*
Graissessac, *Thu*
La Grand-Combe, *Wed*, *Sat*
La Grand-Motte, *Sun* (+ *Thu* Jun–Sep)
Le Grau-d'Agde, *Thu* (summer)
Le Grau-du- Roi/Port-Camargue, daily except *Sun*
Gruissan, *Mon*, *Wed*, *Sat*

I

Ille-sur-Têt, *Wed*, *Fri*
Ispagnac, *Sat* (+ *Tue* Jul/Aug)

J

Juvignac, *Wed*

L

Lamalou-les-Bains, *Tue*
Langogne, *Sat* (+ *Tue* Jul/Aug)

Lansargues, *Tue, Thu*
Lanta, *Wed*
Lapalme, *Tue, Fri*
Laroqne-des-Albères, *Wed*
Lasalle, *Mon*
Latour-de-France, *Fri*
Lattes, *Wed, Sun*, (+ *Tue, Fri* eve in summer)
Laudun, *Mon*
Laurens, *Thu*
Lauret, *Sat*
Ledenon, *Tue*
Lespignan, *Wed*
Lézignan-Corbières, *Wed*
Lieuran-les-Béziars, *Tue, Thu*
Lignan-sur-Orb, *Thu*
Limoux, *Fri*
Lodève, *Sat* (+ *Tue* eve Jun–Sep)
Loupian, *Wed*
Luecate, *Tue, Fri*
Lunel, *Tue–Sun*

M
Le Malzieu-Ville, *Tue*
Les Mages, *Wed*
Manduel, *Wed*
Maraussan, *Tue, Fri*
Margeuritts, *Sat*
Marseillan, daily
Marvejols, *Tue, Sat*
Mauguio, *Tue, Thu, Sun*
Maureilhan, *Wed, Sat*
Maury, *Tue–Sat*
Méjannes-le-Clap, *Mon* (Jun–Sep)
Mende, *Sat*
Meynes, *Wed*
Meyrueis, *Wed*
Mèze, *Thu*
Millas, *Tue, Thu*
Mireval, *Tue, Fri*
Molières-sur-Cèze, *Sun, Fri*
Monoblet, *Sat*
Montady, *Mon*
Montarnaud, *Sun, Wed*
Montbazin, *Sat*
Montblanc, *Mon, Wed, Fri*
Montferrier-sur-Lèz, *Tue, Sat*
Montfrin, *Tue*
Montpellier, see Six of the Best

Montpeyroux, *Thu*
Montredon-des-Corbières, *Mon, Sat*
Moussan, *Thu*
Mudaison, *Wed, Sat*
Murles, *Sun*
Murviel-les-Bèziers, *Tue, Thu, Sat*

N
Nailloux, *Wed*
Narbonne, see Six of the Best
Nasbinals, *Sun* (Jun–Sep)
Nebian, *Tue, Thu, Fri*
Nezignan-l'Evèque, *Fri*
Nîmes, *Mon, Fri*
Nissan-lez-Enserune, *Tue, Thu, Sat*

O
Octon, *Thu* eve (mid-Jun–Aug)
Olonzac, *Tue*
Orsan, *Tue, Thu*
Osseja, *Thu*
Ouveillan, *Tue, Thu, Fri, Sat*

P
Palau-del-Vidre, *Tue, Thu*
Palavas-les-Flots, *Mon, Wed, Fri*
Paulhan, *Thu*
Pépieux, *Fri*
Pérols, *Mon*
Perpignan, daily
Peyriac-de-Mer, *Mon, Thu*
Pézenas, see Six of the Best
Pezilla-la-Rivière, *Tue, Fri*
Pignan, *Tue, Fri*
Pinet, *Tue*
Pollestres, *Mon, Wed, Fri*
Pomerolles, *Mon, Thu*
Pont-de-Montvert, *Wed*
Pont-Saint-Esprit, *Sat*
Portiragnes, *Tue, Thu* (+ *Mon, Wed, Sun* in summer)
Port-la-Nouvelle, *Wed, Sat*
Port-Vendres, *Sat*
Poujaut,,*Thu*
Poulx, *Wed*
Poussan, *Tue, Fri*
Pouzolles,*Wed, Fri*
Pradès, *Tue, Sat*
Prades-le-Lez, *Mon, Sat*

Puimisson, *Mon, Wed, Fri*
Puissalacion, *Tue, Fri*
Puisserguier, *Fri*

Q
Quarente, *Wed, Fri*
Quillan, *Wed, Sat*
Quissac, *Wed*

R
Raissac-d'Aude, *Wed, Thu*
Remoulins, *Fri*
Rennes-les-Bains, *Tue, Thu, Sat*
Revel, *Sat*
Rieux-Minervois, daily
Rivesaltes, *Mon*
Rodilhan, *Wed*
Roquemaure, *Mon*
Roquebrun, *Tue, Fri*
Roquefort-des-Corbières, *Wed, Fri*

S
Saint-Ambroix, *Tue* (+ *Fri* eve Jul/Aug)
Saint-André, *Thu, Sat*
Saint-André-de-Valborgne, *Sat*
Saint-Bauzille-de-Putois, *Wed*
Saint-Brès, *Tue, Sat*
Saint-Chaptes, *Thu, Sat*
Saint-Chély-d'Apcher, *Thu*
Saint-Chinian, *Thu, Sun*
Saint-Clément-de-Rivière, *Sun*
Saint-Cyprien, *Thu, Fri* (+ *Sun, Tue* in summer)
Sainte-Enimie, *Thu* eve (Jul/Aug)
Saint-Estève, *Sat*
Saint-Gély-du-Fesc, *Thu, Sat*
Saint-Geniès-des-Mourgues, *Wed*
Saint-Genis-des-Fontaines, *Mon, Fri*
Saint-Georges-d'Orques, *Wed, Sat*
Saint-Germain-du-Teil, *Fri*
Saint-Gervais-sur-Mare, *Wed*
Saint-Gilles, *Sun, Thu*
Saint-Hippolyte-du-Fort, *Tue, Fri*

Saint-Jean-de-Valériscle, *Thu*

Saint-Jean-de-Védas, *Thu, Sat*

Saint-Jean-du-Gard, *Tue*

Saint-Just, *Tue, Fri*

Saint-Laurent-d'Aigouze, *Mon, Fri*

Saint-Laurent-des-Arbres, *Fri*

Saint-Laurent-la-Salanque, *Thu, Sun*

Sainte-Marie-la-Mer, *Wed, Fri, Sat* (+ *Thu* Jul/Aug)

Saint-Martin-de-Londres, *Tue*

Saint-Martin-de- Valgalgues, *Thu*

Saint-Mathieu-de-Tréviers, *Wed, Thu*

Saint-Michel-d'Euzet, *Sun* (Jul/Aug)

Saint-Paul-de-Fenouillet, *Wed, Sat*

Saint-Pierre-la-Mer, daily

Saint-Pons-de-Thomières, *Sun, Wed*

Saint-Quentin-la-Poterie, *Fri*

Saint-Thibéry, *Tue*

Saissac, *Sun* (Jul/Aug)

Salasc, *Sun* (Jul/Aug)

Saleilles, *Mon–Sat* eve (mid-May–mid-Sep), *Mon, Wed, Fri* eve (mid-Sep–mid-May)

Salles-d'Aude, *Tue, Fri, Sat*

Salles-sur-l'Hers, *Wed*

Salses, *Wed*

La Salvetat-sur-Agout, *Thu, Sun*

Saussan, *Sun*

Sauve, *Thu, Sat*

Sauvian, *Fri*

Serignan, *Mon, Wed, Fri*

Servian, *Tue, Thu, Sat*

Sète, see Six of the Best

Sigean, *Tue, Thu*

Le Soler, *Mon, Tue, Sat*

Sommières, *Wed, Sat*

Sorède, *Tue, Fri*

Sorèze, *Fri*

Soudorgues, *Sat* (Jul/Aug)

Sumén, *Wed*

T

Tautavel, *Tue, Thu*

Tavel, *Tue*

Thézan-lès-Béziers, *Tue, Thu*

Thuir, *Sat*

Torreilles, *Tue, Fri*

Toulouges, *Tue, Fri*

Tourbes, *Wed*

Le Triadou, *Sun*

Trouillas, *Tue, Wed, Fri*

U

Uchaud, *Thu*

Uzès, see Six of the Best

V

Valflaunes, *Sun*

Vallabrègues, *Mon*

Valleraugue, *Wed* and *Sat* in summer

Valras-Plage, *Mon, Fri*

Vauvert, *Wed, Sat*

Vergèze, *Mon, Thu*

Vernet-les-Bains, *Mon, Thu, Sat*

Vézénobres, *Thu*

Vias, *Sat* (+ *Wed* in summer)

Le Vigan, *Sat*

Villefort, *Thu*

Villefranche-de-Lauragais, *Fri*

Villegly, daily (except *Sun*)

Villelongue-de-la-Salanque, *Wed, Thu*

Villeneuve-de-la-Raho, *Thu*

Villeneuve-de-la-Rivière, *Wed*

Villeneuve-lès-Avignon, *Thu*

Villeneuve-les-Béziers, *Tue, Thu, Sat*

Villeneuve-lès-Maguelonne, *Wed, Fri*

Villeveyrac, *Wed, Fri*

Vinca, *Tue, Thu*

Vingrau, *Wed*

LOIRE VALLEY

Great wines, big blonds and upside-down tarts

I have to thank a Frenchman who didn't believe in lunch (a rare animal) for my discovery of some of the Loire Valley's secret gems and, incidentally, its markets. To be fair, Hubert Tissier de Mallerais did stop for sustenance around noon, but he liked to eat light. A gentleman of the *ancien régime*, he was possessed of innate good manners, an unlikely crew cut and formidable energy. Having commissioned me to write a brochure in English for the Loire Valley, he was determined I should see as much of it as possible in the ten days allotted. There simply wasn't time for the traditional bucolic two-hour indulgence in the middle of the day. Which was just as well considering the speed at which Hubert took the corners on the D-roads as we drove from here to there. Drinking would have been disastrous.

Markets, curiously, weren't much on Hubert's agenda but on the days he went back to catch up with running the regional tourist office in Orléans, leaving me to my own devices, I stole time to include them on mine. This was some years ago. Interestingly, Loire Valley is now one of a handful of regions to actually devote a booklet – in English – to regular markets and fairs. And these deserve the spotlight, for not only are many of them blessed with superb settings in famous château towns, the quality of local produce culled from what is known as the Garden of France is impeccable.

It was the lushness of the Loire that first lured the French royals away from smelly Paris. Rumbling southwards for a couple of days in their carriages, they came for the sweetness of the country air and the thrill of the hunt, for the game, the asparagus and the mushrooms. And, as we know, so seductive were the charms of shepherdess-dotted meadows, game-filled forests and well-stocked rivers (Cher, Indre, Loiret, Eure and little Loir as well as the mighty Loire), that before long the entire court relocated here. The great castles of Chambord, Blois and Chenonceaux were built, triggering a property boom on the grandest scale as other aristos followed suit.

Today, well-heeled Parisians, who take barely more than an hour to zap down the autoroute to their weekend retreats, come for much the same reasons as the latterday upper-crust. Perhaps not for the shepherdesses, but certainly for sophisticated country living, the wines of Touraine and the superb food. Doubtless the plethora of Saturday markets in the Loire is to cash in on this influx.

Specialities

Hunting and fishing are both still significant preoccupations – especially as autumn mists wreathe the woods and lakes of the Sologne area east of Orléans, and wild geese make Peter Scott pictures in the wide skies above the Brenne marshlands. Venison, pheasant, partridge and the renowned black hazel grouse all have their season. Wild boar terrines figure on the charcuterie stand and *foie gras* is a given. Also, as in Western Loire, lake fish like *sandre* are transformed into smooth *mousses* in little glass jars – nice on something crisp for nibbles. Superb mushrooms – *girolles*, *cèpes* and fragile little *mousserons* – are harvested from the forest floor, as well as – with the aid of a good dog's expert nose – truffles.

The Loire Valley's cow's milk cheeses – Caillebotte, Frinault, St Benoist – are all worth trying but they are outnumbered by its gourmet goat's cheeses: notably, Ste Maure, with straw running through it, and the AOC Selles-sur-Cher. My favourite is Chavignol-Sancerre. One of my 'light' lunches with Hubert was taken in the dappled shade of old apple trees in the tussocky yard of a *ferme-auberge* near St-Satur. The farmer's wife brought out a simple salad of mixed leaves, this creamiest of goat's cheeses torn in chunks, pieces of fried bacon and, topping the lot, eggs *mollet* – that is, soft-boiled and shelled, so that the yolks when pierced dribbled delectably over everything and blended with the vinaigrette. Watch out for the mature version of this *chèvre* – Crottin de Chavignol. Dry, with a sludge-brown rind and powerful pong, for my liking it comes a bit too close to what it's named after (*crottin* means goat's dung).

When Catherine de Medici arrived on the scene from Florence back in the sixteenth century, her entourage included Italian pastry cooks whose elaborate confections were soon copied and, to this day, the Loire is known for its delicious **gâteaux**. Blois, particularly, is a shrine for the sweet-toothed with its exquisite *pâtisseries* and *chocolatiers*. Pithiviers conjures up those large flaky marzipan-filled pastries (called Pithiviers, of course) and Montargis the crunchy pralines devised by the Duke of Praslin. In the markets, there is more often than not a stall stacked with a tempting array of nutty florentines, feather-light macaroons and varieties of nougat. It was in this region too that one of France's most beloved fruit tarts was invented. In a little town called Lamotte-Beuvron, the Tatin sisters devised an upside-down apple pie which became known forever and throughout the land as Tarte Tatin. The market in Lamotte-Beuvron has been known to sell it.

Aside from the big-name Loire **wines** such as Bourgueil, Chinon, Vouvray, Sancerre, Pouilly-Fumé and the various Touraines, there are some not quite so well known labels worth sampling. Those of Cour-Cheverny, Montlouis, the Orléanais and Côteaux de Giennois make very easy drinking.

Lots of fruit brandies are distilled. Pears from Olivet go into Poire William *eaux de vie* and the leftovers become *poires tapées* when sun- or oven-dried and flattened with a mallet. Quinces from Orléans are turned into *cotignac*, a rather rubbery jelly that's packed in small round boxes. Joan of Arc prancing on horseback is stamped on the top of each jelly, making it look like an old-fashioned wax seal. Don't try to chew *cotignac* or you'll extract your fillings. The thing to do is lick it like a lollipop. I have to admit I find it overrated but they say Louis XV's daughters were crazy for it.

I once struggled home with a beautifully marked Ali-Baba pot from the studio of an English potter called Owen Watson whose rustic lair near Mesland was almost hidden in the undergrowth. Loire potters, weavers, stonemasons and bell-founders aren't always that hard to find and many sell their **craftwork** at markets. Keep an eye open for the pretty china made in Gien and wicker basketry from Villaine-les-Rochers. Green souvenirs are possible too; Loire Valley is full of stunning gardens large and small and their nurseries frequently send a rep to market. Rooted plants and cuttings can be brought back to the UK from other EU countries.

Six of the Best

Blois (Loir-et-Cher)

Every day except Monday and Friday

I have particularly fond memories of Blois because it was my first stop driving south on my very first visit to the Loire Valley and only my second to France. I remember parking close to its incredible château (no restrictions then) and gazing open-mouthed at Francis I's elaborate octagonal spiral stairway with his emblem, the golden salamander, entwined in the stonework. It was not until subsequent visits that I discovered the joys of Place Louis XII, where markets are held (as they have been for centuries) three mornings a week: on Tuesday, Thursday and Saturday.

The cathedral towers above, jugglers and tumblers carved in wood look down from the medieval Maison des Acrobats, and at the top of Rue Pierre-de-Blois a Gothic house sprouts a wooden footbridge which spans the road. This is the house of Denis-Papin who, in the 17th century, invented what amounted to the first pressure cooker.

Fresh produce predominates in Place Louis markets. In spring, the early strawberries (small *gariguettes*) are in abundance, in late summer cherries from Olivet. The vegetables are beautiful – pristine white onions, their roots almost as clean as their skins, white asparagus in season, the slimmest of french beans and sometimes more unusual vegetables like salsify roots, yellow tomatoes and forgotten greens. Plus all the usual marvellous fresh *fromages fermiers*, the potted meats Rabelais raved about (*rillettes* and *rillons*), thick yellow sunflower honey from the Gâtinais and, if you strike lucky, precious shreds of saffron (the Gâtinais once contributed 20 per cent of world production, now the cultivation of *Crocus sativus* bulbs is being revived).

There are other markets in Blois (Wednesday, Rue P et M Curie; Saturday afternoon, Quartier République; Sunday morning, Avenue de l'Europe) but Place Louis XII is the charmer.

Don't miss

○ Catherine de Médici's room in the château, with its painted beams, rich colours and gilding, and her 'study' next door, full of secret panels. Forget Versailles, this castle has been occupied by a series of far more fascinating rulers than the Sun King.

○ The triple-spired Saint Nicolas church.

○ Au Rendez-vous des Pêcheurs, a relaxed little restaurant with well-deserved Michelin star – Rue Foix, close to the river.

○ To-die-for *chocolatiers*, confectioners and pastry shops in Rue Denis-Papin.

○ The Poulain chocolate factory.

○ *Son-et-lumière* in the château courtyard.

ⓘ1 Avenue Jean Laigret.

Somewhere to stay

⌐ Anne de Bretagne, a spruce and cheerful small hotel close to the château. Decor rustic or rattan. No restaurant. ☎ 02 54 78 05 38.

⬐Auberge du Centre, just 10km south of Blois in Chitenay – one of the region's 'Hotels of Character'. Garden terrace. ☎ 02 54 70 42 11.

Montrichard (Cher)
Monday afternoon, Friday morning

When you want to do some serious market shopping, it's sometimes better to avoid the crush of very touristy places. The riverside town of Montrichard, although within easy range of a cluster of A-list châteaux (Amboise, Chenonceau and Azay-le-Rideau, to mention but three) is more laid-back, being less high-profile. It's also a little gem. A grid of cobblestone streets and timbered houses surrounds the Romanesque church of Ste Croix, while at the back rises a square keep in a state of romantic crumblability. Cross the bridge for the best view of it – from an imported sandy beach stretching along the banks of the Cher. From here,

swimmers and canoeists launch themselves, toddlers paddle in the shallows and picnics are spread in the shade of willows. Mark your spot, then forage for ingredients in the Friday food market (the Monday mixed market will not suffice as it is held in the afternoon, though that in itself could come in handy).

In Montrichard one brilliant September morning to do some filming for a TV travel programme, I had eyes only for the marvellous mêlée of Friday stalls in the two main squares, Places de Verdun and Général de Gaulle. There were buxom button mushrooms aptly named '*gros blonds de Touraine*', and ash-covered goat's cheeses shaped in roulades (Ste-Maure), flat rounds (Selles-sur-Cher) and inky-grey cones (Graçay). Pyramids of rosy-cheeked apples wafted cider scents, Chasselas grapes their honeyed perfume. I kept dropping such heavy hints about the looks and quality of what was on offer to the film crew that the cameraman finally gave in with a sigh. 'Oh well, I suppose we could take a few shots of the market too.' And how!

Don't miss

♻ The remains of the donjon – ruined or not, you can climb up inside for the view.

♻ Within easy reach, Amboise, Villandry and its stunning parterres, and Montrésor, one of the *plus beaux villages*, which has a 12th-century covered market abuzz on Saturday.

ⓘ1 Rue du Pont.

Somewhere to stay

↘ Bellevue, comfortable and friendly, where the restaurant and almost every room look out on the river Cher.
☎ 02 54 32 06 17.

↘ Or, a bit more special, about 24km away on the north side of the Loire, the Auberge de Launay, a rustic, creeper-clad inn among the vineyards. Generous traditional cooking.
☎ 02 47 30 16 82.

Bourges (Cher)
Saturday and Sunday

No, it isn't the best-known city in Loire country, but Bourges, capital of the deeply undulating Berry country, is one of the most relaxed and accessible. There is parking near the magnificent Gothic cathedral – a landmark that's unmissable as it is taller than Notre Dame in Paris. The archbishop's garden inevitably waylays visitors, who feel impelled to linger on its shaved lawns and admire the riotous flower beds. But press on into the historic centre via pedestrianized Rue Bourbonnoux, Place Gordaine, the market place in medieval times (wonderful wooden carvings of cabbages and grapes) and Rue Girard – all full of criss-cross timbered buildings and gorgeous shops.

At the end of Rue Girard is the splendid glass-and-steel market hall of Saint Bonnet, said to have inspired the Paris *halles*. This, on Sunday morning, shelters one of the town's two seriously big food markets. On Saturday morning, shoppers flock to the early 19th-century corn exchange (Halle au Blé) in Place de la Nation. Through the glass roof of its central courtyard, daylight bathes its groaning stalls (antique markets are also held here). Specialities to look for? Check out the chickens (*poulets Berrichonnes*), for the Berry area vies with Bresse in Burgundy to rear the tastiest poultry. It also competes with Le Puy in Auvergne to grow quality green lentils. Bourges is also somewhere to seek out that AOC goat's cheese, Crottin de Chavignol, for the farms of Sancerre where it's made aren't far away. And sweets called *forestines* are dangerously moreish: they were created by Georges Forest, the first confectioner to wrap soft centres in hard sugar coatings. If you don't find them in the market, seek out the dedicated shop, Maison de la Forestine, in Place Cujas.

Don't miss

○ The cathedral's interior whose stained glass is as glowingly crimson as Chartres's is startlingly blue.

○ The magnificent Palace of Jacques Coeur, Charles VII's treasurer, who was a whizz at feathering his own as well as the royal nest, for which Charles banished him from court (shades of Louis XIV and Fouquet) and he never got to live in his dream house. *Son-et-lumière* shows are held here in summer.

○ Under an hour's drive away: Nohant, the delightful *manoir* and garden of novelist George Sand, furnished as if she left it yesterday.

ⓘ 21 Rue Victor Hugo.

Somewhere to stay

⌐ Bourbon, a hotel within the walls of an ancient abbey. Its restaurant, Abbaye St-Ambroix, has 1 Michelin star. Hotel ☎ 02 48 70 70 00.

⌐ The Moulin de Chaméron at Bannegon, a little way south (roughly 43km) – worth any detour. Delightful 18th-century watermill, brilliant food, super swimming pool, utterly peaceful. ☎ 02 48 61 83 80.

Vendôme (Loir-et-Cher)
Friday all day

A *ville fleurie*, full of interesting nooks and crannies, the centre of Vendôme exists on islands formed by the little Loir splitting and rejoining itself, flowing under elegant bridges and trailing willows, past weathered stonework and creeper-covered terraces. No cataclysmic event has immortalized Vendôme, but it remembers local hero Maréchal de Rochambeau, the

market in Place du Marché. This is a few steps from an arm of the river and the abbey. In the morning anything goes – food, clothes, household goods, novelties. At lunchtime, the food part packs up and the rest stays. Look for unusual local wines like the AOVDQS Côteaux du Vendômois and the slightly sparkly Crémant de Loire. Also Orléans wine vinegar, and exceedingly pretty local pottery. From October to April the same covered market hosts a trade flea market every third Sunday in the month.

Don't miss

✪ Dining on Le Petit Bilboquet's terrace.

✪ The flamboyant façade of the abbey church, covered in lacy stonework.

✪ A drive along the beguiling valley of the Loir (no 'e'): countryside loved by Ronsard, the 16th-century poet who penned lines about nature, love and fleeting time. Punctuating the route are charming small towns like Lavardin, Montoire and Couture-sur-Loir.

ⓘ47–49 Rue Poterie.

great French soldier who helped the Americans win their Independence. His statue commands a *quartier* named after him. There is a ruined fortress, a fine old abbey, relaxed shopping in pedestrian streets and a glut of restaurants. The approach to Vendôme may be industrialized but this is soon forgotten.

The Friday all-day market is the one to aim for, held in and around the Quartier Rochambeau's 19th-century covered

Somewhere to stay

↘Capricorne, near the train station, a pleasant 2-chimney Logis with rooms around a garden courtyard. Simple restaurant. ☎ 02 54 80 27 00.

↘Domaine de Seillac, a 'small' château hotel half-an-hour's drive to the south, with a lake set in verdant parkland. Dogs welcome. ☎ 02 54 20 72 11.

Chartres (Eure-et-Loir)
Saturday

Chartres is more than just its cathedral windows. So many coach parties hop straight back on the bus as soon as they've seen that acreage of world-famous blue glass in what Rodin called 'the Acropolis of France', but the old-town backwaters are bliss. Cobbled streets twist downhill past timbered houses to where the river Eure flows gently in around their foundations. Gazing at humpback bridges, sagging wash-houses and a profusion of flowers brightening the shadows, you could be in a country village.

On Saturday morning, drift through the flower market in Place du Cygne to the food in Place Billard, an embarrassment of riches under a glass and steel *halle*. Both are in a pedestrianized cat's cradle of streets so the aromas don't have to compete with traffic fumes.

The bread is extra good here, coming as it does from the 'granary of France': the Beauce area where the wheat is much prized. Chartres invented the *baguette rétrodor*, an open-textured crusty loaf that is *sans additif* and tastes like bread used to. Excellent with *feuille de Dreux* cheese, not exactly a local but one that hasn't had to travel far – its chalky white surface sports a single brown leaf. You won't need bread, however, to eat *pâté de Chartres* for it is encased, like a pork pie, in a pastry crust, the pâté comprising partridge, duck, duck liver and truffles. *Une tranche* will go down very nicely with an excellent

Chartres beer as you row along the river (boats are for hire).

The traditional everything-else market (also Saturday morning) has, at the time of writing, been temporarily shifted because of 'works' to the Rue de la Poissonnerie. If it is not there when you go, check with the tourist office. And finally there are old books to browse among in an idyllic setting on Rue de la Tannérie on the banks of the Eure (Sunday also).

Don't miss

❂ Notre Dame de Chartres – as if you would – listed a World Heritage Site by UNESCO.

❂ The Centre International du Vitrail (stained glass), and the studios of various modern glass artists.

❂ The Musée des Beaux Arts.

❂ Lunch or dinner by the waterside at the Moulin de Ponceau, Rue de la Tannerie.

❂ In the *pâtisseries*, macaroons and Mentchikoffs, praline chocolates coated with white meringue.

ⓘ Place de la Cathédral.

Somewhere to stay

⭗ Money no object, Le Grand Monarque, a former post house near the cathedral. Elegant rooms, fine dining in the winter garden or on the terrace in summer. ☎ 02 37 18 15 15.

⭗ Hôtel de la Poste, a welcoming 2-chimney Logis de France, equally close to the cathedral. ☎ 02 37 21 04 27.

Aubigny-sur-Nère (Cher)
Saturday all day

For its curiosity value alone as the one-time HQ of the Stuarts, the ruling family of Scotland, Aubigny is easily a draw – it was awarded to John Stuart of Darnley during the Hundred Years War for helping Charles VII of France grapple with the English. Set on the fringes of the

Sologne's oak, birch and chestnut woods, it is a delightful town. Since I first went there, it has expanded a little, but the centre has lost none of its character. Spacious squares separate the mesh of little streets where old houses garnished with geraniums look coyly out from underneath deeply pitched roofs. A former Stuart castle is now the town hall.

The all-day Saturday market (8.30 to 18.30) has ample room to spread throughout Place Adrien Arnoux, Rue du Charbon and Rue du Prieuré. Always lively, it is especially so in autumn when shooting parties are around and game garnered from the Sologne is on offer. Mornings are reserved for local produce: freshwater fish, game terrines, ewe's milk cheeses, lovely honey – Miel de Sologne in terracotta pots – and forest mushrooms from spindly *mousserons* to the much-prized fleshy *cèpes*.

In the afternoon, a mixed selection of goods: hunters hunt for bargains among racks of gear in which to dress the part – camouflage jackets and khaki hats, wellies and waders, not to mention lethal knives, canvas hampers and seats. Aside from this, there is plenty of cheap and

cheerful fashion for all sexes and ages, sometimes including lingerie 'seconds' from the town's own factory.

Don't miss

✪ The Stuart Pâtisserie and the Auberge des Stuarts.

✪ The Maison du Bailli, one of the oldest houses.

✪ The Stuarts' grandest bit of real estate: the lakeside Renaissance Château de la Verrerie, said to have inspired Alain Fournier's novel *Le Grand Meaulnes*. Medieval Stuarts are seen galloping along the courtyard murals and on the frescoes of the chapel with its little bent steeple. Owned by the Comte de Vogüé, the château is now a very up-market *chambres d'hôtes* (see below).

✪ Within half-an-hour's drive, Gustave Eiffel's wonderful Pont Canal, enabling cruisers on the Canal Latéral to cross the River Loire at Briare.

ⓘ 1 Rue de l'Eglise.

Somewhere to stay

➴ Château de la Verrerie (see above). In one of the bedrooms, the fireplace shows the Stuart coat of arms entwined with *fleurs de lys*. ☎ 02 48 81 51 60. There's also a restaurant in a 17th-century house in the grounds.

➴ La Chaumière, a comfortable small hotel in town, all bricks, beams and tinted plaster – even in the newer annex. ☎ 02 48 58 04 01.

★ **Amboise** The most charming of Loire-side château towns, with markets on Friday and Sunday mornings. Don't miss the Manoir Clos Lucé, where Leonardo da Vinci died. IBM has created working models of his futuristic designs for a tank, swing bridge and helicopter. He is buried in the chapel of the Château d'Amboise.

★ **Azay-le-Rideau** Markets in Place des AFN on Wednesday and Place de la République on Saturday till 14.00. As the site of a favourite smaller-scale château, the town is inevitably packed in season.

★ **Beaulieu-sur-Loire** Peaceful and pretty, on the banks of the Canal-Latéral-à-la-Loire. Wednesday morning (until noon) market.

★ **Gallardon** Combine the Tuesday morning market with a visit to its little 12th-century church which has a beautiful painted wooden ceiling.

★ **Lamotte-Beuvron** Home of the Tatin sisters – a pilgrimage for lovers of Tarte Tatin. Go on Friday for the market and afterwards for lunch at Tatin.

★ **Loches** On a spur above the Indre, a delightful town with a medieval citadel (almost made my best six). In the great hall of the Château, Joan of Arc persuaded the Dauphin to go to Reims to be crowned. Markets are held on Wednesday all day (7.00–17.00) and on Saturday morning. Also, every second Sunday of the month there's a good *brocante* on Esplanade Bas-Clos.

★ **Meung-sur-Loire** Minutes off the A10 just west of Orléans, this rich little commuter town has a tiny but perfectly restored medieval centre and super restaurants. Markets Thursday afternoon and Sunday morning.

★ **Montoire** A relaxed small riverside town on the Loir. Wednesday afternoon and Saturday morning for markets.

★ **Nogent-le-Rotrou** Another appealing town west of Chartres with a market all day Saturday.

★ **Olivet** Leafy suburb/ville outside Orléans in which to start a perfect weekend. Book lunch on Friday at Le Rivage, whose terrace is lapped by the River Loiret, then do the Friday afternoon market.

★ **Orléans** Mostly rebuilt commercial hub, but usually quieter on Saturday. In the pedestrianized area to the south of the cathedral, the Halles de la Charpenterie are open Tuesday, Thursday and Saturday mornings. Also on Saturday mornings, a flea market in Boulevard Alexandre Martin.

★ **Ste-Sévère** Deep in the Berry countryside, where Jacques Tati filmed part of *Monsieur Hulot's Holiday*. Market Wednesday.

★ **Sancerre** Famous wine town on a hill with markets on Tuesday and Saturday mornings.

★ **Sully** Small fruit and vegetable market all day Monday near the fairytale castle which stands admiring its reflection in the waters of the Loire.

★ **Tours** Big city traffic, but the restored medieval centre is pleasant. Produce markets every day except Monday. Flea markets, Boulevard Béranger, fourth Sunday, and Place de la Victoire, Wednesday and Saturday.

★ **Vouvray** A must for wine-buffs. Markets on Tuesday and Friday mornings.

Other significant flea markets

◉ Chinon, Promenade Dr Mattrait, third Sunday.

◉ Châteauroux, Boulevard des Marins, first Sunday.

◉ Vierzon, Place Ancienne Mairie, fourth Sunday.

🖱 www.visaloire.com

Markets at a glance: Loire Valley

A
Les Aix-d'Angillon, *Tue, Fri*
Amboise, *Fri, Sun*
Amilly, *Sun*
Ardentes, *Thu*
Argenton-sur-Creuse, *Thu, Sat*
Argent-sur-Sauldre, *Tue*
Arthenay, *Thu*
Aubigny-sur-Nère, see Six of the Best
Auneau, *Fri*
Authon-du-Perche, *Tue*
Avoine, *Fri*
Avord, *Thu*
Azay-le-Ferron, *Wed*
Azay-sur-Cher, *Sun*
Azay-le-Rideau, *Wed, Sat*
B
Ballan-Miré, *Fri, Sun*
Baugy, *Fri*
La-Bazoche-Gouet, *Sat*
Beaugency, *Sat*
Beaulieu-sur-Loire, *Wed*
Beaumont-en-Veron, *Wed*
Beaune-la-Rolande, *Wed*
Belabre, *Fri*
Bellegarde, *Mon*
Le Blanc, *Wed, Sat*
Bléré, *Tue, Fri*
Blois, see Six of the Best
Boiscommum, *Thu, Sun*
Bonneval, *Mon*
Bonny-sur-Loire, *Sat*
Bourges, see Six of the Best
Bourgueil, *Tue, Sat*
Bracieux, *Thu*
Brezolles, *Thu*
Briare, *Fri*
Brou, *Wed*
Buzançais, *Fri*
C
Cepoy, *Wed*
Chabris, *Sat*
Chaingy, *Sun*
Chalette-sur-Loing, *Tue, Fri*
Chambray-lès-Tours, *Thu, Sun*
La Chapelle-St-Mesmin, *Sun*
Chârost, *Fri*
Chartres, see Six of the Best

Chassignolles, alternate *Wed*
Châteaudun, *Thu*
Château-la-Vallière, *Mon*
Châteaumeillant, *Fri*
Châteauneuf-en-Thymerais, *Wed*
Châteauneuf-sur-Cher, *Sat*
Châteauneuf-sur-Loire, *Fri*
Châteaurenard, *Wed*
Château-Renault, *Tue, Sat*
Châteauroux, *Sat*
Châtillon-Coligny, *Fri*
Châtillon-sur-Indre, *Wed*
La Châtre, *Sat*
Châtres-sur-Cher, *Tue*
Chécy, *Sat*
Chinon, *Thu, Sat, Sun*
Cinq-Mars-la-Pile, *Thu*
Clion-sur-Indre, *Wed*
Cloyes, *Sat*
Contres, *Fri*
Corbeilles-en-Gatinais, *Thu*
Cormery, *Thu*
Coullons, *Fri*
Cour-Cheverney, *Tue*
Courtenay, *Thu*
La Croix-en-Touraine, *Thu*
D
Deols, *Tue, Fri*
Descartes, *Thu, Sun*
Dordives, *Fri*
Dreux, *Mon, Wed, Fri, Sun*
Droué, 1st *Sun*
Dun-sur-Auron, *Sat* (mornings only in winter)
E
Ecueille, 2nd and 4th *Wed*
Eguzon-Chantome, alternate *Wed*
Epernon, *Tue, Sat*
Esvres-sur-Indre, *Sat*
F
Fay-aux-Loges, *Wed*
Ferrières-en-Gatinais, *Fri*
La Ferté-St-Aubin, *Thu*
La Ferté-St-Cyr, *Wed*
Fleury-les-Aubrais, *Tue*
Foëcy, *Fri*
Fondettes, *Wed, Sun*
G
Gallardon, *Tue*

Gidy, *Sun*
Gien, *Wed, Sat*
Gièvres, *Tue*
Graçay, *Thu*
Le Grand-Pressigny, *Thu*
La Guerche-sur-l'Aubois, *Tue*
H
Henrichemont, *Wed*
Herbault, *Mon*
Huisseau-sur-Mauves, *Sat*
I
L'Ile Bouchard, *Tue*
Illiers, *Fri*
Issoudun, *Fri, Sat*
J
Janville, *Tue*
Jargeau, *Wed*
Joué-lès-Tours, *Wed, Thu, Sat, Sun*
L
Ladon, *Sun*
Lamotte-Beuvron, *Fri*
Langeais, *Sun*
Langon, *Fri*
Léré, *Sat*
Levet, *Fri*
Levroux, *Mon*
Lignières, *Mon*
Ligueil, *Mon*
Loches, *Wed, Sat*
Lorris, *Thu*
La Loupe, *Tue*
Lourdoueix-Saint-Michel, alternate *Thu*
Luant, *Wed*
Lucay-le-Male, *Fri*
Lucé, *Wed, Sun*
Luidant, *Sun*
Lureuil, alternate *Fri*
Luynes, *Sat*
M
Maintenon, *Thu*
Mainvilliers, *Thu*
Malesherbes, *Wed, Sun*
Marchenoir, *Tue*
Mardie, *Sun*
Mehun-sur-Yèvre, *Wed*
Menetou-Salon, *Sun*
Mennetou-sur-Cher, *Thu*
Meobecq, 2nd *Thu*
Mer, *Thu*

Messas, *Wed*
Meung-sur-Loire, *Thu*, *Sun*
Mézières-en-Brenne, *Thu*
Mondoubleau, *Mon*
Montargis, *Wed*, *Sat*
Montbazon, *Tue*, *Fri*
Monthou-sur-Cher, *Wed*
Montlouis, *Thu*, *Sat*
Montoire, *Wed*, *Sat*
Mont-près-Chambourd, *Tue*
Montrésor, *Sat*
Montrichard, see Six of the Best
Monts, *Wed*, *Sat*
N
Nazelles-Négron, *Wed*
Nérondes, *Sat*
Neuillé-Pont-Pierre, *Tue*
Neung-sur-Beuvron, *Sat*
Neuvillé-aux-Bois, *Mon*
La Neuville-sur-Essonne, *Fri*
Neuvy-le-Roi, *Fri*
Neuvy-sur-Barangeon, *Tue*
Nogent-le-Roi, *Sat*
Nogent-le-Rotrou, *Sat*
Nogent-sur-Vernisson, *Thu*
Nouan-le-Fuzelier, *Wed*
Nouzilly, *Sat*
Noyer-sur-Cher, *Sun*
O
Olivet, *Fri*
Onzain, *Thu*
Orléans,*Tue*, *Thu*, *Sat*
Orsennes, alternate *Wed*
Oucques, *Wed*
Ouzouer-le-Marché, *Fri*
Ouzouer-sur-Loire, *Sun*
Ouzouer-sur-Trézé, *Sun*
P
Palluau, *Sun*
Pannes, *Sun*
Patay, *Tue*, *Sat*
Pellevoisin, *Tue*
Pithiviers, *Wed*, *Sat*
Preuilly-sur-Claise, *Thu*, *Sat*
Préveranges, *Mon*
Puiseaux, *Mon*
R
Reuilly, *Fri*
La Riche, *Wed*, *Sat*
Richelieu, *Mon*, *Fri*

Romorantin, *Wed*, *Fri*, *Sat*
S
Saint-Aigan, *Sat*
Saint-Amand-Montrond, *Wed*, *Sat*
Saint-Août, *Tue*
Saint-Avertin, *Wed*, *Sat*
Saintay, *Sat*
Saint-Benoit-du-Sault, *Sat*
Saint-Brisson, *Sat*
Saint-Cyr-en-Val, *Sun*
Saint-Cyr-sur-Loire, *Tue*, *Fri*
Saint-Denis-de-Jouhet, *Tue*
Saint-Denis-de-l'Hotel, *Sun*
Saint-Denis-des-Ponts, *Sun*
Saint-Denis-en-Val, *Sun*
Saint-Doulchard, *Tue*
Sainte-Maure-de-Touraine, *Fri*
Sainte-Sévère, *Wed*
Saint-Florent-sur-Cher, *Fri*
Saint-Gaultier, *Fri*
Saint-Genou, *Sat*
Saint-Georges-sur-Cher, *Sat*
Saint-Germain-du-Puy, *Thu*
Saint-Gervais-la-Forêt, *Fri*
Saint-Jean-de-Braye, *Fri*
Saint-Jean-de-la-Ruelle, *Wed*, *Fri*
Saint-Jean-le-Blanc, *Sat*, *Sun*
Saint-Laurent-Nouan, *Fri*
Saint-Martin-d'Auxigny, *Sun*
Saint-Paterne-Racan, *Thu*
Saint-Pierre-des-Corps, *Tue*, *Wed*, *Fri*, *Sat*
Saint-Pryvé-St-Mesmin, *Sat*
Saint-Rémy-sur-Avre, *Sat*
Saint-Satur, *Thu*
Salbris, *Thu*, *Sat*
Sancergues, *Wed*
Sancerre, *Tue*, *Sat*
Sancoins, *Wed*
Sandillon, *Sun*
Savigné-sur-Lathan, *Wed*
Savigny-sur-Braye, *Tue*
Savonnières, 1st *Fri*, *Sat*, *Sun*
Selles-sur-Cher, *Thu*
La Selle-sur-le-Bled, *Sat*
Sermaises-du-Loiret, *Thu*
Sully-sur-Loire, *Mon*

T
Tournon-Saint-Martin, *Tue*, *Fri*
Tours, daily (not *Mon*)
Trainou, *Tue*
V
Vailly-sur-Sauldre, *Fri*
Valençay, *Tue*
Vallenay, *Fri*
Varennes-Changy, *Sun*
Vatan, *Wed*
Veauges, *Fri*
Veigné, *Fri*
Vendôme, see Six of the Best
Vernouillet, *Sat*
Vernou-sur-Brenne, *Thu*
Vesdun, *Wed*
Vierzon, *Tue*, *Wed*, *Thu*, *Sat*, *Sun*
Vigoulant, alternate *Tue*
Vijon, *Mon*, alternate *Tue*
Villedieu-sur-Indre, *Wed*
Villefranche-sur-Cher, *Fri*
Villemandeur, *Tue*
Vitry-aux-Loges, *Wed*
Vouvray, *Tue*, *Fri*
Voves, *Tue*
Y
Yzeures-sur-Creuse, *Tue*, *Thu*, *Sat*

BURGUNDY

The wine Champs-Elysées, patriotic chickens and hot stuff in porcelain

Sooner or later, all *bon viveurs* gravitate to this land of *grand-cru* vineyards and grassy slopes grazed by creamy Charolais cattle. The Burgundians are among Europe's champion trenchermen. They are also great hosts and they assume that everyone is as obsessed with eating as they are. This can sometimes be ever-so-slightly wearing if you're an official guest anywhere from Nuits-St-Georges to Nevers, for trying to avoid the effects of serious overindulgence is a losing battle. The very name of Burgundy suggests corpulence. As the witty Madame de Sévigné once remarked on her return to the court of Louis XIV, 'you only have to breathe the air to get fat'. At a typical gastronomic tour-de-force dinner, I asked the enviably svelte Colette, glossy-haired queen of the regional press office, how she managed to stay so slim in the face of such temptation. Her enigmatic answer was that 'you weel not put on weight eef you only eat good food'. It hasn't done it for me.

Having said that, these days there are many chefs, even in Burgundy, who aim to dispense delicious meals with a lighter touch – like the significantly tall and willowy Jean-Pierre Senelet. At his restaurant, L'Ecusson, just outside Beaune, he sometimes arranges cookery courses. During one of these, I had the privilege of visiting Dijon market on the tails of his immaculate white coat. We went before the dawn haze had barely evaporated and it was fascinating to watch him casting a practised eye over the crates of moist fresh vegetables, looking for inspiration. He pounced on wild celery leaves. '*La saveur est très spéciale*' – stronger than ordinary celery, he explained, and this was the trigger for a memorable starter which he showed us how to prepare.

The finely chopped leaves were added with chopped hard-boiled egg to a smooth potato purée. This filled the two halves of a skinned, deseeded plum tomato. Reassembled, the tomatoes were then briefly warmed through in the oven (not cooked) and each served in a shallow dish with a spoonful of warm chicken stock laced with white wine. I can't tell you how delicate and tasty the combination was – and only vaguely fattening.

Food and wine aside, Burgundy is rich in many other things. Great abbeys, ecclesiastical treasures, stout castles with burly bastions and masterpieces of civic architecture with glittering roofs of glazed tiles. The countryside is also a joy: ramblers on foot or horseback can get lost in Morvan's vast sweep of forested hills where truffles and *cèpes* grow, while less energetic travellers go afloat on canals and navigable rivers into deeply rustic backwaters. Mind you, some canals are quite hard work – the Nivernais, for example. While it may be France's most picturesque, meandering past endless flower-decked lock-keepers' cottages, the locks themselves have to be worked manually and there are 110 on a 173-kilometre stretch. Been there, cranked the handles. Which may explain why on one particular holiday in Burgundy I managed to eat like a horse and not put on an ounce.

Where'er you roam, Burgundy's markets reflect its reputation as the 'belly of France'. In cities like Dijon, Beaune, Auxerre and Avallon, every gastronomic prize from the four corners of the country is available. In rural towns, cattle markets and live chicken markets add their sound effects to weekly gatherings of growers selling grade-A produce. And throughout the year annual fairs celebrating melons and onions, chestnuts and cherries, *cèpes* and *saucissons*, to say nothing of wine, get in on the act.

Specialities

You'll hear a lot about **Charolais beef**. It is excellent. Self-caterers, treat yourselves to a steak or make your own *boeuf bourguignon*. It's not that difficult – provided you use a good cut like sirloin, not scraps of stewing meat, which even some Burgundy restaurants try to get away with. The trouble with many iconic regional dishes is that good restaurants consider them too unimaginative for their menus and lesser ones don't do them well enough. Canned versions are often more reliable. So it is with *boeuf bourguignon* in my experience.

The **charcuterie** is outstanding: cured hams; *jambon persillé*, a melt-in-the-mouth terrine of ham with parsley in winey jelly; sausages for serving hot (*andouillettes* and *boudin*) and cold (air-dried *rosettes du Morvan* and *judru*, which is produced from free-range pigs fed on acorns and matured in *marc*). *Marc*, the spirit distilled from the lees of the wine, is used a lot in the preservation of pork, and cheese. *Tourte* is ever so calorific, a pork pâté baked in pastry, while *bresli*, a very fine air-dried beef – great with Dijon mustard – will be more to the taste of Atkins-dieters. To this protein-rich list add Bresse AOC chickens, saddles of hare, casserole-ready rabbit, pigeon and snails.

Only a few places are synonymous with one product. Dijon equals **mustard**. A legacy of the city's position on the spice route, it was long ago dubbed by the French '*un goût du diable*', a taste of the devil. Today, like the fiend himself, it comes in an infinite number of guises: from the simple *moutarde fine de Dijon* to mustard with tarragon, mustard with red berries, mustard with Marc de Bourgogne and many other variants – as well as the old-style textured grainy mustard, *moutarde à l'ancienne*. Most famously made by Maille (since 1747) and Amora (both of whom put it in those re-usable tumblers – even beer glasses), the condiment is packaged in Dijon itself in distinctive hand-painted porcelain pots. You can also buy the pots without the mustard. And if you can find a menu in Dijon without something in a sauce *à la moutarde de Dijon*, it will be a first.

Gingerbread – *pain d'épices* – dates back to the Crusades when knights took this rather dry and solid cake in their knapsacks. It appears with monotonous regularity throughout the region, though it doesn't belong only in Burgundy. I'm probably not alone in thinking a good ginger-flavoured American brownie or a slice of lovely sticky traditional English gingerbread beats it into a cocked hat. Continental tastes in this kind of cake differ fundamentally from ours. We like our cakes moist and gooey. They don't. *Tartes* and pastries, many packed with blackcurrants and flavoured with *cassis*, are another matter. These are delectable. Some of the **sweets** on offer are very nice too: *nougatines* from Nevers; Anis bonbons in old-fashioned tins from Flavigny (where the film *Chocolat* was shot); and cherries from the Yonne, which are sold both *glacés* and made into divine liqueur chocolates.

If Dijon is mustard, Burgundy itself *is* **burgundy wine**. Let's start with Bourgogne Aligoté, the essential white to make the apéritif, Kir – unless you fancy a Kir Royal, in which case it will have to be champagne. To add the blush: a hefty dash of Crème de Cassis liqueur, made from Burgundy's glut of blackcurrants. In the chalky soils of the Serein valley, the Chardonnay grape produces the most elegant white wines. From the Auxerrois, Tonnerois, Vézelay and Côte Saint-Jacques vineyards comes a full range of reds, whites and rosés, as well as Irancy and the sparkling Crémant de Bourgogne that, to me, rivals champagne at a third of the price.

Then there is the celebrated Côte-d'Or with its Route des Grands Crus, the Champs-Elysées of the wine world. In a market, you will not find stellar names such as Gevry-Chambertin, Clos de Vougeot, Meursault and Puligny-Montrachet, but they are a bonus to seek out and taste if you aim for Dijon and Beaune. The same goes for market-hopping in the Côte Chalonnaise (Rully and Mercurey), the arid Mâconnais (Mâcon, Pouilly-Fuissé) or the west of Burgundy where the smoky-edged Pouilly-Fumé, although not classed as burgundy, is also part of the region's portfolio.

Marc de Bourgogne, distilled from the lees, is the firewater. Some say the best digestif of all; to others it's paint-stripper. Whatever, it's for grown-ups.

To go with full-bodied wine, you need a **cheese** with personality. Epoisses, matured in caves for three months and washed with marc, is certainly that. Wonderful stuff. As are the deliciously creamy Brillat-Savarin and Délice de Bourgogne. Saint-Florentin, spicy yet soft and washed in brine, is akin to the vine-leaf-wrapped Soumaintrain; while Citeaux, made by the Trappist monks of the Abbaye de Citeaux, is worth talking about. There are lots of goat's cheeses of different ages and shapes, plain or rolled in ash, and a good supply of hard cheeses from neighbouring Franche-Comté because the Burgundians are keen on them. Don't miss a very moreish snack – *gougère*: cheese-pastry rings or small squares – and, if you can take it, a taste of *fromage fort*, a very whiffy fermented mix of cheese, butter, herbs and marc.

Dijon (Côte d'Or)

Tuesday, Thursday, Friday and Saturday

Even the stonework of the gourmand's capital is preoccupied with food – swags of grapes and cabbages decorate cornices and lintels, and against a backdrop of burgundy red timbering a verdigrised bronze statue of Bacchus stands out (centrepiece for the Fêtes des Vignes each autumn). Yet, surprisingly, there are only two 1-star Michelin restaurants in the city centre.

The daily food market here is as big a tourist attraction as the Palais des Ducs, and only a few minutes' walk from it. Around classic 19th-century *halles* large enough to accommodate a football pitch, the fruit and vegetable merchants lay out their staggering array with élan – competition is as keen as a butcher's knife. Clumps of whiskery chives decorate the onions, a mist of water is sporadically sprayed mid-air above spinach and lettuces to keep them crisp, tiny wild plums nestle with their leaves in a frayed grape basket.

Inside, it seems, is stashed every edible known to woman or man. Snails ready-stuffed with parsley butter, canned and bottled *coq au chambertin* and rabbit prepared in mustard sauce. Haunches of venison, trussed pigeons and whole *marcassins* (young wild pigs). At the *fromagerie*, mild Roucy in square boxes, strong Charolais, and goat's cheeses like upturned cupcakes. The gingerbread stand has slabs cut like turf to show the different variants – made with honey, whole almonds or covered in chocolate – and then there's the bonanza of everything *cassis* from little and large bottles of the liqueur to *cassissines* sweets laced with it.

Dijon exports its treats all over the world, and the world comes to Dijon. With only an hour by fast train (TGV) from Paris, even Parisian foodies come to shop here. The biggest market days are Tuesday and Friday. Thursday's is just the covered market. Every second Sunday in the month there is a *brocante* in the Quartier des Antiquaires.

Don't miss

✪ The Bistrot des Halles, Rue Bannelier, for lunch, or Chez Nous, Rue Musette, between the *halles* and Notre Dame, a real philosophers' café straight out of an Impressionist painting. The Hôtel Nord, Place Darcy, is a good bet for an authentic *boeuf bourguignon*.

✪ The Palais des Ducs, which houses the Musée des Beaux Arts (full of Flemish masters) and the tombs of the dukes who ruled both Burgundy and Flanders.

✪ The Hôtel de Vogué's magnificent tiled roof.

✪ Mulot et Petitjean, Place Bossuet, if you really like *pain d'épices* – it travels well.

✪ The Grey-Poupon mustard shop in Rue de la Liberté.

✪ On the doorstep, the Côte d'Or vineyards and the Route des Grands Crus.

ⓘ 34 Rue des Forges, itself a magnificent historic building with a Renaissance spiral staircase.

Somewhere to stay

↘ Hôtel Philippe le Bon, 15th-century mansion (now Libertel) beside the museum of Burgundian life. Contains Les Oenophiles, the restaurant of the Company of Burgundian Wine Lovers. ☎ 03 80 30 73 52.

↘ Hôtel Nord, right in the thick of things. Old-fashioned ambiance, cosy updated rooms. Cellar wine bar. ☎ 03 80 50 80 50.

Beaune (Côte d'Or)
Wednesday and Saturday

Half an hour's drive from Dijon – though more if you meander (as you should) through the vineyards instead of taking the boring main road – the old wine town of Beaune snuggles within its walls. Its outer boulevards are pleasant, and the centre, easily walkable, has the relaxed atmosphere of a village. Not, it has to be said, in peak summer season when finding a parking space is a headache – staying centrally is a must so you can wander freely through the narrow streets and choose a pavement table in the intimate Place Monge.

The Saturday market is the major event, spreading outside the market hall in the pedestrianized area almost opposite Beaune's – and Burgundy's – prime architectural attraction, the magnificent Hôtel-Dieu (see Don't miss), where the annual wine auction is held on the third Sunday in November.

This market is almost as good as Dijon's, with many of the same specialities, but on a slightly smaller scale. I remember lots of marvellous bottled fruits and a terrific selection of milky-fresh farm cheeses – try the delightfully named Claquebitou, a goat's cheese with garlic and herbs from just outside town.

Beaune is where *le Beaujolais nouveau* is launched – and where I found a rival to Crème de Cassis: a bottle of Crème de Mûres (wild blackberry liqueur) which makes a different sort of Kir – though not one, I suppose, that the French would recognize.

Don't miss

○ A proper visit to the medieval gem of the Hospices, the Hôtel-Dieu, founded in 1443. The exterior's fabulous roof, a geometric tapestry of red, green and gold glossy tiles, is one thing, but the inside is also amazing with its four-poster beds slotted in around the walls of the Great Hall of the Poor.

○ The wine museum in the Hôtel des Ducs and numerous tasting *caves* around town.

○ The 15th-century tapestries in the collegiate church of Notre Dame.

○ L'Ecusson restaurant, Place Malmédy. ☎ 03 80 24 03 82.

○ Roger Batteault's great little food shop in Rue Monge.

○ The charm of the Beaune wine villages – Meursault, Puligny-Montrachet, Aloxe-Corton and Nolay (which has a 16th-century covered market hall).

ⓘ Rue de l'Hôtel-Dieu.

Somewhere to stay

↘ Hôtel Central, in a 16th/17th-century corner mansion a few steps from the Hospices (☎ 03 80 24 77 24) with good restaurant, Le Cheval Blanc (☎ 03 80 24 69 70).

↘ Hôtel Grillon, pink house in a peaceful garden about a mile from the centre. Comfy, relaxing, easy parking. ☎ 03 80 22 44 25.

Clamecy (Nièvre)

Saturday

I shall always remember Clamecy as a high and dry haven after a very rainy day afloat with friends on the Nivernais Canal. We came to rest here just as the locks were closing and a weak sun was struggling through purple clouds. The swirling cobbles of the street that led from the moorings were drying off even as we walked uphill to the old centre. We registered with pleasure its immaculately preserved timbering, lace-trimmed windows and stone steps shortcutting to different levels. It is a charming little *ville fleurie*, the historic part almost encircled by water – the rivers Yonne and Beuvron as well as the canal – from where, until the mid-19th century, timber was floated all the way to Paris. On Bethléem bridge, you'll see a small statue of one of the *flotteurs*, the men who diced with death jumping from log to log.

It's not hard to guess the location of the Saturday morning market: it's in Rue du Grand Marché and under the splendid Halle Guise. Food, flowers, bijoux and accessories. The specialist shops put out their wares: nutty, candied fruit, chocolate-covered *confits*, *andouillettes* from the artisan butchers, *vin de pays* from the Coteaux de Tannay, and Clamecy's own hand-painted faïence. Among the cheeses, try a lovely cone-shaped goat's from nearby Lormes.

There are plenty of seductive riverbank picnic spots by medieval wash houses – or in the Parc Vauvert.

Don't miss

✪ The splendid Gothic church, part-13th century.

✪ In a wonderful old mansion, the Romain-Rolland museum, which tells you about the timber industry and charcoal production; it also has some Flemish paintings and a collection of Art Deco posters.

✪ The Faïencerie in Place de la Gravière.

✪ The tea and chocolate shop in Rue de la Monnaie.

ⓘ Rue du Grand-Marché.

Somewhere to stay

↘ Auberge de la Chapelle, in the ancient 12th-century chapel of the bishops of Bethléem – a curiosity, but quite comfortable. ☎ 03 86 27 06 21.

↘ Hostellerie de la Poste, a pleasant little Logis with good cooking. ☎ 03 86 27 01 55.

Louhans (Saône-et-Loire)

Monday

Here in the heart of Bresse country is a unique market, its *raison d'être* what the Bresse is famous for – prestigious free-range, maize-fed chickens that are the only poultry in the land to be awarded an AOC pedigree. You can admire them not plucked but in their full clucking glory, for the Marché aux Volailles each Monday morning is a sale of *live* chickens. Red combs quiver, white feathers fluff up and distinctive mauvey-blue legs dangle as sellers and buyers take the birds gently out of their crates to check they're in impeccable order – or should that be peckable? The red-white-and-blue badges they wear carry the name of their producer and silver leg bands his/her identity number. While *les poulets de Bresse* are the stars of this show, the rest of the cast is equally live and twitching: ducks, rabbits, geese, goats, sheep, cows, pigs, small dogs and even the odd horse. Don't worry, non-participants are welcome. The agricultural market in the Champ de Foire has become a big tourist attraction, drawing also a flock of traditional traders. These fill virtually every street of this small town in southern Burgundy, where the Solnan river meets the Seille. Louhans's centre is a historic monument. Its Grande Rue has the longest run of arcades in France (157 altogether). Under these mass the clothes stalls on market day. Food is in Place Général de Gaulle, craftwork in Place St-Jean, pots, pans and assorted cookware behind the church etc etc. You won't need directions.

Look out for beautiful pottery (some chicken-shaped inevitably), ceramics, wrought-iron work and straw-seated chairs from Rancy and Bantanges.

Don't miss

✪ Restaurants featuring the succulent but unfatty Bresse birds, good simply roasted with a potato gratin or most deliciously done with cream and morel mushrooms. Try Cotriade, Rue d'Alsace.

✪ The Hôtel-Dieu Museum, its apothecary and 16th-century lustre ware.

✪ Eglise St-Pierre, part 14th-century (rust-and-gold patterned roof).

✪ The Musée de l'Imprimerie (old newspaper-printing workshop).

ⓘ Place St-Jean.

Somewhere to stay

↘ Cheval Rouge, businesslike 2-star Logis, in town. ☎ 03 85 75 21 42.

↘ Moulin de Bourgchâteau, an atmospheric old mill by the Seille on the road to Chalon. Good small restaurant. ☎ 03 85 75 37 12.

Tournus (Saône-et-Loire)
Saturday

I know it's not far from Louhans (see page 193), but Tournus's Romanesque abbey is very special. And the Saturday morning market is everything it should be.

On a mad drive back to Britain from Provence, I made the mistake of stopping the night in Bourg-en-Bresse, a muddle of a place and noisy, when half an hour beyond was lovely relaxed old Tournus, lying along the banks of the Saône. With its almost Mediterranean air, it is one of southern Burgundy's nicest towns. I'd just hit the road the following morning when I came to it and couldn't resist stopping when I saw canopied stalls.

The market takes up the Rue de la République, the Place de la Hôtel de Ville and streets around. Clothes, a bit of this and that, big food section. As usual, I went looking for things local and sampled an extremely smelly goat's cheese called Chevroton de Mâcon which the *fromager* said was also known, for obvious reasons, as Boutons de Culottes (fly buttons). Gave it a miss. Settled instead for a cylinder of *chèvre frais* and some sun-ripened apricots for the journey. Then, having had no breakfast, I zoomed in on a Galette Bressane. It was so good – a kind of sugary bread dough with custardy filling – that most of it was gone by the time I'd walked round St Philibert's (see below) .

Don't miss

✪ St Philibert's 10th- and 12th-century abbey church, the most beautiful I've ever visited. Although full of massive soaring pillars and barrel-vaulting, it has an incredible lightness of being because of its simplicity and the quality of the soft pink Préty stone.

✪ The Musée Bourguignon, close by (scenes of country life).

✪ Hôtel-Dieu, housing both an apothecary and the Musée Greuze (paintings, mostly).

✪ Streets of Renaissance and medieval houses, and a plethora of antique shops.

ⓘ Place Carnot.

Somewhere to stay

⌦ Hôtel de Greuze, exquisitely renovated mansion opposite St Philibert's clock tower. No restaurant. ☎ 03 85 51 77 77.

⌦ Hôtel de la Paix, 2-star Logis de France on a quiet road leading to the river, near both abbey and market. Tasty, inexpensive food. ☎ 03 85 51 01 85.

Sens (Yonne)
Monday all day, Wednesday, Friday, plus Saturday once a month

At the beginning of Burgundy – if you're coming from Paris – this appealing old city is known to many waterway enthusiasts because of its pleasure-boat port on the Yonne. Marooned here for a week some years ago, I got to know and love its graceful heart, wealth of civic gardens and ring of shady boulevards. Once capital of a Gallo-Roman province, Sens was very powerful right up to the

17th century when its archbishop held sway even over the bishop of Paris. It has one of France's first great Gothic cathedrals and, virtually opposite, one of its most impressive 19th-century covered market halls, a kind of wedge shape which fits snugly into the space available. Here, as well as outside in Place de la République and streets hither and thither, buzzes a superb market all day Monday (food, flowers, clothes), another similar on Friday morning until 13.00, and on the Saturday on or after the 5th of the month the food counters in the market hall itself are busy again with a similar *marché bourguignon*. If you miss these, there is another food-plus market on Wednesday and Sunday morning on the outskirts of town (Promenade des Champs-Plaisants at the ZUP), but the ambiance is not so fun.

I find it hard to remember particular specialities because we ate such a lot in a week, but being within 110-odd kilometres of Paris Sens caters for sophisticated tastes. Lots of inviting pavement tables encourage malingering in the vicinity of the cathedral, their bright parasols singing out against its sombre but spectacular facade.

Don't miss

✪ The treasures inside St Etienne's cathedral (whose head stonemason rebuilt parts of Canterbury's); fabulous windows depict Thomas à Becket (the priest murdered in Canterbury) and there are relics of his vestments, as well as splendid tapestries and ivories.

✪ The pedestrianized Grande Rue and its timbered houses.

✪ Maison d'Abraham.

✪ The rose garden in the Parc du Moulin à Tan.

ⓘ Place Jean-Jaurès.

Somewhere to stay

↘ Hôtel Paris et Poste, cushy comfort in an elegant provincial-style town house. Restaurant with patio. Food good but a tad pretentious. ☎ 03 86 65 17 43.

↘ Relais de Villeroy, about 8km west of Sens, spruce little Logis in Villeroy village. Rustic dining room. ☎ 03 86 88 81 77.

Best of the Rest

★ **Autun** Established by the Romans, this southern Burgundian cathedral town is relatively quiet and untouristy, with good shops and markets on Wednesday and Friday.

★ **Auxerre** Delightful Yonne-side pleasure port with the beautiful old city rising behind, crowned by its Gothic cathedral (easy way up if you arrive by water is to take the *Petit Train*). The most appealing market is in Place Charles Surugue on Wednesday morning, others further out are on Tuesday and Friday.

★ **Auxonne** One-time fortress town on the Saône with a covered market on Friday in what was a Vauban-designed arsenal. Napoleon Bonaparte was stationed here as a young lieutenant.

★ **Brancion** Utterly charming hill village near Tournus with a huge castle, perfect Romanesque church and very old market hall, which hosts a country produce market on the first and third Sunday mornings of the month.

★ **Chablis** A wine town that needs little introduction, it stages a very typical *marché bourguignon* of local products on Sunday mornings. Lots of opportunities to taste and buy the flinty dry white at *caves* throughout town.

★ **Châtillon-en-Bazois** Tiny town on the Nivernais Canal with a 16th-century castle by the water and a super little Logis, Auberge de l'Hôtel de France. Market, Thursday.

★ **Châtillon-sur-Seine** Lots of character, lots of taste in this pleasant and leafy Seine-side town close to the border of Champagne-Ardenne. A relaxed place to go shopping – Saturday market.

★ **Cluny** Home of the Benedictines whose influence spread across medieval Europe. The ruins of the great abbey, Romanesque houses and richly endowed museum of Romanesque art are must-sees. Saturday market.

★ **Corbigny** Monday here sees one of the biggest cattle markets in Burgundy; Friday is traditional market day.

★ **Joigny** Another medieval-hearted gem on the Yonne's bonny banks with markets on Wednesday and Saturday.

★ **Meursault** This small Côte d'Or vineyard village with its rich old houses and elegant wine château has a small market on Friday. But the real attraction is the wonderful full-bodied white wine it produces.

★ **Nevers** Sizeable town on the Loire famous for ceramics. Busy markets on Tuesday, Thursday, Friday and Saturday. Flea market in Place Mossé, third Sunday in the month.

★ **Noyers-sur-Serein** Adorable medieval village with fortified gates, winding streets and museum of naive art. Small market on Wednesday.

★ **Semur-en-Auxois** Peaceful and picturesque, with big round defensive towers and a slender church spire perched above streets crammed with pretty old houses. The rock on which it's built is almost surrounded by the river Armançon. Sunday morning food market in pedestrianized Rue Buffon.

★ **Toucy** Birthplace of Larousse, who compiled the dictionary of food, this small town with a 15th-century church stages a very typical Saturday morning Burgundian market.

🖱 www.burgundy-tourism.com

Markets at a glance: Burgundy

A
Aillant-sur-Tholon, *Tue*
Ancy-la-Franc, *Thu*
Appoigny, *Mon, Sat*
Arnay-le-Duc, *Thu* eve (Jul/Aug)
Autun, *Wed, Fri*
Auxerre, *Tue, Wed, Fri*
Auxonne, *Fri*
Avallon, *Sat*
Azé, *Sun*

B
Beaune, see Six of the Best
Beaurepaire-en-Bresse, *Wed*
Bellevesvre, *Fri*
Blanzy, *Tue*
Bléneau, *Tue*
Bligny-sur-Ouche, *Wed*
Bourbon-Lancy, *Sat*
Brazey-en-Plaine, last *Wed*
Brienon-sur-Armançon, *Tue, Fri*
Brinon-sur-Beuvron, *Sun*
Buxy, *Thu*

C
Cercy-la-Tour, 2nd and 4th *Thu*
Cerisiers, *Sun*
Chablis, *Sun*
Chagny, *Sun*
Chalon-sur-Saône, *Wed, Fri*
Champignelles, *Thu*
La Chapelle-de-Guinchay, *Sun*
La Charité-sur-Loire, *Sat*
Charnay-lès-Mâcon, *Fri, Sun*
Charny, *Tue, Sun*
Charolles, *Wed*
Château-Chinon, *Sat*
Châtel-Censoir, *Thu*
Châtenoy-le-Royal, *Wed*
Châtillon-en-Bazois, *Thu*
Châtillon-sur-Seine, *Sat*
Chaufailles, *Fri*
Chemilly-sur-Yonne, *Tue, Fri*
Chenôve, *Wed, Sun*
Cheny, *Fri*
Chéroy, *Tue*
Cire-le-Noble, *Sat*
Clamecy, see Six of the Best
La Clayette, *Mon*

Cluny, *Sat*
Corbigny, *Fri*
Cosne-sur-Loire, *Wed, Fri*
Couches, *Wed*
Coulanges-sur-Yonne, *Tue*
Courson-les-Carrières, *Thu*
Cravant, *Sat*
Le Creusot, *Tue, Thu, Fri*
Cuisery, *Tue*

D
Decize, *Fri*
Digoin, *Fri, Sun*
Dijon, see Six of the Best
Dixmont, *Sun*
Domats, *Sun*
Dommartin-les-Cuiseaux, *Wed*
Dompierre-les-Ormes, 2nd and 4th *Tue*
Donzy, *Thu, Sat*
Dornes, *Wed*

E
Entrains-sur-Nohain, *Wed*
Escolives-Sainte-Camille, *Sun*

F
Flavigny-sur-Ozerain, *Sun* (Easter to Christmas)
Flogny-la-Chapelle, *Tue*
Fourchambault, *Sun*
Frontenaud, *Wed*

G
Génelard, *Sun*
Genlis, *Sat*
Genouilly, 2nd and 4th *Tue*
Gergy, *Mon*
Gibles, *Sun*
Givry, *Thu*
Guérigny, *Wed, Fri*
Gueugnon, *Thu*

I
Iguerande, *Fri*
Imphy, *Thu*
L'Isle-sur-Serein, *Wed*
Is-sur-Tille, 1st *Wed*

J
Joigny, *Wed, Sat*
Joux-la-Ville, *Tue*

L
Lessard-en-Bresse, *Tue*
Ligny-le-Châtel, *Thu*

Longvic, *Sun*
Lormes, *Thu*
Louhans, see Six of the Best
Lugny, *Fri*
Luzy, *Fri*

M
La Machine, *Sat*
Mâcon, *Sat*
Maligny, *Wed*
Marcigny, *Mon*
Matour, *Thu*
Melay, *Fri*
Mercurey, *Sat*
Mervans, *Fri*
Meursault, *Fri*
Mézilles, *Thu*
Migennes, *Thu*
Mirebeau-sur-Bèze, *Wed*
Monéteau, *Sat*
Montbard, *Fri*
Montceau-les-Mines, *Tue, Sat*
Montchanin, *Wed*
Montpont-en-Bresse, *Thu*
Montsauche-les-Settons, *Mon, Thu, Sat*

N
Neuvy-sur-Loire, *Thu*
Nevers, *Tue, Thu, Fri, Sat*
Nitry, *Wed*
Nolay, *Mon*
Noyers-sur-Serein, *Wed*
Nuits-St-Georges, *Fri*

P
Palinges, *Fri*
Paray-le-Monial, *Fri*
Perrecy-les-Forges, *Sat*
Pierre-de-Bresse, *Mon*
Pougues-les-Eaux, *Thu*
Pontailler-sur-Saône, *Sat*
Pontigny, *Thu*
Pont-sur-Yonne, *Wed, Sun*
Pouilly-en-Auxois, 2nd *Thu*
Pouilly-sur-Loire, *Fri*
Précy-sous-Thil, 3rd *Tue*
Prémery, *Tue, Sat*

Q
Quarré-les-Tombes, *Tue*
Quétigny, *Wed*

R
Ravières, *Tue*

La Roche-Vineuse, *Thu*
Romanèche-Thorins, *Wed*
Romenay, *Fri*
S
Saint-Amand-en-Puisaye,
   Mon
Saint-Benin-d'Azy, *Mon*
Saint-Christophe-en-
   Brionnais, *Thu*
Saint-Clément, *Thu*
Saint-Fargeau, *Fri*
Saint-Florentin, *Mon*, *Sat*
Saint-Gengoux-le-Nal, 1st
   and 3rd *Tue*
Saint-Germain-du-Bois, *Sat*
Saint-Germain-du-Plain, *Thu*
Saint-Honoré-les-Bains, *Tue*,
   Thu, *Sat*
Saint-Julien-du-Sault, *Thu*,
   Sun
Saint-Léger-sur-Dheune,
   Tue
Saint-Marcel, *Wed*
Saint-Martin-du-Tertre, *Sun*
Saint-Martin-en-Bresse, *Wed*
Saint-Pierre-le-Moutier, *Thu*
Saint-Pierre-le-Vieux, 1st
   and 3rd *Sat*
Saint-Saulge, *Fri* and 4th *Tue*
Saint-Sauveur-en-Puisaye,
   Wed
Saint-Valérien, *Sat*
Saint-Vallier, *Tue*, *Wed*, *Fri*
Saint-Yan, 2nd *Sat*
Salornay-sur-Guye, 2nd and
   4th *Thu*
Sanvignes-les-Mines, *Fri*
Saulieu, *Sat*
Seignelay, *Sat*
Selongey, *Sat*
Semur-en-Auxois, *Sun*
Sennecey-le-Grand, *Fri*
Senozan, *Fri*
Sens, see Six of the Best
Simandre, *Wed*
T
Tancon, *Wed* (Jun–Sep)
Tannay, *Sun*
Tonnerre, *Wed*, *Sat*
Torcy, *Wed*
Toucy, *Sat*

Toulon-sur-Arroux, 1st and
   3rd *Mon*
Tournus, see Six of the Best
Tramayes, 1st and 3rd *Fri*
V
Varennes-St-Sauveur, *Thu*
Varzy, *Thu*
Vénarey-les-Laumes, *Wed*
Verdun-sur-le-Doubs, *Thu*

Vermenton, *Fri*
Véron, *Sat*
Villeblevin, *Fri*
Villeneuve-la-Guyard, *Mon*
Villeneuve-l'Archevêque, *Sat*
Villeneuve-sur-Yonne, *Tue*,
   Fri
Vincelles, *Wed*
Viré, *Thu*

LIMOUSIN

Tapestry landscapes, magical night markets, china and chestnuts

Not without reason is Limousin known as the green heart of France. The least populated of all the regions, it presents a bewildering kaleidoscope of empty vistas – wooded pastureland, well watered valleys, thickets of chestnut forest and castles with witch's hat towers reflected in lakes. Lyrical. Fairytale even. Everywhere are scenes straight from an Aubusson tapestry.

Like Picardy, Limousin has only three *départements* and suffers the same fate of being easy to drive through with your sights set beyond its borders. Zapping down towards Cahors in the Lot, I've often bypassed Brive, one of Limousin's big market towns – and its chocolate-covered walnuts, more's the pity. Meandering east of Bergerac, I've strayed into the softly rumpled hills of Corrèze thinking I was still in Dordogne.

You must get deep into the countryside to appreciate Limousin's tranquil beauty. Those who have done so include a sizeable number of British ex-pats – farmers, artists and writers – who quietly congratulate themselves on finding a pot of gold: a life less ordinary in an authentic rural France that's still relatively undiscovered.

On an official press trip to Limoges, the famous china town and regional capital, I got my first sniff of its markets. Educationals organized by the French tourist office are notoriously short on shopping time so, when our people-carrier swerved past the city's attractive glass-roofed covered market, I begged to be allowed to pop in. On the first greengrocer's display, I spied enormous freshly picked *morilles*, or morels – my absolute favourite wild mushrooms. It's not just their earthy taste but the chewy texture of their velvety pleated caps that to me sets them apart. They spent their first night in the confines of the Espace's boot, wrapped in a paper bag. Next day, beginning faintly to advertise their presence, they were transferred to a small chestnut trug to allow the air better to circulate around them. The second night, it was politely suggested that I might take them to my hotel room – which I did, carefully arranging all seven along the cool of a marble mantelpiece. In the morning, a faint grey mould emitting a strong whiff of ammonia had begun to appear in the caps' crevices. They were given a clinical examination over breakfast and Isabelle, one of my French colleagues, broke it to me gently, 'I sink zey are over.'

It wasn't just the expense of the loss. I was going to be deprived of my treat. There was nothing for it but go back to the market to buy more. When I eventually savoured them in a creamy risotto back home, I promise you they were worth every centime.

Specialities

Earth, air, fire and water have contributed to this region's **traditional arts**: the manufacture of porcelain, enamelling, ceramics and tapestry weaving. I cannot pretend even a slightly damaged Limoges dinner service is likely to fall off a market stall (factory shops do the discounts), but this is not to say you won't find the odd old piece in the flea markets – especially in Limoges itself. The same goes for Aubusson tapestries. Rare ones may be in expensive antique shops, but the same techniques are applied today to produce a limitless flow of smart tapestry handbags, cushion covers and dandy waistcoats which do turn up at some markets, as well as tapestry kits to tempt you to do it yourself.

The art of **enamelling** is still alive and thriving. Craftspeople who make pretty artefacts and enamel jewellery bring their wares to market, especially in the summer. And there are some beautiful ceramics too.

Significantly, the power base in Limousin was once held by a group of feisty butcher families who ruled from the picturesque Rue de la Boucherie in Limoges. Today, pasture-rich Limousin still boasts some of the finest **beef** in Europe. Raised on a totally natural, hormone-free diet, the russet Limousin cattle develop thick yet tender fillets and sirloins. If you're camping or in a gîte, don't miss throwing one of these prime cuts on the barbecue. It will reawaken your tastebuds as to how good red meat ought to taste. Seeing it on the hoof at one of the special live cattle markets is pretty impressive too. Local *mairies* or

tourist information offices will tell you if there's one due in the vicinity.

Local **lamb** is of equal quality, and fresh **pork** and *charcuterie* from the cute *culs noirs* (black-bottomed) pigs are a must on the shopping list.

What you will not trip over in Limousin is a huge selection of local **cheese**. Cow's milk is generally for the calves, sheep's for the lambs. Unless there's a surplus, in which case it will be made into a simple *creusois* or *corrézon*, but in the markets most of the cheese from nearby farms is likely to be *chèvre*.

When the **red fruit** season gets under way, you'll see mountains of it everywhere – in the markets, by the roadsides. They grow strawberries for France on the hillsides of Beaulieu-sur-Dordogne, and on 11 May celebrate the Fête de la Fraise with a gargantuan strawberry tart of which all comers get a portion. The currants, gooseberries, raspberries and cherries follow on, with bilberries gathered wild from the Plâteau de Millevaches. Later in the year, it is the turn of **apples** and **plums**, along with *tartes aux pommes*, cider and apple juice, plum *eau de vie* and plum *flaugnarde*, a pudding related to the more widely known *clafoutis*, that delicious spongey dessert studded with bitter black cherries.

Naturally, local inventiveness knows no bounds when it comes to turning any glut of fruit to good use – spinning it into cakes, jams, syrups, fruit drinks and liqueurs. As for **wine**, Limousin does produce a little in the south – though nothing to get wildly excited about. Mille et Une Pierres is a pleasantly fruity country red and Beaulieu-sur-Dordogne's *vin paillé*, or straw wine, is sweet – the grapes are painstakingly dried on a bed of rye straw to produce it, but Monbazillac it

isn't. However, with Dordogne to the west and the Loire to the north, Limousin is well supplied with good labels.

No country market will fail to garner each season's **free harvest** from the surrounding forests and moorland – woodcock, pheasant and partridge, rabbit and hare, and, of course, mushrooms: chanterelles, parasols, horns of plenty, the much-sought-after ceps and truffles as well as those delicious morels. Look too for freshwater fish like rainbow trout and grayling; tench, pike and carp from the lakes; and some nice creamy fish pâtés in jars.

Walnuts are grown with singular dedication, to be sold fresh or salted for aperitifs, transformed into fragrant walnut oil and liqueurs as well as confections like the chocolate-coated temptations from Brive. **Chestnuts** are consumed in even greater quantities. One of the most enjoyable dishes I had in Limousin was a casserole of pigs' cheeks, meltingly tender, served with chestnuts as a vegetable. You can buy this ubiquitous nut puréed, made into liqueurs, brewed as beer or crystallized into delectable *marrons glacés*. But that old chestnut has another role. Haute-Vienne is the *pays des feuillardiers*: craftspeople who work in **chestnut wood**. Groves of saplings flourish like thickets of bamboo. Cut at this stage, they make hoop-work for the frames of those classic, lightweight scoop garden chairs and matching tables. Fine ribbons of wood shaved from the mature trees' trunks are woven to cover seats and table tops – or make trugs and shopping baskets as crisp as biscuits. My bet is you won't come back from Limousin without one of these heirloom *paniers* packed to the rim.

Saint-Léonard-de-Noblat (Haute-Vienne)

Nights in summer; Saturday mornings all year

Here, markets on summer nights are magical. More than just markets, they're celebrations of local food. Everyone gathers not where the regular markets are held, among the old stones of the medieval town itself, but down where the Pont de Noblat crosses the river Vienne. A banner strung aloft announces 'Marché des Producteurs de Pays' – which means farmers come not only to sell their produce direct but set up a barbecue to cook it and long communal tables for everyone to eat at.

By happy coincidence, on an August evening, I caught up with one of these jolly affairs and went shopping for my supper at the stalls. The trio of skewered lamb meatballs that I chose (one laced with chestnuts, the others with sage and ceps) hit the grill with a hiss alongside fellow diners' marbled steaks and spiced sausages. Smoke swirled and chips deep-fried as people tucked into *rillettes* and country bread for starters and opened cider that was fragrant with old varieties of apples. When I ate the entire contents of a jar of preserved *haricots verts*, my table companions were mildly amused, pointing out – rather unnecessarily – that they were cold. My response amused them even more. '*Je suis anglaise et il faut manger les légumes verts.*' (I'm English so I must have my green vegetables!)

As the light faded, midges rose from the river and dew began to fall but no one seemed to mind. Wine was shared, the *entente cordiale* deepened and when a bus crossed the viaduct above, hooting in salute, we all shouted 'Santé!' and raised our plastic cups.

Marchés des producteurs de pays (look for the green casserole logo) alight in lots of Limousin towns throughout July and August (local tourist offices have details and dates). As for Saint-Léonard, it is as noble as its name suggests and worth a stop any time (21km east of Limoges), especially for the Saturday market which throbs around its mellow 11th–13th century church.

Don't miss

✪ A proper look at the church: one of Limousin's Romanesque gems with a very fine tower and the relics of Saint Léonard.

- The Massepains *pâtisserie*, Place de la République, *the* marzipan speciality shop in Limousin.

- Sugared prunes, another local treat.

- Le Maître Pierre restaurant in its idyllic riverside location beyond the bridge.

ⓘ Place du Champ-de-Mars.

Somewhere to stay

↘ The *chambres d'hôtes* of Karen Salmon and Laurent Carayol, a Yorkshire lass and her French partner. Elegant stone country house about 3km outside town. Small children and white Pyrenean sheepdogs much in evidence.
☎ 05 55 56 90 40.

Uzerche (Corrèze)

Tuesday evenings, Saturday mornings

With its spiky array of slate-roofed turrets lording it above the river Vézère, this small, walled town rightly styles itself 'the pearl of Limousin'. Uzerche's medieval fortifications are in splendid condition – partly because they were never breached. It's said that after seven years under siege by the Moors, the townspeople offered the last of their food as a banquet to the enemy who, thinking the town was still well supplied, promptly scarpered.

What really mystifies me is why Uzerche's delights are so unknown. Strolling through almost deserted streets on a glorious August afternoon I assumed

everyone had gone for a siesta. Things do liven up for the markets, however. On Tuesday evenings in summer, the tiny Place de la Libération at the top of the citadel hosts a small *marché paysan* – a mere handful of producers but they sell quality stuff. This is the place to buy freshly made *fromage blanc*, ladled into your own pot, blueberry jam (*confiture de myrtilles*), apple juice and cider. Saturday mornings (year round) see a marvellous big mixed market fill up the Place de la Petite Gare down on the other side of the river – a lovely waterside site, by an immaculately preserved old railway station, with stunning views of the town on its rocky spur above the trees.

Don't miss

✪ The 11th–13th-century abbey church of St-Pierre crowning the summit of the town.

✪ The Porte Bécharie and the Maison Eyssartier, whose pestle-and-mortar insignia means it was once a pharmacy.

✪ Renaissance houses climbing up the hill.

✪ The Clos du Bois Doré antique shop in Ave Ch. de Gaulle for desirable *objets*, linen and lace.

✪ Out of town, great walks in the Gorges de la Vézère.

ⓘPlace de la Libération.

Somewhere to stay

➥ Hôtel/restaurant Jean Teyssier by the Pont Turgot. Tasty regional cooking, cosy rooms without frills.
☎ 05 55 73 10 05.

Limoges (Haute-Vienne)

Daily, antiques second Sunday in the month

I really like Limoges. Regarded by the French – and even the Limogeois themselves – as somewhat provincial, it is for me one of the most relaxed and user-friendly regional capitals. A little confusingly there are two centres: an old town and an older town – plus evidence of the Roman settlement below ground. The best bits are around the cobbled Rue de la Boucherie (lots of half-timbering), the cathedral and the river Vienne.

Limoges is served by several markets, but the main focus is on the 19th-century covered *halle* near the Place des Bancs. The building itself, a *tour de force* in iron and glass, has a wonderful ceramic frieze depicting the good things on sale within. The market is open from 6.00 to 13.00, every day, and is boosted from Tuesday to Saturday by an open-air food and flower market in Place des Bancs itself (5.00 to 18.00). Ready-made dishes available from the *traiteurs* in the covered market are of Michelin-star quality: look for trout with *chanterelles* in lemony butter and *magret de canard* in truffle juice. To pop in your picnic basket, try some simple *galetous* – pancake-shaped flatbreads made from wheat or rye flour that are great rolled around pâté or soft cheese.

A highlight of each month in Limoges is the *puces de la cité* which takes place near the cathedral every second Sunday. This draws enthusiastic crowds from town and around who come to browse among a cornucopia of up-market collectables. On a smaller scale, there's the last-Sunday-of-the-month's *brocante* in Marché Brousseau.

Don't miss

○ The Adrien Dubouché Museum containing exquisite porcelain collections from around the world – Meissen, Sèvres, Ming and Delft as well as Limoges's own.

○ The burnished glory of the 14th-century enamels in the Bishop's Palace, as well as some early paintings by Renoir, who was born in Limoges.

○ The Maison Traditionnelle in Rue de la Boucherie, putting life back into an old butcher's mansion.

○ The porcelain makers' factory shops, such as Bernardaud, Avenue Albert Thomas, where children can paint their own plate and bargain hunters case the seconds department.

○ Lunch or dinner at Le Pont Saint-Etienne restaurant with its view of the river, the cathedral and the handsome Romanesque Saint-Etienne's bridge.

ⓘ Boulevard de Fleurus.

Vieille is taken over on Thursdays either by a marvellous *brocante* or a market for *produits du terroir*. You can try checking which happens when with the tourist office, but they may not know with any degree of accuracy. Better to rely on serendipity, the art of making happy discoveries by accident.

The Thursday I dropped by, it was the *brocante* – one of the best I've come across. All Limousin's yesterdays, from last century to last week, shaken out into the corners of the old *quartier*'s most picturesque street – vintage clothes and rusty warming pans, china and chairs, lanterns and buttons. A wind-up gramophone played Jacques Brel while a mini-*quincaillerie* of antique secateurs, scythes and vices drew virtuous handymen. The familiar market habitués were there too – the ammonite sellers,

Somewhere to stay

↘Royal Limousin, Place République. Smart, modern, comfortable and central. Charming staff. No restaurant. ☎ 05 55 34 55 21.

Aubusson (Creuse)
Thursdays in summer for fleas and farm produce, Saturday mornings all year

The tapestry capital is surprisingly small, with an attractive old town and a rather anonymous newer centre. Throughout July and August, the meandering rue

the girl demonstrating the non-stick pan that needs no lubricant and the man with the wooden toy trains that trail letters spelling names. No threadbare tapestries, but a great little shop on the sidelines called Pêle Mêle which sells covetable leather-trimmed tapestry shoulder bags in traditional and animal prints, fleur-de-lys purses and stacks of cushion covers.

The regular Saturday morning market is large and all-embracing but in a less appealing venue on the edge of town. On Wednesday evenings in July and August, a smaller produce market gathers in the *centre ville* in front of the *mairie*.

Don't miss

✪ The Musée Départemental de la Tapisserie's fascinating contrasts, from

16th-century mythical landscapes, inhabited by winged beasts, griffons and unicorns, to the bold colours and striking themes of modern designs.

✪ The long-established Manufacture St Jean, where traditional tapestries are still woven and mended.

✪ The 16th-century Maison du Vieux Tapissier, which recreates an early workshop.

✪ Charming patches of the old town like Grande Rue and the Vieux Pont over the river Beauze.

Somewhere to stay

↘ Hôtel du Lissier, Grande Rue. Small and friendly with a well-patronized restaurant. ☎ 05 55 66 14 18.

↘ Château de la Chassagne, a 'tapestry' idyll near St-Hilaire-le-Château. 15th–17th century mansion in 12-acre park. Five enchanting *chambres d'hôtes de prestige*. ☎ 05 55 64 55 75.

Beaulieu-sur-Dordogne (Corrèze)
Wednesday and Saturday mornings

The name says it all – a really beautiful village on the banks of the Dordogne, its back snuggled against a wooded hill and a chapel with a 12th-century belfry mirrored in the river. In its heart, around a Benedictine abbey that is softly illuminated at night, wind half-timbered streets of houses with wooden balconies, dovecotes and flowers in every niche.

People wander by the quais, canoe, fish and even swim in the river which, at this point, is wide, calm and clear. Or they take trips in the *garbares* – reconstructions of the lighters that used to ply the route to Bordeaux. With its mild microclimate, Beaulieu has been dubbed the Limousin Riviera.

This is where the strawberry fête takes place in May, but Beaulieu's regular markets are a feast. The Saturday one is the bigger, taking over the centre of town. Few of the gastronomic goodies on offer have had to travel far so they are in a state of perfection whatever the season: *foie gras*, golden corn-fed chickens, honey, milky *chèvre*, mounds of fresh fruit, home-made compôtes and jam. Look out for a moreish potato and onion tart, *pâté de pommes de terres*, which will make a fine lunch with a glass of light Cabernet/Merlot from the nearby Branceilles vineyards. You have to at least try the sweet *vin paillé*. Although unremarkable on its own, with a slice of *gâteau de noix*, it slips down without protest.

On Monday evenings in summer, Beaulieu also hosts a *marché des producteurs de pays*, from 17.00 to 20.00 outside the penitents' chapel.

Don't miss

✪ The enamel shrine and 12th-century virgin and child in the St Pierre abbey church treasure room.

✪ The Chapelle des Pénitents, which houses a small museum about local life.

✪ Collonges-la-Rouge, a classified *plus beau village* within easy reach; built entirely of deep sunset-coloured sandstone, it is unique in Limousin.

ⓘ Place Marbot.

Somewhere to stay

↘ Central Hôtel Fournié, in a lovely setting by the river. Bib Gourmand restaurant. ☎ 05 55 91 01 34.

↘ Hôtel la Turenne, near the church. Traditional ambiance, spacious rooms. ☎ 05 55 91 10 16.

Bourganeuf (Creuse)
Wednesday morning

Bourganeuf's fat, conical copper towers appear deceptively as if in a hollow as you drive along the N141 between Aubusson and Limoges, but the town is halfway up – or down – the hill which falls away to the Thaurion Valley. From the market place in Place du Mail, a classic walled terrace under pollarded plane trees, you have a balcony view of the lovely open countryside undulating away to the north. Casting its welcome shadow on a warm morning is the massive round 15th-century Tour de Zimzim, part of a priory that once belonged to the Knights of Malta in which, it's said, the brother of a sultan was once kept prisoner.

During recent restoration of the tower, the market was moved to the Place du Champ de Foire below but by now should be back in its proper place. Here you can buy superb fresh produce – even fish from the Atlantic coast – as well as Creusois specialities such as wholewheat baguettes, cakes made with chestnut flour or hazelnuts (*gâteau le creusois*) and superb *tarte aux myrtilles* (blueberry pie) in season (July to September). Cantal cheese from nearby Auvergne is often available too and free-range geese and ducks are sometimes still alive and quacking. Bourganeuf is charming, a laid-back little town with lots of antique shops, good places to eat and a pleasant main square to linger in – Café le Central does terrific ice-creams.

Don't miss

✪ A peep at the church with the turquoise door beside the Mairie: Eglise Saint-Jean. It is special, 12th–15th century, with a plain blue cupola, frescoes on the apse and stained glass above the door which is set on fire by the afternoon sun.

✪ The museum of electrification, should this turn you on!

✪ Les Milles Sources, *produits du pays* shop, Rue de la Résistance.

ⓘ Rue Billadour.

Somewhere to stay

↘ Hôtel du Thaurion, not in Bourganeuf itself, but a few miles towards Aubusson in the village of St-Hilaire-le-Château. Well-run, atmospheric old inn whose 'Bottin Gourmand' restaurant offers *saveurs du terroir*. ☎ 05 55 64 50 12.

Best of the Rest

- ★ **Arnac-Pompadour** Nice small town with stalwart château built originally by Louis XV for Madame de Pompadour, who never set foot in it. It is now part of the National Stud. Good markets Saturday mornings and second and fourth Wednesdays in the month.

- ★ **Bellac** Wednesday and Saturday morning markets are especially lively if the regular fair coincides (every 1st of the month) in this otherwise peaceful small town in Haute-Vienne.

- ★ **Bort-les-Orgues** The 15th-century Château du Val on an islet in Lake Bort is one of Limousin's definitive sights – with its six machicolated towers, it is straight out of *Lord of the Rings*. Saturday-morning market in the village.

- ★ **Boussac** Very pretty town, a favourite of writer George Sand. She used to stay in the tapestry-filled château and set many of her novels in the surrounding landscapes – where, later, the painter Claude Monet gleaned inspiration too. Thursday market.

- ★ **Brive** Big market town where the core of the Tuesday, Thursday and Saturday markets shelters under a modern vaulted wooden roof dedicated to the singer George Brassens. Old quarter has an animated buzz and chic restaurants, shops and cafés. There's a coals-to-Newcastle touch about the museum which displays eight English tapestries from Mortlake.

★ **Châlus-Chabrol** On Friday mornings (except the second Friday in the month), vendors cluster in and around a smart new wooden-covered market on the edge of this little town famous for its chestnut weaving. Chestnut wattle fences a rose garden below the spot where Richard the Lionheart was slain by a bolt hurled from the top of the spectacular keep – all that remains of Châlus's fortress. Lunch at the welcoming Auberge Richard Coeur de Lion is an affordable treat.

★ **Felletin** Hugely popular market on Friday mornings in this appealing historic town which is as preoccupied with tapestry-making as nearby Aubusson. Lots of galleries and workshops to visit, a beautiful church and the Château d'Arfeuille.

★ **Guéret** Capital of the Creuse and one of the most attractive larger towns. Super bric-a-brac market once a month from October to June (for dates, call 05 55 41 14 32). Regular markets: Thursday and Saturday. La Senatorerie, a superb museum of decorative arts, is housed in a former private mansion in a lovely park.

★ **Rochechouart** Highlights are its massive château and museum of contemporary art. Markets on Tuesday, Friday and Saturday.

★ **St-Junien** A 12th-century Collegiate adorns this charming town which is renowned for making couture leather gloves. Look for bargain pairs at the regular Saturday morning market as well as direct from the warehouse.

★ **St-Yrieix-la-Perche** Bustling little place with charming river walks and a porcelain museum. The ancient monastery where pilgrims halt en route to Compostela harbours fabulous gold relics. Morning market first and third Saturday in the month.

★ **Ségur-le-Château** One of the *plus beaux villages*, full of timbered houses huddled below a romantic ruin. Monday evening (17.00–20.00) *marché des producteurs de pays* throughout July and August.

★ **Treignac** Another official *plus beau village*, though more a walled town. Perched above the Vézère and crowned by the imposing Château de Combon, it has markets on Tuesday and Saturday mornings. The sweet-toothed shouldn't miss the Comptoir du Chocolat.

★ **Tulle** Much rebuilt after 1944 destruction, Tulle is largely modern and busy, but it has excellent markets on Wednesday and Saturday in Places Gambetta and Smolensk, and on Sundays in Place Albert Faucher.

🖱 www.tourismelimousin.fr

Markets at a glance: Limousin

A
Ahun, *Wed*
Aixe-sur-Vienne, *Fri, Sat*
Allassac, *Fri*
Ambazac, *Fri*
Argentat, *Thu, Sat*
Arnac-la-Poste, 7th of month
Arnac-Pompadour, *Sat*, 2nd and 4th *Wed*
Aubusson, see Six of the Best
Auzances, *Tue*
Ayen, 2nd and 4th *Sat* (+ *Thu* eve Jul/Aug)

B
Beaulieu-sur-Dordogne, see Six of the Best
Bellac, *Wed, Sat*
Bénévent-l'Abbaye, *Tue*
Bersac-sur-Rivalier, *Wed*
Bessines-sur-Gartempe, *Sun*
Beynat, *Sat* (+ *Tue* eve Jul/Aug)
Bonnat, *Sat*
Bort-les-Orgues, *Sat*
Bourganeuf, see Six of the Best
Boussac, *Thu*
Brive, *Tue, Thu, Sat*
Bussière-Dunoise, 16th of month
Bussière-Poitevine, *Tue, Thu, Sat*

C
Châlus-Chabrol, *Fri* (but not 2nd *Fri*)
Chambon-sur-Voueize, *Wed*
Champagnac-la-Rivière, *Tue*
Chartrier-Ferrière, *Wed* eve (Jul/Aug)
Châteauponsac, *Fri, Sat*
Châtelus-Malvaleix, *Fri*
Clugnat, *Wed*
Corrèze, *Sun* (Jul/Aug)
La Courtine, 2nd *Sat*
Couzeix, *Sat*
Crocq, 1st and 3rd *Sun*

D
Donzenac, *Thu*
Le Dorat, *Wed, Fri*
Dournazac, 1st *Sun* (summer)

Dun-le-Palestel, *Thu*
E
Égletons, *Sun*
Évaux-les-Bains, *Mon*
Eymoutiers, *Sat*
F
Faux-la-Montagne, *Mon* (Jul/Aug)
Felletin, *Fri*
Feytiat, *Sat*
G
Genouillac, *Tue*
Gouzon, *Tue*
Grand-Bourg, 2nd and 17th of month
Guéret, *Thu, Sat*
J
Jarnages, 4th *Thu*
La Joncherre-Saint-Maurice, *Sat*
L
Laurière, *Tue*
Limoges, see Six of the Best
Linards, 1st *Sat*
Lupersat, 2nd and 4th *Sun* (every *Sun* in summer)
M
Magnac-Bourg, *Wed*
Magnac-Laval, *Thu*
Mainsat, 4th *Sat*
Malemort, *Sun*
Merlines, *Thu*
Meymac, *Wed* eve (Jul/Aug)
Meyssac, *Tue, Fri*
Mezières-sur-Issoire, 2nd *Mon, Thu*
Monceaux-sur-Dordogne, *Thu* eve (Jul/Aug)
N
Nantiat, *Tue, Sat*
Neuvic, *Wed*
Nexon, 3rd *Fri*
Nieul, 2nd *Sat*
O
Objat, *Sun*
Oradour-sur-Vayres, *Thu*
P
Le Palais-sur-Vienne, *Sun*
Panazol, *Sun*
Perpezac-le-Noir, *Wed*

Peyrat-le-Château, *Tue, Thu, Sat, Sun* (+ daily Jul/Aug)
Peyrilhac, 3rd *Sun*
Pierre-Buffière, *Fri*
Pontarion, 1st *Fri*
R
Rilhacrançon, *Sat*
Rochechouart, *Tue, Fri, Sat*
Royère-de-Vassivière, *Tue*
S
Saint-Étienne-de-Fursac, *Fri*
Sainte-Féréole, *Thu* eve (Jul/Aug)
Sainte-Fortunade, *Fri* eve (Jul/Aug)
Saint-Georges-la-Pouge, 1st *Tue*
Saint-Junien, *Sat*
Saint-Léonard-de-Noblat, see Six of the Best
Saint-Maurice-la-Souterraine, 3rd *Sun*
Saint-Pardoux, *Wed* (Jul/Aug)
Saint-Pardoux-Corbier, *Wed* eve (Jul/Aug)
Saint-Privat, *Wed* (Jul/Aug)
Saint-Sulpice-Laurière, *Fri*
Saint-Sulpice-les-Champs, *Thu*
Saint-Yrieix-la-Perche, 1st and 3rd *Sat*
Sardent, 3rd *Fri*
Ségur-le-Château, *Mon* eve (Jul/Aug)
Seilhac, *Sun*
Sereilhac, *Wed, Sun*
Soursac, *Sun* (Jul/Aug)
La Souterraine, *Thu, Sat*
T
Treignac, *Tue, Sat* (+ *Fri* eve Jul/Aug)
Tulle, *Wed, Sat, Sun*
U
Ussel, *Sat* (+ *Tue* eve Jul/Aug)
Uzerche, see Six of the Best
V
Vallière, 2nd *Thu*
Vigeois, *Thu*
Voutezac-le-Saillant, *Tue* eve (Jul/Aug)

AUVERGNE

Sleeping volcanoes, lively water, AOC lentils and donkey sausages

Had the *Lord of the Rings* movies not employed a Kiwi director determined to shop-window the landscapes of his native New Zealand, Auvergne would have been a mean contender for the backgrounds in Tolkein's epic tale. As dramatic as its neighbour Limousin is gentle, this region in the Massif Central would satisfy anyone in search of scenic grandeur. It is big country where extinct volcanoes loom, high ridges and limitless plateaux suddenly plunge into ravines, rushing rivers tumble and oak forests peter out at the edge of silver lakes. Add Gothic castles straight out of Mordor and rural idylls reminiscent of the Shire, and you'll be in the picture.

Another literary giant, RL Stevenson, started from here when he took his four-footed friend Modestine south towards the Cévennes. I'm sure the book about their journey would have been just as eventful if he and the donkey had stayed in Auvergne and headed instead for the great volcanic sweeps of Puy-de-Dôme or Cantal. These days, little Levades donkeys with hikers in tow are ubiquitous, as are – somewhat disconcertingly – donkey *saucissons* in the markets. No potential source of food is ever unexploited by the French.

I took a while to get around to Auvergne but am now making up for lost time. I love it, and I like the straightforward, no-nonsense Auvergnats. Rarely under pressure from too many tourists, they give you an especially warm welcome and leap to your aid if you exhibit the slightest furrow of concern. Circling Clermont-Ferrand in search of my hotel late one evening, I kept passing the same café. On the third lap, when I stopped the car in its reflected glow to peer at my street map three young men swiftly abandoned their beers to offer advice. Market traders are extra chatty too when they register a foreign accent, so it's a particular pleasure to buy from them, and the markets themselves are as varied and packed with distinctive local produce as in any region whose economy is based largely on agriculture.

You will not find a more rewarding part of *la France profonde*. As well as its great outdoors, over which you can hike, ride, balloon or hang-glide, there are state-of-the-art spas, urban sophistication and a treasure-trove of early Romanesque art and architecture. Pockets of heavy industry do exist but are soon dwarfed by the wide and wild open spaces, the forest, the fertile pastureland and the vineyards of the Bourbonnais, cradle of the French monarchy.

Specialities

You will eat well and heartily. Away-from-home Auvergnats so hanker after the cuisine of their homeland that almost every French city from Paris to Pau has its Auvergnat restaurant or specialist food shop. Restaurants in the region displaying the 'Toques d'Auvergne' sign are good bets if you want to enjoy typical ingredients and dishes, but creating your own simple meals from market buys is particularly easy and fun.

Meat from the Salers cattle that roam the Aubrac plateau is becoming even more desirable than that of Charolais. It is more marbled, with the fat lightly flecked through the flesh – *persillé*, as they say in French – and many contend this gives Salers **beef** a better flavour and texture. Seeing it on the hoof is a pleasure in itself, for the handsome beasts have dark red coats and huge harp-shaped horns. If you see wheat-coloured cows, those are Aubracs. They produce superb beef too. Neither meat-

eating 'rosbifs' nor Texan ranchers – nor even gauchos from Argentina – will fail to be impressed by a seared Salers or Aubrac steak with a dollop of Auvergne's own Charroux grain mustard.

Cantal **lamb** is good too – it's the traditional Easter Sunday roast.

There's a wonderful scent that infuses the air after dark in deeply rural parts of France – it hits you whenever you step into the open and sniff: there's a bit of old cork in it, and moist leaves, but mostly smoke from wood-stoked ovens. It's very prevalent in Auvergne, for here, in *charcuterie* land par excellence, smoking is a regular habit. So is air-drying. The result is huge haunches of ham and an endless variety of *saucisson* – the most versions I've seen on any one market stall is twenty-two. They included goat, donkey, bull, ostrich and wild boar. Some were flavoured with cheese such as Bleu d'Auvergne and Comté, others with wine, hazelnuts and bilberries – my personal favourites. A sceptic might be tempted to guess one or two of the more exotic labels owe more to promotion than truth, but you can certainly see the nuts and the bilberries.

The French don't generally have a passion for **pulses**, but passionate they are around Le-Puy-en-Velay where lentils have been awarded an AOC. A major local earner, the small dark green Le Puy lentils, grown on rich volcanic soil, have a lovely earthy flavour and nutty texture and are bagged in nice style.

Cheese picks up an impressive quota of AOCs too: the famous five being Bleu d'Auvergne, Saint-Nectaire, Salers, Fourme-d'Ambert and Cantal. Creamy Tomme, also from Cantal, may not have the magic letters but is the essential ingredient of much-loved *aligot*. I have only to whisper the name of this purée of potato and cheese to my Auvergnate friend Christine to watch her go misty-eyed. You can buy pre-prepared *aligot*. Ditto other moreish dishes like *truffade* (cheese and pork) and *pounti*, a pork terrine with prunes and beet leaves in it.

Vichy and other bottled waters are commonplace at home. Vichy *pastilles*, on the other hand, make pretty presents in their attractive tin boxes. Sweet, minty and refreshing, they lack the seductive edge of Moulins's Palets d'Or luxury chocolates, but they'll probably travel better.

Thiers has carved itself a small slice of history by producing quality **cutlery** for over five centuries. Keep an eye open for great kitchen knives on hardware stalls, as well as the sleek and sharp Thiers folding knife which rivals the Laguiole of Aveyron. It's known as the 'crime of passion' knife, so that gives you a fair idea of its efficacy.

On a softer theme, fine baskets are woven from hazelnut wood, straw, chestnut, wicker and even bramble. Le Puy lacemakers are still active in creating fine cotton lace, and Ambert makes exquisite pure rag paper, decorated with inserts of flowers and leaves.

As with all landscapes where people have learned to occupy themselves in lonely, isolated places, there is an abundance of **craftwork** in wood, stone, glass and wrought iron. The Allier *département*'s tourist offices have a useful booklet, *La Route des Métiers*, which points you in the direction of talented artisans based in the Livradois-Forez regional nature park. Many take their work to markets throughout the region.

The grapes that grow in Auvergne are not what they used to be – they're better. This was once one of the most important wine-growing regions – in fact the Saint-Pourçain vineyards in the Bourbonnais are the oldest in France. After the phylloxera epidemics, the industry has made a big comeback. Bourbonnais wines are still the classiest, mainly white but there are fruity reds and rosés too. Côtes d'Auvergne are also good – look for Madargue, Châteaugay, Chanturgue, Corent and Boudes. All sorts of sweet and bitter apéritifs are made from herbs, gentian root and verbena, and any number of liqueurs emanate from chestnuts, cherries, bilberries and other fruits.

Bourbon-l'Archambault (Allier)
Saturday morning

A name that resonates – and not just for connoisseurs of Southern Comfort. In the northern part of Auvergne, this was the seat of the Bourbon dukes whose dynasty took over the throne of France. After the royals were done away with, Napoleon III was among those who came to Bourbon-l'Archambault to take the waters. Its spa dates back to Roman times and is Auvergne's oldest. Dominated by the fat round towers of the Bourbons' ruined medieval fortress, the town today is a charming base from which to explore the well-wooded Bourbonnais countryside, its numerous castles and the Saint Pourçain vineyards, a landscape of lyrical perfection which often features in period French films.

Bourbon-l'Archambault is more special than its covered market (19th-century) but when this comes to life on Saturday mornings (Place du Marché Couvert) it adds to the town's appeal. On the first Saturday of each month, a much larger mixed outdoor market occupies Place de l'Hôtel de Ville. This is well worth targeting, for as well as food (specialities such as *foie gras*, Bourbon pâté, *pompe aux grattons* – savoury lardy buns – and honey bread), you can get really nice craftwork: wrought-iron pot stands and mirror frames, wooden jigsaws, paintings on silk, mohair knits, etcetera. Because of the spa connection (it's still thriving), plant-based oils and other beauty products figure too. Picnic in the

delightful Allées Montespan near Les Thermes – or in the municipal gardens where there's an attractive public swimming pool.

Don't miss

✪ The picturesque streets of the old town.

✪ The museum of Augustin Bernard with its collection of blue-and-white pharmacy pots.

✪ Saint Georges' church, an enlarged Benedictine chapel with a rich interior and some superbly jewelled reliquaries.

✪ Les Thermes.

✪ Out of town, the Souvigny Priory, where the Bourbons are entombed.

ⓘ Les Thermes building.

Somewhere to stay

↘ Grand Hôtel Montespan-Talleyrand. Who could resist sending a postcard from here? Mme de Sévigné, as was her wont, sent letters. Talleyrand and Mme de Montespan too. Surprisingly, the charms of the hotel's three disparate ancient buildings are not as pricey as the name implies. Bib Gourmand food. Heated pool.
☎ 04 70 67 00 24.

Clermont-Ferrand (Puy-de-Dôme)

Monday to Saturday (Wednesday and Saturday best), first Sunday flea market

Clermont-Ferrand is a major hub, a pleasant, airy, largely modern city. In the centre, the immense Gothic spires of its black lava cathedral soar above an expanse of red rooftops, while beyond on the skyline you can see the Puy-de-Dôme, the volcanic peak that gives its name to the *département*.

In the mesh of old streets hugging both the cathedral and the stout Romanesque basilica of Notre Dame du Port, an intriguing mix of shops sells naughty underwear, nice pastries, lace, puppets and postcards of local hero Monsieur Bibendum (the Michelin tyre company was founded here in 1830). In this area too is Place du Marché St-Pierre, where a good daily (except Sunday) food market throbs in a functional covered hall: a sure source of typical Auvergne products – cheese, *charcuterie*, chestnut liqueur, bilberry tarts. Look out also for black soap, pink garlic from Billom and crunchy hazelnut *nougatins*. For lunch, the adjacent Brasserie Daniel Bath is a good booking.

However, the market that draws crowds to Clermont-Ferrand is the enormous flea market that alights in Place du Premier Mai at the top of Avenue de la République on the first Sunday of every month. Prices are favourably lower than Paris or Provence and the range is just as all-embracing, from toy soldiers to antique chests fashioned from Tronçais forest oak.

Place St-Victoire, on the south flank of the cathedral, makes a magical setting for the Christmas market (most of December) with lights festooned among the trees and around Pope Urbain the Second's fountain.

Don't miss

- ✪ The tiered black lava Fontaine d'Amboise.
- ✪ Renaissance houses in the placid streets of Montferrand.
- ✪ Church interiors: especially of the 12th-century Notre Dame du Port, a remarkable basilica with crumbly early sculptures and a wonderful raised choir. The cathedral, considered to be the finest Gothic edifice in Auvergne, is a bit doomy but its stained glass is superb (they say it's from the same workshop as Sainte-Chapelle's in Paris).
- ✪ A trip to the top of the Puy-de-Dôme. Hike it, coach it, or ascend the spiral whirl after 6pm in your own car, but do go to see the magnificent panorama of the sleeping volcanoes, the Chaîne des Puys, each extinct crater's hollow accented by sun and shadow.

ⓘ Place de la Victoire.

Somewhere to stay

- ➘ Arverne, a modern 3-chimney Logis with the cathedral and the Puy-de-Dôme in your sights from the breakfast area's roof terrace. ☎ 04 73 91 92 06.
- ➘ Château de Codignat – somewhere to spoil yourself. East of Clermont-Ferrand, in the tiny hamlet of Bort-l'Etang near Lezoux, this 14th-century castle surrounded by lakes is one of the most romantic Relais & Châteaux hotels. Pool. ☎ 04 73 68 93 54.

Langeac (Haute-Loire)

Tuesday and Thursday mormings

An unassuming small market town that has quietly gone about its business for over seven hundred years, Langeac is poised on the brink of my favourite bit of Auvergne – the wild gorges of the upper Allier. In an open patch of the valley, this is a likeable place with an old château and a convent but no particularly riveting focal point. However, it puts on a corker of a market twice a week in and around its collegiate church, Saint Gal.

Streets named after forges, tanners and butchers are clues to the market's *raison d'être* in times past – to serve local farmers who came to buy and sell their animals, have their horses shod and stock up on clothes and supplies. It's still full of sensible gilets and fishing tackle, balls of string and Thiers knives (for which Langeac supplies whetstones cut from the grey boulders of Chadernac

and Chambarret). But nowadays there's plenty to interest passing tourists as well – sports gear for rafters and hikers, souvenir earrings and ashtrays made of basalt, paintings on wood. The farm produce is tops – great cheeses, whole hams and home-baked tarts filled with bilberries, cherries, apples or pears, whatever's in season. *Fougasse*, the fruit-studded brioche – especially good in Auvergne – is an ideal calorific reward after outdoor effort, as is potato pie and the elusive *potée auvergnate*. This last is a gutsy peasant dish of *saucisse*, cabbage and potatoes which many restaurants are becoming too sniffy these days to serve, more's the pity. Langeac is the kind of place you might find it, if not sizzling in the market, perhaps on a local menu.

Don't miss

✪ Maison du Jacquemart with its painted walls, lace-making tableaux and the story of Langeac's artifical pearls.

✪ All the joys of the Allier gorges and their hinterland – the village of Lavaudieu, its stained glass centre and beautiful Romanesque cloister; La Chaise-Dieu and the Danse Macabre murals; Brioude's fabulous old cobbled church; Chanteuges Abbey; the tiny chapels of St Ilpize on its rocky spur and Ste-Marie-des-Chazes in lonely isolation by an Allier towpath, where she watches canoeists careering past on the fast-flowing water.

ⓘ Place Aristide Briand.

Somewhere to stay

⬊ Les Deux Abbesses, 10 minutes out of Langeac. A unique hotel which has reinvented the entire perched village of St-Arcons-d'Allier, where bright hollyhocks waver against dark lava stone buildings. Main reception areas occupy the château and rooms are the village houses. ☎ 04 71 74 03 08.

⬊ Le Val d'Allier, comfortable, convenient and efficient Logis in Reilhac, a few kilometres north of Langeac. ☎ 04 71 77 02 11.

Le Puy-en-Velay (Haute-Loire)

Wednesday and Saturday, plus Thursday evening mid-July to August

Pilgrims' point of departure on the Way of Saint James to Compostela, Le Puy could never be mistaken for any other town. Three extraordinary volcanic cones stick up like birthday candles to give the townscape its arresting profile. On one basalt stack is a shrine, on another a chapel and the third is crowned by a massive Virgin and Child made from cannons melted down after the Battle of Sebastopol. The infant is cradled, curiously, on the right. The story goes that when the sculptor discovered his mistake he threw himself from the top of it. Miniatures of this statue are – predictably – sold as souvenirs, and I have memories of a rather kitsch dessert into which a chocolate Madonna was thrust feet first. As mirth bubbled up in us like spa water, we wondered which would be the less sacrilegious: to bite her head or her toes off first.

Saturday is a double whammy in Le Puy, with both a terrific local-produce market and a *brocante* in adjoining squares. Make for the Hôtel de Ville. The action takes place in Place du Clauzel in front of it and in Place du Plot at the rear. Around Plot's ancient fountain, artisan farmers cluster to sell eggs, honey, bilberry syrup, summer fruits or autumn mushrooms. Clucks and squawks advertise the presence of live chickens, and cuddly rabbits twitch ears and whiskers. Cheese-wise, the famous blues are upstaged by the hand-made farmers' offerings, like an exceptionally good Tomme du Pays from the village of St-Jean-Lachalm. Sacks of AOC Puy lentils are unmissable.

Place du Clauzel does the bric-a-brac as well as some craftwork – sometimes painted sun-dials, biscuit-coloured pottery and enamelled stoneware – plus racks of bargain fashion, footwear and hats. There's a restored 19th-century market hall with more gourmet food shops close by.

Don't miss

✪ The Chapelle St-Michel d'Aiguilhe, on its narrow pillar of rock, built by Bishop Gothescalk in 962 after leading the first Compostela pilgrimage.

✪ The fabulous Romanesque cathedral and its Black Madonna.

✪ The cloister, reckoned to be among Europe's most beautiful.

✪ New lace shops, old lace collections in Musée Crozatier, and the Atelier-Conservatoire National de la Dentelle where it is still made.

✪ Bright green and yellow liqueurs – Verveine and Gentiane.

✪ Smart interiors and fashion shops in Rue Pannesac.

✪ Le Bistrot, small, friendly eatery near the market.

ⓘ Place du Breuil.

Somewhere to stay

➘ Le Val Vert, modest but comfortable, with a striking view of the city stacks from the restaurant. ☎ 04 71 09 09 30.

➘ Le Moulin de Mistou, about 40 minutes away at Pontempeyrat, Craponne-sur-Arzon – the first ever Logis de France, now run by Bernard Roux and his lovely wife. Idyllic, peaceful riverside location. Fishing. Pool. Super food (Toque d'Auvergne). ☎ 04 77 50 62 46.

Salers (Cantal)

Wednesday

High up in the Cantal mountains, where the air is heady and the sense of space intense, Salers merits its place among the exclusive company of France's *plus beaux villages*. Medieval, with both walls and roof tiles of sturdy, sombre stone, pepperpot turrets and Romanesque treasures within and without, it is a fascinating little town. However, it's more than just a pretty face; Salers is also a *'Site Remarkable du Goût'*, celebrating its splendid cattle and AOC cheeses. In Wednesday morning's local produce market, the stars are massive blocks of grey-crusted, pale-hearted Cantal – *jeune*, *entre-deux* or *vieux* – and the firm, slightly sharper Salers, matured in cellars for three months to a year. Two superb cheeses to savour at the end of a meal with some red fruit or an apple and a few nuts. *'Goûtez, goûtez,'* the *fromager* will insist, cutting you not a sliver but such a sizeable chunk to taste that you'll then feel obliged to buy at least half a kilo. It's an old trick!

Big amber bottles of local-recipe gentian apéritif are also labelled Salers, as are scrumptious square shortbready biscuits called *carrés de Salers*. In addition, you may find *fouaces* baked with chestnut flour, *bourriols* (pancakes) made with buckwheat flour, as well as golden farm butter and, in season, blackberry jams and huge dappled parasol mushrooms.

Don't miss

⊙ The Musée du Fromage de la Vache.

⊙ The belfry with its clock and twirly weather vane.

⊙ Eglise St-Mathieu's marvellous *tableau vivant*, a coloured relief of characters grouped round the tomb of Christ – their expressions so lifelike they could be people in the streets today.

⊙ Beautifully preserved Renaissance town houses with interior courtyards, vaulting and stone balconies – Maisons du Bailliage, des Templiers (arts and traditions museum) and de la Ronade. Many are softly aglow at night.

⊙ Beyond the town, the regional volcano park; the basilica at Mauriac; the Château d'Auzers.

ⓘ Place Tyssandier d'Escous.

Somewhere to stay

⬃ Bailliage, in town, with spacious rooms, country furniture, bright welcoming restaurant and pretty terrace. Auvergnate cuisine at reasonable prices. ☎ 04 71 40 71 95.

⬃ Hostellerie de la Maronne, not far west of Salers, near St-Martin-Valmeroux. Delightful 19th-century manor house, classy, cosy and peaceful amid shades of rolling green. Delicious food. ☎ 04 71 69 20 33.

Vichy (Allier)

Daily except Monday

File away images of World War Two and puppet-governments. This elegant queen of the spas has long since swept it all under the Aubusson and today is a highly agreeable town in which to relax and have fun. Vichy has oodles of *fin-de-siècle* (19th) charm, ravishing gardens and river and lakeside walks. There is a feast of art nouveau as well as reviving *eau*, gastronomic restaurants, couture label shops, casinos, horse-racing and golf. The resort atmosphere which prevails seems every bit as invigorating as it must have been when the crowned heads of Europe flocked here in the 1930s to enjoy balneotherapy and balls.

The markets dispense classy stuff, whether in the daily *halles* (Monday excepted) or in Place Jean Epinat just behind: here, a regular *foire* on Wednesday mornings offers *produits du terroir* from the Bourbonnais as well as bargain chic and the rest. This might be Charolais beef country, but much is also made of Duchambais ducks and Jaligny turkeys. If you're not looking to cook dinner, you'll come across plenty of alternatives as edible souvenirs, from the famous Vichy pastilles to decorative pots of Charroux grain mustard, heather and broom honey. If you're munching on the go, give in to glistening tartlets with cherries and bilberries anchored in *crème pâtissière*. Essential oils and perfumes are equally tempting, but they're not Jo Malone.

Two smaller regular food markets gather under the gaze of St-Blaise's old church (Friday mornings) and in the Carreau des Célestins (Tuesday, Thursday and Friday mornings) – both quite near the Parc des Sources.

Flea market passion is unleashed every second Saturday in the month in Place Charles de Gaulle. (No public space has been named after Marshal Pétain.)

Don't miss

✪ A sip or two of the therapeutic waters dispensed from ornate pumps in the Belle Epoque style Parc des Sources (they have an eggy whiff in varying degrees – one is industrial strength).

✪ The original Thermes building, now a shopping mall.

✪ The Opéra – in the theatre of the Grand Casino – a treat even if there's nothing on but especially if there is.

✪ A Sunday session at the Centre Thermal des Dômes – the only place you can go without booking a month in advance. The new Thermes de Vichy are very modern and medical.

ⓘ Rue du Parc.

Somewhere to stay

➘ Pavillon d'Enghien, in town. Intimate ambience, rooms with individual touches and pretty restaurant surrounded by greenery. ☎ 04 70 98 33 30.

➘ La Colombière, 4km south of Vichy, Route de Thiers, a roadside hotel with a personality, parking and very good traditional cooking. ☎ 04 70 98 69 15.

Best of the Rest

★ **Ambert**, of Fourme d'Ambert cheese fame, has a museum telling you about it and a good Thursday market.

★ **Aubière** Sweet little village not far from Clermont-Ferrand with a lovely old church and an extraordinary painted mural of a market in the square where the market is held on Friday and Sunday mornings.

★ **Aurillac** In the heart of the 'Châtaigneraie' (chestnut grove), the capital of Haute-Auvergne. It's a bustling agricultural town with an industrial legacy and a vast and varied market each Saturday and a smaller one on Wednesday.

★ **Billom** Famous for its pink garlic and great Monday market. An attractive medieval *centre ville* swirling around the Rue des Boucheries and Saint-Cerneuf collegiate church.

★ **Brioude** Has the most fabulous Romanesque basilica with gargantuan arches, painted frescoes and cobbles on the floor. I caught a wedding here one Saturday afternoon and it was enchanting, the bride like a delicate angel floating through this spiritual yet physically so earthbound church. Saturday is the regular market day and there's one on Wednesday as well in July and August.

★ **La Chaise-Dieu** On Thursday, the market stalls soften the impact of the massive, overbearing Benedictine abbey which sits on top of this small perched town. The Danse Macabre frescoes are brilliant though.

★ **Le Monastier-sur-Gazielle** A must for fans of RL Stevenson, for this is where he first encountered Modestine. The Sunday market is suitably rustic.

★ **Montluçon** Industrial and businesslike outskirts, but a charming medieval Quartier St Pierre and fascinating museum of musical instruments (housed in yet another Bourbon château). The hotel/restaurant Le Grenier à Sel is the perfect place to pause if you're speeding up or down the A71. On Saturday a picturesque food market clusters in the cathedral quarter and clothes racks spill along the Ave Max Dormoy.

★ **Moulins** On the banks of the Allier, this ancient town succeeded Bourbon-l'Archambault as capital of the Bourbonnais in the 10th century. Members of the Bourbon court mix it with the saints on the cathedral's stained glass. Lots of fine old buildings and great chocolate shops. Superb Friday market.

★ **Pierrefort** in Cantal has a market on Wednesday but the Friday one is more of a spectacle: it's a meat market to which people come from all around just to watch the goings on. Salers beef from the Aubrac plateau is the main ingredient.

★ **St-Flour** Beautifully sited small City of Bishops on a green hill of Cantal above a meander of the river Ander. The Haute-Auvergne Museum has stunning early Romanesque statues, carvings and reliquaries. Market days are Tuesday and Saturday.

★ **St-Nectaire** Centre of AOC cheese-making. Market Sunday.

★ **Thiers** The cutlery capital, a tangle of crooked streets stacked on a hillside above the river Durolle. In its time, Thiers has produced everything that chops from guillotine blades to scissors. Waterfalls used to turn the grindstones. The cutlery museum and cutlers' workshops explain. There are markets on Monday, Wednesday, Thursday and Saturday.

★ **Vic-sur-Cère** Heavenly little town nestling by the Cère. Tuesday is the day.

⌂ www.auvergne-tourisme.info

Markets at a glance: Auvergne

A
Aigueperse, *Tue*
Ainay-le-Château, *Tue*
Allanche, *Tue*
Allègre, *Wed*
Ambert, *Thu*
Les Ancizes, *Wed*
Ardes, 2nd and 4th *Mon*
Arfeuilles, *Wed*
Arlanc, 2nd and 4th *Mon*
Aubière, *Fri, Sun*
Aulnat, *Wed*
Aurec-sur-Loire, *Wed, Fri,*
    Sun
Aurillac, *Wed, Sat*
B
Bas-en-Basset, *Wed, Sun*
Beaulon, 3rd *Thu*
Beaumont, *Wed*
Beauzac, *Tue, Sun*
Bellenaves, *Wed*
Bellerive-sur-Allier, *Tue, Sat*
Bert, *Wed*
Besse, *Mon*
Besse-et-St-Anastaise, *Mon*
Bézenet, *Tue*
Billom, *Mon*
Blesle, *Fri* (Jul/Aug)
Blot-l'Eglise, 4th *Tue*
Boisset, *Sat* eve (Jul/Aug)
Bort-les-Orgues, *Sat*
La Bourboule, *Sat*
Bourbon-l'Archambault, see
    Six of the Best
Bourg-Lastic, 20th of month
Brassac-les-Mines, *Sun*
Le Breuil-sur-Couze, *Wed*
Brioude, *Sat* (+ *Wed,* and *Tue*
    eve Jul/Aug)
Brout-Vernet, *Thu*
Buxières-les-Mines, *Wed*
C
Calvinet, *Fri*
Cebazat, *Thu, Sun*
Le Cendre, *Fri*
Cérilly, *Thu*
Ceyrat, *Sat*
La Chaise-Dieu, *Thu*
Chamalières, *Tue, Thu, Fri, Sat*
Chambon-sur-Lac, *Fri*
    (Jul/Aug)

Le Chambon-sur-Lignon, *Sat*
    (+ *Wed* mid-Jun–mid-Sep)
Champeix, *Fri*
Champs-sur-Tarentaine, *Thu*
Chantelle, *Thu*
Charbonnier-les-Mines, *Fri*
Châteaugay, *Sun*
Châtel-Guyon, *Tue, Fri*
Châtel-Montagne, *Sat* (+ *Sun*
    Jul/Aug)
Chaudes-Aigues, *Mon, Thu*
Chevagnes, 3rd *Mon*
Chomelix, *Thu* eve (Jul/Aug)
Cistrières, *Fri* eve (Jul/Aug)
Clermont-Ferrand, see Six
    of the Best
La Combelle, *Mon*
Commentry, *Fri*
Condat, *Tue*
Cosne-d'Allier, *Tue*
Costaros, *Mon*
Cournon-d'Auvergne, *Thu,*
    Fri, Sat
Courpière, *Tue*
Craponne-sur-Arzon, *Sat*
Cressagnes, *Tue*
Cunlhat, *Tue*
Cusset, *Sat*
D
Domérat, *Fri*
Dompierre-sur-Besbre, *Sat*
Le Donjon, *Tue*
Doyet, *Thu*
E
Ebreuil, *Thu*
Egliseneuve-d'Entraigues,
    Wed
Ennezat, *Wed*
G
Gannat, *Wed, Sat*
Gelles, 1st *Mon*
Gerzat, *Thu, Sun*
H
Hérisson, *Fri*
Huriel, *Tue*
I
Issoire, *Sat*
J
Jaligny-sur-Besbre, *Wed*
Job, *Sun*
Jumeaux, *Wed*

Jussac, *Sun* (Apr–Nov)
L
Landos, 2nd *Tue*
Langeac, see Six of the Best
Lapalisse, *Thu*
Lardquebrou, *Fri* (Jul/Aug)
Lempdes, *Tue, Wed, Fri, Sat*
Lezoux, *Sat*
M
Manzat, *Wed*
Marcenat, *Thu*
Marcillat, *Thu*
Maringues, *Mon*
Mariolles, *Tue*
Martres-de-Veyre, *Wed*
Massiac, *Tue*
Mauriac, *Sat*
Maurs, *Thu*
Mayet-de-Montagne, *Mon*
Meaulne, *Mon*
Menat, *Wed*
Messeix, 14th of month
Le Monastier-sur-Gazeille,
    Sun
Monistrol-sur-Loire, *Fri*
La Monnerie-le-Montel, *Sat*
Montaigut-en-Combrailles,
    Tue
Le Mont-Dore, *Fri*
Le Montet, *Thu*
Montfaucon-en-Velay, *Wed*
Montluçon, *Sat*
Montmarault, *Wed*
Montsalvy, *Thu*
Moulins, *Fri*
Murat, *Fri*
Murol, *Wed*
N
Néris-les-Bains, *Thu, Sun*
Neussargues-Moissac, *Wed*
Nohanent, 1st and 3rd *Tue*
Noyant-d'Allier, *Wed*
O
Olliergues, *Sat*
Orcet, *Tue*
P
Pérignat-les-Sarlièves, *Tue,*
    Fri
Peschadoires, *Sun*
Picherande, alternate *Fri*
Pierrefort, *Wed, Fri*

Pionsat, *Fri*
Pleaux, *Sat*
Pont-du-Château, *Thu* (+ bulb mkt *Tue* Sep–Jan)
Pontgibaud, *Thu*
Le Puy-en-Velay, see Six of the Best
Puy-Guillaume, *Wed*

R
Randan, *Fri*
Retournac, *Wed*
Riom, *Sat*
Riom-ès-Montagne, *Sat*
Rochefort-Montagne, 1st *Tue*
Romagnat, *Thu, Fri*
Rosières, *Sat*
Le Rouget, *Sun*
Royat, *Tue*

S
Saignes, *Tue*
Saint-Amant-Tallende, *Sat*
Saint-Anthème, 2nd and 4th *Tue*
Saint-Beauzire, *Wed*
Saint-Dier-d'Auvergne, *Thu*
Saint-Eloy-les-Mines, *Sat*
Sainte-Sigolène, *Tue*
Saint-Flour, *Tue, Sat*
Saint-Georges-de-Mons, *Thu*
Saint-Germain-des-Fossés, *Fri*
Saint-Germain-Lembron, *Tue*
Saint-Gervais-d'Auvergne, *Mon*
Saint-Julien-Chapteuil, *Mon*
Saint-Maurice-de-Lignon, *Sun*
Saint-Menoux, *Wed*
Saint-Nectaire, *Sun*
Saint-Pal-de-Mons, *Thu, Sun*
Saint-Pal-en-Chalencon, *Wed*
Saint-Paulien, *Sun*
Saint-Pourçain-sur-Sioule, *Sat*
Saint-Rémy-sur-Durolle, *Sun*
Saint-Romain-Lachalm, *Fri* (Jul/Aug)
Saint-Sauves-d'Auvergne, *Sun* (Jul/Aug)
Saint-Sauvier, *Mon*

Saint-Urcize, *Sun*
Saint-Yorre, *Wed*
Salers, see Six of the Best
Sauges, *Fri*
Sauxillanges, 2nd and 4th *Tue*

T
Tauves, *Thu*
Tence, *Tue*
Thiel-sur-Acolin, 1st *Wed*
Thiers, *Mon, Wed, Thu, Sat*
La Tour-d'Auvergne, *Tue, Sat*
Treignat, *Fri*
Trizac, *Tue*
Tronget, *Mon*

U
Urçay, *Fri*

V
Vallon-en-Sully, *Tue*

Valuejols, 1st and 2nd *Tue*
Varennes-sur-Allier, *Tue, Fri*
Le Vernet, *Thu*
Vernet-la-Varenne, 1st and 3rd *Mon*
Vertaizon, *Fri*
Vichy, see Six of the Best
Vic-le-Comte, *Thu*
Vic-sur-Cère, *Tue, Fri*
Viverols, 1st and 3rd *Tue*
Volvic, *Fri, Sun*
Vorey-sur-Arzon, *Sun*

Y
Ydes, *Sat*
Ygrande, *Thu*
Yssingeaux, *Thu* (+ *Sun* Jul/Aug)
Yzeure, *Wed*

Through a glass sparkling, silver trainers, Troyes and Troyes again

Clouds had chased me along the Côtes des Blancs all afternoon, in and out of small wine villages pinned in place by sharp-edged churches. Over the green corduroy patchwork itself, Chardonnay vines grooved this way and that, their leaves sometimes glittering after a fitful shower. Darkness behind, sun still ahead, my car tyres hissed through yet another bright but businesslike bit of bubblyville – was it Cramant or Cuis? – and then the grey canopy finally caught up with me at Epernay. Perhaps this in part was to blame for the fact that I didn't exactly pop my cork with excitement in the 'capital of champagne'. It is single-mindedly focused – as it should be – on making the sublime fizzy and on processing tourists through the chalk caves of Moët et Chandon, Perrier-Jouët, Mercier and the rest, but the town itself is a little dull. To cap it all, the site of the market was overhung by a giant crane and the buildings next to it were in the throes of demolition. As half a wall tumbled, what was hopefully to have been one of my 'six of the best' also bit the dust.

That's how it goes sometimes. This region perversely turns up wonderful markets in unexpected places and often fails to deliver any where one would most like to find them. That said, it was hard enough to select six from a very good haul, and by the time you read this Epernay's may well be worth visiting. I have to admit even the town itself looked beautiful when twinkling in the distance at twilight as I drank a *coupe* of its sparkling best in the sybaritic dining room of the Royal Champagne hotel in Champillon.

There's a big divide between the rich champagne-producing part of Champagne-Ardenne and its non-champagne-producing *département* in the north. Bordering Belgium, Ardennes has not only borne the brunt, down the centuries, of being frontier territory, but suffered the loss of its coal-mining industry. It produces excellent beer, however, enjoys an abundance of wild forest, deep rivers and voluptuous pastureland, and although its markets may not be as numerous as elsewhere in France (tourists here are thinner on the ground), few locations for street trading are as grand as that of Charleville-Mézières's 17th-century Place Ducale.

Marne, Aube and Haute-Marne – the champagne-growing *départements* – have their share of woods and water too, the lake of Der-Chantecoq providing bait for fishing enthusiasts and Lac d'Orient geared for water sports. Between the vineyards and a succession of long, lazy uneventful hills are pockets of intensely rural charm and a generous scattering of charismatic old stones. Nowhere is the choice and quality of market produce better, yet apart from a few individual cheeses and local charcuterie there is surprisingly little that you wouldn't find elsewhere. As a region, Champagne-Ardenne either culls or copies the best from all around – from Burgundy, Ile-de-France, Picardy, the east and the coast – often refining and perfecting the original. For instance, Aube is second only to Alsace as a producer of the nation's supply of choucroute, or sauerkraut, and cooks it most distinctively in – can't you guess? – champagne.

Specialities

While many delicate dishes are created to complement the range of champagnes on offer, low-calorie fare is pretty well upstaged at markets. Pigs' trotters are still a regional favourite and the **charcuterie** stalls generally are loaded with *boudins blancs* from Rethel (fat porky sausages for grilling or frying), *andouillettes* (chitterlings) and smoked and dried Ardennes ham, which really is superb. Special outsize loaves, *miches* or *michettes*, come filled with bits of bacon or studded with garlic cloves. If you're into strenuous action there'll be no problem refuelling. *Traiteurs* often sell the somewhat overrated *quenelles de brochet* (pike in pasta). Much tastier are stuffed young pigeon, packs of snails in butter and *pâté de foie gras*.

Atkins followers should perhaps avoid the small goose **pies** which tend to turn up on special feast days (so *good* though) and the hefty veal pies they make in Reims for New Year's Eve. Cured hams are often baked in puff pastry and, although thinner in shape, the flat bacon, pork and veal pies they call *palettes à la viande* are not exactly slimming either. I don't have too much trouble resisting any of these but it gets harder if I spot *flamiches*, the yummy leek and cream tarts that Aube has adapted from the Flemish north, or *gougères des Riceys*, which to all intents and purposes are morsels of cauliflower cheese wrapped in hot pastry – but they are moreish nevertheless. Finish off with sugar tart – another regular – if you can manage it.

The lightest, most elegant **champagne** is Blanc de Blancs and the Coteaux Champenois still **wines** are all white, but a good blush infuses some of champagne country's other worthwhile labels. There are pink champagnes, of course, but two more unusual wines are the lovely Rosé des Riceys, a still rosé that was a favourite of Louis XIV, and the beguilingly named Bouzy, an excellent light red. Neither of these is likely to fall off a stall, but wine shops and cellars often open their doors on market day. Look too for a slightly fermented redcurrant drink called *rubis de groseilles*. Bumper crops of red berries are the pride of the Argonne and Vouzinois areas, where they are made into wonderful drinks as well as intensely flavoured jams with a very high fruit content.

Truffles are snuffled out in Haute Marne by exactly the same method employed elsewhere – by the requisite pooch trained for the purpose. But the search is not so random. Here, truffles are cultivated: not the classic black diamond, *Tuber melanosporum*, but a variety called *Tuber uncinatum*. Purists maintain this greyish-brown truffle is not the real McCoy but, during its heyday last century, it was supplied to Paris restaurants specializing in truffle dishes. In the winter months, some of these naturalized fungi make sporadic appearances at markets such as Chaumont's. They are pricey.

If you want a representative AOC **cheese** from Champagne-Ardenne, Chaource is it. The vast bulk of production is 32 kilometres from Troyes, but Chaource is also made in Burgundy. Its pinkish white crust hides a lovely creamy

interior that tastes faintly of mushrooms. A *brioche* baked with Chaource inside it makes an ideal picnic treat. Langres, sold in flat rounds, is a sharper cheese and Chaumont is vaguely similar but stronger. They also make a good Emmenthal in Haute-Marne, and Carré de l'Est, a blandish imitation of Brie made in Lorraine, is widely consumed.

I'm mad about **baskets** and find it hard to come back from anywhere without one. If you're a basket case too, you'll love the beautifully woven reed affairs designed to carry anything from bread to bottles of champagne that come from Fayl-Billot. There's a national school of *osiériculture* there. Terracotta **pots** and planters swagged and trimmed in fine 18th-century style were the speciality of the Drouilly brothers from Champagne-Ardenne who supplied Versailles and the Vatican. The tradition continues and some very pretty elaborate pots make their way to market.

Troyes (Aube)

Daily, open-air Saturday

Capital of Aube in medieval times, Troyes possesses one of the nicest city centres in France. Fittingly in the shape of a champagne cork, Vieux Troyes has gradually been restoring its once-crumbling half-timbered buildings to their true colours – pink and pale ochre, almond green, rust and duck-egg blue. Now people with an eye for sympathetic surroundings – architects, painters, art and antique dealers – are relocating here. On a cool but bright August morning, I squandered happy hours strolling through cobbled courtyards and slivers of passageways like the Ruelle des Chats (cat's alley), where a moggy on the roof could easily jump from one side to the other.

With its relaxed pedestrian areas and factory outlets in the suburbs, Troyes also offers great retail therapy. Perhaps it was blessed when Pope Urbain IV built the Basilica on the site of his father's shop?

Unlike Paris, Toulouse and Lyon, Troyes has kept its wonderful 19th-century food *halles* in the very heart of town. These open every day except Sunday and don't even close for lunch on Friday and Saturday. Here is the usual urban feast of everything that isn't local (tankfuls of eels from the Atlantic, olives from Provence) and everything that is: *andouillettes de Troyes* (some made with mutton); *langues fumées* (smoked lamb's tongues); mounds of Chaource cheese – also delicious small and creamy Ervy *fermier*, one I shall seek out again. There are also two good wine merchants, but save yourself for the Cellier St-Pierre (see Don't miss). On Saturday, the decibel level shoots up when the vendors' cries ricochet around the building in counterpoint to the sales patter of the stallholders outside. For it's then that the weekly mixed market piles into the square and around the walls of the church of St Rémy, which has a famously twisted spire. A super location.

Don't miss

✪ The cathedral.

✪ Opposite the cathedral, Cellier St-Pierre, the plum of Troyes wine merchants, for champagne, Coteaux Champenois, Rosés des Riceys and ratafia, a local apéritif made from grape juice and marc.

✪ The rood screen in Ste Madeleine.

✪ Pascal Caffet's Palais du Chocolat, Rue de la Monnaie.

✪ Maison de l'Outil, a fascinating museum in a 16th-century townhouse celebrating workers' tools and different crafts.

✪ 111 Rue Emile Zola – press the buzzer for a peep at a Renaissance courtyard with ox-blood red wooden spiral stairway.

✪ Marques Avenue and McArthur Glen factory outlets selling designer fashion and top names in household linens at well-reduced prices.

ⓘ 16 Boulevard Carnot (near the station) and Rue Mignard (Church of St-Jean).

Somewhere to stay

⤵ Either Maison de Rhodes or Champ des Oiseaux, two stunning hotels under the same ownership which are side by side in a quiet cobbled street a step from the cathedral. Both are in renovated half-timbered 17th-century buildings with open courtyards, typical of medieval Troyes. Breakfast only.
☎ 03 25 43 11 11.

Aix-en-Othe (Aube)
Wednesday and Saturday

A determined Stéphanie Chenet of the Aube tourist office insisted I make time for this market, reckoned to be among the country's 100 best. I hadn't heard of Aix-en-Othe, but I can't wait to go back now that I've discovered both the market and Eddy and Jaqui's marvellous *auberge* (see Somewhere to stay).

The village, tucked away in the mossy hills of the Pays d'Othe, between Troyes and Sens, is pleasant enough. Small, peaceful, one dog-leg and you're through it. Yet its centrepiece is a market hall that would not look out of place in a town twenty times the size. A fully fledged Baltard-style creation in glass and steel with split-level roof and surrounds of glowing ceramic tiles, it stands proudly beside the church. Built 1889, restored to perfection in 1997. Its contents on a Wednesday morning were a revelation. Top quality stuff and an infinite choice. Complete tyres of *boudin noir* flavoured variously with apples, cheese and red pepper. Rabbit pâté. Trotters. River trout.

Oysters. Red mullet from the Mediterranean. Outside, the local farmers' produce: cider; free-range eggs; unusual vegetables like *patissons* (round white courgettes), black radishes and curly spinach. Then, around the war memorial, the general merchandise which ranged from granny slippers to silver trainers, sensible aprons to satin pyjamas, lawnmowers to G-strings. Had it not rained earlier in the morning, this section would have doubled, according to the mattress man who was struggling to prop his unwieldy wares up in a dry spot. I couldn't imagine it being any better.

Don't miss

✪ The 12th-century Chapelle St-Avit near the cemetery.

✪ Chocolates Au Dragon d'Or, 40 Rue St-Avit.

✪ Le Renaissance bar and the bakery beside it.

✪ Parc des Fontaines, laid out like an English garden – perfect for a picnic.

ⓘ In part of an old stocking factory, 21 Rue des Vannes.

Somewhere to stay

⮩Auberge de la Scierie, 5 minutes' drive out of town. Chef Eddy Kansowa used to work at London's Savoy. He and his wife Jaqui have turned the restaurant into one of the best in the area. His food is inspired, but they've kept the ambience low-key, not gussied it up out of character. Rooms are comfortable. A river shushes through leafy grounds and there's a pool. ☎ 03 25 46 71 26.

Charleville-Mézières (Ardennes)

Tuesday, Thursday and Saturday

A tale of two cities, and two towns. Caught in the meanders of the river Meuse are Mézières, the medieval half of Charleville-Mézières, and Charleville to the north, planned in Classical style at the time of Louis III. The two were united in 1966. Charleville stages the thrice-weekly market – plumb in the centre of its star tourist attraction: the Place Ducale. This lovely arcaded square echoes the more famous Place des Vosges in Paris – hardly surprising since the architects of these twin monumental urban spaces were brothers: Clément Métezeau created Place Ducale and Louis Métezeau, Place des Vosges.

The markets on Tuesdays, Thursdays and Saturdays last all day and – bonus – if you're there in August, there's free parking in the square. Merchandise is a grand mêlée of rush-seated chairs and patchwork dresses, shampoo and cleaners, a sprinkling of bric-a-brac and a lot of food. Food increases on Saturday when the country produce comes in – honey from the Thiérache, guinea fowl from Marie Hot's farm, sugar tarts, and sometimes a special breed of red turkey – *dinde rouge* – that is much prized in the Ardennes for its flavour. It's the feathers that are red, of course, not the flesh.

The place to adjourn to for a refreshing Leffe beer after shopping is the Bar du Marché under the arcades – that's if you don't mind sniffing the fishy smells of next door's *poissonnerie*. No one else seems to.

Don't miss

✪ Charleville's favourite citizen, the Grand Marionnettiste (Puppeteer). His golden head is framed by a dormer window, his feet appear on the ground below a clock. As each hour strikes, curtains part and puppets perform as the booming voice of the puppeteer recites lines from an epic poem about four brothers – *Les Quatre Fils Aymon*. At

21.15 on Saturday, you get the whole story. Every three years, Charleville's International Puppet Festival pulls thousands.

✪ Lively drinking spots: La Petite Brasserie Ardennaise, 15 Quai Arthur Rimbaud (closed Sunday), and Le Mawhot, a pub on a converted barge moored permanently on the Meuse.

ⓘ4 Place Ducale.

Somewhere to stay

↘ In Sedan (under half an hour east), the Hôtellerie du Château Fort, a superb new landmark hotel created inside the walls of Europe's largest fortress. Smooth comfort against rough textures. Fusion cooking in the open-plan foyer restaurant. ☎ 03 24 26 11 00.

↘ Auberge de l'Abbaye, an old post house at Signy l'Abbaye, under half an hour's drive west. Family-run (seven generations), good restaurant. Beef and lamb are raised on the farm and vegetables supplied by the kitchen garden. Frédéric does the rest. ☎ 03 24 52 81 27.

Châlons-en-Champagne (Marne)
Wednesday, Friday, Saturday and Sunday

For iconic grandeur and exciting monuments, Châlons may lose out to Reims, but for market connoisseurs, the region's administrative capital is, I think, more user-friendly. Driving in from wheatfields or Blanc de Blancs vineyards, you encounter plenty of outlying sprawl, but once you're in the centre of town, within the arms of the river Marne and its canals, Châlons is delightful. There is an easy charm about its waterside timbered houses, old bridges and peaceful public gardens, and there's a Romanesque-Gothic jewel to explore. Ornate, late-19th century *halles*, just across from the cathedral, burst with a cornucopia of comestibles four times a week – Wednesday, Friday, Saturday and Sunday mornings. On Wednesday and Saturday, the food halls are fenced in by racks of clothes and accessories stalls which fill Place Godart and several adjacent streets. Among the fripperies you can sometimes find superbly made artifical fashion flowers from Orges. There's loads of underground parking, and you only have to walk through to the neighbouring Place de la République for an eclectic selection of bars and restaurants. I love the amiable Les Ardennes whose rustic, beamed interior sports a flickering fire in its big chimney on cold days. From anywhere outside, you can hear the historic carillon of 56 bells from Notre-Dame-en-Vaux.

Don't miss

✪ Notre Dame-en-Vaux, with its Romanesque towers and original cloister within the museum.

✪ Cathedral St-Etienne's windows.

✪ By the canal, Le Petit Jard gardens which incorporate crumbly bits of old city walls and a turreted toll gate.

✪ Boat trips.

✪ A visit to one of the champagne houses, especially the 18th-century Joseph Perrier (Queen Victoria's favourite brand), where the chalk cellars were dug, as most were in Champagne, by Roman slaves. You need to telephone before tasting: 03 26 68 29 51.

ⓘ 3 Quai des Arts.

Somewhere to stay

➽ Royal Champagne, at Champillon – really worth going the 40 minutes out of town for. Looking down on the Epernay vineyards, this old coaching inn is a sublime Relais & Châteaux where Old Boney once slept and Britain's late Queen Mum spent her 80th birthday. Sumptuous dining room, Michelin-starred food.
☎ 03 26 52 87 11.

➽ In town, the Angleterre, whose fresh, pretty rooms seduce almost as much

as master chef Jacky Michel's food (also Michelin-starred). Only drawback is the restaurant is closed for lunch on Saturdays and Mondays and all day Sunday. ☎ 03 26 68 21 51.

Les Riceys (Aube)
Thursday

One of the most picturesque of the wine towns in which to enjoy a market. Les Riceys is, in fact, three small towns nestling in the Côte des Bar. They share a river (the Laignes), four chapels, five wash houses, three classified churches and a château. There's a marvellous viewpoint on the RD17 (the road to Mussy) where you can picnic and, in autumn, when frost is likely, watch little wraiths of smoke arising from the steep, vine-clad slopes – it means the winegrowers have lit their wood-burners among the Pinot Noirs to keep them warm. Les Riceys has the accolade of being the only commune in France boasting three AOC wines, including the very classy Rosé des Riceys which requires such particular conditions it cannot be achieved every year. Louis XIV, the Sun King, adored it. Les Riceys also makes champagnes and Coteaux Champenois, and you have a choice of six different cellars to visit. Once a week, local food producers come to sell their stuff in the purpose-built covered market hall by the river in Ricey-Haut. In summer, when the number of stalls increases they spill out into the surrounding Place des Héros de la Résistance. It's the kind of market that gives some of the region's smaller businesses a showing: those that make fruit compotes and onion jam, country breads and farm cheeses. Look for a nice ash-covered one from Les Riceys itself, also Mussy-L'Evêque, Lacaune *brebis* and the smelly but delicious *soumaintrain* from nearby Burgundy.

Don't miss

- ✿ A walk through the vines – set trails of differing lengths follow a route linking the stone wine huts.

- ✿ The church of St-Pierre-ès-Liens, dating from the 13th century.

- ✿ The vintage car museum in Ricey-Bas, open Sundays, public holidays and every afternoon in July and August.

- ✿ Morize Père et Fils in Ricey-Haut for a tasting in 12th-century vaulted cellars.

ⓘ3 Place des Héros de la Résistance.

Somewhere to stay

⬏ Magny, on the road to Tonnerre, a charmingly renovated stone house whose garden contains a pool that's heated from May to October.
☎ 03 25 29 11 72.

Langres (Haute-Marne)
Friday

I wish I could transport this perfect town somewhere nearer home so I could spend a day in it every week – preferably Friday when the market moves in. You can see Langres, aloft and aloof, on a ridge as you cross the lake-studded countryside of Haute-Marne. But sweep up and into it and you're in a little Shangri-la, the whole town snuggling within its four-kilometre collar of sturdy ramparts, complete with seven towers and six massive gates. Inside is a web of pleasant bourgeois streets and squares lined with Renaissance houses, antiques shops, scented *chocolatiers* and elegant *salons-de-thé*. All is not quite what it seems, however. The 17th-century Chapelle des Oratoriens conceals the theatre. Behind an 18th-century facade, the cathedral dates from the 1100s. And a whimsical old bandstand tucks the public loos underneath. In one small square stands a statue of Diderot, writer and critic. In another, Place de l'Eglise, the weekly market slots in Fruit, vegetables, flowers, fish, chickens and, of course, cheese – especially Langres's own brand. Sometimes in the summer, Georges Decorse, whose traditional distillery is at Millières, brings his prune, raspberry and mirabelle plum

brandies. If Fayl-Billot baskets aren't for sale when you're there, Fayl-Billot isn't far away . . .

Don't miss

✪ Panoramic views from the battlements and the little train ride that takes you on a one-and-a-half hour trip within the walls to see the main monuments.

✪ The Navarre and Orval towers with their wooden roof timbers, vaulted rooms and casemates. The towers were opened by King Francis I in 1521.

✪ Le Nouveau Musée displaying a huge Gallo-Roman mosaic of Bacchus, and sculptures from the Middle Ages and the Renaissance.

ⓘ Square Lahalle.

Somewhere to stay

⬂ Cheval Blanc, 3-star inn converted from a church during the Revolution. Vaulted rooms, plus modern ones in the Diderot pavilion opposite. Good traditional cooking. ☎ 03 25 87 07 00.

⬂ Grand Hôtel de l'Europe. Not terribly grand, but a charming Logis de France in an old post house, quite near the market. ☎ 03 25 87 10 88.

★ **Bar-sur-Aube** A wine town that's a real pleasure. Nice walks by the waterside and in the surrounding woods. Market on Saturday.

★ **Chaumont** Another historic town in the south-east of the region, once the residence of the Counts of Champagne. Its most eye-catching monument is a massive railway viaduct. Complicated to get into but picturesque in the centre, with markets on Wednesday and Saturday.

★ **Essoyes** In the Côte des Bar. The market on the second Tuesday of the month adds a final flourish to this picturesque village much loved by Renoir. It was his wife's home town and the artist often painted by the river Ource. Today you can follow a trail of places he chose as subjects and visit his former studio which is now a workshop for budding artists.

★ **Givet** Lovely old frontier town on the Meuse which at this point is about to flow into Belgium. Has a mammoth ruined fortress, a marvellous arts and crafts museum and a terrific onion fair each November 11. Onions also feature prominently in its Friday market.

★ **Jandun** In the Ardennes foothills (20km south of Charleville-Mézières). Local farmers bring their wares to the village hall every first Friday evening in the month (17.00 to 21.00). Expect the freshest dairy produce, meat, fruit, vegetables, apple juice and cider. Also delicious bread baked

in the renovated traditional bread oven. You can eat on the spot too.

★ **Nogent-sur-Seine** A charming town on the western border of Champagne-Ardenne. It still has one or two *ginguettes* – riverside wine-bar/restaurants where workers used to dance to the accordion – and was a favourite haunt of the novelist Gustave Flaubert, whose father was born here. Markets are on Wednesday and Saturday (Provins, only half an hour away, also has a Saturday market – see chapter on Paris and Ile-de-France).

★ **Reims** Brave the maze of confusing traffic systems to reach the centre. The sight of that awesome Gothic cathedral where the kings of France were traditionally crowned should be worth the effort. Best cellars to visit are Pommery and Piper Heidsieck. Reims has markets every day and hosts a serious flea market the first Sunday of the month (except August) in the Parc des Expositions.

★ **Rocroi** A one-off. An extraordinary star-shaped citadel the size of a village where all roads lead to the central cobbled square. This is where the market gathers on Tuesday mornings (except the beginning of the month on Mondays), in and around an open-sided covered hall.

★ **Sedan** Its colossal fortress – the largest in Europe – dominates the town. The rest is something of a curate's egg, but there are many pleasant corners including the part of town where the market is – just below the Château Fort near St Charles's church. There's a big food hall and a mixed market outside on Wednesday and Saturday.

★ **Signy-le-Petit** A charming little market town amid the lovely Thiérache countryside. The spacious Place de l'Eglise, filled by the market on Thursday, has a church in the middle and on one corner La Hulotte au Lion d'Or which serves delicious organic and original dishes.

★ **Vouziers** A small Ardennes town that keeps busy making baskets and is rightly proud of its magnificent Renaissance church door. Lively Saturday market.

Other significant flea markets

◎ **Launois-sur-Vence**, second Sunday.

◎ **Reims**, first Sunday except in August.

There aren't that many markets devoted purely to antiques in Champagne-Ardenne, but one or two bric-a-brac stalls often set up at regular mixed markets and summer sees a lot of sporadic *vide-greniers*, especially in the Aube. Check for dates at local tourist offices.

🖰 www.tourisme-champagne-ardenne.com

Markets at a glance: Champagne-Ardenne

A
Aix-en-Othe, see Six of the Best
Attigny, *Wed*
Avize, *Thu*
Ay-Champagne, *Fri*
B
Bar-le-Duc, *Tue, Thu, Sat*
Bar-sur-Aube, *Sat*
Bar-sur-Seine, *Fri*
Bazancourt, *Fri*
Betheny, *Tue*
Bogny-sur-Meuse, *Mon*
(Braux), *Wed* (Château-Regnault)
Brienne-le-Château, *Thu*
C

Carignan, *Fri*
Châlons-en-Champagne, see Six of the Best
Chaource, *Mon*
Charleville-Mézières, see Six of the Best
Chaumont, *Wed, Sat*
D
Dienville, *Sun*
Dormans, *Sat*
Doulevant-le-Château, *Mon*
E
Epernay, *Tue, Wed, Thu, Sat*
Ervy-le-Châtel, *Fri*
Essoyes, 2nd *Tue*
Esternay, *Tue*
Estissac, *Sun*

F
Fismes, *Sat*
Fère-Champenoise, *Wed*
Fumay, *Wed*
G
Givet, *Fri*
H
Les Hautes-Rivières, *Wed*
J
Jandun, 1st *Fri* eve (Mar–Dec)
Joinville, *Fri*
Jonchery-sur-Vesle, *Sat*
L
Langres, see Six of the Best
Ligny-en-Barrois, *Fri*
Lusigny-sur-Barse, *Sat*

M
Monthermé, *Mon*
Montier-en-Der, *Fri*
Montmiral, *Mon*
Mourmelon-le-Grand, *Thu*
Muizon, *Sun*
Mussy-sur-Seine, *Thu*
N
Nogent-sur-Seine, *Wed*, *Sat*
Nouzonville, *Mon*
O
Oger, *Wed*
P
Pontfaverger, *Tue*
R
Reims, daily
Renwez, *Thu*

Rethel, *Thu*
Revigny-sur-Ornain, *Wed*
Revin, *Tue*
Les Riceys, see Six of the Best
Rocroi, 1st *Mon*, otherwise *Tue*
Romilly-sur-Seine, *Mon*
S
Saint-Dizier, *Wed*, *Thu*, *Sat*, *Sun*
Sainte-Menehould, *Mon*
Sedan, *Wed*, *Sat*
Sermaize-les-Bains, *Sun*
Sézanne, *Wed*, *Sat*
Signy-le-Petit, *Thu*
Suippes, *Fri*

T
Tinqueux, *Wed*
Troyes, see Six of the Best
V
Venduevre-sur-Barse, *Wed*
Vertus, *Tue*
Verzenay, *Mon*
Vireux-Wallerand, *Thu*
Vitry-le-François, *Thu*, *Sat*
Vouziers, *Sat*
W
Wassy, *Thu*
Witry-lès-Reims, *Sat*

FRANCHE-COMTÉ

Wooden toys, a sausage called Jesus and cheeses big enough to sit on

Where exactly is it? That's the question most often asked when I mention Franche-Comté to friends less familiar with France than I am.

Years ago, I journeyed by car from Calais down to Lake Annecy, just south of that other larger lake known to the world as Geneva but which the French insist on calling Léman. During the last hairpin-bend lap, we crossed the green Jura mountains, squeezing through a series of dramatic steep wooded valleys. This was the southern part of Franche-Comté. Ooh, I thought, I'd like to come back here. Not all of the region is as eye-popping but, as I've discovered since, it has some very beautiful scenery. It's a kind of toned-down Switzerland, which it lies alongside (except for the bit in the north-east that touches Germany).

French film makers looking for costume drama locations often choose Franche-Comté because of its unspoiled landscapes and paucity of industrial eyesores. The lushness of its wine country contrasts with vast tracts of space left to nature. Waterfalls like Hérisson's and the cascades at the sources of the Doubs, Lison and Loue rivers are spectacular targets for intrepid hikers. The Plateau des Milles Etangs in the north is a lovely area studded with small lakes, perfect for cycling. But most appealing, to me, are the wide sweeps of undulating high pastureland. Intensely green and edged with fir trees, they're like perfect golf courses without the bunkers. You want to spread your wings and take off – as many do in microlites and hang-gliders.

It was during a flying visit (on a proper plane via Basle-Mulhouse) with two other writers to the Christmas market in Montbéliard that the germ of the idea for this book began to form. All three of us were bowled over by the town's twinkly concentration of seasonal cheer. I remember packing every page of a fat little notebook with scribbles about the treats we saw and sampled. Mind you, the cumulative mix of ginger cake, cheese, spiced apple juice, hot chocolate and smoked sausage inevitably took its toll, completely ruining our appetite for dinner, but we couldn't offend our hosts by refusing. Barbara and Françoise kept egging us on – 'You have to try everything. It is what everybody does.' They, I noticed, didn't!

Summer in this eastern border region is punctuated with wonderful fairs and festivals but regular markets are not as numerous or as heavily baited to attract tourists as they are in, say, Provence or Midi-Pyrénées. Which is understandable – Franche-Comté is sparsely populated and gets fewer visitors. Even so, it has its gems.

Specialities

Surrounded by a thick cover of fir forest and with long winter evenings to fill before the arrival of television, the people of Franche-Comté took to carving countless everyday objects out of wood – anything from pipes to pepper grinders. Today, the tradition continues with the manufacture of a wonderful assortment of **wooden artefacts**, especially beautiful boxes and imaginative toys. In fact, 'toys are us' could be the Jura's motto. It supplies just under half those sold throughout France (most made in Moirans-en-Montagne).

Watchmaking, as in neighbouring Switzerland, is a big earner too, though beware of flashy timepieces sold in markets – they may have come from Taiwan. Glassware and glasses (of the spectacle variety) are also key products, as are, curiously, buttons. I came across a terrific selection in the market at Ronchamp on a stall devoted to haberdashery – a branch of merchandising that has all but withered away.

Comté, Morbier and Mont-d'Or are the big **cheeses** of Franche-Comté known on the international circuit. There are also many excellent local ones that stay at home, particularly goat's cheeses. Try a particularly good salted one from Saint-Claude. Almost liquid creamy cheese specialities like Cancoillotte and Mamirolle, variations on fondue and raclette, can be eaten cold or hot and are often offered as market snacks. So too is the heartier *tartiflette* or *morbiflette*, a scrumptious scramble of potatoes, cheese, onions and snippets of bacon, the lot spiced with nutmeg – real trencherman's fare to satisfy fresh-air-induced appetites. Look also for large smoky Morteau and Montbéliard **sausages**. They're the size of rounders bats, and Morteau's big brother, the Jesu, weighs in at half-a-kilo. These plus smaller *saucissons* and country terrines are packed with flavour, and the hams of Luxeuil-les-Bains compare with the best from Parma – and so they should after macerating for months in red wine before being hung over the smouldering sawdust of fir trees.

Jura **honey** is rather special: aromatic and a rich deep golden, it brings the breath of conifers and alpine flowers to the table. As for the honey-coloured *vin jaune* or the sweet *vin de paille* ('straw wine'), I'm not the one to go by. They say Franche-Comté wines are an acquired taste, loved by some while they leave others cold. To me they lack personality, but the Romans were sold on them and the region today boasts six AOCs. So my palate may not be sufficiently well educated, or possibly it's just that the best are expensive. The only one I've found that I liked was a red from Arbois. With the delicious wines of neighbouring Alsace featuring on most restaurant menus, it is all too easy to fall back on these. But to be in Jura wine *country* is a particular pleasure. Plenty of tasting opportunities arise at wine village markets.

There is great **fishing** in Franche-Comté and river fish such as crayfish, brown trout, pike and zander feature in moderation at markets. Lake herrings and grayling are rarer. *Friture de carpe* – fried young carp – if crisp and freshly done is good to munch as you saunter round the stalls.

Besançon (Doubs)
Tuesday to Sunday

In Besançon, think of Raymond Blanc. The renowned chef-patron of the legendary Manoir aux Quat' Saisons in Oxfordshire was born here in the Franche-Comté capital. Its covered market exemplifies all he preaches about the importance of local produce and food being 'seasonal, fresh, sharp and bright'. The quality is top notch and the variety far-reaching. Unusual vegetables such as kohlrabi and celeriac join a shrubbery of salad leaves and springy fresh herbs. Exotic fruits – figs from Iran, fresh dates from Israel – flank plump local plums and grapes. And, of course, the region's renowned cheeses are out to impress – massive roundels of Comté big enough to sit on.

The new purpose-built *halle* occupies a corner site (Rue de Paris/Rue Goudimel) near the Pont Battant in the old town. Outside in Place de la Révolution on Tuesday and Friday mornings, a farmers' market offers straight-from-the-earth potatoes, just-picked fruit from the orchard, honey still on the comb and forest mushrooms in season – when I was there, dark *trompettes de la mort* were being snapped up. But to balance all this potential healthiness, Bisontins, as the city-dwellers are known, give in to their sweet tooth. *Pâtisserie* counters are heaped with pretty biscuits – *minutes de Besançon*, *galets du Doubs*, *pavés bisontins* – and *griottes*, the most luscious of cherry liqueur chocolates.

An airy city of parks and gardens with its historic core lassooed by the river Doubs, Besançon has a lot of charm. Especially in Battant, the old wine traders' quarter. A large quota of students keeps things humming and the cobbled streets near the market are well stocked with inexpensive bistros and fun cafés like the 7th Art Café overlooking the river on Quai Vauban.

A terrific Christmas market runs for most of December.

Don't miss

○ Vauban's Citadelle. Quite hard to miss – it towers on a rocky spur above town and is home to several museums including one on the history of the French Resistance movement.

○ Place Victor Hugo, birthplace of both the great novelist and the Lumière brothers who invented cinematography.

○ In the market square, the Beaux Arts Museum, the oldest in France.

○ The animated Horloge Astronomique in the cathedral – a timely reminder that Besançon is France's watchmaking capital.

○ For splashing out, Mungo Park, a Michelin-star eatery in Rue Jean Petit.

○ For tighter budgets, the cosy Le Vin et l'Assiette above a wine cellar in Rue Battant.

ⓘ 2 Place de la 1ère Armée Française.

Somewhere to stay

↘ Hôtel Nord, comfortable old town address, with fresh interiors and garage parking. ☎ 03 81 81 34 56.

↘Hôtel Regina, a 2-star of intimate
spaces and cosy simplicity. Some
rooms look out at the Citadelle. In a
reasonably quiet alley.
☎ 03 81 81 50 22.

Belfort (Territoire de Belfort)

*Daily except Monday, major antiques the
first Sunday in the month*

I keep going back to this likeable town
whose lack of scale is part of its
attraction. It seems to have a portion of
everything you'd find in a much larger city
– except traffic chaos. Striking examples
of 18th- to early 20th-century
architectural styles give the small,
tranquil centre substance. The famous
Lion de Belfort, stretched out under the
walls of the Vauban citadel, has spawned
a rash of references to it – lion heads on
the bandstand, the restaurant 'Au Pied du
Lion' and a baker's called 'La Brioche du
Lion'. There are spacious gardens,
elegant squares, lots of antique shops
and a corker of a flea market once a
month (first Sunday) that draws an
international crowd. It commandeers the
entire *vieille ville*.

Belfort's mix of bygones reflects its
geography and history. Close to the Swiss
and German border, the town was part of
Alsace until 1921. Military memorabilia
abounds, but you'll also find sagging
chaises longues and tarnished
chandeliers, painted headboards and
copper cake moulds, wooden coffee-
grinders and lots of clocks. A peripheral
scattering of snack stalls helps sustain

buyers and sellers with hot sugared peanuts and Chinese tidbits.

Belfort is also served by a sophisticated daily market housed in its Second Empire covered hall (1905) and, every Sunday morning, a market of local Vosges produce that sets up on the edge of town.

Don't miss

✪ The Lion. He commemorates a 103-day siege. Constructed from blocks of Vosges sandstone, like a latterday Lego, he was created by Auguste Bartholdi, who also designed New York's Statue of Liberty.

✪ The citadel, whose grassy confines contain the Museum of Art and History.

✪ The 18th-century town hall, its splendid staircase and paintings that tell the story of Belfort.

✪ The Donation Maurice Jadot, one man's stunning collection of modern art – Jadot knew Picasso's agent and there are photographs of the fiery-eyed genius in his Antibes studio as well as pictures by him, by Léger, Le Corbusier, Braque and Baudin.

✪ Pot au Feu, super little cellar restaurant.

✪ Notre Dame du Haut, Le Corbusier's stark chapel on a hill above Ronchamp, about 16km away.

ⓘ 2 bis, Rue Clemenceau.

Somewhere to stay

↘ Grand Hôtel du Tonneau d'Or. Something of a curiosity but very comfortable. It was the German HQ when Belfort was occupied in 1940, and the Belle Epoque foyer with flamboyant staircase sports, incongruously, photographs of elephants' bottoms on the walls. Newly modernized rooms. ☎ 03 84 58 57 56.

↘ Vauban, small, friendly family hotel covered with paintings by local artists. ☎ 03 84 21 59 37.

Arbois (Jura)
Friday mornings and the first Tuesday in the month

Streamers of stylized bunches of grapes in purple and green polythene flap like Tibetan prayer flags in the central square of this *petite cité de caractère*. It can hardly escape your notice that Arbois is a wine town for it nestles in a carpet of vineyards below a high cliff that drops from the Jura plateau: a sight to sigh at from whichever angle you approach. No boring bits. A busy main throughfare, then quiet alleyways, ancient towers, tumbling weirs and enviable back-of-house terraces perched above the river

Cuisance. A statue of the great chemist Louis Pasteur sits in a little park by the church of Notre-Dame. He was born in Dole but brought up in Arbois and it was the study of wine fermentation that led him to his discoveries in bacteriology.

The Champ de Mars on the edge of town normally acts as a car park. On Friday mornings cars are banished to wherever they can tuck themselves away and this space becomes the market place. Sometimes in the summer the market is held in the town centre, in and around the fountain on Place de la Liberté. Either way, it is a buzzy one. Plenty of fashion, footwear and novelties, but food is the main focus. The pick of hams cured over juniper and pine, and Bresi, the smoked dried beef. Ash-covered goat's cheeses and pots of *fromage blanc* as well as fine locally made Comté. To go with these, there's usually freshly churned butter and rough-hewn loaves of country bread, rather like sourdough. Add a few cherries, or mirabelles in season, and carry your buys up into the vineyards to relish with a bottle of Arbois wine.

Don't miss

❂ Louis Pasteur's father's house.

❂ The church of St Just.

❂ The 16th-century château.

❂ The wine and vine museum.

❂ A tasting at Henri Maire, the 'best wine maker in the Jura' (Place de la Libération) and/or a light meal in Henri's lively wine bar, La Finette.

❂ Pâtisserie Hirsinger in the main square.

❂ Jean-Paul Jeunet's 2-Michelin star cuisine – one of his specialities is *fera* (lake fish) with Savagnin butter, mini turnips, mushrooms and spinach (Rue de l'Hôtel de Ville).

❂ Louis XIV's extravagant Royal Saltworks at Arc-en-Senans, about 16km away.

ⓘ10 Rue de l'Hôtel de Ville.

Somewhere to stay

↘Les Messageries, welcoming old post house (2-chimney Logis) with stone facade in the heart of town near Pasteur's statue. No restaurant.
☎ 03 84 66 15 45.

↘Annexe le Prieuré, linked to Jean-Paul Jeunet's posh restaurant. 17th-century building, 7 charming rooms, small garden. ☎ 03 84 66 05 67.

Montbéliard (Doubs)

Christmas market all of December, weekly markets Tuesday, Wednesday, Saturday

This delightful turreted town is small and walkable yet it hosts one of the most magical Christmas markets in eastern France as part of its Christmas lights festival (end November to Christmas Eve). Over 120 craftspeople from all over the country gather in a glittering village of wooden chalets in the main square by St Martin's Lutheran church. On sale are inspired decorations, pottery and clever wooden toys as well as the usual seasonal fluff of squeaky Santas and tinsel angels. To taste are cartons of hot, melted *cancoillotte* cheese, slabs of ginger cake and cups of spiced apple juice. Or, if you want a more substantial snack, there's *tartiflette*, the mix of cheese, onion, ham and potatoes, to help keep out the cold. Pink-faced chaps with brawny arms cook it by the panful over a flame.

I carried away pretty hand towels, monogrammed on the spot, and slivers of tangy fresh orange dipped in chocolate – these survived until I got back to London but not, I'm afraid, until Christmas!

Montbéliard pulls out all the stops to attract the crowds. There's a wonderful crib, a street theatre giving lively performances of folk tales, a witchy godmother called Tante Airie who doles out treats to the little ones while Père Noël takes them for a trot in his horse-drawn carriage. The best jaunt, however, is by vintage Peugeot to the highly entertaining

Peugeot Museum (see Don't miss).

Year round, there are markets in Montbéliard on Tuesday, Wednesday and Saturday mornings. In August, however, it is almost deserted.

Don't miss

- The château's antique music box collection and, at Christmas, the exhibition of games and toys from Christmases past.
- Dining at Chez Cass'Graine, 4 Rue Général Leclerc, a cosy restaurant liberally strewn with charming bric-a-brac.
- Chocs to-die-for in JP Debrie, Rue de Velotte.
- Bois de Senteurs, 1 Rue de la Souaberie, and Boutique de l'Artisanat d'Art, 29 Rue Cuvier for interiors chic – pretty toile-de-Jouy quilts and fragile light fittings.
- The Peugeot Museum at Sochaux (15 min away – tickets and quirky transport from a booth in a corner of the market). It shows everything Peugeot has ever made, from coffee grinders to sewing machines, and the vintage car showroom echoes to the sound of bronchitic horns and the music of each era.

ⓘ1 Rue Henri-Mouhot.

Somewhere to stay

- Hôtel Bristol, modest and comfortable, a fairly quiet address in a semi-pedestrianized street. ☎ 03 81 94 43 17.
- Hôtel Balance, 16th-century shell, renovated rooms, nice atmospheric restaurant. ☎ 03 81 96 77 41.

Ornans (Doubs)

Third Tuesday in the month

Birthplace and inspiration of the painter Gustave Courbet, Ornans is one of the sweetest towns in the Doubs and the jewel of the endlessly picturesque valley of the Loue. I make no excuse for including it even though it only has a market once a month, because when the stalls assemble under the trees in Place Gustave Courbet they simply complete the picture. Flowers adorn bridges and footbridges and the balconies of houses overhanging the river. It's a place to stand, stare, muse and listen to the hollow bell of St-Laurent's church

reverberating across the water – or, alternatively, the happy shouts of canoeists going with the flow. Inevitably, Ornans has been dubbed the 'little Venice of Franche-Comté', but don't let that put you off. It isn't jammed with tourists. Mid-August, I wandered round sleepy back streets and found a table for lunch at the first try.

The market is a mixed one, with fishing and hiking kit, hardware, lace panels for country windows, pottery and wrought-iron pot-stands. In August the food section had huge boxes of blueberries, mirabelles from Lorraine and melons from Cavaillon, down in Provence. There were glistening river fish to cook (Ornans is a big freshwater fishing centre) and hot appetizers of small fry to eat on the spot. I bagged a delicious home-made mushroom pie.

The market ends at lunchtime, but you won't want to leave Ornans in a hurry.

Don't miss

✪ The museum in Gustave Courbet's atmospheric former home. Many of his sombre canvases need restoring, but his blurry impressions of the town, and of other beauty spots in the valley, show how little it has changed. You can go on a Courbet route that includes subjects such as *Le Miroir de la Loue*.

✪ The museum of freshwater fishing (Maison Nationale de l'Eau et de la Pêche).

✪ The magnificent view from the Rocher du Château above town.

✪ Lods, further along the valley, one of the *plus beaux villages*.

✪ The waterfall at the source of the Lison, which joins the Loue.

✪ A scary moment at the Pont du Diable!

ⓘ 7 Rue Pierre Vernier.

Somewhere to stay

⬊ Hôtel de France, 3-star Logis de France facing the main bridge. Nice rustic dining room with regional cooking, some rooms renovated.
☎ 03 81 62 24 44.

⬊ La Truite d'Or, Lods, a simple 2-star Logis in this pretty village a short drive from Ornans. Dining terrace by the river. ☎ 03 81 60 95 48.

Dole (Jura)
Tuesday, Thursday and Friday

I gravitate to riverside cities. Here, within sniffing distance of Burgundy, is another agreeable one sited where the Rhône-Rhine canal joins the river Doubs. Once the old Comtoise capital, under the Burgundian dukes, Dole became part of Louis the Sun King's realm in the late 1600s. Today it is a busy place. Hovering on the outskirts, you might be inclined to bypass it, but the well-preserved historic quarter is too delightful to miss. Vieux Dole, part pedestrianized, is full of cobbled alleys, peaceful courtyards and fountains. Beautiful town houses and public buildings, some dating back to the 15th century, flaunt splendid carved doorways, wrought-iron grilles and other engaging details.

Three times a week, the Baltard-style market hall and Place Nationale (aka Charles-de-Gaulle) throb with commerce, blessed – as is so often the case – by the looming presence of an ancient church: the mossy-roofed Collégiale Notre Dame. While Our Lady's lofty belfry touches the heavens, Dole's consumers attend to their material needs below. As in all big city markets, the choice of food (especially in the *halle*) is eclectic – it comes from everywhere. Outside, it's a mixed bag, with stands displaying the usual chain-store variety of outerwear, underwear, hardware, craftwork and flowers.

There's parking near the Hôtel Dieu and in Place Grevy where the tourist office is.

Don't miss

✪ Place aux Fleurs, the most charming corner of the pedestrian precinct.

✪ The house where Pasteur was born, now a museum, 43 Rue Pasteur.

✪ The 16th-century Collégiale Notre Dame.

✪ A gastronomic treat at Au Bec Fin, Rue Pasteur.

✪ The Royal Saltworks at Arc-en-Senans which are within 48km of Dole.

ⓘ6 Place Grevy.

★ **Baume-les-Dames** Where the Doubs and Cusancin rivers meet, an ancient Benedictine Abbey holds sway and there's a pipe museum. Market on Thursday mornings.

★ **Faucogney-et-la-Mer** Oddly named village nothing to do with the sea but in the 'thousand lakes' district. Regular small markets are held twice a month (first and third Thursday) but throughout July and August there's a country fare and craft market every Saturday evening from 16.00–20.00.

★ **Faverney** Wednesday is market day in this romantic small town sleeping in the lee of its enormous abbey. Nice stretches by the banks of the canal and the Lanterne.

★ **Fougerolles** The kirsch capital. Interesting stop if you like fruit liqueurs and *eaux de vie* (distillery visits). A good fruit and vegetable market every Friday morning with loads of cherries in season.

★ **Lure** Traditional market every Tuesday morning takes over the Esplanade Charles de Gaulle.

★ **Luxeuil-les-Bains** A quaint old town at the southern tip of the Vosges mountains with 14th- to 16th-century architectural gems, a spa known since Roman times and a casino. Saturday market.

★ **Morteau** Home of the great Franche-Comté sausage. The village has a nice priory church, a fascinating museum of clocks and automatons and markets on Tuesday and Thursday mornings. Adrien Bouheret and La Fruitière sell prime quality Morteaux.

★ **Pesmes** Its location, with the ramparts of the citadel reflected in the waters of the Ognon, is always serene. Things liven up during the Tuesday market. Stairways and passages lead to the site of the old castle from where you can look out on the Serre hills.

★ **Poligny** A 'poem in stone', fortified Poligny is all towers, steeples, courtyards and cloisters. There's a stained-glass workshop and you can visit cheese-making dairies. Markets on Monday and Friday.

★ **Ronchamp** Two birds to kill with one stone if you visit on a Saturday. Le Corbusier's famous chapel up on the hill and the traditional country market down in the village. It's behind a church with beautiful blue stained-glass windows.

★ **St-Amour** Ruined ramparts, a castle, fountains and flowery streets make this a very appealing town. Its curvy roof tiles hint at the south. Good Saturday morning market.

★ **Salins-les-Bains** Thursday and Saturday markets are held in the pleasant setting of a spa town which has an undergound cathedral of salt. Lots of nice walks, steep narrow streets, potters' studios.

★ **Sellières** Cider country. A lovely, peaceful old staging-post in which to hang out and do some shopping in the Wednesday market. Both high town and lower town, straddling the river Brenne, are full of elegant houses.

★ **Vesoul** The heart of this town is a historic monument which has recently been renovated. Markets held here on Thursday and Saturday.

🖱 www.franche-comte.org

Markets at a glance: Franche-Comté

A
Aillevillers, *Thu*
Arbois, see Six of the Best
Arinthod, *Tue*
Audincourt, *Wed*, *Fri*, *Sat*, *Sun*
B
Baume-les-Dames, *Thu*
Beaucourt, *Thu*
**Belfort, see Six of the
Best**
**Besançon, see Six of the
Best**
Bletterans, *Tue*
C
Champagnole, *Sat*
Champlitte, 1st *Wed*
Chaumergy, *Thu*
Clairvaux, *Wed*, *Sat*
Cousance, *Sat*
D
Dampierre-sur-Salon, *Fri*
Damprichard, *Wed*, *Sat*
Delle, *Wed*, *Sat*
Dole, see Six of the Best
E
Echenoz-la-Méline, *Sun*
F
Faucogney-et-la-Mer, 1st
and 3rd *Thu* (+ *Sat* eve
Jul/Aug)
Faverney, *Wed*
Fesches-le-Châtel, *Fri*
Fougerolles, *Fri*
G
Giromagny, *Sat*
Grand-Charmont, *Wed*
Grandvillars, *Sat*
Gray, *Fri*
Grosmagny, 2nd *Sat*
H
Héricourt, *Wed*, *Sat*
Hérimoncourt, *Tue*
Les Hopitaux-Neufs, *Wed*
(Jul/Aug)
I
L'Isle-sur-le-Doubs, *Fri*
J
Jussey, *Tue*
L
Lévier, *Wed*
Lons-le-Saunier, *Thu*, *Sat*
Lure, *Tue*
Luxeuil-les-Bains, *Sat*

M
Maîche, *Sat*
Malbuisson, *Fri* (mid-
Jun–Aug)
Mandeure, *Sat*
Marnay, 1st *Mon*
Mélisey, *Wed*
Moirans, *Fri*
Moirans-en-Montagne, *Fri*
**Montbéliard, see Six of the
Best**
Montbozon, 1st *Tue*
Montferrand-le-Château, *Fri*
Montmorot, *Sat*
Mont-sous-Vaudrey, *Thu*
Morez, *Sat*
Morteau, *Tue*, *Thu*
Mouthe, *Fri* (May–Oct)
O
Ornans, see Six of the Best
P
Pesmes, *Tue*
Plancher-les-Mines, *Fri*
Poligny, *Mon*, *Fri*
Pontarlier, *Thu*, *Sat*
Pont-de-Roide, *Fri*
Port-sur-Saône, *Tue*
R
Recologne, *Sun*
Ronchamp, *Sat*
Rothau, *Sat*
Rougemont, 2nd and 4th *Fri*
Les Rousses, *Fri*
Le Russey, *Wed*, *Sat*
S
Saint-Amour, *Sat*
Saint-Aubin, *Wed*
Saint-Claude, *Thu*, *Sat*
Saint-Loup-sur-Sémouse,
Mon
Saint-Sauveur, *Sun*
Salins-les-Bains, *Thu*, *Sat*
Sellières, *Wed*
Seloncourt, *Fri*
Sochaux, *Thu*
T
Tavaux-Villages, *Wed*, *Fri*
V
Valdoie, *Sat*
Valentigney, *Tue*
Vesoul, *Thu*, *Sat*
Villersexel, 1st and 3rd *Wed*
Voujeaucourt, *Fri*

ALSACE

Painted chests, a peck of pickled cabbage and Riesling with everything

Alsace: a tiny strip of France running between the western flank of the Rhine and the well-forested Vosges mountains. It may be one of the smallest regions, but it packs in more Michelin stars than any other and hosts some of the country's most scintillating markets. Strasbourg's at Christmas ranks unchallenged as the star of Yuletide fairs while cuckoo-clock wine villages provide market backdrops so fairytale they outdo Disney. Once, when I dropped into Riquewihr for a day during the *vendange* in late September, I couldn't believe anywhere could be so cute and still work for its living. But there, at the far end of every street that tottered off the cobbled main drag, rows of russet and golden vines were nudging garden fences, and the 'angel's share', the intoxicating sweet-sour odour of fermenting grapes, swirled around every flower-garnished balcony and twirly shop sign. The season's harvest had just been safely garnered.

Through the centuries, what is now Alsace has found itself on the German side of the border countless times, the last briefly during the Second World War. As a result, it owes much of its sense of order, place names, art, architecture, cuisine and country style to the influence of its neighbours. Yet it has an identity and charm of its own that it uses, like a beautiful woman modestly aware of her attractions, with quiet confidence to draw the world to its feet. Everyone is beguiled by Alsace.

As the Route du Vin inevitably lures you into the folds of the Vosges foothills, you tend to forget that the greater part of the region is actually flat. Flat and very fertile, the alluvial plain allotted to rich farms and fruit orchards. Local produce is exceptionally good. Take into account also a long tradition of almost gypsy exuberance in decorating anything that stands still long enough to be ornamented – and indeed anything that moves, from cow bells to Rhine cruisers – and you can expect to find some very pretty souvenirs.

Specialities

Oh, the **wines**, the fragrant Rieslings, the elegant Tokay Pinots Gris, the thrusting Pinots Noirs . . . Alsace is not too bothered that its labels have lost ground on British wine lists. Consumption elsewhere – in Germany, in the States – is more than healthy and at home guaranteed by the Alsatians themselves, their glut of visitors and the neighbours in Lorraine and Franche-Comté. You're in for a treat – both in the drinking and in the cooking. Memories still linger on my palate of a lovely Boeckel Riesling Brandluft accompanying chicken with a cream and Riesling sauce in one of Strasbourg's waterside restaurants. Even Edelzwicker, the everyday wine that comes in a blue-and-white earthenware pitcher, is a *vin ordinaire* less ordinary. As for something fruity and golden to partner *foie gras* (about which Alsace is as fanatical as the Dordogne), they do it with the late-grape Gewürztraminer Tardive.

Cellars never waste an opportunity to open on market days and **eaux de vie** made from plums, apples, cherries, raspberries and even rosehips are often on display to be snapped up. They do wondrous things for simple puddings and desserts, either as an ingredient or to sip on the side. The **beer** is, of course, brilliant. The aristocratic Kronenbourg and Heineken are brewed in Strasbourg, but there are hundreds of local brews.

It was an Irish Benedictine monk, Columbanus, who invented Münster **cheese**, circa 600, hence the name of this old province of the Emerald Isle cropping up as a town in Alsace. Served seasoned with cumin seed or steeped in kirsch, it's a cheese with a boisterous personality.

The wealth of cabbages in the fields is mostly destined for conversion into **choucroute** (sauerkraut), that pickled cabbage dish that's served with salted pork and spiced sausages – often steamed up on a market booth. There's even a Route de la Choucroute, if you're minded to follow it. (Only in April does another vegetable take precedence – the white asparagus from Hoerdt.) Alsace **sausages**, or *saucisses* – the ones you have to cook as opposed to smoked *saucisson* – are big, fat and often packed with more than meat. *Gfilter söymage* is a whole pig's stomach stuffed with potatoes, carrots, leeks and onions as well as precooked meat – a kind of Cornish pasty in a skin. Look too for beer sausage, *cervelas*, and *kassler*. A favourite way to cook these is to roast them with pickled turnips.

You will be unable to escape **kougelhopf**. When Marie-Antoinette decided to let the Alsatians eat cake, she introduced this deep whirl of a brioche with raisins and sometimes almonds in it. It's a cake sold in every bakery as well as in the markets. The tin in which it's baked resembles a jelly mould with a hole in the middle and this cavity can on high days and holy days be filled with cream or ice-cream, fresh fruit, extra nuts, glacé fruits or anything else that's festive. The moulds themselves, which come in decorated pottery as well as copper and tin, are a speciality to take away.

Although much touted everywhere, *flammeküche* or *tarte flambé* is simply pizza by another name. More special are the biscuits, *bretzels* and wide variety of breads on offer – spelt bread, poppy-seed bread, Molzer bread, *sübrôt* . . .

Alsatians are highly skilled in the art of **table setting**. Printed traditional cloths, napkins, place mats and a host of other

peasanty designs similer to those you see on barges. Kougelhopf moulds, wine pitchers, casseroles and bowls are all gaily ornamented. For quality blue on grey-glazed Betschdorf and the tawnier Soufflenheim pottery, you need to go to specialist shops, but lots of very pleasing

dainty accessories are irresistible. Kelsch linen, in indigo and madder-red check patterns, and cotton with recurring embroidered motifs are turned to a hundred decorative uses. Glazed **earthenware** also bears a very individual stamp with its strong colours and

older pieces can be picked up at flea markets. It's fun to visit the two pottery towns where you can watch it being thrown and fired. The craftwork in general, whether in ceramics, wood, wrought-iron or any other medium, is always eye-catching.

Strasbourg (Bas-Rhin)

Tuesday, Wednesday, Friday and Saturday, plus Christmas market all of December

Alsace does Christmas to a crisp – indeed it claims to have started the custom of decorating fir trees – and nowhere conveys both the magic and the spiritual essence of it better than Strasbourg. Just imagine the thrill of turning a corner to find a living crib, complete with mooing cow and braying donkey. It happens during the city's centuries-old Christkindelsmärik – the Christ Child market – which each year runs for the whole of December in this appealing old border capital. From the foot of the soaring Gothic cathedral in Place Kléber, stalls spread through other streets and squares of Vieux Strasbourg. The air is filled with the scent of cinnamon, musicians play, bells peal and carols drift out from the inner glow of churches. Huge Christmas trees dwarf the waves of muffled shoppers as they wander among the chalets, warming up with mulled wine and nibbling roast chestnuts or tiny Christmas cakes called *bredelas*. Each stall, trimmed with fairy-lights, seems more enticing than the last. There are clockwork toys, fabulous baubles and heart- and tree-shaped biscuits studded with crystallized cherries and nuts. No shop is unfestooned, no architectural highlight unilluminated. It's unbelievably enchanting.

But Strasbourg's historic heart, a World Heritage Site, will enchant at any time. Enclosed by a canalized eyelet of the river Ill, it is all walkable – no more than a square mile – and the Petite France area with its boat trips, covered bridges and waterside restaurants is a joy. A very picturesque weekly market takes place near the cathedral on Saturday. The *brocante* section collects around an ivy-smothered well in the Place du Marché aux Cochons de Lait, while chefs jostle locals to get the best local produce in the adjoining Marché aux Poissons by the canal. There's also a good mixed market on Wednesday in Place Broglie.

Don't miss

✪ The sound-and-light show on the cathedral's intricate stone façade on summer nights.

✪ The permanent Christmas shop, Un Noël en Alsace, 10 Rue des Dentelles.

- Musée Alsacien, in an old timbered house, for a glimpse of traditional costumes and painted furniture – truckle beds, tiled stoves, tableaux of brides in black decked in artificial flowers.

- Maison Kammerzell, a most original Renaissance building, splendidly carved, now a gastronomic restaurant.

- Dinner at Maison des Tanneurs overlooking the canal – the place for *choucroute*, fine river fish and slick service by white-aproned waiters.

- Almost any *winstub*, a unique Alsatian blend of bierkeller/wine bar/bistro.

- Poterie d'Alsace, Rue des Frères.

- A river boat trip.

- The European Parliament and Human Rights buildings.

- Place Kléber.

Somewhere to stay

- Hôtel Hannong, a step from the cathedral, on the site of an old porcelain factory. Fresh interior with blond wooden floors and bright red accents. Parking close by.
  ☎ 03 88 32 16 22.

- Hôtel des Arts, in the Place du Marché aux Cochons de Lait, a small 2-star of character in one of the prettiest of La Petite France's squares.
  ☎ 03 88 37 98 37.

Riquewihr (Haut-Rhin)
Friday

Twenty years after my first visit during the October wine harvest, I went back here recently on a hot morning in August. Nothing had changed – except the streets were packed with trippers. Riquewihr is still a picture, its 15th-century Hansel and Gretel houses leaning chummily against each other, lace and geraniums at their dark-shuttered windows. I'd forgotten the fortified gates and the sculpted balconies – and the scent of coconut wafting from the open-fronted *pâtisseries* that bake macaroons on the premises and sell them warm in small paper bags. The vines, still green at the end of summer, were loaded with grapes and, just as I remembered, crept to the end of each side street.

Friday's market awnings were just the final flourish. A small market, in keeping with the scale of the town, squeezes in under the pink sandstone Protestant church in Place des 3 Eglises (though I could only see one). Some staples – vegetables, fruit, cheese – are joined by the inevitable plastic watches and hardware. But mostly it's small producers' offerings. Smoked sausages encrusted with herbs, honey the colour of treacle from the pinewoods – *miel de sapins* – and logs of spice bread. Also pretty aprons appliquéd with geese, grapes, and twee boys and girls bearing posies.

By the time the stalls packed up, every eatery was crammed, so I bought a wedge of *tarte flambée* and sat munching on a bench in the sun.

Don't miss

- ✪ Booking a restaurant ahead! If you collect Michelin-stars, there are two with one apiece – Table du Gourmet and Auberge du Schoenenbourg. But lots of lesser tables await.

- ✪ A tasting of the local wines at Domaine Baumann.

- ✪ In the shops: clever metal mobiles of knights on horseback; green-stemmed Riesling glasses at the Cristallerie de Riquewihr; decorated gingerbread hearts – and macaroons.

- ✪ The Feerie de Noël Christmas shop.

- ⓘ In the middle of the main cobbled street which is rather pompously named Général de Gaulle.

Somewhere to stay

- ↘ Hôtel l'Oriel, in a quiet alley behind the church. Spotless rustic style. No restaurant. ☎ 03 89 49 03 13.

- ↘ Hôtel Riquewihr on the road that crosses the vines to Ribeauvillé. Modern, with a pool. No restaurant. ☎ 03 89 86 03 00.

Colmar (Haut-Rhin)

Wednesday, Thursday and Saturday, plus Friday flea market

Don't expect to drive your car through the centre. Colmar's medieval inner core is the most intact in Alsace and well protected. In the 16th century, wine merchants shipped the local Riesling along the river Lauch and the canal. Today, pleasure boats putter through its winsome Petite Venise quarter, their passengers captivated by the so-picturesque jostle of timbered houses tinted powder blue, dark blue and pale sand. Most of the central cobbled alleys, squares and waterside streets are pedestrianized, so once you've ditched your wheels (plenty of car parks), it's a pleasure to wander in relative calm.

At its most animated during the wine fair in August, Colmar is incredibly popular year round, but its allure is undiminished by tourism. There are masses of antiques shops, and every Friday in the long summer season, a great *brocante* alights in Place des Dominicains. The pickings range from carved fruit-wood picture frames to assorted chocolate moulds. On Thursday morning, it's the food market:

the old covered hall by the river opens and local producers set up in the surrounding streets. Delicacies in Colmar come in rich and super rich – not content just with *foie gras*, here they layer it with truffles (*pain de Colmar*). Other local goodies to consider include *saucissons* made from wild boar, and tiny smoked *filets mignons*. Meanwhile, in Place des Dominicains and the cathedral square, clothes and marvellous textiles are sold all day Thursday. This market is back again on Saturday. There are two other general markets: Saturday and Wednesday mornings on the outskirts. Colmar's Christmas market is a stunner too.

Don't miss

✪ The town at night delicately floodlit.

✪ Musée d'Unterlinden to see Matthias Grünewald's awesome Issenheim altarpiece.

✪ Musée Bartholdi, the house where the sculptor of New York's Statue of Liberty was born.

✪ Musée du Jouet – antique wind-up toys and trains.

✪ Maison Pfister and Maison des Têtes for their magnificently elaborate exteriors. The latter, with over a hundred stone-carved creatures on its facade, is now a hotel with a superb restaurant.

✪ The Dominican church's 'Virgin and the Rose Bush' by Schongauer – birdlovers will spot a robin, chaffinch and goldfinch among the roses.

✪ The Route du Vin – Colmar is the capital of wine country.

ⓘ 4 Rue des Unterlinden.

Somewhere to stay

➥ Hostellerie le Maréchal, 3-star in a 16th-century Alsatian-style house overlooking the Petite Venise. ☎ 03 89 41 60 32.

➥ Hôtel Le Colombier offers contemporary charm in a Renaissance setting around a quiet courtyard. ☎ 03 89 23 97 27.

Gueberschwihr (Haut-Rhin)
Wednesday

Not to be confused with the much larger Guebwiller, Gueberschwihr oozes as much charm as Riquewihr but is more low-profile – perhaps its name is harder to pronounce! Just south-west of Colmar, this little village on the Route du Vin is one to relax in, even kick off your shoes while flopping at a café table to sample a *ballon* from the local cooperative. Even the Wednesday morning market doesn't disturb the peace too much, slotting in among the plethora of dark terracotta houses. Gueberschwihr is the kind of place it's a pleasure to shop when you've had your fill of fighting for a parking space. Just leave the car by the vineyards on the fringe of town and amble in. The market mostly comprises stuff brought in by local farmers. Lovely jams and fruit purées, butter, eggs, bunches of earthy horseradish (a regular ingredient in Alsace cuisine) and a small selection of handicrafts in summer.

Take your time over tasting in the local caves and play the game of spotting symbols on the buildings' carved timbers: diamonds for fertility, St Andrew's cross for prosperity, the sun for a good harvest and hearts for virgins. I didn't spot many hearts.

Don't miss

✪ A rather nice Romanesque tower.

ⓘ No tourist office.

Somewhere to stay

⬐ Relais du Vignoble, a pleasant, unassuming roadside stop. Newish building with a *cave* attached. Rooms look out on the vines. Tasty inexpensive menus. ☎ 03 89 49 22 22.

Obernai (Bas-Rhin)
Thursday morning

In the northern vineyards, Obernai once served as the HQ of the dukes of Alsace. Set within walled ramparts with three medieval gates still holding, it is more truly Alsatian than most other towns – its residents speak Alsatian and national costume is shaken out and donned at the drop of a flamboyantly brimmed black hat.

Obernai revolves around its ancient Place du Marché and the 16th-century Halle aux Blés (corn exchange). The Thursday morning market couldn't have a more atmospheric setting. Stands almost smother the marvellous Renaissance fountain, the overflow (stalls not fountain)

spilling into neighbouring *places* du Beffroi and de l'Eglise. Delicious country produce, river fish such as *sandre* and *omble chevalier* and a feast of flowers mix it with bargain fashion, fabrics and table accessories. If you want to lunch in one of the well-patronized *winstubs* (a very popular one is now ensconced in the Halle aux Blés), get there early or be prepared to veer off into one of the quieter flower-filled courtyards. *Winstubs* are the places to enjoy simple filling dishes such as *bäckoffe*, in which layers of three different meats, potatoes and onion rings are cooked in Riesling – what else?

Don't miss

✪ A walk along the ramparts to view the vineyards and the waves of Vosges forest beyond.

✪ Eglise St-Pierre-et-St-Paul.

✪ The 16th-century town hall and the Kapellturm Gothic belfry.

✪ La Dime *winstub*, Rue des Pèlerins.

✪ La Maison du Lin (household linens).

✪ Gross Chocolatier, Rue de Général Gouraud.

✪ The Chapelle Sainte-Odile, last resting place of Alsace's 7th-century patron saint, on Mont Sainte-Odile to the west.

ⓘ Place du Beffroi.

Somewhere to stay

↘ La Diligence, Place de la Mairie, comfortable, small hotel in a very pretty central area. ☎ 03 88 95 55 69.

↘ Les Jardins d'Adairic, in the residential quarter. Nice newish hotel with a stream at the bottom of its garden. ☎ 03 88 47 64 77.

Sélestat (Haut-Rhin)

Tuesday and Saturday

I could easily have picked six of the best among the wine villages, but Sélestat is an interesting Renaissance town and, rather as wine-tasters grab a chunk of bread between takes to clear their palates, it's almost a relief to pause somewhere that's less intensely gussied up. Once, this was a great centre of learning. Charlemagne came for Christmas in 775. The Bibliothèqe Humaniste, which contains illuminated manuscripts and some of the earliest printed leather-bound books, is reason enough to stop here. Another is the bread museum (see Don't miss). And another is the Tuesday market.

This has been unfurling throughout the streets of the town centre since 1435. It's a terrific market affording an excellent mix. Clothes and cabbages, great glass jars of preserved *foie gras* and humble pies, dainty fruit tarts and a whole range of country breads. The handicrafts, from gaudy painted tiles to expertly fashioned silk flowers, make present-buying a breeze.

If you miss Tuesday, on Saturday morning there's a smaller market of local produce in Rue Galiéni and a *marché bio* (organically grown stuff and herbal potions) in the St Hilaire arsenal, Rue des Chevaliers.

Don't miss

❍ The Humanist Library, Rue de la Bibliothèque.

❍ The turreted Cour des Prélats.

❍ Two wonderful churches within a step of each other – Ste-Foy, 12th-century with an octagonal belfry, and St-Georges whose green-and-gold ceramic roof tiles echo those of Burgundy.

❍ La Maison du Pain, Rue du Sel, a museum, café and bakery all in one where visiting bakers from around the world drop by to demonstrate their methods of bread-making.

❍ Towering in the hills to the west, Haut-Koenigsbourg castle, the fortress recreated by Kaiser Wilhelm II at the end of the 19th century.

ⓘ Boulevard de Général Leclerc.

Somewhere to stay

➘ The very special Hostellerie de l'Abbaye la Pommeraie, a Relais & Châteaux in the old town with Michelin-starred restaurant and welcoming *winstub*. ☎ 03 88 92 07 84.

➘ The affable and more easily affordable Auberge des Alliés, near Ste-Foy. ☎ 03 88 92 09 34.

Best of the Rest

★ **Betschdorf** Very lively village north of Strasbourg on the edge of the Hagenau forest, famous for its blue-patterned, grey-glazed pottery and the only timber-framed church in Alsace, the Lutheran Kuhlendorf. Monday is market day.

★ **Dambach-la-Ville** Distinguished by ramparts and fortified gates, another pleasant wine town with important growers. Has a market on Wednesday.

★ **Molsheim** Streets are packed with Renaissance houses and the land beyond with vines. Good stop on a Monday or Friday for marketing.

★ **Mulhouse** A busy industrial city, but if you have occasion to be there it does have very good markets (Tuesday, Thursday, Friday and Saturday) as well as some splendid museums (fabrics, railway history) and the Schlumpf collection of vintage cars including several Bugattis and Charlie Chaplin's Roller. Significant flea market last Sunday in the month.

★ **Neuf-Brisach** Its amazingly intact octagonal citadel is one of military architect Vauban's most remarkable star-shaped accomplishments, complete with church dedicated to St Louis (sucking up to the Sun King). On Friday mornings there's a small market of fish, local vegetables, roast chickens etc, in the central square. On the first and third Mondays of the month, a big mixed market.

★ **Ribeauvillé** Arguably even more of a tourist honeypot than its near neighbour Riquewihr, this village known for the quality of its Riesling and Traminer wine also boasts the ruins of three medieval castles, an extraordinary butcher's tower in the town hall square and a very jolly Saturday market.

★ **Saverne** Once the summer retreat of the prince-bishops of Strasbourg, a town beautifully sited on the Marne-Rhine canal and the river Zorn. Lots of timbered Renaissance houses and gourmet eating places along its main street. Market Tuesday and Thursday, also Saturday in summer.

★ **Soufflenheim** Home of the terracotta-coloured pottery decorated with bold flowers. Quite near (9km) Betschdorf. Monday and Wednesday markets.

⌂ www.tourisme-alsace.com

Markets at a glance: Alsace

A
Altkirch, *Thu*, *Sat*
Andlau, *Wed*
B
Barr, *Sat*
Bartenheim, *Fri*
Benfeld, *Mon*, *Sat* (Apr–Sep)
Bergheim, *Mon*
Betschdorf, *Mon*
Bischheim, *Fri*
Bischwiller, *Sat*
Bletterans, *Tue*, *Sat*
Brumath, *Wed*
C
Cernay, *Tue*, *Fri*
Châtenois, *Thu*
Colmar, see Six of the Best
D
Dambach-la-Ville, *Wed*
Dettwiller, *Wed*
Diemeringen, *Wed*
Drulingen, *Wed*
Duttlenheim, *Wed*
E
Erstein, *Thu*
F
Fegersheim, *Tue*, *Thu*, *Sat*
G
Gueberschwihr, see Six of the Best
Guebwiller, *Tue*, *Fri*
H
Hachimette, daily (not *Tue*)
Haguenau, *Tue*, *Fri*
Hindisheim, *Wed*
Hochfelden, *Tue*
Hoerdt, *Wed*
I
Illkirch-Graffenstaden, *Sat*
Ingersheim, *Wed*
Ingwiller, *Thu*
K
Kaysersberg, *Mon*, *Fri*
L
Labaroche, *Sat*
Lauterbourg, *Tue*, *Fri*
Lembach, *Wed*
Logelbach, *Wed*
M
Marckholsheim, *Tue*, *Wed*, *Fri*, *Sat*

Marlenheim, *Sat*
Masevaux, *Wed*
Molsheim, *Mon*, *Fri*
Mertzwiller, *Thu*
Mulhouse, *Tue*, *Thu*, *Sat*
Munster, *Tue*, *Sat*
Mutzig, *Fri*
N
Neuf-Brisach, *Fri*, 1st and 3rd *Mon*
Niederbronn-les-Bains, *Fri*
O
Obernai, see Six of the Best
Orbey, *Wed*, *Sat*
Ostwald, *Fri*
P
Pfaffenhoffen, *Sat*
Plobsheim, *Tue*, *Fri*
R
Reichshoffen, *Thu*
Rhinau, *Thu*
Ribeauvillé, *Sat*
Riquewihr, see Six of the Best
Rosheim, *Fri*
Rothau, *Sat*
Rouffach, *Sat*
Russ, *Fri*

S
Saales, *Mon*
Sainte-Croix-en-Plaine, *Tue*
Sainte-Marie-aux-Mines, *Sat*
Saint-Louis, *Sat*
Sarre-Union, *Fri*
Saverne, *Tue*, *Thu*
Schiltigheim, *Thu*
Schirmeck, *Wed*
Sélestat, see Six of the Best
Souffelweyersheim, *Thu*
Soufflenheim, *Mon*, *Wed*
Soultzmatt, *Tue*
Strasbourg, see Six of the Best
T
Thann, *Wed*, *Sat*
Turckheim, *Fri*
V
Villé, *Wed* (+ *Thu* eve Jun–Sep)
W
Wasselonne, *Mon*
Wettolsheim, *Wed*
Wintzenheim, *Fri*
Wissembourg, *Sat*
Woerth, *Thu*

LORRAINE

The elusive quiche, soldiers' caps, miracles in glass and mirabelles

When your region is known to the rest of the world mainly for an egg, cream and bacon tart, I suppose out of perversity you might at times be in denial about it. 'Where do you come from?' 'Lorraine.' 'Oh – quiche!' Getting a reaction like a sneeze must be a tad irritating. I wonder if that's why Lorraine's traditional savoury is so hard to come by? In my experience, quiche is no more and no less prevalent here than anywhere else. You see the usual rather stodgy versions in *traiteurs* and bakeries but rarely does it feature on restaurant menus. Once, after three days in and around the delightful city of Metz, eating – it has to be said – superb food, my search for quiche was unrequited. So I ordered one in a bistrot behind the cathedral. It had cheese in it – supposedly a no-no – and was, well . . . disappointing. Then, one summer evening I happened upon a tiny market of local produce in the village of Girmont-Val-d'Ajol in the Vosges and met the definitive article. In melt-in-the mouth pastry hand-crafted at the edges, this quiche was luxuriously creamy, with that all-important hint of nutmeg. An invention to be proud of.

The Vosges, shared by Lorraine with Alsace and Franche-Comté, are more a flow of thickly wooded hills than a 'mountain range' and, from a distance, resemble a rumpled carpet that the dog has burrowed under. They run for 100 kilometres and are 50 kilometres wide. In among the folds, you can see only fir trees. But get to the summits, where there are copses of beech and clearings scattered with wildflowers, and on a clear day you can see across Alsace to Germany on the far side of the Rhine.

To the west, the rest of Lorraine sprawls until it meets Champagne-Ardenne, over two-thirds of it napped in forest, with huge protected wilderness areas and lakes set aside for migrating birds. Although firmly established as a cog in the works of the industrial east, concerned – at one time – with coal, iron, salt and steel, this undeservedly little-known region is also surprisingly rural. Where the river Meuse meanders above Verdun, the pastureland is of a green so intense it could have been painted in pure viridian.

Some wine is produced in the Pays de Metz and around Toul, but you won't find village after picturesque village as you do in Alsace. Aside from the exceptional glories of the main cities and the delights of the spa centres, many towns are a hotchpotch of drab architecture, still dented by the ravages of 20th-century warfare. Markets here are fewer than anywhere else in France but there are some definitely worth hitting if you go to see Lorraine's resonant military sites, Art Nouveau treasures or untrammelled nature.

Specialities

For all kinds of reasons, hunters after **militaria** will find a rich seam in Lorraine. The region has historically been a battleground. Until the 16th century it was ruled by powerful dukes. Part of it then became France, part Germany and the borders have since shifted back and forth. Vestiges remain of the Maginot Line, the notoriously ineffective World War One defence, limitless acres of white crosses mark the graves of unknown soldiers and, today, the HQ of the French army are in Metz. Flea markets often throw up old weapons and armour, dusty braided tunics and assorted caps, as well as soldiers' water bottles and other items of personal equipment.

In the cradle of Art Nouveau, the skills associated with this sinuous style – of glass-making, enamelling, ironwork and ceramics – are still going strong. **Craftwork** in Lorraine is often stunning. Pretty and practical bargain glassware may sparkle at markets, but not the latest and finest Daum, Baccarat, St-Louis or Portieux crystal – not even seconds; they're all smashed at birth. Antique pieces can be found in the flea markets. An Emile Gallé vase, perhaps? But it won't be a bargain. Keep an eye open for enamelled artefacts and glazed earthenware from Longwy, Niderviller, Sarreguemines and Lunéville.

The admirable **mirabelle**, a tiny yellow plum originally introduced from Italy, could qualify as Lorraine's regional emblem – 80 per cent of the national crop is harvested here. Mirabelles appear in every guise from fresh fruit in season to jam, juice, sugar syrup, plum brandy, bonbons, *tartes* and liqueur chocolates. Possibly the most exquisite treat of all is mirabelles in marzipan with mirabelle *eau de vie* in the centre. On the savoury side, rabbit in mirabelle plum aspic is an inspired combination. *Traiteurs* do it, ready to be sliced thickly like a terrine.

Hand-made redcurrant jam from Bar-le-Duc is another 'special'. Otherwise known as 'Lorraine's caviar', it may not

sound so unusual, but what makes it unique is a) the fact that people sit winkling the seeds out of the fruit with goose feathers, and b) the taste, which is tartly sweet and sensationally good. Alfred Hitchcock was a great fan of this *confiture de groseilles* – not jelly, please note; the texture of the fruit remains. Only one factory in the little town of Bar-le-Duc still makes it the time-honoured way, but passable imitations are offered up at farmers' markets. With cream cheese, it makes a lovely dessert.

The invention of the **madeleine**, the little cake which caused Marcel Proust to wallow in such waves of nostalgia in *Remembrance of Things Past*, has been claimed most tenaciously by the citizens of Commercy. Their version of its origin is that at a banquet hosted by Duke Stanislas (he who commissioned the fabulous Place Stanislas in Nancy), the chef flounced out of the kitchen leaving a minion to rustle up dessert. The minion's name was Madeleine and she simply whipped up a few of the cookies her mother made at home. *Et, voila!* Immortality. Essentially a lemony Victoria sponge mix – though this being France rather drier – *madeleines* are but one of a long list of Lorraine confections. There doesn't seem to be a town that hasn't pinned its name on some kind of toothsome tea cake, biscuit or bonbon, whether it's gingerbread from Remiremont, Boulay macaroons, St-Mihiel almond biscuits, golden Bergamotes de Nancy or sugared almonds from Verdun.

Metz (Moselle)
Daily except Sunday and Monday

First night in Metz, I hung up my clothes in a romantic toile-de-Jouy'd room with a view – right outside the Gothic wonder of the floodlit cathedral. I decided instantly that this was a city of obvious charm and never had reason to change my mind. Because of its Germanic past, the capital of Lorraine feels more mid-European, and wide, tree-lined boulevards, flower gardens, fountains and engaging river walks by the Moselle and Seille give it a green and pleasant air.

The Hôtel de la Cathédrale (see below) hits the spot for the open-air market that pitches up on Tuesday, Thursday and Saturday mornings in the cobbled square outside. The adjacent food hall functions daily (except Sunday and Monday). Here, the forest fare from the Vosges is something to marvel at. Suckling pig in aspic. Wild boar. Venison. *Saucisson* spiked with spices, pistachios or truffles. And mushrooms – ceps, morels and chanterelles, depending on the season. Big-city sophistication, of course, demands – and is satisfied by – goodies from *partout*. Olives from Provence. Pickles from Poland. Black-forest gateau.

What Metz is a real mecca for, however, is antiques. Not only is it bursting with dedicated shops, it boasts (along with Isle-sur-la-Sorgue in Provence) that it hosts the country's second largest flea market, after Clignancourt in Paris. At least once and often twice a month, dealers and buyers from all over eastern France and the border countries cram into the Metz Congress Centre. A key source of 19th- and 20th-century furniture and objects, it also throws up a mixed bag of everything from comic strips to mechanical spare parts. To check the programme of dates for the *puces* (they're not on fixed days), call the organizers on 03 87 55 66 00. There are additional second-hand trade fairs from time to time in the Outre Seille district.

Don't miss

○ St Etienne's cathedral: known as 'God's lantern' because of its expanse of stained glass, some by Chagall. Carvings of naughty peasants can be seen mooning high up inside the vaulted roof.

○ The oldest still-used theatre in its lovely neo-classical square.

○ The Templars' chapel – one of the oldest churches in the land.

○ The railway station, built during Wilhelm II's Second Reich – Cecil B de Mille could not have done it better. Philippe Starck designed the new street lights outside.

ⓘ Place d'Armes.

Somewhere to stay

↘ Hôtel de la Cathédrale, 17th-century, cosy. Chateaubriand once slept here. Breakfast only, but good restaurants nearby (like L'Ecluse, which does Breton specialities). ☎ 03 87 75 00 02.

↘ Hôtel Cécil, pleasant 1920s (an Englishman built it) 2-star with subdued decor near the station. ☎ 03 87 66 66 13.

Nancy (Meurthe-et-Moselle)

Tuesday to Saturday, antiques market first Saturday in the month

The cradle of Art Nouveau, Nancy is where Emile Gallé designed his inimitable vases and Louis Majorelle his sinuous furniture. A distinctly French city, Nancy contains one of the most harmonious urban spaces in Europe, Place Stanislas. To admire its elegance, scale and magnificent gilded wrought-iron gates, the best vantage point is a table at the Café Foy. On a city walking tour, this old coffee house festooned with Bacchanalia was, I remember, welcome respite from the verbal torrent of a too-knowledgeable guide! Later, led into the narrow Grande Rue, we again managed to lose her in the delightful muddle of the flea market (monthly, first Saturday). Giggling like schoolchildren off the leash, we tried on old *gendarmes'* caps smelling of mothballs and fusty Foreign Legion kepis, and pounced on anything that looked vaguely Art Nouveau. I bought an enamelled saucer which turned out to be genuine but not wildly valuable. This is a fun market full of pretty trinkets and bric-a-brac in a very picturesque setting.

Nancy's big covered market is in Place Henri Mengin and open Tuesday to Saturday all day. Its contents are eclectic. Don't forget to buy a box of Bergamotes de Nancy, the biscuits flavoured with bergamot that score for their packaging alone.

This so-rewarding city has but one drawback. Parking is a nightmare. Go by train (Eurostar to Paris, TGV to Nancy).

Don't miss

✪ The Musée des Beaux Arts, a fine 18th-century mansion on Place Stanislas which has a superb collection of antique Daum crystal.

✪ Crystal boutiques around the square sell modern Daum and Baccarat.

✪ The Villa Majorelle, Louis Majorelle's totally Art Nouveau house.

✪ Museum of the Nancy School, again a large house of the appropriate period, where entire rooms are embellished with work by the exponents of 'the spaghetti style' – Majorelle, Prouvé, Vallin, Gallé, Grüber and Daum. Pillars writhe and twist like unknown trees and butterflies alight on lamps.

✪ The elegant symmetry of the Cours Léopold.

✪ Brasserie Excelsior for its Art Nouveau/Deco interior, exquisite food (try the wild boar terrine with chestnuts and forest berries).

ⓘ Place Stanislas.

Somewhere to stay

↘ Grand Hôtel de la Reine – to stay in Place Stanislas and bask in its floodlit gleam at night is the ultimate treat.

Marie-Antoinette slept in this svelte *pavillon* – but don't consider that an ill omen. Expensive but a wonderful experience. ☎ 03 83 35 03 01.

↘ Hôtel Résidence, oddly attired rather folksy 3-star that's comfortable and welcoming. It's a *Bon Weekend en Villes* hotel where you can at times stay 2 nights for the price of one.
☎ 03 83 40 33 56.

Vittel (Vosges)
Wednesday and Saturday

I was prepared for this famous spa resort to veer towards the antiseptic. Far from it. Vittel is, in reality, lush, sophisticated and full of architectural curiosities. Like an inland Le Touquet. On the August day I was in town, everything was bathed in a buttery golden light and I half expected to turn the corner and find the sea. In fact, I came very near to downing tools and squandering a few days here. Public gardens with fizzing fountains garnish the opulence of the thermal establishments, while a miniature train snakes past main-street chic and along quiet, leafy avenues of idiosyncratic villas – all early-20th-century. There's a small market mostly of fresh produce on Wednesday and Saturday mornings in Place Général de Gaulle, within a few minutes' walk of the town centre and the Parc Thermal. Farmers bring in lovely fresh cheeses with herbs, and Brouère, another good local one. With summer red fruits or a few golden mirabelles, you'll be well-equipped for a picnic and have no problem finding a spot somewhere in Vittel's green and flowery acres.

Craftspeople and small producers also sometimes sell their wares in the arcaded spa gallery during the summer, but not on a regular basis.

Don't miss

✪ The sumptuous baths and gallery where you taste the waters. The town was designed all-of-a-piece by, among others, Charles Garnier, who did the Paris Opéra.

✪ Coffee or a drink at the Grand Hôtel des Thermes (and Casino), now owned by Club Méditérranée.

✪ The neighbouring spa, Contrexéville, only 5 minutes' drive away.

✪ The Imagerie at Epinal (45 minutes – see Best of the Rest).

✪ The Roman amphitheatre and mosaics at Grand (30 minutes).

✪ Domrémy-la-Pucelle (30 minutes), the village where Joan of Arc was born, and the Centre Johannique.

ⓘ Avenue Bouloumié.

Somewhere to stay

◥ Hôtel d'Angleterre is very charming – a not overwhelming 'grand' with a wooded garden, pool, fitness packages and unpretentious regional cooking. ☎ 03 29 08 08 42.

◥ Le Chalet Vittelius, comfortable 2-chimney Logis within walking distance of the centre. ☎ 03 29 08 07 21.

Verdun (Meuse)
Friday morning

It's the town that invented sugared almonds (*dragées*), but this is hardly the first fact that surfaces when the name of Verdun is mentioned. The apocalyptic Battle for Verdun was one of the most devastating of World War One. The loss of life on both sides was horrific in its proportions – over 800,000 in the space of 18 months. At the end of which, the evacuated town was razed. France's Unknown Soldier was chosen from the remains of those slaughtered.

Today, Verdun remembers – the museum in the underground citadel contains a shattering but superb memorial – but the attractive Meuse-side town doesn't live in the past. Sensitively rebuilt, it's an arresting town to arrive at,

with an animated river frontage guarded by the restored 15th-century Chaussée gateway. The stunning Monument aux Morts of five soldiers standing shoulder to shoulder says it all.

When I was here in 2004, the old covered market was also being restored and the Friday morning market temporarily at a remove. By the time you read this, the work should be well finished and the site promises to be yet another shiny facet of the new Verdun. It's on Rue Victor Hugo just below the cathedral and a step from the river. Don't forget the sugared almonds.

Don't miss

- ○ La Citadelle Souterrain. Prepare to be emotionally rocked. The conception is only too brilliantly effective – battery-powered cars take you through 15 galleries of Vauban's ancient fortifications which reveal through inspired audio-visuals the story of the brutal battle's carnage.

- ○ The World Peace Centre in the former Bishop's Palace.

- ○ In the battlefields, the Ossuary at Douaumont, with its forest of crosses where 130,000 unknown soldiers lie.

- ○ A tour of the sugared almond makers, Dragées Braquier, Rue du Fort.

- ○ Aux Délices, Rue Mazel, for a tasty range of quiches with different additions – cheese, onion, snails, etc (open 7.15 to 19.15).

- ○ A local Stenay beer on Les Copains d'Abord – this jolly barge in the marina makes an original watering hole.

- ⓘ Place de la Nation, by the Monument.

Somewhere to stay

- ◿ In the little town of St-Mihiel, between Verdun and Commercy, the delightful Hôtel Restaurant Rive Gauche. Good restaurant (try the home-made terrine of *foie gras*). ☎ 03 29 89 15 83.

- ◿ In the Argonne forest, a few miles to the west, a haven of an auberge: Hôtel Restaurant à l'Orée du Bois in Futeau. Enchanting spot. Food superb.
☎ 03 29 88 28 41.

Gérardmer (Vosges)
Thursday and Saturday mornings

The 'pearl of the Vosges'? I'm nervous of such precious labels, but Gérardmer deserves it – and who am I to gainsay the claim of an Office du Tourisme which has been at it longer than any other town's in France (since 1875)?

Actually, it was Victor Hugo's brother Abel who coined the phrase (obviously not as original as his sibling) but it is as apt today. The appeal of this garden-filled lakeside resort, anchored in fleecy Vosges pinewoods, can be summed up in three words – 'location, location, location'. Gérardmer has been custom-built for leisure, be it winter sports in the mountains or sailing on the lake in summer. More or less obliterated by the Nazi scorched-earth policy, it was totally rebuilt in the late 1940s.

Tourism is now the town's pivot and the Thursday market reflects this, with plenty of souvenir-sized objects to buy. The craftspeople from Liézey, a *village artisanal* a few miles away, bring in hand-made wooden toys, ceramics and pottery, as well as delicious concentrated fruit drinks and Petit Cru Vosgien, a semi-sparkling apéritif made from wild herbs and plants. The local cheese, Géromé, is Lorraine's version of Munster, so this can be mild and creamy or pungent beyond taking home. With lots of outdoor action in the offing, backpacks and suitable clothes for boating and hiking mix with more fashionable threads and rustic clogs. And although Gérardmer's textile industry is not what it used to be, there are bargains in fabrics and pretty household linens – as in Alsace.

The Saturday market is smaller and more angled towards food. Both materialize in Place du 8 Mai behind the church.

Don't miss

✪ Boat trips and pedaloes on Lake Gérardmer, the largest in the Vosges, and on Lake Longemer nearby.

✪ The Musée du Textile des Vosges.

✪ Endless waterside walks.

✪ For energetic hikers and pony-trekkers, the Route des Crêtes which takes you over the top of the Vosges into Alsace – access at the Col de la Schlucht.

✪ The craft village of Liézey, 8km from Gérardmer, where you can watch skilled hands fashioning all kinds of beautiful work.

ⓘ Place des Déportés.

Somewhere to stay

↘ Le Grand Hôtel, in the centre of town, a very well-run establishment with indoor and outdoor pools, fitness centre and two restaurants. ☎ 03 29 63 06 31.

↘ Hôtel Beau Rivage, a modern '*hôtel du lac*' whose gourmet restaurant's windows frame panoramic views of glassy water. Heated outdoor pool. ☎ 03 29 63 22 28.

Plombières-les-Bains (Vosges)
Friday plus Christmas market weekends in December

This small spa town nestling in a cleft of the Vosges has an incongruous grandeur.

As you tumble down into its time warp (modern spread having been hindered by the enclosure of the valley), the cool of its deep shadows, rose gardens and graceful architecture instantly soothes and refreshes. The Romans first exploited the source of Plombières' radioactive water which spurts out in 27 different places. The town was then redeveloped in the 17th century and luminaries such as the Empress Joséphine, Scotland's James Stuart (the 'Old Pretender'), Baudelaire and Berlioz have come to be steamed, detoxed, pummelled and plastered with mud.

Beyond the thermal establishments, the palatial spa hotels and the casino, an engagingly ordinary little bit of bourgeois town enjoys a small weekly market on Friday mornings, but it's the Christmas markets in Plombières that put it on the map. Held over the four weekends of December in a tree-lined *allée* hung with winking lights, they add extra sparkle to a few days' winter spa indulgence. Present lists can be wiped out in a trice with enamelled jewellery, pinewood honey, kirsch chocolates and delightful craftwork (lots from neighbouring Alsace), while golden bonbons which imprison thistle heads soaked in *eau de vie* make novel stocking fillers.

Don't miss

✪ The Pavillon des Princes.

✪ Les Thermes Napoléon.

✪ Les Bains Impériaux.

ⓘ Place Maurice Janot.

Somewhere to stay

↘ Le Prestige Impérial – opulent common parts in *fin-de-siècle* style, modern rooms. The cavernous dining room, where people pad about in towelling, is not above serving cottage pie (*hachis parmentier*). Direct access to Les Thermes. ☎ 03 29 30 07 07.

↘ Le Commerce. Open April to September only. Simple rooms, country-house dining room, swimming pool and solarium. ☎ 03 29 66 00 47.

Best of the Rest

★ **Baccarat** Pleasant town on the Meurthe whose name is synonymous with exquisite crystal – and, of course, a card game, but it's the glass that's trumps here. No factory visits, but the museum has demos and sparkling exhibits which range from designs for Tsar Nicholas II to tiny paperweights. Market Friday morning.

★ **Bar-le-Duc** The River Ornain flows between the low town and the high town where there are some beautiful Renaissance mansions. If you want to watch the depipping of the redcurrants with a goose feather at the jam factory, taking in a market (Tuesday, Thursday or Saturday) will give added interest.

★ **Epinal** Unmissable for its riveting museum of printing, the Imagerie, which houses a Gutenburg press and Harris linotype machine from England. Artisan-printers still produce fabulous posters and cards in the traditional way on hand-made paper. The town's outskirts are fairly dull, but there's a little bit of old town left and some nice areas by the Moselle. Markets on Wednesday and Saturday.

★ **Girmont-Val d'Ajol** Pleasant Vosges village which holds a market of local produce and crafts every Friday evening in July and August.

★ **Lunéville** boasts a château known as Le Petit Versailles, where Duke Stanislas ended his days, and two excellent museums: one devoted to *faïence* (glazed earthenware), the other to motorbikes. Markets Tuesday,

Thursday and Saturday in Place Léopold.

★ **Mirecourt** Centre of violin-making and home to the National School for the skill. Also to a museum. The

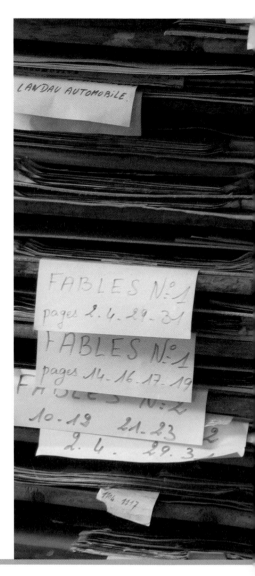

Lutherie's collection of ancient strings and mechanical instruments includes an organ whose repertoire features ten-note tunes to teach your pet canary. The Saturday market is a

bonus if you happen to be here.

★ **Montmédy** A border town, or rather two. Le Bas is unremarkable. Tiny Montmédy-le-Haut is extraordinary. Fortified to the hilt. It had changed hands so often before France took it in the mid-1600s that Louis XIV is said to have instructed Vauban, 'Enough is enough! Make sure we don't lose it!' Tuesday is market day.

★ **St-Dié-des-Vosges** Worth a visit for its cathedral and church connected by cloisters as well as a museum on Vosges life. Markets on Tuesday, Friday and Saturday.

★ **St-Mihiel** An appealing small town in the Meuse valley whose pride and joy is a wonderful 17th-century Benedictine Library. Saturday market.

★ **Stenay** A shrine for beer lovers, this small town on the Meuse not only makes a very good brew, downed with gusto throughout Lorraine, it houses the intriguing Musée Européen de la Bière in a former maltings in the old town. Friday is market day.

★ **Toul** The wine town, surrounded by forest plus vineyards to the north, then by the Moselle and the Canal de la Marne, and finally by Vauban ramparts. Among its highlights are the cathedral's Renaissance chapels. Gris de Toul is the local label. The sparkling version with a dash of Mirabelle liqueur makes 'Kir Lorraine'. Markets on Wednesday and Friday.

🖱 www.cr-lorraine.fr

Markets at a glance: Lorraine

B
Baccarat, *Fri*
Bains-les-Bains, *Fri*
Ban-de-Laveline, *Sat*
Bar-le-Duc, *Tue, Thu, Sat*
Bleurville, 1st *Sat* (*bio*)
Bouligny, *Wed*
Bruyères, *Wed*
C
Châtel-sur-Moselle, *Fri*
Commercy, *Mon, Fri*
Contrexéville, *Tue, Fri*
Corcieux, *Mon*
Cornimont, *Thu*
D
Dabo, *Sat*
Damvillers, *Sat*
Darney, *Fri*
Dun-sur-Meuse, *Wed*
E
Éloyes, *Sun*
Epinal, *Wed, Sat*
Étain, *Thu*
Étival-Clairefontaine, *Wed*
F
Falck, *Wed*
Faulquemont, *Thu*
Fenétrange, *Wed*
Fraize, *Fri* (+ *Wed* eve mid-Jul–mid-Aug)
G
Gérardmer, see Six of the Best
Girmont-Val-d'Ajol, *Fri* eve (end Jun–Aug)
Gondrecourt-le-Château, *Fri*
H
Haussonville, *Tue, Thu, Fri, Sat*
Hennezel, last *Wed*
L
Lamarche, *Fri*
Liffol-le-Grand, *Thu*
Ligny-en-Barrois, *Fri*
Lunéville, *Tue,Thu, Sat*
M
Maizières-lès-Metz, *Thu*
Marly, *Tue*
Martigny-les-Bains, *Fri*
Metz, see Six of the Best
Mirecourt, *Sat*

Monthureux-sur-Saône, *Sat*
Montmédy, *Tue*
Moyenmoutier, *Thu* (+ *Sun* Apr–Oct)
N
Nancy, see Six of the Best
Neufchâteau, *Sat*
Nomexy, *Sat*
P
Phalsbourg, *Fri, Sat*
Plombières-les-Bains, see Six of the Best
R
Rambervilliers, *Thu*
Raon-l'Etape, *Sat*
Remiremont, *Tue, Fri*
Revigny-sur-Ornain, *Wed, Sat*
S
Saint-Amié, *Wed* (Jul–Sep)
Saint-Dié-des-Vosges, *Tue, Fri, Sat*
Saint-Mihiel, *Sat*
Sarrebourg, *Tue, Fri*
Sarreguemines, *Tue, Fri*
Serémange-Erzange, *Wed*
Stenay, *Fri*
T
Le Thillot, *Sat*
Toul, *Wed, Fri*
V
Le Val-d'Ajol, *Sun* (+ last *Sat* for flea market Apr–Sep)
Vandoeuvre-lès-Nancy, *Fri, Sun*
Vaucouleurs, *Sat*
Verdun, see Six of the Best
Vigneulles-lès-Hattonchâtel, *Sun* (+ *Sat* Jul/Aug)
Vittel, see Six of the Best
Volmerange-les-Mines, *Wed*
Y
Yutz, *Fri*
Z
Zoufftgen, *Fri*

PROVENCE & CÔTE D'AZUR

Olive passion, lavender bees in stereo and the southern capital of fleas

Marseille, the Mediterranean port with a somewhat less-than-warranted 'wicked' reputation, was the scene of my first-ever encounter with a full-blown French market. Feeling grey around the gills after a night travelling south *sans couchette* on the old Blue Sky Express (long since shunted into the sidings of railway history), I walked into the September light of Provence and a frenzy of buying and selling in the Place des Capucins.

The impact was like a shot of adrenalin. Never had I seen anything like it. Stalls canopied against the already sizzling heat crowded this little square just off the city's main boulevard, La Canebière, which runs uphill from the Vieux Port. Under the awnings lay heaps of glistening olives, black and purple and green, and wooden bowls full of *tapenade*, the paste made from them that has a taste as old as time. Gaudy peppers and dark satiny aubergines jostled plump peaches, apricots and melons. Red mullet and huge whiskery prawns fixed me with their little black eyes. Such fish and shellfish were a revelation.

But it wasn't just the abundance and quality of the food or even the aroma of Gitanes cigarettes laced with roasting chicken that excited me; it was the clamour and glamour of it all, a bit of theatre that represented, to my newfangled teenage eyes, the exotic otherness of 'the south of France'. Every detail is still sharp in my memory: the balletic movements of lithe young hunks in tight T-shirts unloading vans to top up supplies, the manicured bronzed hands of local women expertly picking over the produce, the merchants' gypsy looks and strong Provençal accents. '*Très bieng, madameuh – vous n'avez pas une centime? De rieng.*' Even back in the 1960s, a centime was written off with a shrug.

Since then, I've got to know Provence and neighbouring Côte d'Azur, the smallest region of all, probably better than any other part of France, and their markets are a source of endless delight. There are also more of them here than anywhere else. This is marketsville ad infinitum – from the Luberon's *villages perchés*, immortalized by writers from Frédéric Mistral to Peter Mayle, to the lofty Vauban-fortified towns of the Hautes Alpes (remember that Provence, like Côte d'Azur, reaches right up into ski territory) to the Italianate resorts of the Riviera. The goodies on offer remain largely the same but the emphasis, as ever, changes according to what's grown locally. Olive groves, vines, cherry orchards, swathes of lavender, herb-covered *causses* and herds of goats are heavy clues. And the thicket of holm oak and undergrowth that covers the craggy hills of the Vaucluse and Alpes-de-Haute-Provence hides the most precious treasure of all – the black truffle.

Specialities

Provence grows the biggest share of the aristocrat of the fungus world, *Tuber melanosporum*. **Truffle** markets are surrounded by a mystique that is hard to penetrate. The buyers are almost exclusively restaurateurs, chefs and hoteliers who know the form. A casual observer will not even be aware of the prices – usually passed to and fro on scraps of paper. But the ritual is riveting to watch if you happen to be market-trawling in winter – November to March is the optimum time for truffle sales. And a few of the 'black diamonds' make their way to general markets to be snapped up by those with sharp eyes, quick reactions and deep pockets.

Up in the back country, where the big commercial **lavender** fields (at their peak in mid-July) stretch across the Plateau de Valensole and westwards towards Mont Ventoux, lavender bags/soap/essence/oil are a given. So is that famous Provençal mix of **herbs**, indispensable to good cooks, which includes a sniff of lavender in its blend of rosemary, mint, savory, sage, marjoram, tarragon and thyme. Alas, the lovely terracotta pots with the words *herbes de Provence* scrawled across them are now a rarity but, bagged in rustic sacking or more cheaply in clear plastic, these indigenous flavourings which grow wild in the hills are still the essential souvenir, transporting the seductive scents of southern France back to less-fragrant London or Long Island.

The bees that hum among the lavender contribute lavender **honey**, as well as golden beeswax candles, which are fine if you don't mind a gunge of melted wax building up on your candlesticks – it's unbudgeable on brass. Clones of the cicadas that rasp unseen alight on everything – they're a Provençal thing. Large ceramic ones are designed to cling to the wall, smaller versions to use as fridge magnets or brooches.

Since Picasso founded a **ceramics** industry at Vallauris, the potters of Côte d'Azur and Provence have never looked back. Some beautiful work by artist-craftspeople is sold at markets and you pay for what pleases you. Less expensive but with its own appeal is the mass-produced stuff, often decorated with olive motifs, while the plain glazed terracotta cooking pots and tableware displayed in bumper bundles are incredibly good value – who cares if some of it is made in Spain?

There's also the arm-and-a-leg patterned porcelain of Moustiers-Ste-Marie – though its rather fussy designs are an acquired taste. Choosing something small, like an egg cup, limits both the price and scope for decoration. The thing to do is look out for old pieces in antique markets as these are generally much more subtle and desirable.

No market from Antibes to Avignon is complete without its swags of sprigged, **hand-blocked cottons**. Originally from Tarascon, these were inspired by Indian prints and known as *les Indiennes*. Quality fabrics by Souleiado and Les Olivades are pricy but there are bales of imitations such as Valduras which are cheaper, cheerful and wash just as well. Tablecloths, quilts, tiered skirts – like those worn by the gypsies of the Camargue – festoon market stalls, and the same cotton is also run up into endless fripperies from aprons to oven gloves.

The famous *boutis* quilts are also much sought after, both second-hand and new ones in plain colours and subtler patterns – especially toile-de-Jouy. If you can't afford a bed cover, there are table mats and runners in *boutis* style too.

Plenty of good **wine** is grown on the basking slopes of the Côtes du Luberon, Côtes de Ventoux and especially the Var, which is now littered with AOC labels. The rosés and reds are best, good-value and quaffable, and there are some quite memorable labels like Bandol, Château La-Tour-l'Evêque (from Pierrefeu) and Le Grand Pigoudet (Rians). While wine doesn't, as a rule, take happily to being

sold off a sunny market stall, *caves* usually open their doors on market day and tempt buyers inside with a few bottles on display.

As for the **olive oil**, some of the world's best comes from Provence; several producers boast the AOC accolade. Beautifully turned olive wood salad bowls, cheese boards and pincers for *cornichons* (gherkins) make perfect presents. Olive oil soap is an affordable luxury while the olives themselves are both an essential drinks nibble and staple of any dish *provençal*. Aside from the chestnut, no tree can be more generous with its gifts than the olive.

Six of the Best

Forcalquier (Alpes-de-Haute-Provence)
Monday

This is one of the most popular markets in Haute Provence and one of my all-time favourites.

About an hour or so north of Aix, Forcalquier lies between the Valensole plateau (purple with lavender in July) and the Montagne de Lure (still tipped with snow in April). It was once the capital of the Counts of Provence, the last of whom, Raymond Bérenger V, had no sons but managed to marry off all four of his daughters to kings, including Eléanore to Henry III of England. So the dynasty went out with a royal flush. The Bérenger castle has long since crumbled, but today a domed sanctuary tops this small hill town, giving it a Hobbiton-like air from a distance.

The A to Z of Provencal specialities can be found at Forcalquier's market. The fact that it is held on a Monday, normally closing day, only partly explains its attraction. Centred on the Place du Bourguet under the gaze of a stately Gothic-Romanesque cathedral and an 18th-century picture house straight out of *Cinema Paradiso*, the stalls spread everywhere, up through the winding streets of the old town and down towards several free parking areas.

In addition to all the usual cottons, pottery, *miel de lavande* and bonanza of fruit, vegetables, fish and fowl, Forcalquier is a magnet for skilled artisans and budding dress designers, especially in the little *boulodrome* where wonderful knits, craft jewellery, accessories and avante-garde clothes stalls cluster around massive old plane trees.

You begin by buying a rope basket and end up weighed down with plastic carrier bags as well because the specialities are so tempting: a whole range of Banon *chèvre* cheeses – the little fresh discs decorated with a single sprig of savory, the pungent wrapped in dried chestnut leaves and tied with raffia; aubergine *caviar* and *tapenade* olive paste from the olive stall, and *pain de campagne* to spread it on; herb *tisanes* and, in high summer, big bunches of fresh thyme and tarragon; air-dried *saucissons* galore and aromatic chunks of spit-roasted pork complete with *jus* for lunch. But well before the cathedral bell sounds one-o'clock, you must find a seat at either the Café du Commerce or du Bourguet – *au soleil* if it's spring or autumn, under a parasol in July or August – to people watch and slake your thirst. If you like the flavour of aniseed, try a *pastis* or one of the curious herb-based *apéritifs de Provence*, made in Forcalquier's own unique distillery. Who could resist a drink called Rinquinquin?

Don't miss

○ The flagship shop of the now worldwide Olivier & Co, Place Vieille, whose proprietor Olivier Baussan hails from nearby Mane.

○ The Caves de Régusse, behind the cathedral, for local wines.

○ The ancient 16th-century Couvent des Cordelliers.

○ Further afield, the Monastery of Ganagobie, perched above the Durance Valley; the Romanesque priory of Notre Dame de Salagon with its medieval herb garden, and the anachronistic Château de Sauvan, styled after the Trianon at Versailles.

○ Award-winning AOC olive oil straight from the press at the Abrizzi grove near Les Mées, and the Moulin de l'Olivette shop in Manosque (35 and 20 minutes away respectively).

○ The Gorges du Verdon (about an hour's drive).

ⓘ Place du Bourguet.

Somewhere to stay

◢ Mas du Pont Roman, about 3km. Renovated 18th-century mill by a Romanesque bridge. Indoor and outdoor pools. No restaurant ☎ 04 92 75 49 46.

◢ Grand Hôtel, tiny 1-star that's spic, span and welcoming, in the main street. ☎ 04 92 75 00 35.

Nice (Côte-d'Azur)

Tuesday to Saturday

Like Queen Victoria, who wintered here, I prefer the Riviera resort of Nice in February. Around carnival fortnight, which varies from year to year, skies are often bluer than in summer, temperatures hover around 17°C and the light is cut-glass sharp.

You have to start early to get the best of it, striding along the Marché aux Fleurs in the *vieille ville* as the flower sellers assemble under their striped canopies wafting the delicate fragrance of yellow mimosa. It's the scent of spring on the Côte d'Azur just as Britain's is daffodils. Then the Cours Saleya and Place Pierre Gautier, focus of Nice's fruit and vegetable market, open up in an edible blur of Impressionist colour against the ochre stucco of baroque Italianate palaces (Nice was ruled by the Dukes of Savoy until the mid-19th century).

Before you do anything, it's compulsory to queue for *socca*, a savoury pancake made with chickpea flour. A jolly Niçoise regular flips it in a huge pan over a brazier, wraiths of smoke and steam rising in the cool air. Thus fuelled, you wander round the market's cartloads of olives and garlic, spices, nuts and winter squash, plus a haul of normally unseasonal produce from all around the Mediterranean. '*Allez, mesdames, m'sieurs, voici des fraises très bon marché. Essayez mes bonnes fraises!*' And people eagerly pop delicious strawberries from North Africa into their mouths, roll their eyes and nod.

As your digestive juices flow, the restaurants along the Cours Saleya grill peppers, stuff courgettes and prepare Niçois specialities like *ratatouille* or *trucha*, a tasty omelette with chopped green chard in it, so that on the dot of noon you will be unable to stop yourself flopping down on one of their terraces for lunch. Nice is one place where non-carnivores can veg out – always providing they're not hooked by the platters of fresh anchovies, sea urchins and lobster.

Every day there's also a small fish market in Place Saint-François and locally grown fruit and vegetables in Place Général-de-Gaulle. On Monday mornings, the Cours Saleya hosts a flea market.

It goes without saying, it's all equally marvellous in the summer. Just busier.

Don't miss

○ Specialist food shops in Rue St François de Paule, near the Cours Saleya: Confiserie Henri Auer, with its pretty rococo tearoom, for wonderful chocolates and candied rose petals and jasmine; Alziari for locally pressed olive oil and soap.

○ The Palais Lascaris, with its grand vaulted stairways and open courtyards, for an insight into how the Niçois nobility once lived.

○ The glories of the Russian Orthodox Church.

○ Museums devoted to the works of Matisse and Chagall in the suburb of Cimiez.

Somewhere to stay

⬎ Château des Ollières, affordable magic in the leafy Quartier des Beaumettes, once the sumptuous villa of a Russian prince. Still sumptuous as a hotel but prices not punishing. ☎ 04 92 15 77 99.

⬎ Hôtel Windsor, a few blocks back from the Promenade des Anglais, quiet, with a pool and small walled garden. ☎ 04 93 88 59 35.

Isle-sur-la-Sorgue (Vaucluse)

Saturday, Sunday, Monday

After Les Puces de Clignancourt in Paris, the picturesque Vaucluse town of Isle-sur-la-Sorgue, half an hour south-east of Avignon, claims to host the second largest flea market in France. This is not difficult to believe – even if Metz makes the same claim! On any day of the week,

Isle-sur-la-Sorgue is worth visiting for it is a feast of antiques and bric-a-brac shops and there are endless attractive little restaurants with terraces fronting or backing onto the river Sorgue and its offshoot canals which vein the town.

At weekends, however, Isle-sur-la-Sorgue's cup runneth over. On Saturday, Sunday and Monday it expands into a mammoth flea market, spreading its wares along the river's *quais*, across bridges and through sunny courtyards. The optimum day to go is Sunday, when from 8.00 to 13.00 the bygones are augmented by a bourgeoning traditional Provençal market with all the usual – or, more accurately, unusual – specialities and crafts.

If you want to carry off, as I have, frilly glass pendant lampshades, old French bedlinen, classic Ricard carafes and handsome Provençal country chairs, this is the place. And the characters are as varied as the goods. A Geordie lady from Newcastle has the best selection of enamel cafetières, and an eccentric Irishman flogs cut-price china from Stoke. The choice of courtyards and passageways to comb, from Le Cour St Francois to Le Village des Antiquaires, Place Gambetta to Le Carré de l'Isle, is inexhaustible on any one day. Don't miss the old station, Le Quai de la Gare, which houses two floors of stalls as well as bistros to refuel in when retail fatigue sets in.

My own favourite space, L'Ile aux Brocantes, has a great selection of wirework and metal garden furniture outside and an indoor cavern of really classy stuff. After you've run the gamut of Louis XV mirrors and Second Empire chaises longues, you slip through to the dappled shade of the little bistrot Chez Nane's waterside terrace. Here, to the accompaniment of quacking ducks excited by the prospect of occasional tidbits, you can lunch well for not a lot of euros.

Don't miss

✪ The 18th-century Hôtel Dieu whose pharmacy has 17th-century faïence from Moustiers.

✪ Nearby Fontaine-de-Vaucluse (10 minutes' drive), another pretty town with a rushing stream (a canoeists' paradise) and a still pool where the spring is below a towering cliff.

✪ About 12km away, Gordes, one of the Vaucluse's archetypal and much-photographed perched villages, and the Cistercian Abbaye de Sénanque in its secret valley carpeted in lavender in June and July.

Somewhere to stay

↘ The Hôtel les Bories, Gordes, a new but traditionally-built 4-star with pool and 1-Michelin-star restaurant.
☎ 04 90 72 00 51.

Marseille (Bouches-du-Rhône)

Garlic market Monday to Saturday, mid-June to mid-July. Also daily markets

Marseille has many markets, but until you've been to the summer garlic market, you won't believe how many different kinds of this pungent bulb there are. Pink garlic, mottled garlic, purple garlic, garlic with great busty cloves covered in pristine white tissue, tiny bulbs packing a concentrated punch. All combine to make this a garlic fest beyond imagination. Held for four weeks between mid-June and mid-July in and around the Cours Belsunce, the market's bulbous bouquets and knotted strings of assorted *Allium sativum* fill the area – as you'd expect – with a glorious odour. Where else to celebrate this feisty member of the onion family – regarded universally as the national flavour of France – than in the city that invented *bouillabaisse*, a dish that would have remained a mere fish stew without its assertive accompaniment of *sauce rouille*, the chillied garlic mayonnaise?

During the month of the garlic market – Monday to Saturday, 8.00 to 13.00 – the restaurants of Marseille outdo each other to gild with garlic, but the best – and simplest – way to enjoy it is to rub a lightly crushed clove on a chunk of crusty bread, then drizzle with olive oil and munch.

Marseille's daily morning markets are the fish market on the Vieux Port's quai des Belges, where the latest catch is unloaded every morning, and the food markets in Place des Capucins, Cours Joseph-Thierry, Avenue du Prado and Cours Pierre-Puget.

Don't miss

❂ The Musée du Santon. *Santons* are tiny Provençal figurines of crib and village characters invented during the Revolution when enacting the Nativity was forbidden. In the adjoining *atelier*, *santons* are still made.

❂ Notre-Dame-de-la-Garde, an over-the-top basilica in more senses than one, topping the hill above the harbour.

❂ Boat trips to the Château d'If, the 16th-century island prison which inspired Alexandre Dumas's *The Count of Monte Cristo*.

❂ *Bouillabaisse* – or another seafood special – at one of the Vieux Port restaurants. Miramar, for instance. The Michel-Brasserie des Catalans, Rue Catalans, does a Michelin-starred version.

ⓘ4 La Canebière.

Somewhere to stay

⬎Lutétia, a friendly central hotel in a quiet street. ☎ 04 91 50 81 78.

⬎Le Corbusier, style icon in the famous architect's pilot development, Cité Radieuse. ☎ 04 91 77 18 15.

Grasse (Alpes-Maritimes)
Tuesday to Sunday

With the sea in sniffing distance and fields of lavender, jasmine and roses beyond its suburbs, the perfume capital high above the Côte d'Azur is, as you might expect, full of seductive fragrances. But the aromas that swirl, most mornings, around the handsome fountain in the centre of the *vieille ville*'s Place aux Aires are not the kind you dab behind the ears. They are the scents of spices, of sweet onions on *pissaladière* and of fruity *fougasette*, the local cake; the smell of honey and olive oil soap and the briny tang of Mediterranean fish. In other words, Grasse's daily market. Here, all the abundance of the south is heaped in tempting array. Morsels of cut melon, paper-thin dried ham or whiffy mountain cheeses are offered for you to taste – sometimes on the point of a knife. I remember it was in Grasse that I first encountered ewe's milk cheese. 'Qu'est-ce-que c'est, *brebis*?' I asked the *fromagère*, my poor French accent giving me away. Helpfully, she replied, 'C'est la femme du mouton – ze wife of ze sheep.' For me, *brebis* has been 'sheep's wife' ever since.

Grasse continues to grow among the surrounding pine-clad hills and hollows, but the Renaissance old town, whose cobbled stairways and steep alleys accommodate its different levels, is small and delightfully unspoiled. You will not be allowed to forget that the painter Jean-Honoré Fragonard was born here. His name is given to one of the perfume museums, the main boulevard and several bars, and there are countless sleepily shuttered, rust-tiled mansions whose stucco is washed with one of his favourite colours: a beautiful buttery yellow.

Don't miss

✪ The perfumeries – Fragonard, Molinard or Galimard (just out of town), and the international museum of perfume behind its Second Empire facade.

✪ The Musée Provençal du Costume et du Bijou in the Hôtel de Clapiers Cabris, a private mansion that once belonged to Mirabeau's sister.

✪ The cathedral, Notre Dame du Puy, mainly for the two Rubens and Fragonard's 'Washing of the Feet'.

✪ Le Baltus, an appealing yet affordable small restaurant in Rue de la Fontinette near the market.

ⓘ Palais des Congrès.

Somewhere to stay

↘ Hôtel l'Horizon, in the charming medieval village of Cabris, about 6km from Grasse. Modest, well run and well named – there's an opera-box view of the distant Mediterranean from the breakfast terrace. ☎ 04 93 60 51 69.

Arles (Bouches-du-Rhône)
Wednesday and Saturday

On the edge of the Camargue, this ancient Roman town on the River Rhône embodies the spirit of southern Provence.

Here, Van Gogh painted 'Night Café', and lived in a yellow house with Gauguin until he sliced off part of his ear. And here, late on a June evening, I once ventured in with nowhere booked to stay. My car seemed to have a life of its own, nosing through the streets of the old centre until it almost crashed into the courtyard of the venerable Hôtel d'Arlatan. Swiftly registering swags of expensive fabric, lavender-scented furniture polish and Roman ruins visible through a thick glass panel in the foyer floor, I couldn't believe my luck. Only one room was available. 'I'll take it!'

Within a stroll of the d'Arlatan next morning was an explosion of colour, chatter and jolly-sounding brass filling the Boulevard des Lices. The Saturday market. Merchants occupy the entire length of this broad tree-lined avenue and the Boulevard Georges Clemenceau as well. Hot, peppery Provençal cottons drape counters and cover pots of jams, pesto and *anchoïade*, the anchovy and oil paste. Curtains of gypsy skirts and tops hang from canopies, while black felt fedoras like those worn by the *gardians*, the Camargue rangers, vie with Van Gogh sunhats. There are old clothes, new clothes, collectables and ceramics, hardware and compact discs. And, of course, the local specialities: pungent *saucisson d'Arles* and Arles Tomme cheese, sea salt and red rice from the Camargue marshes. The olive seller mans a stall as long as a stair carpet, where basins of black, green, grey and purple olives rest in brine or oil, flavoured with garlic, herbs, chilli or just

themselves. The fish vans also sell dry salted cod to make *brandade de morue*, a creamy garlicky pâté that was once a Christmas treat but is now popular year round. And, at the sweet end of the spectrum, nougat, marzipan sweets and crunchy *croquants* biscuits come from the almond trees whose ethereal blossom sparkles against the ploughed red earth of the surrounding hills in spring.

On Wednesday, the market moves outside the walls to Place Emile-Combes, and on the first Wednesday in the month Boulevard des Lices hosts a bric-a-brac market.

Don't miss

○ The Roman arena. It seated 20,000 in Julius Caesar's day and still packs in 12,000 for bullfights and other spectacles. Also the Théâtre Antique and Les Alyscamps Roman necropolis, a kilometre or so out of town.

○ The 11th/12th-century Eglise Saint Trophime.

○ Shady Place du Forum, presided over by a dapper statue of writer Frédéric Mistral. The bright yellow Café Van Gogh clearly mimics the artist's famous work, 'Night Café'.

○ The Museon Arlaten, founded by Mistral, full of everyday objects, costumes and furniture evoking traditional Provençal life.

Somewhere to stay

↘ Hôtel d'Arlatan (see above). No restaurant. ☎ 04 90 93 56 66.

↘ Hôtel Nord Pinus, in Place du Forum, with antique columns embedded in its facade. Long the haunt of artists and writers. Chic interior, excellent food. ☎ 04 90 93 44 44.

★ **Aix-en-Provence** The town of Cézanne has fountains and charm overload, a daily market in Place Richelme and others on Wednesdays, Thursdays and Saturdays in Place de la Madeleine. These abound in food, local crafts and bric-a-brac.

★ **Antibes** Atmospheric walled port where the château has a collection of Picassos. Covered market daily from June to August in Cours Massena, Tuesday to Sunday from September to May. Craft market in the afternoons. Regular antiques markets on Place Audiberti on Thursdays and Saturdays.

★ **Apt** Famous for its glacé fruits. A big Saturday market runs the length of the Rue des Marchands and into squares either end of it. Bric-a-brac market on Fridays.

★ **Aubagne** Nice hill town with a month-long pre-Christmas market of *santons*, the little figurines. Regular markets Tuesday, Thursday, Saturday, Sunday, plus Friday from May to November.

★ **Avignon** Tuesday to Sunday, covered halls on Place Pie; Friday mornings, Place Crillon. Antiques every Saturday in Place Crillon and flea market on Sunday in the Cloître des Carmes. One of the starriest Christmas markets of the region lights up the Place de l'Horloge from the first weekend in December to the end of the month.

★ **Carpentras** Busy but characterful town close to the Rhone where Friday mornings from the end of November to

March are devoted to truffles in Place du 24 Août 1944. Friday is also the day of the traditional weekly market in the town centre. Antiques and bric-a-brac: Sunday in Allée Jean-Jaurès.

★ **Draguignan** Very typical Provençal country town with good markets Wednesday and Saturday.

★ **Le Muy** In Saint Tropez back country, with one of the biggest Sunday markets in the eastern Var. Also one on Thursday.

★ **Manosque** Marvellous Saturday market of everything under the sun in every square of this old walled town at the eastern end of the Luberon.

★ **Richerenches** In the north of the Vaucluse. Very big on truffles on Saturdays in winter. They even hold a truffle mass here on the third Sunday in January.

★ **St-Rémy-de-Provence** Paradise for shoppers in search of interiors chic. Wednesday and Saturday morning markets in several leafy squares. Place de la République is heaped with *boutis*, the traditional quilts. Food begins in the shady narrow streets and Place Jules Pellissier has the fresh stuff. Lovely craftwork and small paintings.

★ **Sanary-sur-Mer** Traditional fishing port/resort west of Bandol with old-fashioned ambiance and enormous, really colourful market on Wednesday near the marina. Loads of parking space close by.

★ **Sault** Idyllic *village perché* in Vaucluse with stunning view of Mont Ventoux. Small but picturesque Wednesday morning market.

★ **Sospel** Dreamy Italianate town in the mountains with general market Thursday and one for local products like Alpine liqueurs on Sunday.

★ **Vaison-la-Romaine** One of the most delightful towns in the upper Vaucluse, originally a Roman watering hole. Its attractive pedestrianized shopping area bursts at the seams on Tuesday morning when the market adds to the fun.

★ **Valréas** Key truffle market venue on Wednesdays mid-November to mid-March.

★ **Villefranche** Very picturesque port with a 17th-century chapel decorated by Jean Cocteau and quayside antiques market on Sunday mornings.

Other significant flea markets

◎ **Aubagne**, fourth Sunday.

◎ **Brignoles**, Sunday.

◎ **Cabannes**, second Saturday.

◎ **Cannet-des-Maures**, Saturday.

◎ **Grimaud**, Sunday.

◎ **Istres**, second Sunday.

◎ **Jonquières**, Sunday.

◎ **Lançon**, Saturday and Sunday.

◎ **La Seyne-sur-Mer**, second Sunday.

◎ **Marseille**, Saturday and Sunday.

◎ **Mornas**, Saturday and Sunday.

◎ **Orange**, Sunday afternoon and Thurs morning.

◎ **Riez-la-Romaine**, first Sunday.

◎ **Roquebrune**, Saturday and Sunday.

◎ **St-Mitre-les-Remparts**, Saturday.

◎ **St-Raphaël**, Tuesday.

◎ **St-Rémy**, Tuesday and Sunday.

◎ **Salon**, first Sunday.

◎ **Six-Fours**, Sunday.

◎ **Toulon**, Friday.

◎ **Vaison-la-Romaine**, third Sunday.

🖱 www.crt-paca.fr and
www.guideriviera.com

Markets at a glance: Provence

A
Agay, *Wed*
Agnières-en-Dévoluy, *Tue*
  (July/Aug)
Aiguilles, *Thu*
Aix-en-Provence, daily
Allauch, *Wed*
Alleins, *Tue*
Allemagne-en-Provence, *Thu*
Allos, *Thu*
Ancelle, *Sun*
Annot, *Tue*
Apt, *Sat*
Les Arcs-sur-Argens, *Thu*
L'Argentière-La-Bessée, *Fri*
Arles, see Six of the Best
Aspres-sur-Buëch, *Sat*
Aubagne, *Tue*, *Thu*, *Fri*
  (May–Nov), *Sat*, *Sun*
Aubignan, *Thu*
Aups, *Wed*, *Sat*
Aureille, *Thu*
Auriol, *Thu*, *Sat*
Avignon, daily (except *Mon*)
B
Bagnières-en-Devolut, *Tue*
  (Jul/Aug)
Bagnois-en-Forêt, *Wed*, *Sat*
Bandol, *Tue*
Banon, *Tue*
Barbentane, *Fri*
Barcelonnette, *Wed*, *Sat*
Bargemon, *Thu*
Barjois, *Sat*
Bauduen, *Sun* (summer)
Beaucaire, *Thu*
Beaumes-de-Venise, *Tue*
Le Beausset, *Fri*, *Sun*
Bédarrides, *Mon*
Bédoin, *Mon*
Belgentier, *Mon*, *Sat*
Berre-l'Etang, *Thu*, *Sun*
Besse-sur-Issole, *Wed*
Bollène, *Mon*
Bonnieux, *Fri*
Bormes-les-Mimosas, *Wed*
Bouc-Bel-Air, *Thu*, *Sun*
La Bouilladisse, *Thu*
Briançon, *Wed*
Brignoles, *Wed*, *Sat*
C

Cabannes, *Tue*
Cadenet, *Mon*
Caderousse, *Tue*
La Cadière-d'Azur, *Thu*
Cadolive, *Wed*
Callas, *Tue*, *Sat*
Callian, *Fri*
Canadel, *Tue* (Jul/Aug)
Carcès, *Sat*
Carnioules, *Fri*
Carnoux, *Thu*, *Sat*
Caromb, *Tue*
Carpentras, *Fri*
Carqueiranne, *Thu*
Carry-le-Rouet, *Tue*, *Fri*
Cassis, *Wed*, *Fri* (+ fish
  Mon–Fri)
Castellane, *Wed*, *Sat*
Caumont-sur-Durance, *Thu*
Cavaillon, *Mon*, *Fri*
Cavalaire-sur-Mer, *Wed*
Cavalière, *Mon* (Jul/Aug)
Ceillac, *Thu*
Céreste, *Thu*
Ceyreste, *Fri*
Charleval, *Sat*
Château-Arnoux, *Sun*
Châteauneuf-de-Gadagne,
  Wed
Châteauneuf-du-Pape, *Fri*
Châteauneuf-le-Rouge, *Fri*
  eve
Châteauneuf-les-Martigues,
  Tue, *Fri*
Châteaurenard, daily
Cheval-Blanc, *Sat*
Chorges, *Sun* (Jul/Aug)
La Ciotat, *Tue*, *Sun* (+ daily
  eve Jul/Aug)
Cogolin, *Wed*, *Sat*
Collobrières, *Sun*
Colmars-les-Alps, *Tue*, *Fri*
Cornillon-Confoux, *Tue*
Cotignac, *Tue*
Coudoux, *Fri*
Courthézon, *Fri*
Le Crau, *Wed*
La Croix-Valmer, *Sun*
Cucuron, *Tue*
Cuers, *Fri*
Cuges-les-Pins, *Wed*

D
La Destrousse, *Fri*
Digne-les-Bains, *Wed*, *Sat*
Draguignan, *Wed*, *Sat*
E
Eguilles, *Tue*, *Fri*
Embrun, *Wed*, *Sat*
Ensuès-la-Redonne, *Wed*
Entraigues, *Wed*
Entrecasteaux, *Fri*
Entrevaux, *Fri*
Eygalières, *Fri*
Eyguières, *Tue* (+ *Tue* eve
  May-Sep)
Eyragues, *Fri*
F
La Fare-les-Oliviers, *Sat*
La Farlède, *Tue*, *Fri*
Fayence, *Tue*, *Thu*, *Sat*
Figanières, *Tue*
Flassans-sur-Issole, *Fri*
Flayosc, *Mon*
Fontaine-de-Vaucluse, *Tue*,
  Thu
Fontvieille, *Mon*, *Fri*
**Forcalquier, see Six of the
  Best**
Fos-sur-Mer, *Wed*, *Thu*, *Fri*
Fréjus, *Wed*
Fuveau, *Mon*, *Thu*
G
Gap, *Wed*, *Sat*
Gardanne, *Wed*, *Fri*
La Garde, *Tue*, *Fri*, *Sat*
La Garde Freinet, *Wed*, *Sun*
Gargas, *Wed*
Gémenos, *Wed*
Gignac-la-Nerthe, *Sun*
Gordes, *Tue*
Goult, *Mon*
Grans, *Fri*
La Grave, *Thu*
Graveson, *Fri*
Gréasque, *Mon*, *Fri*
Gréoux-les-Bains, *Thu*
Grimaud old village, *Thu*
H
Hyères, *Tue*, *Sat*, *Sun*
I
**Isle-sur-la-Sorgue, see Six
  of the Best**

Markets at a glance: Provence

Les Issambres, *Mon*
Istres, *Tue, Fri*
J
Jonquières, *Sun*
Jouques, *Sun*
L
Lagnes, *Fri*
Lambesc, *Fri* (+ *Tue* May–mid-Sep)
Lançon-de-Provence, *Tue*
Laragne, *Thu*
Lauris, *Mon*
Le Lavandou, *Thu*
La Londe-des-Maures, *Sun*
Lorgues, *Tue*
Lourmarin, *Fri*
M
Maillane, *Thu*
Malaucène, *Wed*
Malemort-du-Comtat, *Thu*
Malijai, *Thu*
Mallemort, *Thu*
Manosque, *Sat*
Marignane, *Tue, Thu, Sat*
Marseille, see Six of the Best
Martigues, *Wed, Sat* (+ fish daily)
Maussane-les-Alpilles, *Thu*
Mazan, *Mon*
Mazaugues, *Tue*
Mérindol, *Wed*
Mes Mées, *Tue, Fri*
Meyrargues, *Sun*
Meyreuil, *Tue*
Mézel, *Sat*
Mimet, *Tue*
Mirabeau, *Thu*
Miramas, *Thu, Sat*
Môlines-en-Queyras, *Tue* (Feb, Jul/Aug)
Mollégès, *Wed*
Mondragon, *Tue*
Monêtier-les-Bains, *Fri* (Jul/Aug)
Montauroux, *Tue*
Monteux, *Sun*
Montfavet, *Tue*
Montgenèvre, *Wed* (Dec–Apr)
Montmeyan, *Tue, Fri*
Morières, *Wed*

Mormoiron, *Tue*
Mornas, *Sat*
Mouriès, *Wed*
Moustiers-Sainte-Marie, *Fri*
Le Muy, *Thu, Sun*
N
Nans-les-Pins, *Sun*
Néoules, *Sun*
Noves, *Wed, Thu, Fri*
O
Ollioules, *Thu, Sat*
Oppède, *Sat*
Oraison, *Tue*
Orange, *Thu*

Orcières, *Thu* (mid-Dec–mid-Apr and Jul/Aug)
Orgon, *Wed*
P
La Palud, *Tue*
Pélissane, *Sun*
Pelvoux, *Sun* (summer)
La Penne-sur-Huveaune, *Thu*
Pernes-les-Fontaines, *Sat*
Pertuis, *Fri*
Peynier, *Fri*
Peypin, *Mon*
Peyrolles, *Wed, Sat*
Pierrefeu, *Tue, Sat*
Pierrevert, *Wed*
Piolenc, *Mon*

Plan-de-Cuques, *Sat*
Plan-de-la-Tour, *Thu*
Le Pontet, *Thu*
Port-de-Bouc, daily
Port-Saint-Louis-du-Rhône, *Wed, Sat*
Le Pradet, *Fri*
Puget-Ville, *Sat*
Le Puy-Sainte-Réparade, *Wed, Sun*
Puy-Saint-Vincent, *Mon* (end Dec–Apr), *Tue* (Jul/Aug)
Q
Quinson, *Fri*
R
Ramateulle, *Thu, Sun*
Le Rayol, *Fri*
Régusse, *Sun*
Reillanne, *Thu, Sun*
Le Revest-les-Eaux, *Sat*
Rians, *Fri*
Ribiers, *Tue*
Riez, *Wed, Sat*
La Roche-des-Arnauds, *Fri*
Rognac, *Wed*
Rognes, *Wed, Sat*
Rognonas, *Tue*
Roquebrune-sur-Argens, *Tue, Fri*
La Roquebrussanne, *Sat*
La Roque-d'Anthiéron, *Thu*

Roquefort-la-Bédoule, *Thu*
Roquevaire, *Fri*
Rosans, *Sun*
Rousset, *Wed*
Roussillon, *Thu*
S
Saint-Andiol, *Fri*
Saint-André-les-Alpes, *Wed*, *Sat*
Saint-Aygulf, *Tue*, *Fri*
Saint-Bonnet, *Mon* (+ *Thu* Jul/Aug)
Saint-Cannat, *Wed*
Saint-Chaffrey, *Thu*
Saint-Chamas, *Sat*
Saint-Didier, *Mon*
Sainte-Cécile-les-Vignes, *Sat*
Saintes-Maries-de-la-Mer, *Mon*, *Fri* (+ flea market *Mon*, Apr–Oct)
Saint-Etienne-du-Grès, flea market daily (except *Sun*)
Saint-Etienne-les-Orgues, *Wed*, *Sat*
Saint-Firmin-en-Valgodemard, *Tue*
Saint-Jean-St-Nicolas, *Fri*
Saint-Mandrier-sur-Mer, *Wed*, *Sat*
Saint-Martin-de-Crau, *Fri*
Saint-Maxime, *Thu*, *Fri*
Saint-Maximin-la-Sainte-Baume, *Wed*
Saint-Michel-de-Chaillol, *Wed* (Jul/Aug and end Dec)
Saint-Mitre-les-Remparts, *Wed*
Saint-Paul-lez-Durance, *Tue*
Saint-Rémy-de-Provence, *Wed*, *Sat*
Saint-Saturnin-les-Avignon, *Mon*
Saint-Savournin, *Tue*
Saint-Tropez, *Tue*, *Sat*
Saint-Zacharie, *Wed*
Salernes, *Wed*, *Sun*
La Salle-les-Alpes, *Tue*
Les Salles-du-Verdon, *Thu*
Salon-de-Provence, *Tue*, *Wed*, *Fri*, *Sat*, *Sun*
Sanary-sur-Mer, *Wed*

Sarrians, *Sun*
Sault, *Wed*
Sausset-les-Pins, daily
Savines-le-Lac, *Fri*
Seillans, *Wed*
Sénas, *Thu* (+ daily Jun–Sep)
Septèmes-les-Vallons, *Thu*, *Sat*
Sérignan-du-Comtat, *Wed*
Seyne-les-Alpes, *Tue*, *Fri*
Simiane-Collongue, *Wed*, *Sat*
Sisteron, *Wed*, *Sat*
Solliès-Pont, *Wed*
Solliès-Toucas, *Fri*
Sorgues, *Sun*
T
Tallard, *Fri*
Taradeau, *Sun*
Tarascon, *Tue*, *Fri*
Thoard, *Sun*
Le Tholonet, *Tue*, *Sat*
Le Thor, *Wed*, *Sat*
Le Thoronet, *Thu*
La Tour-d'Aigues, *Tue*
Tourtour, *Wed*, *Sat*
Tourves, *Tue*
Trans-en-Provence, *Mon*, *Thu*, *Sun*
Trets, *Wed* (+ *Sun* Apr–Sep)
V
Vacqueyras, *Thu*
Vaison-la-Romaine, *Tue*
La Valette, *Mon*
Vallouise, *Thu*
Valréas, *Wed*
Varages, *Mon*, *Thu*
Vars, *Tue* (Dec–Apr)
Vedène, *Tue*
Velaux, *Thu*, *Sat*
Velleron, *Wed*, *Fri*
Venelles, *Sat*
Ventabren, *Tue*, *Fri*
Videauban, *Wed*, *Sun*
Villecroze, *Thu*
Villes-sur-Auzon, *Wed*
Vinon-sur-Verdon, *Sun*
Violès, *Wed*
Visan, *Fri*
Vitrolles, *Tue*, *Wed*, *Thu*, *Fri*, *Sun*
Volx, *Tue*

A
Antibes-Juan-les-Pins, daily (not *Mon* except Jun–Aug)
B
Beaulieu-sur-Mer, daily (except *Sun* in winter)
Beausoleil, daily
Breil/Roya, *Tue*
La Brigue, *Fri*, *Sat*, *Sun*
C
Cagnes-sur-Mer, daily (except *Mon*)
Cannes-et-le-Cannet, daily in various locations
Carros, *Thu*, *Sat*
F
Fontan, *Fri*
G
Golfe-Juan, *Fri*
Grasse, see Six of the Best
M
Mandelieu-la-Napoule, *Wed*, *Thu*, *Fri*, *Sat*
Menton, daily
Mouans-Sartoux, daily
N
Nice, see Six of the Best
P
Puget-Theniers, *Sun*
S
Saint-Laurent-du-Var, *Tue*, *Fri*, *Sun*
Saorge, *Tue*, *Sat*, *Sun*
Sospel, *Thu*, *Sun*
T
Tende, *Tue*, *Wed*, *Sat*, *Sun*
Théoule-sur-Mer, *Fri*
Tourettes-sur-Loup, *Wed*
V
Valbonne-Sophia-Antipolis, *Tue*, *Thu*, *Fri*, *Sun*
Vallauris, daily (not *Mon*)
Vence, daily
Villefranche-sur-Mer, *Sat*
Villeneuve-Loubet, *Wed*, *Sat*

RHÔNE-ALPES

Beer made from chestnuts, great ski clothes and silk-weavers' brains

Of all nationalities, the French surely take the gold for being the most resourceful and inventive of eaters. Whether out of necessity or innate gastronomic curiosity, they have tried and erred for mankind, and can probably claim the richest variety of comestibles on the planet. Nowhere is this more evident than in France's second city, the foodie's favourite, Lyon. Here, in the capital of the Rhône-Alpes region, it's a well-known maxim that the only unused part of a pig is the squeak. '*Dans le cochon tout est bon!*' insists the writing on the window of the Café des Fédérations, a favourite *bouchon*. As in most *bouchons* (friendly bars-cum-bistros peculiar to Lyon), a feast of *charcuterie* dangles above the zinc counter, and pork in all its guises, from snout to tail and ears to trotters, appears on the menu. As it does in the markets.

Of course, pigs are not alone in giving their all. Stumped by '*joyeuses d'agneau*' on a butcher's stall in the Croix-Rousse *quartier*, I was enlightened by a barrel-chested chap with a saucy twinkle. 'Ze lamb's – how you say? – crown jewels.' I hardly dared ask about *cervelles de canut*, aware that *cervelles* meant brains and a *canut* was a worker in Lyon's once-thriving silk industry. All it turned out to be was a creamy *fromage blanc* scramble with garlic and chives added.

Rhône-Alpes is massive. It's France's largest region, and full of phenomenal scenery, especially in the high valleys and plateaux. Contrasts are acute. Eight *départements* sprawl from the bucolic folds of southern Burgundy to the lavender fields of northern Provence and from the ancient uplands of Auvergne to the tip of Mont Blanc. The eternally snowy French Alps, of which Rhône-Alpes encompasses the lion's share, form a Shangri-la backdrop for hundreds of miles. France's longest river, the Loire, rises in the Ardèche and the mightiest, the Rhône, gushes out of Lake Geneva (Lac Léman) before widening at Lyon to flow down a wide corridor to the Mediterranean.

Life in Rhône-Alpes ricochets from deeply rustic to supremely sophisticated. Cow-bells clonk peacefully on the high pastures as Belle-Epoque lake resorts fizz with watersport action and *joie de vivre*. Primitive communal bread ovens are still ignited in isolated villages while city restaurants collect Michelin stars.

There is immense variety in the markets too. When traditional ski resorts thaw into postcard villages in summer, the emphasis of their merchandise shifts accordingly. In the southern Drôme, market days are as vibrant as in the Vaucluse or on the Riviera. And cities such as Lyon, Grenoble and Saint-Etienne present as bewildering a choice as Paris.

Specialities

Much is made of the crispness and lightness of the baguette and its derivatives, but for my euros yeasty thick-crusted **country bread** or *pain paysan* is an altogether better prospect. The kind that rises to perfection in Rhône-Alpes' old arched village bakehouses fired with vine clippings is a prize indeed. Made of strong white flour, roughed up on the surface with a dusting of rye and bran, the round finished loaves are like well-worn stepping stones across some impetuous stream. Flatter roundels of softer bread, more brioche in texture, are sprinkled with walnuts, onions or fruit – easy eating for lunch on a mountainside. There is also the rather dry *pogne*, boosted with eggs and sugar, and there's bread made with chestnut flour – which is why the chestnut tree was known in the Cévennes as the bread tree.

The Ardèche *département* is the main **chestnut** producer of France. If you're confused about the allusion to them as both *châtaignes* and *marrons*, the *marron* is the variety with a single nut encased inside the spiny outer burr – the one for divine *marrons glacés*. You will be hard put to find a market without chestnuts in some form or other. They go into cakes, chocolates, apéritifs, liqueur and even beer.

The other great M is Montélimar **nougat**, packed with almonds and pistachios and flavoured with honey. A pretty tale explains how it got its name. There once was an old lady from Montélimar known to one and all as Tante Manon. A pastry cook, she used to slip her nephews and nieces a special treat, at which they would exclaim, '*Tante Manon, tu nous gâtes*' (you're spoiling us). Before she died, she left the recipe to her youngest niece with the instruction to call it nougat 'to immortalize the joyous cry with which you used to greet my delicacy'.

It was a great publicity stunt, the race for the 'new Beaujolais'. This pretty average light red **wine** is still released with a fanfare at the beginning of November but the superior quality *crus* such as Juliénas, Fleurie, Morgon and Brouilly give Beaujolais a better name. Robust or rare, Beaujolais wines can be all things to all people. But there are other wines to enjoy in the Rhône Valley: Hermitage, Crozes-Hermitage, Côtes du Rhône and du Vivarais, and the lovely light whites of Viognier and Condrieu. Not forgetting the sparkling Clairette de Die. Chilled well enough and served on a summer evening in the garden, it's as acceptable as bubbly at a third of the price. Also on the lighter side is Bourganel blonde, the beer from the Ardèche that comes *au nature* as well as flavoured with blueberries or chestnuts. The monks of the Chartreuse still distil their golden (or green) liqueur (only three at any one time know the recipe for this botanical elixir) and, in the Baronnies, lime flowers are harvested by the bundle to make the sedative infusion of *tilleul*.

This is big **cheese** country – few regions of France aren't. You only have to look at those pampered cows marshalled up and down the mountains twice a year in pursuit of the juiciest grass to know the quality of their milk is going to be ace. If Roquefort from Midi-Pyrénées is the king of French cheeses, I would rank St-

Marcellin from Rhône-Alpes as consort. With a delectable tang, it comes in flat chalky discs and is at its best when beginning to weep. Better than Camembert – better than Brie. Tomme de Savoie, seasoned with herbs or black pepper, and Beaufort are mountain cheeses. Then comes Reblochon, Bleu de Gex, Fourme de Montbrison (another blue) and Raclette to serve melted over a flame with potatoes in their skins to mop it up and gherkins on the side. The celebrated goat's cheese of the region is Picodon from the Drôme, extra good macerated in olive oil or flavoured with herbs, but there are other *chèvres* from small producers.

Symbol of peace and fidelity, the olive tree with its arthritic branches and fine silver-backed leaves spells the seduction of the Mediterranean. Yet some of the best **olives** come from the southern reaches of the Rhône Valley where they grow on 1,000-year-old trees around Nyons, Buis-les-Baronnies, Mirabel-aux-Baronnies and Mérindol-les-Oliviers. They flourish on terraces edged with dry stone walls and are harvested from November to January when ripe and black. The large ones for eating soak in brine for six months, the smaller ones are pressed for their oil.

A huge variety of both olives and olive oils appears at markets, along with **tapenade**, to which I am addicted. This paste of mashed black olives, herbs and capers is good with bread, brilliant with St-Marcellin cheese and, I remember, was inspired in a potato purée with garlicky roast lamb at Michel Chabran's

Michelin-starred restaurant in Pont-de-l'Isère. In Nyons, they make an olive tart, and bitter-sweet *scourtins*, shortbready biscuits studded with snippets of black olives.

With a galaxy of A-list celebrities on the ski circuit, the snow gear on sale in the winter markets of anywhere within reach of Savoie and Dauphiné is almost as slick as it is in expensive boutiques. The same goes for hiking, biking and other sportswear in summer. Elsewhere, especially in the Drôme Provençale, chic individual **clothes** are brought to market by talented designers working on their own – not just tops, trousers and dresses but accessories too.

Six of the Best

Lyon (Rhône)

Food markets, daily except Monday.
Antiques and crafts, Sunday

Poised where the Saône joins the Rhône, France's second city offers river strolls, a Milky Way of Michelin stars, hip night spots and exceptional architecture. The entire centre is a World Heritage Site in which Roman theatres mix with Renaissance mansions and Baroque department stores. And it's welcoming. Somehow, that breath of the south, the *brin de sud*, brings a mildness to both the air and local temperaments.

Food-market-wise, there are three top locations. The covered *halles* are in the financial district (these resemble a multi-storey car park but their contents are encyclopaedic, and tiny eateries tacked on to the stands invite you to snack as you go). The most charmingly sited is on Quai St-Antoine by the Saône. But the gourmet's favourite runs along the Boulevard de la Croix-Rousse in the old silk workers' *quartier*. In this I became embedded, boggling at the detail. Small was clearly desirable for there were marble-sized new potatoes from the Ardèche, *petite apéro* cigar-shaped *saucissons* and cocktail *chèvres* hardly bigger than a euro. As well as the already mentioned lamb's 'crown jewels', I found pig's snouts (*museaux*) and donkey's noses (*groins d'âne* – actually, silky winter dandelion leaves also known as *pissenlits*). And there was plenty of help for lazy cooks – ready-prepared *quenelles de brochet* (pike dumplings), pork sausages in red wine and *goujons* of lake trout. But the whiskery mushroom man was determined to educate, his sales patter peppered with recipes for the *pleurottes* and morels he was popping into brown paper bags. '*Un petit peu d'ail, un petit peu de crème fraîche . . .*'

For bric-a-brac browsers, Sunday is the day. The Puces du Canal in Villeurbanne start at 6am – in winter early birds have to wield torches to scour the 400 stalls. It's mainly small collectables but lovely pieces of period walnut furniture also surface. A few minutes away, the Cité des Antiquaires beckons on Boulevard Stalingrad. Also on Sunday, back in Vieux Lyon, the Marché de la Création on Quai Romain Rolland sells small artworks – paintings, pottery and other crafts.

There's a Christmas market throughout December in Place Carnot.

Don't miss

✪ Lyon's painted murals.

✪ The Roman theatre and 19th-century basilica on Fourvière hill.

✪ *Traboules* (passageways) and Renaissance mansions in Old Lyon – press the buzzers to get into their open courtyards.

✪ The pedestrianized 'Rue de la Ré' (République) where the boutique chic outsmarts Paris.

✪ Musée des Tissus with its extravagant pre-Revolution court dresses and silk artefacts from ancient Persia, medieval England and many other periods and places.

- Best *bouchons*: Café des Fédérations; Au Petit Bouchon. Note: *bouchons* usually close Saturday and Sunday and for a month in the summer.

- Signature restaurants: Paul Bocuse; La Mère Brazier.

- Atelier de la Soierie, Rue Romain, for fab silk scarves.

- Villa Lumière, where the world's first movie was shot by the Lumière brothers.

- ⓘ Place Bellecour.

Somewhere to stay

- Grand Hôtel des Terreaux, central, charming, reasonably priced. ☎ 04 72 40 45 45.

- Cour des Loges, most exclusive Vieux Lyon address, with rooms off a Renaissance courtyard. Lyon's bright young things rendezvous in the bar. ☎ 04 72 40 93 61.

Annecy (Haute-Savoie)
Tuesday, Friday and Sunday

Ever since an all-too-brief stop near Lake Annecy en route south a few summers ago, I've been dying to return to this adorable water-veined city. Getting into it in high season was a bit of a sweat, but the rewards of the old centre soon deleted the memory. It's utterly magical, with canal-side walks and little bridges leading you on a merry dance to streets that twine around pastel-painted houses, a four-towered castle and the Palais de l'Isle, the most picturesque of ex-prisons. Pelargoniums cascade from railings, hanging baskets and niches. Painters park on corners. Swans tread the green water. And with every glance cast in the direction of the lake and its wall of tall Savoy peaks comes an involuntary sigh. In the August heat, I remember too the bonus of strolling around in an alpine freshness in the evenings.

Three mornings a week, the food market adds extra bustle to the *vieille ville* along its main pedestrian thoroughfare, the arcaded Rue Sainte Claire. This is full of restaurants and shops selling summer fripperies: scraps of bikinis, frivolous hair ornaments and stunning costume jewellery – plus the kind of decorative 'alpine' artefacts that Heidi would have been proud of (cuckoo-clock money-boxes even). Then the fresh produce arrives. Farm stuff that has come down the mountains: crisp vegetables from cooler earth, honey, fruit compotes and Sarasson curd cheese to be eaten fresh with chives, oil and vinegar or for dessert with sugar, jam or honey.

Every last Saturday in the month, it's the turn of the antique peddlars to take over the old town with a huge *brocante* that lasts all day.

Don't miss

- The waterside Jardins de l'Europe shaded by giant redwoods.

- The castle museum where there's a beautiful 15th-century wooden sculpture of St James of Compostela.

- St Maurice church with its *trompe l'oeil* mural.

- Cycling or rollerblading around the lake shore *piste* or a lake cruise.

- The beaches – Plage Impérial is fee-paying; Plage d'Annecy-le-Vieux and des Marquisats (nicest) are free, both 1km out of town.

- Talloires, on the far side of the lake, for its 11th-century priory and Père Bise inn's Michelin-starred tasting menu.

ⓘ Rue Jean Jaurès.

Somewhere to stay

⤥ Marquisats, 200m from the Marquisats beach. An ancient but restored *hôtel du lac* with lovely views. No restaurant.
☎ 04 50 51 52 34.

⤥ L'Abbaye, sheer heaven, a Relais & Châteaux hotel converted from an elegant Benedictine abbey on the lakeshore at Talloires. The painter Cézanne used to stay.
☎ 04 50 60 77 33.

Valence (Drôme)
Tuesday, Thursday and Saturday

The French say southern France starts in Valence. One glance at the market in full swing under the protection of St Appolinaire, its big Romanesque cathedral, and I don't doubt it. It's May, the light is already hard, the shadows intense. Plane trees rustle, cobbles swirl and flanking houses have ochre walls and blue and olive shutters. At a bistrot called Le Marché, jowly chaps in caps are meeting, greeting, lighting Gitanes and overdoing the hand gestures. And the abundant vegetables, fruit and flowers have that fulsome, warm-climate lusciousness about them. There are Picodon goat's cheeses and plump guinea fowl – the local way to cook these tasty *pintadeaux de la Drôme* is with Nyons black olives. There's a stack of those too, glistening like oversized caviar in wooden crates.

We're in the old heart of this sizeable city south of Lyon, but the feeling is of a village, helped by the fact that much of the centre is pedestrian. You can get a car close to the market by heading for the *parking payant* in Place des Ormeaux.

The St Appolinaire market is on Thursday and Saturday mornings. On Tuesdays, it's Place St Jean, where a modest *halle* – more a glass-and-steel pergola – shades local produce. Two charming restaurants, L'Epicerie and La Table de St-Jean, make the most of the market's fresh herbs, mushrooms and cheeses.

There are many things that make Valence an engaging place: its lacy balconies, roomy boulevards and spacious Champ de Mars, a vast terrace from which you can look down on one of the Rhône Valley's finest public parks and beyond to the distant wooded hills.

Don't miss

- The big heart hung from the Champ de Mars bandstand; it was donated by Peynet, the artist who drew 'the lovers'.

- ✪ Maison des Têtes, a Renaissance mansion with a cast of characters tucked in among the stonework.

- ✪ Pogne, reinforced bread in little soldier shapes which commemorate the Vatican Swiss guards who stood vigil over Pope Pius VI when he died in the city.

- ✪ Hubert Robert's beautiful red chalk drawings in the Valence Museum.

- ✪ Michel Chabran's Bistrot des Clercs.

- ✪ Within easy reach, the Hermitage vineyards, and Romans, the couture shoe capital with its superb museum and factory shops selling cut-price Clergerie, Jourdan and Kélian – see Best of the Rest.

- ⓘ Parvis de la Gare.

Somewhere to stay

↘ Michel Chabran, roughly 9km away in the village of Pont-de-l'Isère. This Michelin-star chef's restaurant with rooms is a must-stop on the N7. Quietly luxurious rooms enfold you, dining in the garden on warm evenings is heavenly and the food is an agile balance between traditional and original. (See Best of the Rest for the market.) ☎ 04 75 84 60 09.

Grignan (Drôme)
Tuesday

This very special little village (one of the designated '*plus beaux*') perches in the heart of the Drôme Provençale, a heavenly landscape bordering the Vaucluse. Both areas share acres of rolling lavender fields and sunflowers. Medieval Grignan bursts at the seams with old roses in summer, and its crowning château is regarded as the finest Renaissance castle in south-east France. Madame de Sévigné, that compulsive letter writer, used to stay here – and in fact died here. Her daughter was the Comtesse de Grignan.

'Small but beautiful' was how my friend Isabelle Faure described the Tuesday market which gathers in Place de Mail. In summer, bright canopies shade the cream of country produce, vegetables and fruit, and a confectioner's stand will usually be piled high with blocks of honeyed nougat from nearby Montélimar. In winter, from mid-November to mid-March, Grignan's market is a hub for Tricastin truffles. If you can afford just a shaving, savour it on a thick slice of country bread with a drizzle of olive oil and a sprinkling of freshly milled salt.

Don't miss

- ✪ The beautifully restored Château.

- ✪ St Sauveur church, where Mme de Sévigné's tomb is sited.

- ✪ Village Provençal Miniature – 100 houses, all different, and figurines representing village characters.

- ✪ The typography and book museum which tells the story of printing; it has some fabulous old printing presses and a workshop.

- ⓘ Grande Rue.

Somewhere to stay

↘ Manoir de la Roseraie. According to Mme de Sévigné, it was 'exquisite'. It still is as a hotel. Pricey but last-word with a lovely pool, elegant restaurant and wooded park. On the way to Valréas. ☎ 04 75 46 58 15.

↘ Hôtel Le Clair de la Plume, a romantic 18th-century mansion opposite an ancient wash house. Rooms done out in fresh fabrics and pretty 19th-century furniture. Breakfast in the garden arbour. No restaurant.
☎ 04 75 91 81 30.

La Clusaz (Haute-Savoie)
Monday

No habitual skier will need a thumbnail sketch of La Clusaz, one of the prettiest traditional winter sports villages in the Aravis Massif, its wooden chalet-style buildings tightly packed around a big old church with an onion-domed spire. The name means 'gorge' – it's further down where the Nom torrent crashes through the pine forest.

When the sun sparkles on the snow, the pace of the Monday market in the central square crackles. You need to keep your goggles on to confront dazzling white cotton shirts trimmed with embroidery and bright kitchen cloths printed with Mont Blanc. Chic puffas rub shoulders with hand-knitted alpine sweaters, while faïence outshines fondue sets – with the former you may risk breakage on the way home, but it's a safe bet the latter will never be out of its box!

In summer, the scene changes. Now there are Mont Blanc T-shirts and lycra shorts, sun-tops and hiking boots. Local farmers line up with their hand-made *saucissons* and big millstones of Beaufort cheese – firm-textured with tiny cracks, it has a lovely sweet milkiness that catches the back of the throat: a cheese made in summer when the cows graze the green alps above town but which takes two years to age. '*Essayez!*' Morsels spiked with toothpicks are passed across. What's this? Chambéry, a vermouthy apéritif, and other plant-based *eaux de vie*. You sniff, but the alluring odour of cheese still intrudes – this time Reblochon melting with potatoes and onions in a big wide pan. *Tartiflette*. Isn't it time for lunch?

Don't miss

✪ Magical walks in the forest.

✪ Bercail restaurant, a few miles further up in an old shepherd's house with an airy terrace and Rolls-Royce views of the jagged Aravis peaks.

✪ Scenic routes – the Vallon des Confins, Vallée de Manigod and Col des Aravis.

ⓘ Maison du Tourisme, La Clusaz.

Somewhere to stay

↘ Les Sapins, bright chalet-style facing the Aravis chain, snug in winter, airy in summer. ☎ 04 50 63 33 34.

↘ Le Christiana, in the centre, large and friendly with terraces outside some rooms. ☎ 04 50 02 60 60.

Privas (Ardèche)

Wednesday and Saturday, Thursday evenings in summer

The administrative centre of Ardèche and the world capital of *marrons glacés*, Privas revels in the accolade 'Site Remarquable du Goût' – town of remarkable tastes. The optimum time to hit it is during the last weekend of October when the chestnut festival is on. Chestnuts are roasted, sold by the basket, exploited avidly by local restaurants, and the Brotherhood of the Chestnut enthrones a local luminary (happily not lumbered with the title Big Chestnut).

Chestnuts aside, Privas is good at any time. An old Huguenot town lying along a ridge between two rivers, it was all but wiped out by Louis XIII and Cardinal Richelieu after a Protestant uprising in the 1600s. The scintillating Diane de Poitiers, Henri II's mistress, used to own it and one of the market squares is named after her. Wednesday and Saturday mornings, the shady centre fills with stands. In addition, there's a Thursday evening market in July and August when the fruit picking is at its height. The peaches, nectarines and apricots that thrive on the arid terraces of the Eyrieux Valley are unrivalled for their flavour and juiciness. The red fruit is luscious too and real fruit sorbets made from quinces, figs, plums and even rhubarb are an Ardéchois speciality.

There's a Provençal accent to the merchandise, with cotton prints, soap, honey and lavender products; even the first cicadas alight among the ranges of pottery from Balazuc and Dieulefit. Silk production – once big in the Cévennes – has all but died out, yet screenprinted scarves often waft in the summer air. And look for chic leather stuff, for the tanneries which serve the shoe couturiers in Romans (Jourdan, Clergerie, Kélian et al) also turn out the makings of inexpensive but smart bags, belts and sandals.

Privas hosts one of the region's best flea markets every second Sunday in the month, and a Christmas market in December.

Don't miss

○ As if you would – the *confiseries* stuffed with *marrons glacés*, Lou Pisadou crisp chestnut cake and nougat in attractive packages.

○ The jolly Gourmandin restaurant, Rue P Filliat, where generous regional dishes aren't overpriced.

○ The remains of the 16th-century Tour de Diane de Poitiers and the 17th-century bridge over the Ouvèze.

○ Montélimar, about half-an-hour's drive, for its enchanting Musée de la Miniature, 300 examples from the barely visible to exquisitely detailed tiny scenes from everyday life.

ⓘ3 Place du Général de Gaulle.

Somewhere to stay

↘ Hôtel la Chaumette, modern with a nice atmosphere, lovely secluded outdoor dining terrace and pool. A few minutes' walk from the town centre.
☎ 04 75 64 30 66.

Best of the Rest

★ **Aix-les-Bains** Like Chambéry (below), its Italian period has left its mark. Luxurious spa hotels, decorative villas and café terraces line Lake Bourget. Queen Victoria came for the waters in 1885. Wednesday and Saturday markets.

★ **Ambierle** A joyous little town with a colourful church and the Côtes Roannaises vineyards sloping immediately below. Thursday market.

★ **Beaufort** Where the mountain cheese comes from. Very pretty, tiny Alpine village with a market on Wednesday.

★ **Bourg-en-Bresse** Busy market town on the edge of Burgundy. Neatly trussed Bresse *poulets* abound on Wednesday and Saturday mornings in the Halle du Marché.

★ **Bourg-St-Maurice** Similar to La Clusaz if not quite as pretty. Saturday market.

★ **Buis-les-Baronnies** Lovely village (on the *plus beaux* list) nestling among the hills of the Drôme. Centre of lime-flower production. Wednesday and Saturday markets held under the shade of lime trees.

★ **Chambéry** With Roman beginnings and Belle Epoque heyday, the old Savoy capital offers spas by Lake Bourget and many delights in its old quarter. Students from the university keep things lively in term time. Daily covered market plus Saturday outdoor market which sometimes welcomes cattle from the Bauges pastures. Kill two birds by taking in the delightful nearby village of St-Jean-de-Maurienne's Saturday market too.

★ **Charlieu** In its historic centre, streets of half-timbered houses and shops selling gastronomic delights cluster around a Benedictine abbey and cloistered Franciscan convent. Markets on Wednesday and Saturday morning.

★ **Châtillon-sur-Chalaronne** Its 15th-century wooden covered market is well stocked each Saturday morning by local producers.

★ **Crémieu** Village in the north of the Isère (another *plus beau*) which preserves a magnificently beamed wooden market hall and old stone grain-measuring instruments. Wednesday traders still mass under the 14th-century rafters.

★ **Montbrison** An attractive old town with a castle, tree-lined boulevards, humpbacked bridges over the river and a famous doll museum. Saturday morning market.

★ **Nyons** holds possibly the biggest market in the Drôme every Thursday, plus on Sundays from June to September (it could have made my Six of the Best but I chose Grignan for contrast). Very Provençal in atmosphere, with the famous black olives making their appearance on several stands and a terrific selection of original clothes and accessories adding to the gaiety of the mix. There's a medieval Quartier des Forts, a nice old *place* and venerable olive trees everywhere.

★ **Pont-de-l'Isère** Next to Michel Chabran's restaurant, a wholesale fruit and vegetable market operates daily except Sunday and is thrown open to the public in summer at 18.30.

★ **Roanne** For foodies making a pilgimage to the famous Michelin-starred restaurant, Troisgros, the markets on Tuesday, Friday, Saturday or Sunday would add interest.

★ **Romans** The old part is delightful with its 12th-century sandstone Gothic church. New Romans is a shoe-buyer's mecca, with factory shops full of reduced couture labels and a riveting shoe museum. Markets on Tuesday, Wednesday, Saturday and Sunday.

★ **St-Bonnet-le-Château** enjoys sensational views from its promontory on the edge of the Monts du Forez. Check out the intriguing *boules* museum if you go to the Friday morning market.

★ **St-Etienne** In the past, it made bicycles, arms and ribbons, and invented mail-order. Today it has produced 'the Greens', one of France's star football teams. Much nicer in the centre than the outskirts suggest. Terrific modern art collection in the Beaux Arts. Good local produce markets on Tuesdays and Saturdays in Place Albert Thomas.

★ **Les Vans** Another gem of the Drôme Provençale. Saturday market year round. Plus Tuesday evening in July and August.

★ **Vienne** Ancient Rhône-side market town with a superbly preserved Roman temple in its midst and other fascinating relics. The remains of the antique theatre are less impressive but look better when filled with an audience during the annual jazz festival at the beginning of summer. Markets daily, but an especially good one on Saturday in the centre.

Other truffle markets
(November to March)

◎ **Chamaret**, Monday.

◎ **Dieulefit**, Friday.

◎ **Montségur**, Thursday.

◎ **St-Paul**, Tuesday.

Other significant flea markets

◎ **Annonay**, second Sunday.

◎ **Bourg-Saint-Andéol**, first Saturday.

◎ **Vallon-Pont-d'Arc**, first Sunday (very good).

◎ **La Voultz-sur-Rhône**, fourth Sunday (very good).

🖰 www.rhonealpes-tourism.com

Markets at a glance: Rhône-Alpes

A

Abondance, *Sun*
Aiguebelle, *Tue*
Aigueblanche, *Sat*
Aime, *Thur*
Aix-les-Bains, *Wed*, *Sat*
Alba-la-Romaine, *Sun*
Albens, *Fri*
Albertville, *Thu*, *Sat*
Allex, *Mon*, *Thu* (winter)
Les Allues, *Tue* and *Fri* (mid-Dec–mid-Apr and mid-Jul–mid-Aug)
Ambièrle, *Thu*
Ambilly, *Sat*
Annecy, see Six of the Best
Annecy-le-Vieux, *Wed*
Annemasse, *Tue*, *Fri*
Anneyron, *Tue*
Annonay, *Wed*, *Sat*
Aoûste-sur-Sye, *Sat*
Aubenas, *Sat* (+ *Wed* eve Jul/Aug)
Aussois, *Tue*
Les Avanchers-Valmorel, *Mon*, *Fri*

B

La Balme-de-Sillingy, *Sun*
Barby, *Fri*
Bassenay, *Thu*
La Bathie, *Sat*
Beauchastel, *Tue*
Beaufort, *Wed*
Beaufort-sur-Gervanne, *Wed*
Beaumont-lès-Valence, *Sat*
La Bégude-de-Mazenc, *Tue*
Bellegarde, *Thu*
Belleville-sur-Saône, *Tue*
Bessans, *Mon*
Boëge, *Tue*
Bois-d'Oingt, *Tue*
Bonne, *Fri*
Bonneville, *Tue*, *Fri*
Bons-en-Chablais, *Sat*
Bourdeaux, *Thu*
Bourg-de-Péage, *Thu*
Bourg-en-Bresse, *Wed*, *Sat*
Le Bourget-du-Lac, *Thu* (+ *Sun* mid-Jul–mid-Sep)
Bourgoin-Jallieu, *Wed*, *Thu*, *Sat*, *Sun*

Bourg-St-Andéol, *Wed*, *Sat*
Bourg-St-Maurice, *Sat*
Bozel, *Wed*
Brides-les-Bains, *Wed*
Brignous, *Sat*
Bron, *Mon*
Buis-les-Baronnies, *Wed*, *Sat*
Burzet, *Wed*, *Sun*

C

Carroz-d'Arâches, *Tue*
Chabeuil, *Tue*
Challes-les-Eaux, *Tue*, *Fri*
Chamaret, *Fri* (+ *Mon* mid-Nov–mid-Mar)
Chambéry, daily (outdoors *Sat*)
Chamonix, *Sat*
Champagny-en-Vanoise, *Tue*
La Chapelle-d'Abondance, *Fri*
La Chapelle-en-Vercors, *Thu* (+ *Sat* in summer)
Charavines, *Sun*
Charlieu, *Wed*, *Sat*
Charvieu-Chavagnieux, *Sat*
Châtel, *Wed*
Le Châtelard, *Fri* (Jul/Aug)
Châtillon-en-Diois, *Fri*
Châtillon-sur-Chalaronne, *Sat*
Chedde, *Tue*
Le Cheylard, *Wed*
Chomérac, *Thu*
Cléon-d'Andran, *Tue*
Clérieux, *Sat*
La Clusaz, see Six of the Best
Cluses, *Mon*, *Thu*
Collonge-sous-Salève, *Sun*
Combioux, *Wed*
Contamines-Montjoie, *Tue*
La Côte-Saint-André, *Thu*
Coucouron, *Wed*
Courchevel, *Thu*
Cran-Gevrier, *Thu*, *Sun*
Craponne, *Sat*
Crémieu, *Wed*
Crest, *Tue*, *Wed*, *Sat*
Crest-Voland, *Fri*
Crolles, *Sun*
Cruas, *Fri* (+ *Tue* eve Jul)
Cruseilles, *Thu*

D

Davezieux, *Fri*
Desaignes, *Sun* (Jul/Aug)
Die, *Wed*, *Sat*
Dieulefit, *Fri*
Divonne-les-Bains, *Fri*, *Sun*
Donzère, *Sat*
Doussard, *Mon*
Douvaine, *Sun*

E

Les Eschelles, *Tue*
Etoile, *Wed*
Evian, *Tue*
Evian-les-Bains, *Fri*
Excenevex, *Thu*

F

Faverges, *Wed*
Le Fayet, *Wed*
Ferney-Voltaire, *Sat*
Feurs, *Tue*, *Sat*
Flumet, *Tue*
Fontcouverte-la-Toussuire, *Fri*
Fourneaux, *Wed*
Francheville, *Fri*
Frangy, *Wed*

G

Gaillard, *Sat*
Les Gets, *Thu*
Gex, *Sat*
Gigors-et-Lozeron, *Sun* in summer
Givors, *Wed*, *Thu*, *Sun*
Le Grand-Bornand, *Wed*
Le Grand-Serre, *Fri*
Grane, *Thu*
Les Granges-Gontardes, *Wed*
Grenoble, daily (except *Mon*)
Grignan, see Six of the Best
Groisy, *Tue*

H

Hauterives, *Tue*
Les Houches, *Mon*

J

Jaujac, *Tue*, *Fri*
Joyeuse, *Wed* (+ some eves Jul/Aug)
Juliénas, *Mon*

L

Lablachère, *Sun*
Lagorce, *Tue*

Markets at a glance: Rhône-Alpes

Lalevade-d'Ardèche, *Tue*
Lamastre, *Tue*, *Sat* (+ some eves Jul/Aug)
Lanslebourg-Mt-Cenis, *Wed*
Lanslevillard, *Wed*
L'Arbresle, *Fri*
Largentière, *Tue* (+ *Fri* eve Jul/Aug)
Lavilledieu, *Thu*
La Lechère, *Mon* (Mar–Nov)
Lepin-le-Lac, *Sat* (Jul/Aug)
Lescheraines, *Tue* (Jul/Aug)
Livron, *Tue*, *Sat*
Longessaigne, *Thu*
Loriol, *Mon*, *Fri*
La Louvesc, *Thu*
Luc-en-Diois, *Fri*
Lus-la-Croix-Haute, *Wed* and *Sun* (in summer)
Lyon, see Six of the Best
M
Malissard, *Wed*
Marignier, *Fri*
Marsanne, *Fri*
Mègève, *Fri*
Meximieux, *Wed*
Meyras, *Wed*
Meythet, *Wed*
Mieussy, *Sat*
Modane, *Thu*
Montbrison, *Sat*
Montbrun-les-Bains, *Sat*
Montélimar, *Wed*, *Sat*
Montmélian, *Mon*
Montmeyran, *Tue*
Montpezat-sous-Bauzon, *Thu*
Montségur-sur-Lauzon, *Thu*
Montvalezan, *Thu* (+ *Sat* in summer, *Tue* in winter)
Morestel, *Sun*
Morzine, *Wed*
La Motte-Chalançon, *Mon* (Jul/Aug)
La Motte-Servolex, *Tue*
Moutiers, *Tue*, *Fri*
La Mure, *Mon*
N
Neyrac-les-Bains, *Wed*
Neuville-sur-Saône, *Fri*
Notre-Dame-de-Bellecombe, *Mon* (summer and winter seasons)
Novalaise, *Wed*, *Sun*
Nyons, *Thu*, *Sun* (Jun–Sep)
O
Les Ollières-sur-Eyneux, *Tue* (Jul/Aug)
Oullins, *Tue*, *Thu*
P
La Péage-de-Roussillon, *Thu*, *Sat*
Peisey-Nancroix, *Mon* in summer
Pélussin, *Sat*
Pierre-Bénite, *Wed*, *Sun*
Pierrelatte, *Fri*
Plateau d'Assy, *Wed*
Pont-de-Barret, *Fri*
Pont-de-Beauvoisin, *Mon*, *Sat*
Pont-de-l'Isère, *Tue* to *Sun*, summer eves (see text)
Pont-en-Royans, *Wed*
Le Pouzin, *Wed*
Pralognan-la-Vanoise, *Tue*, *Fri*
Praz-sur-Arly, *Wed*
Privas, see Six of the Best
Puy-St-Martin, *Wed*
R
La Ravoire, *Wed*, *Fri*
Reignier, *Sat*
Rémuzat, *Wed*
Renaison, *Sat*
Rillieux-la-Pape, *Wed*, *Fri*, *Sun*
Rives, *Thu*, *Sat*
Roanne, *Tue*, *Fri*, *Sat*, *Sun*
La Roche-de-Glun, *Wed*
Rochegude, *Thu*
La Roche-sur-Foron, *Thu*
La Rochette, *Wed*
Romans, *Tue*, *Wed*, *Sat*, *Sun*
Rosières, *Mon* (Jul/Aug)
Roussillon, *Wed*, *Sun*
Rumilly, *Thu*
Ruoms, *Fri* (+ *Wed* eve Jul/Aug)
S
Saillans, *Sun*
Saint Galmier, *Mon*
Saint Rambert-d'Albon, *Fri*
Saint-Agrève, *Mon*
Saint-Alban-d'Auriolles, *Mon* (Jul/Aug)
Saint-Bonnet-le-Château, *Fri*
Saint-Bon-Tarentaise, *Wed* (*Thu* at Courchevel)
Saint-Cirgues-en-Montagne, *Sun* (Jul/Aug)
Saint-Donat-sur-l'Herbasse, *Mon*
Sainte-Foy-l'Argentière, *Thu*, *Sat*
Sainte-François-Longchamp, *Sat*
Saint-Egrève, *Tue*, *Wed*, *Fri*, *Sat*
Saint-Etienne, *Tue*, *Sat*
Saint-Etienne-de-Lugardarès, *Tue*
Saint-Félicien, *Fri*, *Sun*
Saint-Fons, *Sat*
Saint-Genix-sur-Guiers, *Wed*
Saint-Gervais, *Thu*
Saint-Gervais-sur-Roubion, *Tue*
Saint-Jean-de-Maurienne, *Sat*
Saint-Jean-de-Sixt, *Sun*
Saint-Jean-de-Tholome, *Sat*
Saint-Jean-en-Royans, *Sat*
Saint-Jeoire, *Fri*
Saint-Jorioz, *Thu*
Saint-Julien-en-Genevois, *Fri*
Saint-Just-St-Rambert, *Thu*, *Sat*, *Sun*
Saint-Laurent-de-Chamousset, *Mon*
Saint-Laurent-du-Pape, *Sun* (Jul/Aug)
Saint-Laurent-du-Pont, *Thu*
Saint-Marcellin, *Tue*, *Fri*, *Sat*
Saint-Martin-d'Ardèche, *Wed* and *Sun* (mid-Jun–mid-Sep)
Saint-Martin-de-Belleville, *Tue*, *Thu* (Val-Thorens); *Wed*, *Fri* (Menuires)
Saint-Martin-de-Valamas, *Thu*
Saint-Martin-d'Hères, *Tue*, *Wed*, *Fri*, *Sat*

Saint-Martin-en-Haut, *Sat*
Saint-Mélany, *Sun*
Saint-Michel-de-Maurienne, *Fri*
Saint-Paul-le-Jeune, *Mon* (Jul/Aug)
Saint-Paul-Trois-Châteaux, *Tue*
Saint-Péray, *Wed*
Saint-Pierre-d'Albigny, *Wed*
Saint-Pierre-de-Chartreuse, *Sun*
Saint-Pierre-en-Faucigny, *Sat*
Saint-Pierreville, *Sun* (May–Sep)
Saint-Priest, *Tue, Wed, Fri, Sat*
Saint-Rémy-de-Maurienne, *Tue*
Saint-Sauveur-de-Montagut, *Sat*
Saint-Sorlin-en-Valloire, *Mon*
Saint-Symphorian-sur-Loire, *Wed*
Saint-Uze, *Sun*
Saint-Vallier, *Thu*
Sallanches, *Sat*
Salles-sous-Bois, *Tue*
Samoëns, *Wed*
Saou, *Sat*
Sarras, *Thu*
Satillieu, *Tue*
Saulce, *Thu*
Sauzet, *Sat*
Sciez, *Sat*
Sclonzier, *Sat*
Séez, *Thu* (eve Jul/Aug)
Serrières, *Fri*
Seynod, *Wed*
Seyssel, *Mon*
Suze-la-Rousse, *Fri*
T
Tain-l'Hermitage, *Sat*
Taninges, *Thu*
Tarare, *Thu, Sat*
Tassin-la-Demi-Lune, *Fri*
Taulignan, *Fri*
Le Teil, *Thu*
Termignon, *Tue*
Thoiry, *Sun*

Thônes, *Sat*
Thonon-les-Bains, *Mon, Thu*
Thueyts, *Fri*
Tignes, *Thu, Sun*
La Tour-du-Pin, *Tue, Sat*
Tulette, *Mon*
Tullins, *Mon, Sat*
V
Val d'Isère, *Mon*
Valaurie, *Sun*
Valence, see Six of the Best
Valgorge, *Sun*
Valleiry, *Sun*
Valloire, *Fri*
Vallon-Pont-d'Arc, *Thu, Sun* (Jul/Aug)
Vals-les-Bains, *Thu, Sun* (+ *Wed* and *Thu* eves Jul/Aug)
Les Vans, *Sat* (+ *Tue* eves Jul/Aug)
Vaulx-en-Velin, *Wed, Thu*,

Sat, Sun
Veigy-Foncenex, *Fri*
Vénissieux, *Thu, Fri, Sat, Sun*
Vernaison, *Sat*
Vernoux, *Thu, Sun* (Jun–Sep)
Vienne, daily
Villard-de-Lans, *Wed, Sun*
Villefontaine, *Wed, Sat*
Villefranche-sur-Saône, *Mon, Tue, Wed, Fri, Sat*
Ville-la-Grand, *Sun*
Villeneuve-de-Berg, *Wed* (+ *Tue* eves Jul/Aug)
Viuz-en-Sallaz, *Mon*
Viviers, *Tue*
Vogüé, *Mon* (Jul/Aug), *Sun* (Sep/Jun)
Voiron, *Wed, Sat*
La Voulte-sur-Rhône, *Fri*

CORSICA

Orange wine, resort chic, pork flavoured with chestnuts, and blackbird pâté

It pains me to make such short work of beloved Corsica, the most stunningly beautiful of all Mediterranean islands, but you hardly need a guide to its markets. There are only half a dozen. However, if you don't know Corsica, let me say a little to whip up your interest.

Imagine a chunk of the Alps flung into the Mediterranean, sky-scraping peaks tumbling down through forests of pine, oak and sweet chestnut. Then, where the land can be cultivated, vineyards, citrus orchards or olive groves. And where it cannot, the dense fleece of *maquis*. The perfume of this tenacious undergrowth of cistus, myrtle, juniper, gorse, arbutus and wild thyme even drifts out to sea. Sailing for home, Napoleon Bonaparte, Corsica's most illustrious local hero, is said to have been able to tell he was near his island before he could actually make out its silhouette on the horizon. I shall never forget inhaling it for the first time as I drove from Ajaccio airport up into the hills, a breeze as hot as a hairdryer buffeting my bare arm propped through the open car window, and every so often gusts of that intoxicating scent wafting in.

It's impossible to oversell this French island. It is scenically breathtaking, the coast encircled by a necklace of gulfs, bays and fabulous white sand beaches. Fishing ports have somehow managed to evolve into smart resorts without losing their character. The only major connurbations are Ajaccio and Bastia, and even they can provide the iconic snapshot of old salts (or handsome young salts) mending their nets against a backdrop of brightly painted bobbing boats.

Away from the increasingly sophisticated pleasures of resorts like Porto-Vecchio, St-Florent, Calvi, Propriano and Bonifacio, the otherness of the island's interior still casts its spell. Here, red-roofed villages with Baroque churches still cling by their toenails to the living rock. The age-old ritual of the Cattenacciu, a reenactment of the Crucifixion, is still followed in Sartène at Easter time. Prehistoric menhirs stand immutable at Filitosa and Palaggiu. And the cult of the vendetta, long since outlawed, lives on in the romance of island folklore.

The Corsicans themselves are special. Slow to smile, but in my experience if you learn to utter merely a greeting in the Corsican language, their sombre faces light up and you'll be well looked after. Their fiercely independent spirit has at times been a thorn in the side of the French body politic, but with visitors the islanders have a record of pretty good relations.

Specialities

With half-wild **pigs** flavouring themselves with *maquis* herbs, acorns and chestnuts, the air-dried hams (*prisuttu*) and *saucisson* (*salamu*) are as good as they get. *Figatellu* is the most strongly flavoured sausage. Made from wild boar liver, it's best split lengthwise and fried in its own fattiness.

Goat and sheep **cheeses** dominate the cheeseboard. *Brocciu*, made with either goat's or ewe's milk – or a mix of both – is the best known. Cubed, it makes an ideal addition for an omelette – just go easy on the salt when you season the mixture, and put in a little chopped mint. *Brocciu* also goes into cannelloni and a rather good cheesecake called *fiadone*.

The **fish** and **shellfish** are, of course, fantastic – especially the *langouste*, or crayfish, found in the deep gulf waters, and the sea urchins (*orsinades*). From the rivers there are trout, often available smoked.

Corsican **wines**, particularly from the Patrimonio area, are a cut above the rest – quite a few AOCs. Look for grape varieties Nielluciu, Sciacarellu and Vermentino. And there's no shortage of interesting *eaux de vie* and liqueurs made from herbs, chestnuts and fruit. Not normally attuned to sweetish apéritifs, I did however take to *vin d'orange*. A handy souvenir – also great in fruit desserts.

For tasty snacks 'to go', try *chaussons* – a kind of pastry filled with swiss chard, onions and courgettes; and *ambrucciate*, small quiches made with *brocciu* cheese.

The **olive oil** from the Balagne area is tops, in particular any marked 'Niellaghja'. **Honey** from Asco and Murzo is delectable. So are the *marrons glacés* of Evisa, Sant' Antonio *croquants* (almond biscuits) and *oliosi* (biscuits made with olive oil). You may hear rumours of blackbird pâté. I think the sensitivities of tourists and keen birdwatchers have put paid to its visibility on menus or at markets. There was a time, perhaps when Corsica was poorer and families had to be resourceful . . . But I've personally never come across it.

Six Markets

Ajaccio
Daily

The few cigarette-lighter apartment blocks in the centre don't take away the appeal of the island's main port and capital. It has great beaches nearby, sophisticated shopping and a casino. The picturesque old quarter by the fishing harbour is filled with statues of Old Boney, as well as gastronomic restaurants and delightful shady squares. One right by the port, Square César Campinchi, otherwise known as Place du Marché, hosts a market of fruit, vegetables, charcuterie and other local goodies every day in summer from 7.00 to 13.00. It closes on Monday from October to May. Fresh fish is sold in the dark ochre building behind, on the corner of Place Foch and Quai l'Herminier.

There's also a flea market every Sunday (7.00–13.00) along the seafront on Boulevard Pascal Rossini, close to Fesch secondary school.

Bastia
Daily except Monday

Bastia can be a bit off-putting on the outskirts with the plethora of industrial grot and storage depots that is part and parcel of any busy large working port. But the ancient harbour has a raffish Neopolitan air, fantastic old bars and atmospheric eating places. Bastia is not generally perceived as a tourist haunt but for that reason it's all the more interesting, and truly Corsican in character. Every day except Monday, an excellent traditional food market (including fresh fish) enlivens Place de l'Hôtel de Ville, near Saint Jean Baptiste church in Terra Vecchio. Sunday morning is the liveliest, with a flea market adding to the bustle.

Calvi
Daily except Sunday

I love Calvi. Admiral Nelson probably didn't, for he lost his eye in a great naval battle just off the coast. But what a location. The old citadel with its fortress rises on a promontory and there are beaches either side. To sit by a harbour bar at sunset watching the Balagne hills turn a misty purple across the bay is entertainment enough for me, but there are plenty of buzzy night spots for cooler customers. A tiny covered market hides in the lower town a couple of streets back from the front. It's near the Eglise Sainte Marie Majeure which is on Boulevard Wilson. Open 8am to noon and closed Sunday. Also, on the first and third Thursday of the month, there's a bigger market of clothes, crafts and souvenirs opposite the Super U supermarket.

Corté
Friday

Tucked away in the mountains, the old-time capital, with its stepped cobbled passageways and air of mystery, has a resonance nowhere else on the island possesses. In the 18th century, Corte was the headquarters of national hero Pasquale Paoli, who led a rebellion to unhitch Corsica from the mother country. The university that it was his dream to set up only came into being 30 years ago, and Corté today is as lively in term time as it is in summer when it becomes a centre for hiking and other mountain activities. Every Friday, there's a traditional food market on Avenue Jean Nicoli.

L'Ile-Rousse
Daily

Aside from Place Paoli, L'Ile-Rousse's palm-shaded main square, this businesslike little port lacks anything historical worth exploring. However, as it's surrounded by marvellous beaches, it's a place for villa-based holidaymakers to find restaurants and shop for food. Place Paoli is the target for both. There's a big traditional covered market every day which overflows into the square from 7.00 to 13.00. On the first and third Friday of each month, this is augmented by a flea and clothes market.

St-Florent
Monthly on Wednesday

The fortunes of St-Florent, nestling below the mountains on the west side of Cap Corse, have soared in the past twenty years in tandem with the rejuvenation of the surrounding Patrimonio winelands. This is Corsica's St Tropez, once a beautiful but peaceful fishing village, now 'discovered' by the Riviera French who steam across in their sleek yachts to anchor in the marina. What St-Florent lacks in the way of beaches (fabulous ones within easy reach, though), it makes up for in atmosphere with its smart cafés, shops and waterside fun, and you can still enjoy a quiet stroll past its little church and up to the round fortress above town. When the market arrives in the main square on the first Wednesday in the

month, St-Florent is complete. For sale are local produce, wine, souvenirs and charming pottery and craftwork. This is an area packed with artists and artisans.

 www.visit-corsica.com

chocolates (*cont.*)
296, 310
liqueur 250, 278, 285
chouchen 78
chouchou 161
choucroute (sauerkraut)
233, 265, 267
Ciboure 131
cider 33, 58, 59, 75, 78,
122, 202, 204, 206,
237, 243
cider vinegar 63
clafoutis 202
Clamecy 190
clams 74
Clermont-Ferrand
222-3
Clisson 98
Cluny 196
cod, salt 152, 301
cognac 106, 112, 114
Cognac (town) 106, 114
Cointreau 90, 97
Collioure 161
Colmar 269-70
Compiègne 38-40
compotes, fruit 241, 313
Concarneau 73, 83
Condom 146
confit 40, 121, 125, 136,
144
onion 161
confits 190
Confolens 113
coq au chambertin 188
Corbières 150
Corbigny 196
Cordes-sur-Ciel 138
cornichons 79, 89
corrézon 202
Corté 328-9
cotignac 171
coupetado 152
courgettes 296
Courseulles 69
crabs 16, 60, 74, 108
crayfish 248, 326
cream 59
Crème de Cassis 187
Crème de Mûres 189
Crémieux 319
crêpes *see* pancakes

crépinettes 120
creusois 202
crevettes roses 34
croissants 55
croquants 326
croque madame 49
croustades 126
currants 202
custard tarts 90, 96

Dambach-la-Ville 274
dandelion leaves 312
dates 52, 250
Dax 131
Dieppe 62-3
Dieulefit 320
Dijon 188
Dinan 81-2
Dinard 83
dinde rouge 238
Dole 257-8
Domme 131
Douai 27
Douarnenez 84
Draguignan 303
ducks 65, 121, 136, 144,
161
Duchambais 227

eaux de vie, see brandies
eels 89, 109, 120, 236
eggs 77, 120, 171, 225,
237, 270
endive (chicory) 16
Epernay 232
Epinal 286
Espalion 146
Essoyes 242
Etaples 18-19
Etretat 69

Les Fabuleuses Terrines
d'Amélie-les-Bains
161
Falaise 58, 70
farci Poitevin 109
far(z) forn 74
Faucogney-et-la-Mer 258
Faverney 258
Felletin 214
fera 253
Fère-en-Tardenois 37-8

fiadone 326
ficelle 46
ficelle picarde 36
figatellu 326
figs 250, 318
fion 90, 96
fish 18-19, 26, 34, 41,
60, 62, 65, 66, 74, 78,
80, 83, 89, 94, 96,
113, 120, 152, 160,
161, 178, 203, 212,
237, 242, 248, 253,
257, 267, 271, 274,
290, 300, 326, 328
see also bream, carp,
etc.
fish soup 78
flamiches 234
flammeküche (tarte flambé)
265
flaugnarde 202
Fleurance 146
Floc de Gascogne 137
foie gras 32, 40, 125, 134,
136, 138, 170, 211,
220, 264, 270, 273,
283
fondue 248
Fontainebleau 49
Forcalquier 294
forestines 175
fouaces 226
fougasette 299
fougasse 156, 224
Fougères 73, 83
Fougerolles 260
Fouras 114
fraises des bois 49
friture de carpe 248
Fronsac 131
fruit purée 95, 270
fruits
glacé 302
soft 90

galantines 59
galetous 207
galets du Doubs 250
Galette Bressane 194
Gallardon 180
garbure 119
garlic 16, 75, 109, 139,

222, 296, 298-9
gâteaux 171, 279
gâteau basque 121
gâteau de noix 211
genièvre 16
Gérardmer 283-4
gfilter söymage 265
gherkins 311
Gimont 146
ginger cake 246, 254
gingerbread 279
gingerbread (*pain d'épices*)
186, 189
Girmont-Val-d'Ajol 276,
286
Givet 242
goat's milk curd 152
goose 121, 136, 234
livers 308
gooseberries 202
gougère 187
gougères des Riceys 234
Granville 70
grapes 121, 143, 161,
173, 188, 220, 250
Grasse 299-300
Gravelines 27
grayling 203, 248
greengages 136
greens 172
Grignan 316-17
grillons 108
Grimaud 304
griottes 250
Gueberschwihr 270-1
Guérande 93-4
Guéret 214
guinea fowl 34, 238, 315
Guingamp 72

hachis parmentier 32, 285
haddock 74
halibut 74
ham 96, 126, 152, 160,
219, 234, 248, 253,
300, 326
hams 224
hare 113, 186, 203
hazelnuts 212, 219
herbs 77, 122, 152, 159,
220, 250, 292, 294,
315